Buddhism and
Christianity in Japan

Buddhism and Christianity in Japan

From Conflict to Dialogue, 1854–1899

Notto R. Thelle

UNIVERSITY OF HAWAII PRESS

HONOLULU

This book has been published with the help of a grant from the Norwegian
Research Council for Science and the Humanities.

Library of Congress Cataloging-in-Publication Data

Thelle, Notto R., 1941–
　Buddhism and Christianity in Japan.

　Bibliography: p.
　Includes index.
　1.　Japan—Church history.　2.　Missions to
Buddhists—Japan.　3.　Christianity and other
religions—Buddhism.　4.　Buddhism—Relations—
Christianity.　I.　Title.
BR1307.T48　　　1987　　　261.2'43'0952　　　86–16147
ISBN 0–8248–1006–6

Contents

Preface

IT HAS BEEN REPEATED over and over again that the present dialogue between Buddhists and Christians in Japan has introduced a radically new stage in the relationship between the two religions. One is often left with the impression that the encounter is a recent phenomenon, stimulated by trends in the World Council of Churches or inspired by the Second Vatican Council. It is certainly true that the dialogue in recent years has been characterized by a new intensity and depth, but the exaggerated emphasis on the uniqueness of the present situation reveals a lack of historical perspective.

My study of Buddhist-Christian relations in Japan convinced me that the radical transformation—from conflict to dialogue—took place primarily in the 1890s. The major part of the present study, therefore, consists of an examination of the dramatic and traumatic development in those years; it was a decade of bitter hostility and conflict, but it also became the starting point for dialogue and cooperation. My primary concern has been historical: to detect the origin of the peaceful dialogue, to examine its motives and trends, and to uncover the process through which dialogue became possible. This inevitably forced me to search further back: to the initial contact after the opening of Japan in the mid-nineteenth century, and even to the so-called Christian Century, which began with the arrival of Francis Xavier in 1549 and ended with the seclusion of the country and the proscription of Christianity. The relationship between Buddhism and Christianity at that early stage, however, will only be referred to as far as it bears upon the religious development in the nineteenth century.

History is a story to be told: about events, conflicts, meetings, persons, ideas. This narration is not only a record of historical events; I also hope to convey some of the atmosphere of the process through which bitter animosity was gradually transformed into reluctant recognition and open dialogue. Furthermore, the story has to be understood in a context. The development will partly be interpreted in the context of theological and ideological changes within the respective religious communities. Religious confrontations, however, never take place in isolation from the rest of society. Buddhist-Christian relations were so strongly influenced by the transformation of the entire Japanese society that, to a great extent, I have found it necessary to interpret the religious development within the framework of political and social changes, on the national as well as on the international level. The scope of the study, from 1854 to 1899, is in itself a clear indication of how deeply religious interactions were influenced by diplomatic relations and foreign affairs. The forced opening of Japan in 1854, symbolized by the advent of Commodore Perry and the subsequent treaties, and the revised treaties, leading to the opening of the interior of Japan to foreign trade, travel, and residence in 1899, were major milestones in Buddhist-Christian relations. Two other events that strongly affected the relationship between the two religions, the tacit recognition of Christianity in 1873 and the nationalistic reaction around 1889, were also related to both home affairs and international affairs.

For the examination of Buddhist-Christian relations in the 1890s, the most crucial time of conflict and reconciliation, I have made use of a number of available studies, by Otis Cary, Ebisawa Arimichi, Kashiwabara Yūsen, Kishimoto Hideo, Kōsaka Masaaki, Mori Ryūkichi, Ozawa Saburō, Saba Wataru, Sakurai Hisashi, Suzuki Norihisa, Yoshida Kyūichi, and others who in various ways have covered aspects of Buddhist-Christian relations in this period. The major research, however, is based on original sources: a wealth of books and pamphlets, written by Buddhists and Christians; articles and reports in the contemporary press, primarily religious journals and newspapers; and to a certain degree the secular press. At this point I feel obliged to express my gratitude to the late Ozawa Saburō. His studies have already been mentioned, but his contribution as a collector of books and journals is also impressive. His extensive library, now included in the library of the Institute for the Study of Humanities and Social Sciences at Doshisha University, provided much of the literature needed for my study. Furthermore, his collections of excerpts from journals and newspapers, copied by hand, one for each year of the Meiji period, proved extremely useful, both as a source of information and as a help in locating important material in the contemporary press. Apart from the above-mentioned library, I have found valuable material in the library of the Theological Seminary and the main library of Doshisha University and in the libraries of Ōtani University and Ryūkoku University, all in Kyoto; and, further, in the libraries of Aoyama Gakuin, Japan Foundation, Kandadera, Tokyo Union Theological Seminary, Tokyo University, and the National Diet Library, all in Tokyo.

Compared to the thorough examination of the 1890s in the major part of the book, the first six chapters are of a more introductory character, originally written to give a historical perspective on the development in the 1890s. Nevertheless, the decades after the opening of Japan offer important clues to the understanding of both conflict and reconciliation. Because of the more introductory character of the initial chapters, I have, as far as possible, based my research on available studies, and only to a limited degree made use of original sources. In addition to the scholars referred to above, I would like to mention studies by Abe Yoshiya, C. R. Boxer, George Elison, Morioka Kiyomi, Tamamuro Taijō, and Tokushige Asakichi.

Given the abundant material, scattered in various libraries and collections without a unified library service system, and mostly written in a style heavily influenced by the old literary language, the major task has been analytical: to reach an understanding of the main trends of Buddhist-Christian relations within the historical context. It has been suggested that I should also adopt a comparative method, seeing the characteristics of the Japanese development through comparisons with similar phenomena in other Asian cultures. Compared to the detailed information about the development in Japan, however, the material available to me about the development in other Asian countries is so fragmentary that it would be presumptuous of me to make any comparison beyond generalities. In the main it seems more enlightening to clarify the nature of the development by comparing the similarities and contrasts between the different stages of development within the Japanese context.

The Epilogue will also include a few issues somewhat outside the immediate scope of the study: a sketch of the main trends in Buddhist-Christian relations in the twentieth century and, further, some reflections of a more general character, relevant to the present dialogue. Since the study was initiated as a result of my involvement in dialogue with Buddhists, my interest has never been purely historical or academic. I am convinced that we need both a historical perspective and critical reflection in order to make the dialogue more than a pleasant conversation or interesting pastime. There are certainly useful lessons to be learned, positively and negatively, from the experiences of those who pioneered the dialogue eighty or ninety years ago.

The present book is a revised version of my doctoral dissertation,

"From Conflict to Dialogue: Buddhism and Christianity in Japan, 1854–1899," presented to the University of Oslo in 1983. The original study emphasized more strongly the differences between the various stages of Buddhist-Christian contact and included more documentation of actual confrontations, in addition to detailed analyses of interfaith relationships. In the present book I have put more emphasis on the flow of events, omitting material that would be of little concern outside the small circle of scholars with particular interest in details of local church history and Buddhist history.

The initial stages of locating and collecting material were done in connection with my work as Associate Director of the National Christian Council (NCC) Center for the Study of Japanese Religions in Kyoto, where I have worked since 1974. A scholarship from the Norwegian Masonic Order in 1974 enabled me to spend some weeks in Tokyo and to collect valuable material. A three-year grant from the Norwegian Research Council for Science and the Humanities from 1979 to 1981 gave me the necessary freedom to concentrate and to complete the study. I also want to express my gratitude to the leadership of the Scandinavian East Asia Mission for their evaluation of religious dialogue as a vital aspect of Christian mission; to Professor Nils E. Bloch-Hoell of the Theological Department of Oslo University; and to Professor Doi Masatoshi and other co-workers at the NCC Study Center for their understanding and support. During my study I had the opportunity to meet with Professors Fukushima Hirotaka, Kashiwabara Yūsen, Sumiya Mikio, Tamura Yoshirō, Yoshida Kyūichi, and with Dr. Imamura Shin'ichirō, who in various ways shared their insights and supported my work. A special word of thanks goes to my friends Professor Beverley D. Tucker of Doshisha University, for his revision and proofreading of my dissertation, and Linda Crawford, who offered many valuable suggestions. I would also like to express my thanks to the editorial staff of the University of Hawaii Press and to Joanne Sandstrom, the copy editor, for their advice and assistance.

Being convinced that this kind of study deserves to be read outside the circle of specialists, I have included some information of general character and have tried to avoid too specialized language. Japanese terminology is introduced only to a limited degree, when it seemed important for understanding. Japanese names are written in the traditional Japanese way, family name first and personal name last, except for bibliographical data where a Japanese author is introduced according to Western tradition. For various reasons I have chosen to be somewhat inconsistent in the transcription of names: personal names are consistently transcribed with signs indicating long vowels (Yūsen, Kyūichi, etc.), while geographical names are consistently written without such signs (Tokyo, Kyoto,

Kobe, etc.); the same is the case with terms that have been included into the English language, such as Bushido (Way of the Warrior); Shinto, Tenrikyo, and other religions; and a well-known institution such as Doshisha.

This study is dedicated to my wife, Mona, and our five children, Rannfrid, Olav, Anne, Notto Johannes, and Ellen Mari. Our sharing of responsibility and time in work and leisure has been a constant reminder that people are more important than books.

CHAPTER ONE

The Religious
Implications of the
Opening of Japan

I shall be both proud and happy if I can be the humble
means of once more opening Japan to the blessed rule of
Christianity.

American Consul General Townsend Harris

THE FIRST TREATY between Japan and the United States, concluded
in March 1854, signified the formal end of more than two centuries of
almost total seclusion, during which Christianity had been proscribed as
the "evil religion" *(jashū)* of the West. The first limited treaties were gradually expanded, and a number of ports were opened for foreign trade and
residence. Extraterritorial privileges were granted, and customs duties
were fixed at moderate rates.[1] The implications of the opening of Japan
can hardly be overestimated. It coincided with and to a great extent contributed to the final collapse of the Tokugawa regime and the subsequent
restoration of Imperial rule in 1868. The last years of the Tokugawa
period (1600–1867) were characterized by the conflict between the advocates of open intercourse with the West and those who wanted to return
to seclusion and expel the foreigners. The conflict continued in the Meiji
period (1868–1912) as a tension between the main trend to adopt Western ideas and institutions and the opposite trend to maintain or reaffirm
national traditions.

For the Buddhists it was particularly important that contact with the
West inevitably implied contact with Christianity. The Western powers
identified themselves more or less as "Christian countries" and supported
the cause of Christianity. The first Christian missionaries arrived in
1859. Their avowed purpose was to serve the Western residents in the
treaty ports, but they were also aiming at missionary work among the
Japanese population. The confrontation with Christianity overshadowed
most other concerns of the Buddhists in the years after the opening of

Japan, as it is depicted humorously in the picture of the "worrying priest" in Figure 1: "Since the disgraceful doctrine of Yaso [Jesus] entered, the fate of the Dharma is my constant concern."

Even though Japan opened its ports and the Western powers gradually expanded their rights to trade and settlement in the treaty ports, Christianity was still a proscribed religion. The Japanese government emphasized that the opening of the country did not imply any change in its anti-Christian policy. Anti-Christian and antiforeign sentiment actually increased in the years after 1854. The enemies of the Tokugawa regime stimulated the exclusionist sentiment expressed in the cry *sonnō jōi*, "Revere the Emperor! Expel the Barbarians!" The politics of expulsion finally failed in the last years of the Tokugawa period, and anti-Christian sentiment subsided somewhat.[2] After the Restoration in 1868, however, the oppression of Christianity was intensified. The notice boards proscribing Christianity were again posted all over the country, and thousands of underground Christians were rounded up, persecuted, arrested, and exiled to distant provinces. In 1873 the boards wee finally removed. The government maintained that Christianity was still proscribed, but the decision was accompanied by so many other changes that the public quite appropriately understood the removal of the boards as a tacit recognition of Christianity. This recognition gradually initiated a new era of Buddhist-Christian relations, as we shall see later. In short, the initial period of contact, from 1854 to 1873, was characterized by these somewhat contradictory facts: Japan was opened for contact with the rest of the world, including Christianity; missionary work was started in the open ports; but Christianity was still proscribed as an evil religion.

The contact between Buddhism and Christianity was not only a religious encounter; it was part of a major cultural and political confrontation. In the broad context of political changes, the interactions between Buddhism and Christianity had only limited significance and did not, apart from some diplomatic complications, exercise any decisive influence upon the course of history. Hence many studies of the period after the opening of Japan pay only slight attention to Buddhist-Christian relations. On the other hand, it is impossible to understand the relationship between the two religious without considering their respective roles in the historic drama.

As Japan emerged from more than two centuries of seclusion, memories of past interactions with the West mingled with abundant new knowledge and experiences. The past offered models for interpreting what was happening, and new developments to a certain extent modified traditional attitudes. To understand the relationship between Buddhism and Christianity we need to consider the religious implications of the opening of the country. In this chapter I shall, therefore, describe the set-

Fig. 1. *Kiyūsō* (the worrying priest): "Since the disgraceful doctrine of Yaso [Jesus] entered, the fate of the Dharma is my constant concern." From Nishikata Kandō, *Buppō gyōshōka* [Buddhist songs at the morning bell] (Tokyo, 1889). Courtesy of Aoyama Gakuin University, Tokyo.

ting of the drama by examining the Tokugawa background and the situation created by the presence of Western (Christian) powers. Against this background it will be easier to understand both the aggressive Buddhist response to Christianity and the Christians' disregard of Buddhism.

THE TOKUGAWA BACKGROUND

The Japanese contact with Iberian traders and missionaries in the sixteenth and seventeenth centuries was an ambiguous experience, characterized by both fascination and fear, openness and rejection. Interpreted by the official ideologists of the Tokugawa period, however, the encounter became a negative experience, traumatic and destructive. Their views, impressed upon the Japanese people throughout the centuries of seclusion, became an important part of the collective memory of the people. Two aspects of the early contact had particular bearing upon the relationship between the two religions after the opening of Japan: (1) the close connection between the policy of seclusion and the proscription of Christianity and (2) the role of Buddhism in the anti-Christian policy of the Tokugawa regime.

SECLUSION POLICY AND THE PROSCRIPTION OF CHRISTIANITY

For more than two decades the centralized power of the Tokugawa shogunate managed to establish and maintain an unprecedented political and social stability. The Imperial Court was kept powerless; the nobility had to pledge their allegiance to the Tokugawa rulers and were kept in place through an effective system of espionage and control. In order to maintain political stability a policy of social stability was adopted. A hierarchy of four social classes was created: the samurai (or warrior-administrator), the peasant, the artisan, and the merchant. All aspects of social life were regulated, even minute details concerning food and clothing. The Tokugawa shogunate has quite appropriately been described as "a government by prohibition which attempted to regulate all human activities by means of ordinances."[3]

Religious life was also regulated. Confucianism, primarily the Neo-Confucian Chu Hsi philosophy, with its static view of social life and its emphasis on loyalty and filial piety, provided the official philosophy and contributed to the stability of intellectual life.[4] Buddhism, although protected as a quasi-national religion, was also strictly controlled in order to serve the political aims of the regime and was used to suppress Christianity, as we shall see later.

The policy of seclusion and the proscription of Christianity were intimately related and can best be understood in relation to the political and social background. Christian propagation and foreign trade, as they developed from the late sixteenth century, were regarded as threats to the political stability of the country; both could become weapons in the hands of feudal lords who wished to challenge the suzerainty of the shogunate or even pave the way for a foreign invasion.[5]

The anti-Christian policy was begun under Toyotomi Hideyoshi (1536–1598), who issued a ban on missionaries in 1587 and prohibited Christianity entirely in 1591. Before that, Christianity had been supported by powerful feudal lords and even by the supreme ruler, Oda Nobunaga (1534–1582). Under the first three Tokugawa rulers, Ieyasu (1542–1616), Hidetada (1579–1632), and Iemitsu (1603–1651), the oppression of Christianity was enforced more and more severely, until the entire Christian population had been exterminated or driven underground by the mid-1640s.[6]

The first decree directed against foreign trade, issued in 1616, restricted it to the two ports of Nagasaki and Hirado; the fear of foreign interference and military intervention gradually led to complete seclusion. In 1635, overseas trading by Japanese ships came to an end: "No Japanese ship may leave for foreign countries. No Japanese may go abroad secretly. If anybody tries to do this, he will be killed. . . . Any Japanese now living abroad who tries to return to Japan will be put to death." Furthermore, all foreigners were ordered to leave Japan: "No offspring of Southern Barbarians will be allowed to remain. Anyone violating this order will be killed, and all relatives punished according to the gravity of the offence."[7] The Shimabara insurrection in 1637–1638, when nearly forty thousand Christian peasants, fishermen, and warriors were defeated and killed, led to the final seclusion of Japan. The last and ultimate decree about seclusion was issued in 1639; apart from a limited and strictly regulated commerce with the Dutch and the Chinese at Nagasaki from 1641, contact with the outside world was strictly prohibited.[8]

We are not concerned here with verifying to what degree Christian propagation and Western trade posed a real threat to the Tokugawa shogunate. Historians generally agree that the charges of hidden motives of territorial aggression made against Roman Catholic missionaries were groundless.[9] What is important in our context is to notice that the denunciation of Christianity as a means of political conquest "was common to all critics of Christianity and was unquestioningly accepted by the whole of the people during the centuries of seclusion and prohibition."[10]

As the Western countries began to press for renewed contact with Japan in the early nineteenth century, the implicit danger of trade and Christian propagation was again used as a powerful argument against such changes. For instance, Aizawa Seishisai (1782–1863) wrote in *Shinron* [New proposals] in 1825:

When those barbarians plan to subdue a country not their own, they start by opening commerce and watch for a sign of weakness. If an opportunity is presented, they will preach their alien religion to captivate the people's hearts. Once the people's allegiance has been shifted, they can be manipulated and nothing can be done to stop it. The people will be only too glad to die for the sake of the alien God. . . . The subversion of the people and overthrowing of the state are taught as being in accord with the God's will. So in the name of all-embracing love the subjugation of the land is accomplished.[11]

Of course conciliatory voices, such as those of Sakuma Shōzan, Yokoi Shōnan, and Yoshida Shōin, and others who had studied Western methods with the Dutch at Nagasaki, advocated contact with the West, combining the emphasis on Eastern ethics with the pursuit of Western science and art.[12] Aizawa's apprehensions, however, were representative of a way of thinking that had been fostered during two centuries of seclusion; they were shared by the population at large, and notably by the Buddhists. The official policy of prohibition, Buddhist and Confucian criticism of Christianity, and numerous popular anti-Christian tales had created among the people a profound aversion to and dreadful abhorrence of Christianity. Such a sentiment was strong not only until the early Meiji era,[13] but maintained popularity and was revived at important times throughout the nineteenth century.

Considering that the Western nations in the mid-nineteenth century were rapidly expanding their influence in the Far East through military force, trade, colonization, and Christian propagation, the Japanese suspicion was hardly unreasonable. The Opium War in 1842 and the forced opening of China especially alarmed the shogunate and stimulated the improvement of military defense in Japan.[14]

In sum, just as the prohibition of Christianity and the policy of seclusion had been intimately related in the beginning of the Tokugawa period, it was almost inevitable that the forced opening of Japan at the end of the period would renew the suspicion, fear, and hostility toward Christianity among politicians, scholars, and religious leaders.

BUDDHISM AND THE PROSCRIPTION OF CHRISTIANITY

We have already seen that the Tokugawa shogunate effectively used religion to cement its absolute control over the country. Through ruthless attacks on Buddhist strongholds in the late sixteenth century, Oda Nobunaga had brought Buddhism to submission, and the Tokugawa rulers maintained and strengthened the control. A number of ordinances regarding sects and temples brought Buddhism under the strict supervision of the shogunate, and at the same time it was favored with financial support and included in the administrative system. This policy of "strict interference" and "excessive protection"[15] forced Buddhism into active support of and cooperation with the shogunate, making it a central organ for the government's anti-Christian policy. Although the government also commanded other means of thought control and oppression of Christianity through officials, secret informers, and neighborhood associations, the Buddhist temples and priests played a central role in the anti-Christian policy of the regime.

One of Ieyasu's highest advisors, for example, was the Buddhist scholar Konchiin Sūden (or Sōden), who advised Ieyasu not only in his management of Buddhist temples but in religious matters generally. Sūden probably had a hand in the famous edict against Christianity, published on January 27, 1614. C. R. Boxer characterizes the edict as a "curious medley of Buddhist and Confucian ideas, with a few passing allusions to Shinto."[16] After referring to the principle of yang and yin and alluding to various Buddhist texts, the edict denounced Christianity in the following terms:

> The Kirishitan band have come to Japan, not only sending their merchant vessels to exchange commodities, but also longing to disseminate an evil law, to overthrow true doctrine, so that they may change the government of the country and obtain possession of the land. This is the germ of great disaster, and must be crushed.[17]

Japan was extolled as "the country of the Gods and of Buddha" and the Christians denounced as "the enemies of the Gods and of Buddha."

To secure the enforcement of the edict, fifteen rules for guidance of the Buddhist priesthood were attached, including one directing that every Japanese citizen be registered as a parishioner of a Buddhist temple.[18] This regulation was eventually developed into a census system, according to which every Japanese was registered at a temple and received a temple certificate *(tera-uke),* which served as a sort of identification card needed for weddings, travel, changes of residence, and the employment of servants. The express purpose of the system was to detect Christians and ensure that they abandoned their faith. Thus the Buddhist temples were entrusted with the official census, the supervision of religious matters, and the investigation of Christianity and other "evil religions."[19] The practice was intact throughout the Tokugawa era, and was witnessed by Townsend Harris in Shimoda as late as 1857.[20]

The control through the annual census was supplemented with another practice that intensified the subjugation of the Christians, the ceremony of *efumi,* or "picture stepping."[21] Sacred pictures of Christ or the Virgin Mary were placed on the ground, and people were ordered to trample on them to demonstrate that they were rejecting the Christian faith. The practice had been used as early as 1631, but the official Inquisition Office (Kirishitan Shūmon Aratameyaku), which was established in 1640, introduced *efumi* as a practice to be performed by all the inhabitants of cities and villages, notably in certain districts in Kyushu where Christianity had been strong. The practice was used not only to detect hidden Christians or to confirm their apostasy but also to "impress on the mind of the non-Christians a profound abhorrence for the forbidden religion."[22] In addition to *efumi,* former Christians had to make a solemn oath that they had revoked Christianity and to join a Buddhist temple. Especially in the countryside the Buddhists played an important role in this connection; the ceremonies were often held in a Buddhist temple and supervised by the Buddhist priest who also confirmed the apostasy. At a later stage *efumi* was not only practiced in areas of strong Christian influence but was included in the religious investigation in many other places as well, as part of the so-called *shūmon aratame seido,* or "conversion system."[23] The practice of *efumi* was abandoned in 1857, under pressure from the Western powers.

In addition to such practices, we should also take note of a few Buddhist anti-Christian scriptures that provided material for Buddhist criticism and strengthened its prejudice against Christianity. The first major Buddhist anti-Christian work was *Ha-Daiusu* or *Ha-Deusu* [Refutation of Deus],[24] written in 1620 by Fabian Fucan, the apostate Jesuit brother. Fabian had previously written an apology for Christianity, *Myōtei mondō* [Myōtei dialogue],[25] which purported to demonstrate the superiority of Christianity over Buddhism, Confucianism, and Shinto. *Ha-Daiusu* represented a sort of formal retraction of his previous defense of Christianity;[26] it was a passionate and eloquent expression of Buddhist anti-Christian thought, reflecting the Buddhist-Christian controversies of the previous decades and the Buddhist animosity toward Christianity in the early Tokugawa period. In *Ha-Daiusu,* Fabian rejected the Christian doctrines in seven steps, describing God and his creation, reward and punishment, the fall of the angels and heaven and hell, the fall of Adam and original sin, God's promise to send a savior, the incarnation and the life of Christ, and, finally, the commandments and the sacraments. The Christian doctrine was, according to Fabian, not only ridiculous and childish, but dangerous, for absolute loyalty to God implied the right to revolt. In the First Commandment "lurks the intention to subvert and usurp the country, to extinguish Buddha's Law and Royal Sway," he warned. "Quick, quick! Put this gang in stocks and shackles!"[27] With Fabian's inside knowledge of Christianity as a previous Jesuit brother, his refutation naturally made a decisive impact on the Buddhist community and became a source of information for later Buddhist attacks on Christianity.[28]

Two anti-Christian tracts written by Buddhists in the middle of the seventeenth century denounced Christianity as inferior to Buddhism and supported the policy of prohibition by alleging that the Christians held secret motives of aggression and conquest. *Taiji jashūron* [Extermination of the evil attachment], composed by a Zen Buddhist named Sessō in 1668 but not published until 1861, branded Christianity as a Buddhist heresy: "Jesus secretly studied Buddhism; but he could not penetrate its wondrous hidden depths."[29] It also criticized the traditional Christian doctrines of monotheism, Adam's fall, redemption, the sacraments, and future life.[30] In *Ha-Kirishitan* [Refutation of Christianity], Suzuki Shō-san, another Zen Buddhist monk, criticized the Christian God as a "foolscap Buddha,"[31] ridiculed the doctrines of creation, redemption, and others, and denounced the Christians for their lack of respect for Buddhism and Japanese religions.

> Japan is the Land of the Gods. To be born in the Land of the Gods and refuse to adore and worship the gods is the ultimate of irreverence. . . . The One Buddha of Original Illumination and Thusness appears in transformation and pursues his work of salvation in accommodation with the mind of man. And thus, the mind which esteems and worships the gods is but acknowledging and worshipping this One Buddha.[32]

Shōsan's attack on Christianity was based on his understanding of the universality of Buddha nature, an idea that naturally prejudiced him against the Christian views of a personal God and an individual soul. According to Anesaki Masaharu, Shōsan's polemic was "the most typical representative of the Buddhist pantheistic stand taken against Christian monotheism, and no one before him or after him in this country has so clearly stated the gap existing between the two religions."[33]

A famous anonymous collection of tales about the Christians, *Kirishi-tan monogatari* [Tales of the Christians], was composed by a Buddhist monk; it was published in Kyoto in 1639 and reprinted in 1665 under the title *Kirishitan taiji monogatari* [Tales of the extermination of the Christians].[34] The tales included a popular account of the advent of the Catholic missionaries and a description of Christianity as a perversion of Buddhist doctrine; they depicted Christian controversies with Buddhist scholars and the final destruction of Christianity in the Shimabara insurrection, and concluded with references to the subjugation of Christianity.

> During this reign the Kirishitan religion has been cut down at its root and cast out of our land. Such must indeed have been the judgment of the Buddhas, Gods, and Bodhisattvas. . . .
> Barbarians from foreign lands came here, to spread their cursed doctrine and, despising the Buddhas and the Gods, to destroy them and do away with them, determined thereby to make of Japan a domain of devils. How wretched it was, how lamentable![35]

Considering the central role of Buddhism in the subjugation of Christianity, it may be argued that the number of anti-Christian writings was small and their impact on the general public limited. Elison, for instance, makes the following evaluation: "Sessō, however, was just one Buddhist monk, and his influence was limited by that very fact. Suzuki Shōsan was an outsider even from his own sect; the direct effects of his activity were felt in Amakusa but hardly extended beyond the islands."[36] On the other hand, Buddhist propaganda was supported by both official policy and a number of other anti-Christian writings. Confucian scholars wrote few explicit refutations of Christianity, but their writings exhibit a consistently critical attitude to Christianity, beginning with Hayashi Razan's *Hai-Yaso* [Anti-Jesuit, or Anti-Jesus] in 1606[37] and continuing throughout the Tokugawa period. In addition to more scholarly works came a great number of popular anti-Christian tales that spread all over the country and found their way to the libraries of feudal lords and Buddhist temples as well as to the homes of the common people.[38]

In summary we may say that the religious policy of the Tokugawa period gave Buddhism a central position as a seminational religion and main agent for the oppression of Christianity. With this consistent anti-Christian policy the Buddhist world could hardly avoid confronting Christianity with bitter opposition as Japan again opened its ports in the mid-nineteenth century. And then the seventeenth-century literature provided Buddhism with important material for opposition to Christianity.

THE TREATIES: COMMERCE AND PRESENCE OF CHRISTIAN NATIONS

Knowing the Japanese attitude to Christianity, the United States approached Japan by emphasizing a policy of strict noninterference in religious matters. In the directions sent by President Fillmore to the Secretary of the Navy in connection with Commodore Perry's expedition to Japan in 1853 it was emphasized that the government of the United States, "unlike those of every other Christian country, does not interfere with the religion of its own people, much less with that of other nations." The same principle was reiterated in a letter from the President to the Emperor of Japan, which assured him that the Americans did not plan to disseminate Christianity among the Japanese, that the objective of the expedition was only to establish friendship and commerce, to secure safety and supplies for stranded sailors, and so on: "The Constitution and laws of the United States forbid all interference with the religious or political concerns of other nations. I have particularly charged Commodore Perry to abstain from every act which could possibly disturb the tranquility of your Imperial Majesty's dominion."[39]

DIPLOMATIC PRESSURE

In spite of this basic principle of noninterference, which was formally maintained in the following years, the presence of the Western nations in Japan was accompanied by consistent and sometimes humiliating demonstrations of their concern for the cause of Christianity. The following description of Perry's arrival in Japan in July 1853 relates vividly the expectations of Western Christians and indicates in its somewhat romantic and exaggerated way the religious implications of what Westerners tended to regard as the "dawn of Japan."

> In the very midnight, then, of Japan's moral and spiritual darkness, in July, 1853, appeared the peaceful armada led by Commodore Perry. The first sound which the people heard, after the sunrise and evening guns, was the invitation given, in music and hearty song, to forsake idols and acknowledge God, the one Father of all. Was it accident, that on the Lord's Day, on which the commodore would transact no business with the Japanese authorities,[40] the church flag—the one ensign allowed above the stars and stripes—was hoisted on the flag-ship for prayer and worship? No! for this was the rule and custom. Nevertheless, it was noteworthy, even prophetic, that the hymn sung on that Sabbath morning was this invitation to the people living in what was then an idol and priest cursed land, but which is now open to the gospel, and where conscience is free:
>
> > "Before Jehovah's awful throne
> > Ye nations bow with sacred joy;
> > Know that the Lord is God alone,
> > He can create and he destroy."[41]

Furthermore, the gifts presented to the Japanese officials and interpreters included a Bible and other Christian literature. The Japanese criticized this as a violation of the principle of noninterference in religious matters and finally returned the gifts.[42] When the first treaty was signed on March 31, 1854, the date was given "in the year of our Lord Jesus Christ" as well as in the traditional Japanese way, but the Japanese refused to enclose the first designation in the Japanese version of the treaty.[43]

When the Russians negotiated a treaty with Japan, they managed to avoid a clause affirming the prohibition of Christianity; promising that they would not propagate Christianity or interfere with the religion of the Japanese, they also obtained a guarantee for Russians to practice their religion in Japan. The Dutch, likewise, refused to insert a clause prejudicial to Christianity, and even managed to press the shogunate to abandon the practice of *efumi* in December 1857.[44] The American Consul General, Townsend Harris, who arrived in 1856, argued that while the object of the Portuguese 250 years before had been "trade, conquest and proselytization," most countries of the West stood for the principle of freedom of conscience, and that "at the present day no nation desired to propagate its religious faith by force of arms."[45] The final treaty between Japan and the United States, concluded on July 29, 1858, guaranteed the right for Americans to practice their religion and to erect suitable places for worship. On the other hand, the principle of noninterference was again confirmed: "American citizens shall not injure any Japanese temple or mia [sic], or offer any insult or injury to Japanese religious ceremonies, or to the object of their worship. The Americans and Japanese shall not do anything that may be calculated to excite religious animosity."[46] Similar articles were included in the treaties with the Netherlands, Russia, Great Britain, and France. Abe Yoshiya summarizes the government policy in the following way:

> The unequal treaties thus secured for foreigners the right to practice Christianity in Japan. The shogunate naively understood the treaties as stipulating that foreigners, within their concessions, might follow their own laws and exercise the freedom to practice Christianity, but the Japanese authorities would be free from the threat of foreign interference in the enforcement of Japanese laws, including the prohibition of Christianity. The Japanese government never suspected that these agreements would facilitate the dissemination of Christianity among the Japanese.[47]

The right for foreigners to practice their religion had far greater consequences than the Japanese authorities had anticipated. Christian worship services and funeral ceremonies were often conducted in a way that intentionally aimed at demonstrating the presence of Christianity. This was notably the case with Townsend Harris, even before the treaty guaranteed the right to such practices.[48] As we shall see later, the right to worship was used systematically by missionaries as a means to propagate their faith among the Japanese.

We have previously referred to the importance attached to the observance of Sundays. Townsend Harris refused to conduct any business or even to attend official ceremonies on Sundays, in order to "set an example of a proper observance of the Sabbath."[49] The so-called Sabbath Question thus became an inevitable issue in the relationship between foreigners and Japanese. Foreigners employed by the government were generally allowed to have Sunday as a day of rest.[50] In 1868 the Customs House in Yokohama announced that it was to be closed on "the Western Sundays and Christmas." In 1872 the military academy and the school for military medicine made Sunday a holiday for the convenience of their foreign teachers. Finally, in December 1872, the government proclaimed that the Gregorian calendar should be adopted as of January 1, 1873; Sunday should be a legal holiday and Japanese holidays abandoned, except New Year's Day and the Emperor's Birthday.[51] A strong reaction against this move led to a temporary return to the old calendar, and foreigners employed by the government were ordered to work on Sundays; however, diplomatic pressure eventually led to the final adoption of Sunday as a public holiday.[52]

The Western representatives in Japan not only insisted on such consequences of the right of foreigners to practice their religion but demonstrated a strong concern for the cause of Christianity in Japan as well. Townsend Harris, a pious Christian, regarded himself as a "humble means of once more opening Japan to the blessed rule of Christianity."[53] Furthermore, he had been instructed by the American Secretary of State "to do his best, by all judicious measures and kind influence, to obtain the full toleration of the Christian religion in Japan, and protection for all missionaries and others who should go there to promulgate it."[54] According to the China missionary Dr. W. A. P. Martin, Harris received more than one hundred geographies for distribution among the officials and asked for Bibles for the same purpose.[55] The American treaty allowed the Japanese to buy anything Americans might wish to sell, except opium and firearms, and Harris explained to Christian missionaries that he had the article worded in that way "expressly to cover the sale of Scriptures and other Christian books by the missionaries, and that he should interfere at once if there were any attempt to violate it."[56]

The most conspicuous demonstration of the Western concern for the cause of Christianity was probably the untiring effort to force the Japanese government to abandon its policy of prohibition. We have already noticed the vain efforts to include passages about religious toleration in the treaties, as well as the successful effort of the Dutch to press the government to abandon the practice of *efumi*. The government, however, not only refused to change its policy but even intensified the persecution of Japanese Christians after the Restoration in 1868. The treaty powers reacted strongly when the new government renewed the traditional anti-Christian policy by posting anew at major intersections throughout the country notice boards with the following: "Evil religions like Christianity are strictly forbidden. Suspicious persons should be reported to the proper office. Rewards will be granted."[57] The foreign representatives could not accept the insulting term "evil religion." They did not intend to interfere with the internal affairs of Japan, they argued, but they could not remain indifferent to such an offense against the religion they represented. In the words of the American consul: "While disclaiming any intention of interfering with the internal affairs of Japan, I deem it my duty to call Your Excellencies' attention to the fact that the Christian religion is the religion of the Country I have the honor to represent."[58] The government defended its policy by referring to the widespread anti-Christian sentiment, the long-established practice of prohibition, and the principle of noninterference accepted by the treaty powers. It further explained that the notice, as written in Japanese, consisted of two distinct parts, the one referring to Christianity and the other to evil religions, and modified the text of the edict to clarify the meaning: "The ban on Christianity will be strictly observed as in the past. Evil religions are strictly forbidden."[59]

Along with renewing the ban on Christianity, the new government intensified its suppression of the so-called hidden Christians, descendants of the seventeenth-century Christians who had been discovered in great numbers since 1865, especially in the districts and islands around Nagasaki. The appearance of the Japanese Christians and their contact with Catholic missionaries alarmed the government, and conflict seemed inevitable. After warnings and various sorts of harassment and reprisals in 1866 and 1867, a severe persecution began in 1868, leading to the arrest and decapitation of a number of the leaders of the Japanese Christians and the deportation of several thousands to other provinces. The Urakami Incident, in which approximately three thousand Christians from Urakami were deported, especially aroused the sentiment of the foreigners in Japan.[60] As the rumors of persecution spread, the treaty consuls in Nagasaki stated in a letter to the Governor General of Kyushu that even though they did not want to interfere in the internal affairs of Japan, "in the name of humanity" it was their duty "to make earnest remonstrances against a step which certainly would prevent all civilized nations from regarding Japan as heretofore, a civilized nation."[61] The deportation plan was, nevertheless, enforced, and the consuls again warned that "any outrage against humanity committed against innocent persons only because they profess the Christian faith cannot but injure the reputation of the Japanese government in the eyes of the civilized world."[62] Ōkuma Shigenobu later recollected that the French minister at a meeting in Osaka in 1869 had threatened to intervene militarily to protect the Christians, to which Ōkuma had rejoined: "Your threat shows how good reason we have to fear Christianity; for as soon as trouble arises, there is instantly talk about gunboats."[63] The question of toleration for Christianity apparently received more attention from the treaty power representatives than any other single issue in the period from 1868 to 1870.[64]

Generally it could be said that the demand for religious toleration became the ultimate condition for the conclusion of treaties based on the principle of equality. This became particularly evident when Japan sent a diplomatic mission, the Iwakura Mission, to the West in 1871 to negotiate a revision of the humiliating unequal treaties. The Japanese envoys were met with strong criticism in the United States and Europe; mass demonstrations were held in London, Paris, and The Hague; and the

Japanese government finally realized that it had to change its policy toward Christianity. In 1872 and 1873 the deported Christians were gradually released; and finally, on February 24, 1873, the government ordered that the notice boards prohibiting Christianity be removed. Even though it was explained that this was done because the content of the edict was generally known, the decision symbolized the beginning of a policy of tacit recognition of Christianity in Japan.[65]

MISSIONARY ACTIVITY

The missionary presence in Japan in the years before 1873 was an open violation of Japanese law, which proscribed Christianity, and with the principle of noninterference in religious matters, accepted by the treaty powers. Nevertheless, from the Western point of view, missionary work was regarded as a natural consequence of the opening of Japan. Even though the consuls from time to time felt obliged to urge zealous missionaries to refrain from propagation among Japanese outside the foreign concessions,[66] the treaty powers generally supported the missionaries and shared their concern for the Christianization of Japan, as we have already observed. The successful mission of the Russian Orthodox Church was even started by a priest employed by the Russian consulate at Hakodate, the later so famous Archbishop Nicolai.[67]

The first missionaries arrived in 1859, when the new treaties allowed foreign residence in Nagasaki and Kanagawa, the present Yokohama. Actually, Japan had been considered a prospective mission field many years before the opening of the ports,[68] and it was characteristic that some of the members of Perry's expedition in 1853 were deeply concerned about missionary work in Japan and later returned as missionaries.[69] In spite of the strict prohibition of Christianity, missionary circles generally expected that the opening of Japan would make it possible to "lay the foundations of a church."[70] It was even suggested that the Japanese were aware of such consequences.

> The Japanese are shrewd, and know enough, experimentally, about Christianity, to understand that the license to its followers to reside on their soil, and to enjoy their own forms of worship, must be followed by its propagation: in other words, that the exercise of our religion involves making converts and planting churches. . . . As you, or I should rather say, we, were the first to occupy China, so your missionaries were the earliest Protestant explorers to cast a wistful eye over the then inaccessible fields of Japan.[71]

Since the ban on Christianity prevented the missionaries from direct propagation, they generally depended on teaching and medical work as the most efficient methods for contact and propagation. Some missionaries established small schools in their homes. The government seemed to approve such teaching, sent students to the missionaries, and even employed some missionaries as teachers of English and Western learning in its own schools.[72] In a similar way, Catholic missionaries taught French, and the Orthodox Father Nicolai taught Russian and English.[73]

Since Christian scriptures were strictly prohibited, the missionaries made use of "scientific works containing an admixture of Christianity," as it was explained by a missionary in Nagasaki. Geographical, historical, and scientific works translated into Chinese were considered "the pioneer literature for Japan." Works in Chinese are understood by all well-educated Japanese, it was explained, and "these works are destined to be eminently useful in doing away with this people's misconception of Christianity and thus preparing the way for the circulation of the Scriptures."[74] From 1857 to 1873 more than twenty different Chinese books had been reproduced in Japan for missionary purposes; a Buddhist priest made a list of ninety-six Christian scriptures imported to Nagasaki by 1865.[75] As one might expect, such methods were condemned by the critics of Christianity, as in the following section from an anti-Christian pamphlet that circulated in Kyushu in 1868:

> In the same way the Americans and English have built Jesus halls, and five or six priests coming, try to lead astray the talented and clever men of Japan. These priests of the Jesus doctrine live mostly in private houses, and under the pretence of teaching astronomy, geography, and the use of fire-arms, and medicine desire in actual fact to spread about the abominable poison of Jesus.[76]

The freedom of religious worship and practice guaranteed to foreigners was systematically used as a basis for missionary expansion among the Japanese. The first Protestant church was built in Nagasaki in 1861, and the first Catholic church was dedicated in Yokohama in 1862. They were formally built for the exclusive use of foreigners, but actually also aimed at the Japanese. When the latter was opened to the public in 1862, it was visited by large numbers of Japanese, giving the missionaries opportunities to respond to questions and to preach. After one month of undisturbed activity, thirty-three visitors were suddenly arrested. They were finally released at the demand of the French consul, but the missionaries had to promise to abstain from preaching to the Japanese. We have already noticed the fervent activity on the part of Catholic missionaries when a great number of hidden Christians sought contact with them after the completion of the church in Nagasaki in 1865. The work eventually resulted in brutal persecution of the Christians; the foreign consuls had to acknowledge the illegal character of the missionary activity and to promise to do their utmost to prevent propagation to Japanese outside the foreign concession.[77] In spite of such serious warnings, the work of the Catholic, Orthodox, and Protestant missions continued, and the years before 1873 can generally be seen as the time when the foundation was laid for the respective churches.

The missionary presence naturally alarmed the government; the missionaries were under constant surveillance through spies who enrolled as their students and collected information about their activities.[78] Both missionaries and Western diplomats emphasized the radical difference between the ambitions of the Portuguese traders and missionaries in earlier centuries and the peaceful objectives of the present Western powers;[79] but the government, still suspicious, opposed and interfered with missionary work until 1872–1873.

In sum, in spite of the strict prohibition of Christianity and the basic principle that the treaty powers should avoid anything that could "excite religious animosity," the presence of the Western powers in Japan made a great impact upon the religious situation: Christianity was openly practiced by the foreigners; the treaty powers exercised a constant pressure on the Japanese authorities to abandon their anti-Christian policy; and a number of missionaries engaged, directly and indirectly, in propagation among the Japanese. The implications of these developments for the Buddhist reaction to Christianity will be discussed in the following chapter.

CHAPTER TWO

Buddhist Defenses against Christianity

> They [the Buddhist priests] are certainly a strange set of
> men, if my suspicions are founded; for they have bought
> whole boxes of Chinese Bibles and Christian books and
> tracts, and all, as they said, for the purpose of teaching
> their scholars. These books, perhaps gotten for bad pur-
> poses only, may yet turn out a blessing to many, quite
> contrary to the wicked intentions.
>
> Guido F. Verbeck, Reformed missionary in Nagasaki

THE EXAMINATION of the Tokugawa background and the religious
implications of the opening of Japan has clarified some of the reasons
why Buddhism identified itself with the anti-Christian forces. The critical
state of Buddhism in the mid-nineteenth century further explains its vehement reaction against Christianity and the defense measures it adopted
against the alien religion.

THE CRISIS OF BUDDHISM

INNER CORRUPTION

More than two centuries of government support and supervision during
the Tokugawa period had brought Buddhism into an extremely demoral-
ized state. Certainly, there had appeared a number of outstanding Buddhist leaders, scholars, and pious priests who are still respected for their
great contributions to Japanese Buddhism; moreover, the compulsory
affiliation with Buddhist temples had enabled Buddhism to penetrate to
all classes of the population, and Buddhist scholarship was flourishing.[1]
Historians are, however, unanimous in concluding that the privileged
status of Buddhism had been accompanied by spiritual and moral decay;
rather than promoting Buddhism, the result seemed to be formalism,
stagnation, and lack of spiritual vigor. The priests became tools of feudal
administration, and their religious function was often limited to funerals
and memorial services. Even Buddhist scholarship lacked creativity and

was characterized by formalistic exegesis. Many of the priests lived in luxury, protected and controlled by the government and supported by offerings from parishioners. Many times the government had to issue regulations against the sexual debauchery of the priests, and in extreme cases imposed sentences of exile, forced retirement, and house arrest.[2] Consequently, Buddhists were often despised for their depravity; in the words of a critic in the late Tokugawa period: "The priests are all stupid; they confuse the people, waste national resources, and offend morality."[3] Tsuji Zennosuke, who devotes the last volume of his history of Japanese Buddhism to a thorough analysis of anti-Buddhist thought and Buddhist decay in the Tokugawa period, concludes that Buddhism became entirely formalistic, a trend that was intensified by the class system and the administrative structure of head temples and subtemples; the status of the priests and temples was fixed, leading to a complicated difference between high and low.

> Even the sects which had originally arisen among the common people became prejudiced by a remarkable class conception; the priests became increasingly aristocratic, Buddhism was alienated from the people, and anti-Buddhist thought arose with a terrible power. Buddhism was almost paralyzed; only because of inertia temples and priests barely managed to protect their social position.[4]

According to Kishimoto Hideo, Buddhism "faced the epoch-making events of the Meiji Restoration with no concern about its own degeneracy or the future."[5] The statement is somewhat exaggerated, as there were, in fact, a number of deeply concerned Buddhists; the general trend was, nevertheless, characterized by indifference, spiritual weakness, and moral corruption. This remained a constant problem for Buddhist reformers throughout the nineteenth century, and made Buddhism an easy target for criticism.

ANTI-BUDDHIST THOUGHT

In addition to inner corruption, Buddhism was threatened from without by several trends of anti-Buddhist thought that had gained momentum during the Tokugawa period, notably among Confucian and Shinto scholars.

Even though Buddhism and Confucianism are usually able to coexist harmoniously and even support each other, there is in Confucianism a latent anti-Buddhist tendency that was clearly spelled out in the Tokugawa period. This was all the more threatening to Buddhism because the Confucian influence penetrated the entire society. A number of outstanding Confucian scholars functioned as advisors to the shogunate, and Confucianism became the official philosophy of state; it dominated all levels of intellectual and social activity of the government and the ruling class and regulated the pattern for social relations and family life.[6]

Among adherents to the Chu Hsi school, Hayashi Razan (1583–1657) criticized Buddha for neglecting benevolence and obligation and for rejecting loyalty and filial piety in order to seek the Way. Yamazaki Ansai (1618–1682) blamed Buddhism for neglecting the five social relationships and the five Confucian virtues.[7] Such criticism from a moral and social point of view was generally shared by Confucian critics.[8]

A great number of Confucians combined their rejection of Buddhism with an attempt to unify Confucianism and Shinto. Japan was regarded as the divine land where the two religions should unite against Christianity and Buddhism. For instance, Hayashi Razan blamed Buddhism for the decline of the nation and of Shinto, and advocated the restoration of the nation through rejection of Buddhism and worship of the Shinto gods. With its historical interest Confucianism shared with Shinto its tendency to glorify the past, and contributed to the renewal of Shinto and the development of Kokugaku, or the school of National Learning.[9]

Confucian critics further rejected the Buddhist world view as illusory; the belief in transmigration, heavens and hells, and the Buddhist concern for the next world seemed incompatible with the Confucian emphasis on the present world. The geocentric (Ptolemaic) theory, which had originally been introduced by Jesuit missionaries, was also used to attack Buddhist cosmology, according to which the mythological Mount Sumeru was believed to be at the center of the world, surrounded by concentric circles of continents and oceans. Historical criticism, introduced by Tominaga Nakamoto (1715–1746), was also used to question the authenticity of Mahayana Buddhism.[10]

The strongest attacks on Buddhism were more practical, based on economic and political arguments although they were often combined with the more esoteric types of criticism. Buddhist priests were denounced as idle and useless elements in society, representing a financial drain. "The temples serve no function," Kumazawa Bansan wrote. "They are an extravagant drain on the national treasury."[11] It was suggested that rather than government protection Buddhism deserved to lose its privileges and to be submitted to severe restrictions.[12] The members of the nationalistic Mito school were particularly harsh in their criticism; they denounced Buddhism as detrimental to the state. Such criticism increased as the financial and political situation in the country deteriorated toward the end of the Tokugawa period. It became especially harsh in the 1830s, and led to the first violent efforts to destroy Buddhism in the fief of Mito in the 1840s.[13] The lord of Mito, Tokugawa Nariaki (1800–1860), expressed his strong aversion to the Buddhist priests in the following way: "My retainers and my people regard the priests as traitors and should never, as long as my rule lasts, devote themselves to Buddhism. . . . The bonzes are my enemies. My retainers and my people should hate the bonzes who [leave their homes and] betray the country with their eternal world."[14]

Shinto also developed anti-Buddhist tendencies, especially through the rediscovery of classical literature and history in the school of National Learning, represented by such scholars as Motoori Norinaga (1730–1801) and Hirata Atsutane (1776–1843). While Shinto and Buddhism had long been unified in a syncretistic whole, called Ryōbu Shinto, or "Dual Aspect Shinto," Buddhism was now rejected as an alien, non-Japanese element, and the integration of Shinto into Buddhism was regarded as a defilement of Shinto. The otherworldliness of Buddhism with its longing for the Pure Land was criticized as incompatible with the affirmative nature of Shinto, and the traditional Buddhist cosmology was also rejected from the point of view of Shinto mythology and scientific knowledge.[15]

These two currents of anti-Buddhist thought—Confucianism, represented primarily by the Mito school, and Shinto, represented by the school of National Learning—together prepared the ground for a wave of anti-Buddhist violence that reached its peak in the first years of the Meiji period and threatened the very existence of Buddhism.

GOVERNMENT PRESSURE AND ANTI-BUDDHIST VIOLENCE

In the attack on Buddhism in the fief of Mito in the 1840s, 196 temples were abandoned, and a great number of priests were forced back to secular life. At the same time Shinto was restored to power; Shinto funerals were adopted and cremation was forbidden. Similar attacks on Buddhism took place in the 1850s and early 1860s in domains where the influence of the Mito school and the school of National Learning was strong, such as Satsuma and Tsuwano. The real blow to Buddhism came with the restoration of Imperial rule in 1868, when the new government ordered the separation of Buddhism from Shinto and the disestablishment of Buddhism, and began to favor Shinto at the expense of Buddhism. Buddhist priests attached to Shinto shrines returned to secular life or had to become Shinto priests; all Buddhist statues, bells, and implements of worship had to be removed from the shrines and were often destroyed by zealous Shinto priests. Buddhist names attached to shrines were abandoned and revised according to Shinto traditions. In 1870 an Imperial Rescript announced the adoption of the so-called Great Doctrine, or Daikyō, proclaiming the exalted Way of the (Shinto) Gods and promoting Shinto as a national religion.[16] In an attempt to restore the ancient traditions, the government had established the Department of Shinto (Jingikan), which in 1869 was given a position in the government above the Grand Council of State (Dajōkan). In 1871 the Department of Shinto was replaced by the Ministry of Shinto (Jingishō), which was in turn replaced by the Ministry of Religious Education (Kyōbushō) in 1872. The latter changes represented a gradual lowering of the status of Shinto; for the government modified its policy as it realized that the attempt to establish Shinto as a state religion was unpopular.[17] Nevertheless, the influence of Shinto was still predominant when the Ministry of Religious Education in 1872 and 1873 issued further instructions about the dissemination of the Great Doctrine. The essence of the Great Doctrine was, for instance, defined in three articles:

1. To make veneration of the Gods and love of the country the basic principle
2. To propagate the rule of Heaven and the way of man
3. To teach reverence of the Emperor and respect for the Imperial instructions[18]

A hierarchy of teachers or moral instructors *(kyōdōshoku)*, including Shinto and Buddhist priests, was appointed by the ministry to propagate the principles of the Great Doctrine. Its ultimate aim was to create a unified national education in which both Shinto and Buddhism were integrated; however, it was characterized by a one-sided emphasis on reverence for the Emperor and worship of the Shinto gods. In January 1873 the Academy of the Great Teaching, or Daikyōin, was opened in Tokyo as a training center for the moral instructors. Originally proposed by the Buddhists, it was marred by tensions and conflicts between Buddhists and Shintoists; but the general purpose and the curriculum of the academy resulted in a Shinto dominance in the academy itself and in similar branch institutions in the provinces. Many Buddhists cooperated willingly in the dissemination of the Great Doctrine, but some found the Shinto dominance intolerable. For instance, Shimaji Mokurai and Ōzu Tetsunen criticized the unification of (Shinto) worship and government, and advocated that Buddhism separate from the Academy of the Great Doctrine. In 1875 four branches of Shin Buddhism were granted permission to separate from the academy, which was abolished later the same year.[19] The system of moral instructors was not abolished until 1884.

The government did not aim at eliminating Buddhism. The official policy and the popular anti-Buddhist sentiment, however, touched off a series of violent anti-Buddhist movements all over the country; these virtually aimed at the "extermination of Buddhism," as the catchword *haibutsu kishaku* could be translated. The most ruthless persecution took place in the domains of Satsuma and Oki. In 1869, 1,066 temples in Satsuma were ordered abolished, 2,964 priests were ordered to return to secular life, and all subjects were forced to become Shintoists. Officials

Fig. 2. A drawing of a scene in which a moral instructor teaches the three articles of the Great Doctrine to children, emphasizing patriotic values and Emperor worship. Included in Shigeyoshi Murakami, *Japanese Religion in the Modern Century* (Tokyo, 1980). Courtesy of University of Tokyo Press.

destroyed Buddhist images, sutras, and accessories, and at least on the surface Buddhism disappeared.[20] In Oki, Buddhism was totally destroyed. Strong waves of anti-Buddhist violence occurred also in the domains of Mino, Matsumoto, Sado, Tosa, and Toyama.[21] In Toyama, a stronghold of Shin Buddhism, the Buddhists were ordered to abolish more than 1,630 temples, leaving only eight temples intact, one for each Buddhist sect. Buddhist statues, bells, and other metal implements were collected in great quantities and melted down to produce guns. The temples were finally restored in 1872, after strong protests from the Buddhist priesthood. In many places where Buddhism was strong the efforts to destroy it provoked riots among the Buddhist population.[22]

Ienaga Saburō has characterized the anti-Buddhist movement in those years as the first extensive persecution ever experienced by the Buddhist world in Japan.[23] A contemporary Buddhist priest, Fukuda Gyōkai, expressed his view on the desperate situation in the following way:

> At the present, provincial temples are being destroyed; people are withdrawing their membership and this causes temple revenues to decline; priests are gladly returning to secular life. Although there is no demand to destroy Buddhism, there probably has been nothing to compare with this situation in the fourteen or fifteen centuries during which Buddhism has been in Japan. In my opinion, there will be an Imperial Rescript eradicating Buddhism within five to seven years.[24]

The position of Buddhism was of course too strong and deep-rooted to allow total destruction. Nevertheless, the inner decay, the strong current of anti-Buddhist thought, and the anti-Buddhist policy of the Meiji government seemed to many observers to represent the final blows to Buddhism, reducing it to a crumbling remnant of the past, unable to respond to the challenges of the new age.

DEFENSE AND AGGRESSION

Under such circumstances it was hardly surprising that the Buddhist world reacted to Christianity both defensively and aggressively. Actually, it is difficult to distinguish between the two reactions; the very existence of Buddhism was at stake, and defense and aggression were two aspects of the same matter. Even though Christianity was only one of the enemies Buddhism had to confront in its struggle for survival and revival,[25] only Christianity was confronted as a real enemy; consequently, the reaction against Christianity was all the more vehement. Buddhist apologists responded to Confucianism, Shinto, and popular movements not by rejecting these but by defending themselves against the charges and advocating peaceful coexistence, as in the past.[26] They also went out of their

Fig. 3. A drawing showing Buddhist sutras being burned during the anti-Buddhist campaigns in the early Meiji period. Included in Shigeyoshi Murakami, *Japanese Religion in the Modern Century* (Tokyo, 1980). Courtesy of University of Tokyo Press.

way to adapt themselves to the religious policy of the new Meiji government. The relationship to Christianity, on the other hand, was one-sidedly negative. The oppressed "evil religion" now appeared again as the spiritual backbone of the encroaching Western civilization. Compromise seemed impossible.

MORAL AND SPIRITUAL REFORM

The natural response of sensible Buddhist leaders to inner corruption and external criticism was to emphasize moral and spiritual reform of the priesthood.[27] Two of the most outstanding leaders of the period, Shaku Unshō (1827–1909) and Fukuda Gyōkai (1806–1888), interpreted the contemporary anti-Buddhist movement as the inevitable result of Buddhist decay. Unshō wrote: "Worldly pleasures have made the priests forget their duty and so seduced them that the authorities have reprimanded them. We cannot endure this shame." Gyōkai argued that the real tragedy was not that temples had been destroyed and that Buddhism was losing its position. Instead, "We grieve before heaven and man that we have lost the greatest Good. In order to regain this Good, and for this reason only, priests should pray for the elevation of truth and the prevention of *haibutsu kishaku*."[28]

In such cases of self-examination and call for reform the major challenge came not primarily from Christianity but from other anti-Buddhist movements. The Christian impact on the early reform movements was rather limited, compared to that on later Buddhist reformers and reform movements.[29] Rather than stimulating reform, the presence of Christianity provoked negative reactions and drew the attention to defensive measures: the foreign religion should be destroyed.[30] Only Fukuda Gyōkai seemed to keep aloof from emotional denunciations, warning against superficial attacks on Christianity.[31]

BUDDHIST APOLOGETICS AND THE STUDY OF CHRISTIANITY

While the positive call for reform was only to a limited degree related to the advent of Christianity, Buddhist apologetics was more and more characterized by a strong anti-Christian zeal. After the opening of Japan hardly any apologetic work was published that did not include a criticism of Christianity. The rejection of Christianity became the primary duty of the Buddhist world; it remained a central concern until the enforcement of mixed residence in 1899. A prominent Buddhist priest wrote around 1865 that while the people were occupied with coastal defenses, the Buddhist priests devoted themselves to the defense against Christianity.[32]

Considering the strong anti-Christian trend of Tokugawa Buddhism, it is not surprising that Buddhist propagators not only maintained traditional attitudes to Christianity, but also made use of and published old anti-Christian literature, such as Fabian's *Ha-Daiusu* [Refutation of Deus], Suzuki Shōsan's *Ha-Kirishitan* [Refutation of Christianity], Sessō's *Taiji jashūron* [Extermination of the evil attachment], and others.[33] Chinese literature written by Confucian and Buddhist scholars was also introduced. For instance, a collection of anti-Christian literature from the late Ming dynasty, entitled *Hajashū* [A collection of refutations of the evil religion], was published in 1855.[34] A prominent Pure Land Buddhist, Ugai Tetsujō (1814–1891), published two collections, *Hekijashū* [A collection of refutations of the evil religion] in 1860, consisting of Chinese treatises, and *Hekija kankenroku* [A personal record of refutations of the evil religion] in 1861, consisting of both Chinese and Japanese writings.[35]

The Chinese anti-Christian literature thus introduced was primarily the product of the vehement Buddhist opposition to the Jesuit mission in the late Ming dynasty, notably in the early seventeenth century. While the Jesuits in China, under the leadership of Matteo Ricci, had established a harmonious relationship with Confucianism, Buddhism and Taoism had been rejected as incompatible with both Christianity and Confucianism. The doctrine of Emptiness was denounced as nihilistic, and the doctrines of transmigration and annihilation (Nirvana) were criticized as incompatible with social obligations. The Buddhists responded by defending Buddhist doctrines against Christian misinterpretations and by publishing a great number of anti-Christian treatises. They criticized the Christian doctrine of God by identifying him with lower divinities in the Buddhist pantheon or by arguing that Christian faith was superfluous in China where the worship of Heaven had been instituted from ancient times.[36]

Even though such old literature exercized a formative influence on the Buddhist attitudes to Christianity after the opening of Japan, it was no longer adequate; it lacked depth and was one-sidedly concerned with Christianity as a threat to the state. Moreover, the situation had changed after 1854; Japan was no longer a secluded country, and Protestantism represented a type of Christianity different from the Catholicism criticized in the old Chinese and Japanese literature.[37] Consequently, to obtain relevant material for anti-Christian propaganda, a number of Buddhists engaged in a more direct study of Christianity. As early as 1861 the officials of the Gakurin, or seminary, of Nishi Honganji, the head temple of the Honganji sect of Shin Buddhism, argued in a petition to the head temple that the arrival of foreign ships and the beginning of Christian propagation necessitated an up-to-date study of Christianity.[38] That same year the Episcopal missionary in Nagasaki, C. M. Williams, reported that an old priest had made detailed inquiries about the Christian faith, including such matters as the differences between Catholicism and Protestantism, and that he borrowed a great number of books which he studied thoroughly.[39] This was probably Haraguchi Shinsui, a priest who in 1862 was employed at the Gakurin and who, through his studies, contributed to the increasing concern about Christianity among Buddhist priests.[40]

In 1862 Chief Abbot Ōtani Kōei (1852–1923) of Higashi Honganji, head temple of the Ōtani sect of Shin Buddhism, attended a sermon in Japanese in the new Catholic church in Yokohama, accompanied by a scholar priest named Higuchi Ryūon (1800–1885). Even though the preaching was finally stopped and a number of Japanese visitors arrested, the Buddhists were alarmed at the bold attempt to propagate the proscribed religion, and Ryūon was put in charge of anti-Christian apologetics. He collected Christian literature, and his studies resulted in a number of anti-Christian writings.[41] Another priest from the same sect who also distinguished himself as an early student of the Bible and Christian literature was Ishikawa Shuntai (1842–1931).[42] Ugai Tetsujō has already been mentioned as a compiler of old Chinese and Japanese anti-Christian literature. He also wrote a number of refutations of Christianity, including a criticism of the only Christian treatise that in this period introduced a substantial criticism of Buddhism.[43]

The discovery of the hidden Christians in the Nagasaki area in 1865 and the fervent activity of the Catholic missionaries among them aroused the resentment of the Buddhists and increased their suspicion and animosity against Christianity. In 1867–1868 the Honganji sect dispatched twenty priests to enroll as students of the missionaries and report on their activities, especially in the Nagasaki area. The Ōtani sect followed their example in 1869. Some of the spies even submitted to baptism to conceal their secret purpose; a few actually became Christians.[44] The missionaries naturally were disgusted when they discovered the secret purpose of some of their students. After he realized that one of his students had published an extremely abusive tract, Guido F. Verbeck, a Reformed missionary in Nagasaki, wrote:

> They are certainly a strange set of men, if my suspicions are founded; for they have bought whole boxes of Chinese Bibles and Christian books and tracts, in fact, hundreds of volumes, and all, as they said, for the purpose of teaching their scholars. These books, perhaps got for bad purposes only, may yet turn out a blessing to many, quite contrary to the wicked intention. For any one comparing the pamphlet with the original sources of all Christian knowledge must see what a bold and wicked perversion of the truth has been practiced.[45]

The study of Christianity was not only the concern of a few scholars, but was in 1868 officially integrated in the curriculum of the seminaries of Higashi Honganji and Nishi Honganji.[46] In addition to the study of

orthodox Shin Buddhism, the Gakurin of Nishi Honganji introduced six
new subjects; two were concerned with the study of other Buddhist traditions, while the four others included the study of the calendar, the
National Learning (including Shinto), Confucianism, and the refutation
of Christianity *(hajagaku).*[47] In a similar way an Institute for Apologetic
Studies (Gohōjō, or Gohōgakujō) was established within the seminary of
Higashi Honganji, under the leadership of Higuchi Ryūon and Senshōin
Kūkaku.[48] In addition to the study of Protestantism and Catholicism,
designated as *yōgaku,* or "Western Learning," the institute devoted itself
to the study of the National Learning, Confucianism, and astronomy,
including arithmetic and astronomical observations; Christianity, however, seemed to attract almost the entire attention.[49] The somewhat
strange combination of subjects is not surprising when we consider the
anti-Buddhist trend of the National Learning and Confucianism, and further, that astronomy, geography, and Western science were used by the
missionaries as important means of undermining traditional beliefs and
promoting Christian understanding.[50] Hence the Buddhists found it necessary to defend the classical Buddhist cosmology against the more
advanced knowledge of the missionaries.[51]

In this way a number of Buddhist scholars and priests gathered a considerable amount of knowledge about the Bible, Christian doctrines,
church history, and Christian denominations.[52] In spite of its defensive
character, the study of Christianity stimulated reform efforts, which in
turn provoked friction with the officials of the head temples. Shimaji
Mokurai and Ōzu Tetsunen were even suspected of heresy, for in an
effort to stop the drift away from temples to churches they had encouraged the easy practice of *nenbutsu,* or the invocation of Amida Buddha,
and paid less attention to the complicated nuances concerning the pure
faith.[53] Because of such problems the "non-Buddhist studies" *(gegaku)*
were abandoned at the Gakurin of Nishi Honganji in 1870. The same
year one of the leaders of the Institute for Apologetic Studies at Higashi
Honganji, Senshōin Kūkaku, was assassinated, and the institute was
closed.[54] Nevertheless, similar studies were pursued with great zeal during the rest of the century.

An additional source of information that provided abundant material
for anti-Christian propaganda should also be mentioned in this context:
Buddhist travels to the West. The first Buddhist delegation was sent to
Europe as early as 1872; since such travels represented a new trend,
however, they will more appropriately be dealt with in the examination
of Buddhist-Christian relations after 1873.

Some further examination of the numerous tracts and books used in
anti-Christian propaganda after the opening of Japan will clarify what
type of criticism the Buddhists leveled against Christianity. Actually, it is

almost impossible to distinguish clearly between the study of Christianity, preaching and lectures, and anti-Christian literature. For the study aimed at propaganda, and a great bulk of the literature was based on lectures and speeches.[55]

The dominant trend of Buddhist propaganda was characterized by the effort to identify "defense of Buddhism" *(gohō)* with "defense of the state" *(gokoku)* and "opposition to the evil religion" *(bōja)*. Christian expansion, it was argued, should be precluded through forcible prohibition; and the most effective argument still seemed to be the traditional charge from the early Tokugawa period that Christianity endangered national security. Perhaps because Buddhism itself was under heavy attack for similar charges, the Buddhists responded by combining their anti-Christian propagation with a heavy emphasis on the beneficial role of Buddhism for the sake of the State. Even though the Buddhist world was caught in the conflict between the support of the shogunate and the call for Imperial restoration, the Buddhists based their activity on a foundation that unified the two camps: the antiforeign and anti-Christian sentiment.[56] Especially within the Honganji sect, which had a strong foothold in Choshu, a number of so-called loyalist priests *(kinnōsō)* combined their loyalist emphasis with warnings against the danger of Christianity.[57] A loyalist priest named Gesshō wrote in his *Buppō gokokuron* [A Buddhist defense of the country] in 1856 that the supreme doctrine of Buddhism was inseparably linked with the national destiny and would perish if the nation perished. Buddhist apologetics consisted, according to Gesshō, "exclusively in protecting the nation through the Buddhist doctrine."

> If the Land of the Gods is held by the barbarians and the [Christian] heresy prospers, how can we protect Buddhism from decay? . . . I am really afraid that the present trend will finally result in fraternization between the foreigners and the ignorant coastal population. . . . They will be led astray by the heresy and become a [rebellious] band of brutes. Hence, as for the urgent need of coastal defense, today nothing compares to resisting religion [Christianity] with religion [Buddhism].[58]

Even though the new Meiji government favored Shinto at the expense of Buddhism, the Buddhist priests consistently identified Buddhism with loyalism. The first two issues recommended for study by the Association of Buddhist Sects in 1868 were the "indivisibility of Imperial and Buddhist law" and the "study and refutation of Christianity."[59] This explains why most Buddhists easily transferred their allegiance from the shogunate to the Meiji government and compromised with, and even supported, the religious policy of the government, in spite of its bias toward Shinto.[60] Even Fukuda Gyōkai, who distinguished sharply between secular and religious concerns, argued that the "Imperial Way" and the "Ways of Confucius and Buddha" were as intimately related as warp and woof, beginning and end.[61]

One might have expected that the renewed study of Christianity, which involved direct contact with the missionaries and acquaintance with the Bible and recent Christian literature, would have led to a modification of traditional prejudices. Its only function, however, was to add new arguments to the old charges.[62] Those who enrolled as students of the missionaries mixed factual information with rumors and badly founded suspicions, and the missionaries quite appropriately rejected their writings as "bold and wicked" perversions.[63] Ryōgen, a Buddhist priest who published his observations in *Sakiyō chabanashi* [Tales of Nagasaki] in 1868, warned that Christianity would ultimately lead to insurrection and thus destroy the country. Christianity was irreconcilably antagonistic to loyalty and filial piety, he argued; because the Christian God was regarded as "the Great Prince and the Great Father," other princes and fathers were reduced to "little princes and little fathers."[64] Jesus was depicted by Ryōgen as a poor man who, banished in his youth, traveled through many countries learning about magic arts.

> He deceived the ignorant lower classes, making them follow himself until his evil design of murdering the sovereign of the country and seizing the country and people for himself being discovered, he was put to death by crucifixion. He was a most traitorous animal. . . . Considering that the foundation lay in such violent wickedness, it is impossible that any of his believers can be either filial or loyal. They say that the most unfilial and disloyal can go to the very top place in heaven if they only love the Lord of Heaven.[65]

Similar charges of destruction of social relations, notably filial piety and loyalty, were also expressed in *Gokoku shinron* [A new treatise about the protection of the country], written by Yasukuni Tan'un in 1868. Tan'un also warned that the commandment against worship of graven images would lead to the destruction of the shrines where the emperors were worshipped and of the sacred images of the gods and of the ancestral tablets. The leaders of the country were challenged to expel the Christians and prevent "this necromantic doctrine" from throwing the country into confusion.[66]

There existed, of course, nuances and shifting emphases in Buddhist apologetics on this point.[67] The dual theme of praising Buddhism for its beneficial role and condemning Christianity for its detrimental influence, however, was carried on by Buddhist propagators in a surprisingly monotonous way until the end of the nineteenth century.

A second trend in Buddhist propagation was represented by a variety of attacks on the Bible and Christian doctrines. The direct contact with missionaries and acquaintance with recent literature increased the knowledge of Christianity among Buddhist apologists; several of them actually claimed to have studied the Bible from first to last page.[68] But this increased knowledge was not accompanied by deeper understanding. In addition to attempting to prove the destructive character of Christianity, Buddhist apologists quoted and commented on biblical passages solely to expose the numerous contradictions of the Bible and to demonstrate the foolishness and shortcomings of its doctrines. The passages and issues selected for discussion were extremely limited and almost identical in the various books: from the Old Testament, usually the stories of the creation, Adam and Eve and the fall, Noah and the flood, and the Ten Commandments; from the New Testament, the birth of Jesus, his unbelievable miracles, a few of his sayings that seemed antagonistic to loyalty and filial piety, and his crucifixion and resurrection.[69] The creation story was rejected as inadequate; God was described as a jealous Lord who ruled the world through arbitrary decisions and emotional whims and who failed even to keep his own commandments; Jesus was portrayed as a parvenu who taught insurrection and propagated a subversive morality; and so on.[70]

This rather one-sided selection was probably the result of a variety of causes. It reflected older anti-Christian literature, which often dealt with similar themes; it corresponded generally to what the missionaries emphasized in their teaching; it represented elements that were particularly incompatible with Buddhist doctrines; and, finally, even though some Buddhists claimed to have studied the whole Bible, the Buddhist students of Christianity seemed to have had a predilection for Genesis, Exodus (the Ten Commandments), and the Gospels.[71]

A third theme in Buddhist apologetics was related to the confrontation with modern science, expressed particularly in the defense of the ancient Buddhist cosmology against the heliocentric theory of Copernicus. The latter was by now accepted by Christianity and adopted by the missionaries as an effective tool for undermining traditional beliefs. For the Buddhists, therefore, the defense of the old cosmology became a central issue.[72] According to the traditional Buddhist ideas, inherited from Indian cosmography, Mount Sumeru was a magnificent mountain of gold and gems in the center of the world, the abode of gods and Buddhas. It was surrounded by concentric circles of mountains and oceans, and the planets revolved around it.[73] From the Buddhist point of view, the negation of this cosmology implied nothing less than the collapse of the entire Buddhist universe, including the innumerable Buddha-lands, heavens, and hells; the doctrines of transmigration and rebirth in the Pure Land; and even the existence of the Pure Land itself, which was believed to be a geographical reality, situated as a Paradise in the West. D. Thompson, a

Presbyterian missionary, reported in 1870 about his instruction of Buddhist priests: "A few facts these men have learned, in Geography and Astronomy, have taken from them some of the fixed dogmas of their faith, and they are now ready to doubt the whole system which included such absurdities."[74] The problem was most painful for the adherents of the Pure Land tradition, the most powerful segment of Japanese Buddhism.[75]

The efforts of Buddhist scholars to undertake a serious study of astronomy in order to prove the fallacy of the Western theories have already been mentioned. One of the most zealous apologists for the old view was Sada Kaiseki (1818–1882), who wrote a number of treatises defending the Buddhist cosmology, including *Buppō sōseiki* [The Buddhist genesis] in 1878. Sada and his supporters, however, were fighting against heavy odds, and the issue lost its attraction as soon as the Buddhist enlightenment movement gained strength.[76] The defeat of the old Buddhist cosmology was a painful experience for traditionally minded Buddhists, but introduced, on the other hand, a new relationship to Western thought. Hitherto Christians and other critics had made use of Western science to prove the inadequacy of Buddhism; once the Buddhist scholars recovered from the traumatic confrontation with the heliocentric theory, they discovered that rather than threatening Buddhism, modern science provided them with effective weapons against Christianity.[77]

Finally, Buddhist anti-Christian propagation was characterized by a strong reaction to a book entitled *Shakkyō seibyū* [Correcting the errors of Buddhism], a systematic criticism of Buddhism from the Christian point of view written by Joseph Edkins (1823–1905), a missionary in China from the London Missionary Society; it was first published in Shanghai in 1857 and later revised and published several times.[78] Just as Chinese anti-Christian literature was used by Japanese Buddhists, Chinese Christian literature was in the beginning one of the major sources of Christian propagation in Japan. Edkins' book was not referred to specifically until 1865, but, according to Ebisawa Arimichi, it might have been brought to Japan by missionaries in Nagasaki as early as 1861.[79] The apprehensions about the book grew gradually among the Buddhists until in 1868 they took a number of counter-measures to neutralize its influence.

Since Edkins' charges to a great extent corresponded to the criticism Japanese Buddhists had encountered from Confucian and Shinto scholars, one might have expected that they would not pay so much attention to his writings. The reaction was, however, extremely strong. In 1868 the book was singled out by a Shin Buddhist apologist as one of the most troublesome treatises against Buddhism, along with Hirata Atsutane's Shinto-based refutation of Buddhism and one Confucian treatise.[80] The refutation of Edkins' book was, consequently, given the highest priority, and was in 1868 included in the curriculum of the apologetic studies at Higashi Honganji and Nishi Honganji.[81] The demand for the book was so great that the Buddhists themselves printed new editions to use as material for further studies, probably as early as 1868.[82] The first refutation of Edkins' treatise, written by Ugai Tetsujō, appeared in April 1868. With his prominent position in Buddhist circles, his counter-attack was representative of the Buddhist response to Edkins. His refutation was entitled *Shakkyō seibyū shoha* [The first attack on *Shakkyō seibyū*] and was, as the title indicated, followed by a second attack in 1873. He followed Edkins' pattern, commenting on and criticizing each of the twenty chapters in Edkins' book. In addition to rejecting the charges against Buddhism, he attacked Christianity for its neglect of filial piety and respect for superiors and argued that the Ten Commandments were imitations of Buddhist precepts.[83] A great number of subsequent attacks on Edkins in the following years were mainly written by Shin Buddhist priests, who most painfully felt the need of defense against Edkins' charges. They generally reiterated traditional arguments and were lacking in originality; as a phenomenon, however, the reaction reveals how sensitive the Buddhist world was to Christian criticism.

It is difficult to evaluate exactly what significance the missionaries attached to *Shakkyō seibyū* and what impact it made on the missionary community. They probably shared Edkins' negative view of Buddhism; and the fact that the book was brought to Japan indicates that a criticism of Buddhism was welcome as a useful source for potential confrontations.[84] As a set of religious doctrines, however, Buddhism was hardly felt to be a problem. The missionaries were certainly aware that Buddhism still had a grip on the common people, and they knew from personal experience that the priests could be troublemakers; but generally they considered it to be only a question of time before Buddhism would lose its power and be extinguished.[85] Thus Edkins' book hardly did more than confirm their bias against Buddhism.

In the first two decades after the opening of Japan, then, Buddhist anti-Christian propaganda was characterized by the identification of defense of Buddhism with national defense and opposition to Christianity, attacks on the Bible and Christian doctrines, defense of the traditional Buddhist cosmology against the heliocentric theory, and a strong reaction against Edkins' criticism of Buddhism. Rather than promoting understanding, the direct contact with missionaries and the increasing knowledge of Christianity deepened traditional prejudices and suspicions. Apart from specific issues of temporary importance, such as the defense of Buddhist cosmology and the reaction to Edkins' criticism, the main arguments and the general way of thinking hardly transcended the pattern inherited from the Tokugawa period. As we shall see, this remained very much the dominant trend of anti-Christian propaganda even to the end of the nineteenth century. For a Buddhism struggling for existence, Christianity represented such a threat that a more comprehensive understanding could hardly be expected.

OTHER ANTI-CHRISTIAN ACTIVITY

The Buddhists did not limit themselves to studying, preaching, and writing about Christianity. Their traditional role as agents for the enforcement of the proscription policy has already been depicted and will not be repeated here. Only a few observations will be added regarding the Buddhist activity after the Meiji Restoration in 1868, when Buddhism lost its privileged position and Shinto instead was established as a semiofficial state religion.

The disestablishment of Buddhism was accompanied by a renewal of the proscription of Christianity; and the Buddhists actually seemed to be more concerned about strict enforcement of the ban on Christianity than on Buddhism itself being thrown into a severe crisis. They adapted themselves to the Shinto-dominated policy of the government and at the same time put pressure upon the government to maintain its anti-Christian policy.[86] For instance, Shaku Unshō wrote in a memorial to the government in 1868 that while Buddhism and Confucianism were "assisting Shinto," Christianity should be excluded as a great evil.[87] The next year the members of the Association of Buddhist Sects pledged that they would "lay down their lives for the country" in the defense against Christianity, and presented a petition to the government against introducing Christianity; to their great relief they received an affirmative response.[88] It might also be noted in this connection that a draft constitution made under the supervision of Kido Kōin in 1872 not only maintained the proscription of Christianity and other alien religions, but even included a paragraph stating that the doctrine of Buddha should be the main religion of Japan.[89] As a politician of Choshu descent, Kido was closely related to such prominent Buddhists as Shimaji Mokurai, Akamatsu Renjō, and Ōzu Tetsunen, who also came from Choshu,[90] and the exceptional draft may partly have resulted from pressure from such Buddhist leaders.[91]

The most conspicuous case of anti-Christian activity took place mainly in the Nagasaki area, where thousands of hidden Christians after 1865 were seeking contact with French Catholic missionaries. The very existence of these Christians and the fervent activity of the Catholic missionaries posed an open challenge to the policy of prohibition, and the Buddhists were eager to suppress the movement. The first persecution occurred as the Christians in Urakami in 1867 refused to make contributions to the temples or to let the deceased be buried according to Buddhist rites.[92] Interrogations and arrests in Urakami and other places were followed by executions of Christian leaders in 1868 and the final deportation of more than three thousand Christians to distant provinces in 1870 and 1871.[93] With their traditional role as supervisors in religious matters the Buddhist priests found it natural that they should be entrusted with the task of exhorting or coercing the Christians to abandon their faith and embrace Buddhism. In July 1868 five sects of Shin Buddhism submitted a petition to the government demanding that their priests be authorized as instructors among the Christians. The fervent study of Christianity in the apologetic institutes of Nishi Honganji and Higashi Honganji began soon after, and was to a great extent meant to prepare the priests for propagation among the Christians in the Nagasaki area. Even though the petition was finally rejected by the government,[94] a number of Buddhist priests were actively attempting to convert the Christians both in Urakami and other places in the Nagasaki area and in the provinces to which the Christians had been deported.[95]

When the government hesitated to yield to foreign pressure demanding the abolishment of its anti-Christian policy and the release of arrested and deported Christians, it was explained that "Shintoists and Buddhists would rise up in anger and there would be a great disturbance" as the result of such changes.[96] When the notice boards against Christianity were finally removed in 1873, the Buddhists actually instigated protest riots among the peasants in some districts.[97] Two decades after Japan was opened for contact with the rest of the world, the Buddhist relationship to Christianity was still characterized by the attitudes that had been nurtured during the centuries of seclusion.

CHAPTER THREE

Christian Disregard of Buddhism

The Kingdom of Satan is already divided against itself. The people favor Buddhism, but they are not allowed to even repair their Buddhist temples, except with a special and exceptional permit from the government. The government favors Sintooism, while many, at least not a few who are destined to be the leading minds, think that Christianity is better than either.

O. H. Gulick, American missionary

MISSIONARY ATTITUDES

THE MISSIONARY MOVEMENT in Japan in the nineteenth century comprised at least three distinct traditions: the Roman Catholic missionaries of the Paris Missionary Society; the mission of the Orthodox Church, represented primarily by Father Nicolai, who later became archbishop; and the Protestant missions, represented by Anglican missionaries from England and the United States and by American missionaries of various Protestant denominations deeply rooted in New England piety.

Because of the tragic history of Buddhist oppression of Christianity during the Tokugawa period, the Catholic missionaries in the modern era could hardly see Buddhism as other than one of the oppressive forces of the *ancien régime*.[1] The only Catholic missionary in the Meiji period who attempted to establish friendly relations with the Buddhist priesthood was Father A. Villion, whose contribution will be discussed in Chapter Five. Because of insufficient material, the Orthodox mission will not be commented on.[2] The following description of missionary attitudes toward Buddhism is therefore primarily based on material concerning Protestant missionaries.

CHRISTIAN EXPANSION AND CIVILIZATION

Apart from their common concern for Christian expansion, the factor that unified all missionaries in Japan was their being in Japan as the religious representatives of the treaty powers. The opening of Japan was understood as the "dawn of Japan," and the prohibition of Christianity was seen as an intolerable barrier against progress, a barbaric remnant of the past that had to be removed before Japan could be treated as a civilized nation. At the same time the Protestant missionaries dissociated themselves from the earlier Catholic missions. They expected that the "repugnance to foreigners, too largely founded on their fear of Jesuitical treachery and mercantile rapacity," would yield to "the more genuine and just procedures of Americans and Europeans promoting trade and propagating Christianity."[3]

It seemed to be the consensus of missionaries and other Western representatives that Christianization and Westernization were two aspects of the same movement. Townsend Harris aspired once more to open Japan to "the blessed rule of Christianity." The missionaries combined propagation with medical work and instruction in Western learning and Western languages. Chinese translations of Western books on geography, history, and science were used as prominent tools for propagation. "The history of the United States, down to the time of the Revolutionary War, is but the history of Christian sects—of the progress of Christianity," O. H. Gulick wrote in 1871. He argued that the study of history brought the Japanese "straight to the Bible, the proscribed book." "It is vain for them to strive to enter the light of modern civilization and reject the light of Christianity."[4] As the Japanese leaders began to respond positively to Western ideas, the missionaries regarded Westernization as a step toward the adoption of Christianity, or at least "the outward forms of the Christian religion."[5] It was believed that the "desire to obtain knowledge and to understand the great causes of Christian civilization" would pave the way for Christianity.[6]

SPIRITUAL WARFARE

One of the most common words used by Buddhists about Christian missionary work was *shinnyū,* meaning "invasion," "intrusion," or "aggression." The Christian expansion was felt as an intrusion upon the time-honored rights of Buddhism and other indigenous religions. Even though historians tend to regard the Buddhist opposition to Christianity as a disgraceful and embarrassing chapter of Buddhist history, it should be noted that the Buddhist reaction was not entirely unreasonable. In fact, it corresponded to a great extent to the methods and the theological outlook of the Christian propagators.

Expressed in traditional terms, the missionary expansion was conceived by the missionaries as the "occupation of Japan,"[7] and the missionaries regarded themselves as "religious invaders."[8] Such expressions certainly did not sound as belligerent in nineteenth-century missionary ears as their literal meanings suggest, and they were easily combined with more peaceful words such as those about "the joy of the reaper in the day of harvest";[9] nevertheless, they certainly implied expectations of a spiritual warfare with conflicting religions and ideologies.

> The religion of Japan, it is hoped, will offer less resistance to missions than that of India or China. It does not hold its votaries with such an iron grasp as Hindooism. It is less compact and exacting than that which prevails in the Middle Kingdom. Already the missionary societies which were first on the ground, have attained to the joy of the reaper in the day of harvest. At this early stage of their warfare, a few, apparently, have cast away their idols, and chosen instead the only living and true God.[10]

We have already seen how the missionaries established themselves in Japan under the protection of the treaty powers, often resorting to diplomatic pressure and violating what the Japanese authorities regarded as an undisputable agreement about noninterference in religious matters. Moreover, since the passport regulations allowed the missionaries a certain degree of travel in the interior, they increasingly combined travel with systematic propagation, ignoring the fact that the purpose of such travel was strictly limited to scientific research and recreation. At a later stage a missionary justified such activity, arguing, in a statement that probably reflected the opinion of the majority of the missionaries, that the "aggressive spirit of Christianity has its source not only in the essential principles of the Christian system, but also in the personal example and instructions of its Divine Author."[11] The heated controversies about treaty revision, extraterritoriality, and the related questions of mixed residence and missionary activity in the interior of Japan in the 1880s and 1890s revealed among many Japanese a latent fear of aggression.[12]

Most of the American missionaries came from small towns in areas that were dominated by New England piety. They held to strict Puritan ideals, emphasizing "personal conversion, implicit faith in the Bible, moral rigor, and a sense of mission."[13] According to Howes, the missionaries for the most part took small-town New England attitudes with them and retained these while in Japan.[14] In addition to the sense of mission already referred to, certain aspects of their theological outlook could easily prevent a sympathetic understanding of Japanese religions in general and of Buddhism in particular.

The most obvious theological factor was the strict monotheism of the missionaries, combined with an uncompromising rejection of all sorts of idolatry. Faith in the One, True God and rejection of ancestor worship, Emperor worship, and Shinto and Buddhist rituals as incompatible with the biblical injunction against idol worship represented, in positive terms, liberation from superstition and oppressive traditions;[15] in negative terms, it implied an inevitable conflict with traditional religious practices. In Japan folk religion, Shinto, Buddhism, and Confucianism traditionally coexisted in a fairly harmonious relationship, according to quite well-defined patterns. The main concern has traditionally been to maintain the harmony of the community; even oppression of religious traditions sought primarily to preserve social and religious stability.[16] When Christianity, in contrast, claimed total allegiance from its converts and rejected other religions as idolatry and superstition, the intruding religion was inevitably felt as a threat to the entire structure of the society.[17]

Such theological exclusiveness was further strengthened by the strong emphasis upon the redemption of Christ as the unique basis of salvation, a doctrine that even the Christian converts found hard to comprehend.[18] The Puritan morality also created a feeling of distance from Japanese religions. The missionaries aimed at fostering strong individuals and found it difficult to understand the collectiveness of Japanese religions, where the individual seemed to be of secondary importance to the community. The emphasis on moral rectitude, strict sexual ethics, abstinence from liquor and tobacco, and observance of the Sabbath represented striking contrasts to the moral laxity and spiritual decay in religious circles, especially in Buddhism.[19] The missionaries' simplicity in religious matters also disposed them negatively to the ornate ceremonies in Buddhism, which perhaps reminded them too much of Catholicism.[20]

In his discussion of the Meiji missionaries, Howes concludes that they went "half way around the world to share their faith and to try to recreate in Japan the world they had known at home," and generally failed to acquire the intellectual breadth usually associated with such travel.[21] It would be misleading, however, to conclude that the missionaries failed to appreciate and understand the Japanese, or that they were entirely negative in their evaluation of Japanese culture and religion. The missionaries included a number of outstanding personalities who not only contributed to the dissemination of Christianity and Western ideas, but also took great interest in the study of things Japanese. Some even distinguished themselves as pioneers in the study of the Japanese language, literature, history, and also religion, especially Confucianism.[22] As for Buddhism, the missionaries were certainly not more biased than most other Western observers, and they were perhaps less categorical than most Japanese intellectuals.

OBSERVATIONS ABOUT BUDDHISM

Apart from generalities about idol worship and spiritual warfare, the early Protestant missionaries made surprisingly few references to Buddhism. They were probably acquainted with the ideas expressed in

Joseph Edkins' treatise about Buddhism, imported to Japan in the 1860s; but there is no evidence that his detailed criticism of Buddhism was of great interest to the missionary community. Rather than systematic studies their comments about Buddhism were based on random observations and incidental encounters or on secondary information regarding the state of Buddhism.[23] The most characteristic types of observations can be summarized as follows:

First, the missionaries soon discovered that Buddhism was generally held in low esteem by the political and intellectual leaders. Guido F. Verbeck observed that perhaps most of the higher classes "had no faith in Buddhism, the religion of the common people."[24] Missionaries in Yokohama referred in 1866 to the openness toward Christianity among the young samurai and concluded, "They despise the Buddhist creed and the Buddhist priest."[25] In short, the popular Confucian charge that the Buddhist priests were "pleasure-seekers, idle and useless beings . . . given to the vices of wine and women," must have been well known among the missionaries.[26]

Second, the fact that many of the early missionaries began their work in rented Buddhist temples must have strengthened their impression of the corruption of Buddhism and Buddhist priests. The priests vacated their temples not because they welcomed the new doctrine, but mainly because they needed the money; some temples may have been abandoned in connection with the anti-Buddhist movement.[27] William Elliot Griffis, in his biography of Samuel Robbins Brown, commented on the use of a temple in Yokohama in 1859:

> It seems curious that the Japanese should so readily lend their temples as residences to foreigners, but so they did, for even then these canny islanders loved lucre, and they love it more now. Indeed they are in the world's race for dollars. The idols, tables, temple furniture, incense burners, and what-not had been stowed away in a recess beside the main altar and shut up there in darkness and disuse by a board partition.[28]

The very fact that the temples were "cleared of idols" and used for Christian worship certainly aroused the feeling that Buddhism was yielding to the superior power of the Christian religion.[29]

Third, the missionaries observed the active role of the Buddhist priests in the suppression of Christianity,[30] especially in connection with the persecution of the hidden Christians after the Restoration in 1868.[31] Their own experiences with Buddhist spies who pretended to be sincere students were certainly disappointing. Verbeck referred to them as "a strange set of men," and characterized their writings as the result of "the instigation of the Father of lies himself."[32] In 1870 missionaries referred to the watchful "eyes of the authorities and the priesthood" as a constant reminder of opposition and possible persecution.[33] In Griffis' words, Christianity was still "accursed by priests, outlawed by government, and in popular notion a system of sorcery and diabolical magic."[34]

Finally, the missionaries interpreted the Shinto-dominated policy of the Meiji government and the disestablishment of Buddhism as the "death-blow" to Buddhism,[35] or at least as an attempt to "root out Buddhism."[36] A missionary report in 1873 referred to the "utter disregard" for Buddhism by the government and described the result of the government policy in the following way:

> Many of the temples have been secularized by a government which does not hesitate for a moment to take a temple for the purpose of a hospital, a school-house, or for a reception palace for the nation's guests. The temple bells have been taken, without number, sold and exported for the bronze of which they are made. One ship alone took to England six hundred tons of bronze, the larger portion of which was old temple bells.[37]

One of the first missionaries to visit Kyoto after the opening of Japan commented in 1873:

> As I saw these surging millions in the interior, and as I wandered all one afternoon among the ancient and beautiful Buddhist temples on the east of Kioto, and found the paths leading to them and the works about them grass-grown, and the temples almost deserted, even by the priests, so that we could wander among the halls, corridors, and rooms, as in deserted ruins, I could not refrain from thinking,—and wishing and praying, for the men ready to go up and possess this land.[38]

Generally, Buddhism was regarded as hopelessly behind the times, ready to be replaced by a faith that could promote civilization and progress. A certain Dr. Chaplin summarized in the *Baptist Missionary Bulletin* what seemed to be the common view of most missionaries:

> Shintooism and Buddhism, as religions, are radically defective, and cannot stand against an enlightened civilization, while Confucianism, as being un-religious, if not anti-religious, leaving God quite out of the account, fails to meet the deepest wants of man. All these must therefore give place to a better system.[39]

It was hoped that the deficiency of traditional religions and the confusion and conflict created by the government policy would provide "space . . . for the introduction of Christianity," as D. C. Greene suggested in 1871.[40] O. H. Gulick expressed similar ideas.

> The Kingdom of Satan is already divided against itself. The people favor Buddhism, but they are not allowed to even repair their Buddhist temples, except with a special and exceptional permit from the government. The government favors Sintooism, while many, at least not a few who are destined to be the leading minds, think that Christianity is better than either.[41]

In short, when the missionaries from time to time referred to Buddhism, they generally depicted it as a power that had lost or was losing its meaning in the new age; Buddhism was, consequently, ignored as a potential rival.

REASONS FOR IGNORING BUDDHISM

The disregard of Buddhism cannot be explained merely by referring to narrow-minded and insensitive missionaries unable to appreciate the spiritual essence of the Japanese people. It seems more appropriate to say that the missionaries were too sensitive to the prevalent intellectual and political trends to realize the latent power of Buddhism. They had a number of reasons for ignoring it.

First, the missionaries' conclusions about Buddhist decay were generally well founded. Because of inner corruption, anti-Buddhist thought, and government pressure and violence against Buddhism, the very existence of Buddhism was at stake. The exaggerated antagonism against Christianity only emphasized the desperate situation of Buddhism.

Second, while Buddhism had been protected during the Tokugawa period, the general trend of the early Meiji period was antagonistic. The anti-Buddhist ideas of Confucian and Shinto scholars were transformed into an official policy of religion, according to which Buddhist doctrines were almost relegated to oblivion.

Third, the missionaries were acquainted almost solely with Japanese intellectuals whose zealous pursuit of Western ideas strengthened the missionaries' confidence in the Christian (Western) civilization. The samurai background and Confucian training of most Japanese leaders confirmed their feeling that Buddhism was doomed. The first Japanese converts were mainly recruited among such people, and the anti-Buddhist prejudice was consequently quite strong in the Japanese churches as well, even without the help of the missionaries.[42]

Fourth, as a consequence of the dominant trend in intellectual and political circles, the missionaries were concerned about more vital challenges than what they could see in Buddhism. Confucianism rather than Buddhism was singled out as the spiritual and moral backbone of the Japanese people, with negative and positive implications. Japanese Confucianism included, to a certain degree, a religious understanding of God, humankind, and the universe; but primarily it provided the ideological framework for social and political life, expressed in such virtues as patriotism, loyalty, and filial piety. Most of the Buddhist anti-Christian propaganda referred to above depended more on Confucian ideas than on Buddhist doctrines. One of the most characteristic expressions of Confucian criticism of Christianity in the early Meiji period was Yasui

Sokken's *Benmō* [An exposition of error], published in 1873.[43] The author was an influential Confucian scholar, and his attempt to revive the traditional charges against Christianity created a great deal of uneasiness in Christian circles. Such challenges from people in powerful positions could not be ignored in the same way as criticism from the Buddhist priesthood.

On the other hand, the missionaries also discovered that Confucianism was not necessarily antagonistic to Christianity but could promote a certain understanding of Christian doctrines and thus serve as a sort of preparation for Christian faith.[44] The more religiously oriented Wang Yang-ming philosophy, especially, served in a number of cases as a mediator between traditional ideas and Christianity.[45] The Confucian spirit and morality also had much in common with the Puritan ideals of the missionaries. In spite of criticism from the Confucian side, then, the Christians were generally not antagonistic to Confucianism but rather regarded Christianity as a fulfillment of Confucian ideas.[46] This perception also explains why many of the missionaries devoted so much energy to the study of Confucianism rather than Buddhism.

Fifth, another phenomenon in addition to Confucianism drew the attention of the Christian propagators: the trend of religious indifference, atheism, materialism, and the atheistic element of Western science. The inherent element of rationalism, utilitarianism, and this-worldliness in Confucianism easily disposed Japanese intellectuals toward a negative attitude toward religion, especially Buddhism. Townsend Harris observed in the late 1850s that "all the higher classes are in reality *atheists*."[47] Such a leading intellectual as Fukuzawa Yukichi (1834–1901) found it impossible to combine modern learning with belief in gods or Buddhas,[48] and Nishi Amane (1829–1897) regarded religions as "foolish faiths and superstitions" which would be dissolved with enlightened education.[49] The challenge from antireligious ideologies, which became much more serious as the enlightenment movement gained strength during the 1870s, will be discussed more thoroughly later. It was, however, serious enough in the early 1870s to make some missionaries realize that the crisis of traditional religions did not necessarily favor Christianity, but might involve a choice between religion and irreligion, or, as the missionaries saw it, between Christianity and "infidelity."[50] In 1873 alarmed Christian leaders realized that theological education had to pay more attention also to Western atheism.

> The native preachers, it is said, will need an education sufficiently thorough to enable them to meet the objections of scientific atheists. There is now a strong tendency to infidelity. Idolatry is at a discount; but atheism, not Christianity is taking its place. This is largely due to the influence of German physicians, employed as medical instructors.[51]

Against this background of Buddhist decay and challenges from more powerful ideologies one could hardly expect the missionaries to consider Buddhism a major challenge.

THE POTENTIAL OF BUDDHISM

The only missionary who at this early stage seemed to apprehend the potential of Buddhism was D. C. Greene, Congregational missionary in Kobe. Even though he hoped that the conflict between Buddhism and Shinto would benefit the missionary work, he was convinced that the government would never manage to root out Buddhism. He had observed that Buddhism had a "far stronger hold upon the people than the Sintooism which the rulers wish to uphold and strengthen," and that "whatever a Japanese may be while he lives, he is a Buddhist when he dies."[52] Referring to the failure of the Shinto-dominated policy, he wrote in a letter in 1872: "Our great fight in Japan, it becomes more and more clear every day, is to be with B[uddhism] which I suspect presents itself in a far more vigorous form here than in China or any other part of the world."[53] Consequently, in 1872 he recommended further studies of Buddhism and asked for the purchase of books on the subject for his own use, and wrote: "The fact that at so many points it touches Christianity makes it of vital importance that we have clear views as to what its teachings are and as to its relation to Christianity."[54]

Greene's awareness of Buddhism as a potential rival for supremacy was still a singular phenomenon and was apparently not followed up with further studies or counter-measures. His clear-sighted understanding of the power of Buddhism, however, anticipated the increasing concern toward Buddhism among Christians in Japan in the 1880s and 1890s.

CHAPTER FOUR

Christianity and Buddhism in the 1870s and 1880s

The Cross was adored and "Amens" resounded in every city and every town of the land. An ancient Buddhist country was on the verge of being converted into a Christian country.

Shaku Sōen, prominent Buddhist priest

THE OPENING of Japan and the advent of Christianity in the mid-nineteenth century aroused complex feelings among Japanese Buddhists: resentment, animosity and fear, aggression and resignation. One might also have expected a touch of admiration of or fascination with the foreign faith. The available material about the initial contact, however, reveals only negative reactions. There was no room for concessions. The history of proscription and seclusion and the forced opening of the country had created a situation in which opposing Christianity seemed the only possible reaction.

The year 1873 introduced a new epoch in the history of the Christian church in Japan, which also led to changes in Buddhist-Christian relations. The removal of the notice boards against Christianity was accompanied by a number of changes in official policy, indicating that Christianity was tacitly recognized by the government. Although official recognition was not obtained until 1889, when the Constitution granted that "Japanese subjects shall . . . enjoy freedom of religious belief," after 1873, religious toleration was more and more regarded as an indispensable condition for friendly intercourse with the rest of the world, and Japan entered a period of progressive modernization and Westernization. The government no longer regarded Christianity as an evil doctrine, tolerated among the foreigners but prohibited for the Japanese; it was freely propagated and it gradually spread. Christianity's rapid growth in the 1880s challenged and alarmed the Buddhist world.

The pattern of relationship between Buddhism and Christianity depicted in the previous chapters was to a great extent maintained also after 1873, but changing circumstances gradually brought about new constellations and other types of relationships between the two religions. While the initial period had been characterized by a one-sided Buddhist concern with Christianity, in contrast to the almost total disregard of Buddhism on the part of the Christians, the relationship after 1873 was characterized by increasing mutual antagonism. This situation is graphically expressed in Figure 8, where both Buddhist and Christian priests are involved in quite aggressive confrontations. A few trends had particular bearing upon the relationship between Buddhism and Christianity in the 1870s and 1880s.

WESTERNIZATION AND CHRISTIANITY

When the Japanese government in 1873 ordered the notice boards against Christianity removed and introduced a policy of tacit recognition of Christianity, it was, to a great extent, the result of diplomatic pressure. Religious toleration seemed an indispensable condition for the international recognition of Japan as a civilized nation.[1] The change had immediate consequences for the relationship between Buddhism and Christianity. The Buddhists had actively supported the proscription of Christianity and had even, to a certain degree, been used by the government in its suppression of Christianity. The policy of proscription had given official sanction to the Buddhists' anti-Christian propaganda. The tacit recognition of Christianity, consequently, meant that the Buddhist opposition to Christianity lost a great deal of its motivation and vigor. Christianity, on the other hand, could expand without fear of reprisals, and was supported by a general trend favorable to the adoption of Western traditions and institutions.

The relationship with the West had traditionally been conceived as a compromise between Western technology and Eastern spirituality or, as expressed by Sakuma Shōzan, "Eastern morality, Western technique."[2] Such distinctions, however, proved deceptive; international trade and the rapid expansion of contacts with the rest of the world inevitably resulted in a degree of Westernization that went far beyond a purely technological development. The adoption of the new technology itself was, of course, never a question of merely outward changes. The modernization of industry and economy, and of the political, administrative, communication, military, and educational systems brought about great changes in social life and the general way of thinking. Even such a minor change as the abolition of the old lunar calendar and traditional holidays and the adoption of the Gregorian calendar, including Sunday as a public holiday, was not merely a change to a more rational system; it symbolized the recognition of Western priorities and values in the daily rhythm of the people.[3] The details of the process of modernization and Westernization cannot be presented here; but a few comments must be made about two movements that made a considerable impact upon the Japanese society in the 1870s and 1880s: the enlightenment movement, which stood for "civilization and enlightenment" *(bunmei kaika)*, and the liberal political movement, which advocated "freedom and people's rights" *(jiyū minken)*.

The most prominent forum for the enlightenment movement was the speaking society Meirokusha, which was named after the year it was founded, Meiji six *(meiroku)*, or 1873, and its journal, *Meiroku zasshi*, published from 1874 until 1875, when it was suspended. The society counted among its members almost the entire intellectual elite of the 1870s, including Fukuzawa Yukichi, Nishi Amane, Mori Arinori, Nishimura Shigeki, Nakamura Keiu (Masanao), and others.[4] Apart from a general agreement that Japan had to develop from "barbarism" toward civilization, identified with Western civilization, Meirokusha did not represent any consensus in politics, religion, or philosophy. The members included Christians and supporters of Christianity as well as people who opposed Christianity. The most prominent advocate of Christianity was Nakamura Keiu (1832–1891), who in 1872 published a memorial to the Emperor entitled "Memorial on the Imitation of Westerners." He argued that the adoption of Western patterns and behaviors had to be accompanied by a true appreciation of the source of the Western civilization, Christianity. "To delight in branch streams or tributaries, while forgetting the source of these, is, I feel, a delusion," he wrote; he even argued that the Emperor should receive baptism and become the "lord of the church."[5] Some members of the enlightenment movement were Buddhists who combined their concern for religious freedom with opposition to Christianity.[6] Many of the members were indifferent to religion, evaluating it on a narrowly rationalistic or utilitarian basis. Tsuda Masamichi suggested, for instance, that the question of Japan's future religion should be settled through a discussion between Christian missionaries and Buddhist priests, and even suggested the adoption of Christianity as state religion.[7] Their Confucian background and the predominantly rationalistic tendency among the members generally did not dispose them toward appreciation of the Christian faith. They were apparently much more concerned with what the missionaries called the modern Western infidelity, that is, Western thought critical of Christianity.[8] As we shall see, Fukuzawa Yukichi and his disciples temporarily lent their support to Buddhism and Shinto, against Christianity.[9] Fukuzawa's sudden support of Christianity in 1884 was not based on a new appreciation of Christianity but on the opportunistic conclusion that the adoption of Christianity would facilitate the process of Westernization.[10] Thus the direct support of Christianity by those in the enlightenment movement was ambiguous, even contradictory. Nevertheless, as one of the most influential movements in the years after 1873 it contributed to the increasing interest in Western culture, which gained momentum in the 1870s and reached a peak in the mid-1880s.

The Popular Rights Movement, or more accurately, The Movement for Freedom and People's Rights (Jiyū Minken Undō), was more closely related to Christian circles than the enlightenment movement had been. It came into prominence in the late 1870s and made a great impact on the political life of the 1880s.[11] While the enlightenment movement had been dominated by scholars and intellectuals with a wide range of cultural and political interests, the Popular Rights Movement was more one-sidedly political and caused a great deal of political agitation and struggle. Kōsaka Masaaki has characterized the decade from 1877 to 1887 as "a period of political frenzy, of gales and raging seas," "an age of disruption, of dismemberment."[12] Newspapers and public opinion were preoccupied with freedom and popular rights.

With its emphasis on natural rights, equality, and democratic ideas the Popular Rights Movement shared a common ideological concern with Protestant Christianity. The movement was critical of the government and of the Buddhist, Shinto, and Confucian establishment, as well as of the politically reactionary trend among scholars who rejected natural rights on the basis of Darwinian ideas.[13] The Popular Rights Movement and Christianity tended to draw their membership from people with similar social backgrounds, such as former samurai who were estranged from government circles, prosperous landowners, and merchants;[14] and the alliance between the two movements developed quite naturally. A great number of prominent Christians were involved in the Popular Rights Movement; some left the church and devoted themselves to political activity, while others became Christians as a result of their concern for popular rights.[15] Even though most of the leaders of the Popular Rights Movement and the Liberal party (Jiyūtō), founded in 1881, were not Christians, they were often defamed as if they were. And although not Christians, they were generally supportive of the Christian church. For instance, the leader of the Liberal party, Itagaki Taisuke, cooperated with missionaries and Japanese pastors. In 1882 he denounced Shinto, Buddhism, and Confucianism as detrimental to national progress, and openly asserted his sympathy for Christianity at a time when the people were using the epithet "Christian" to stigmatize political opponents.[16] He advocated publicly the adoption of Christianity and did all he could to aid the Christian movement from outside, but without committing himself to Christianity.[17]

Fig. 4. Gamblers were often hired by the police to disturb public meetings. Illustration included in Miyatake Gaikotsu, *Meiji enzetsushi* [A history of Meiji oratory] (Tokyo, 1929). Courtesy of the main library of Doshisha University, Tokyo.

The relationship with the Popular Rights Movement was a strong incentive to the Christian movement. It contributed to the popular interest in Western and Christian political ideas and also strengthened the Christian commitment to social and political goals. It is thus not surprising that the Christians were well prepared for the political changes introduced by the Meiji Constitution (1889) and the National Diet (1890).[18] On the other hand, the relationship gave Christianity a political profile that nurtured apprehensions in conservative circles that Christianity had political ideas and goals in disharmony with the established values and the national polity. Such criticism became, as we shall see later, an important element in the anti-Christian propaganda from the end of the 1880s. Since Buddhism tended to adhere to conservative trends, the Christian involvement in the Popular Rights Movement contributed to the increasing polarization between Buddhism and Christianity in the 1880s.

As for the government, no consistent policy had been followed in relation to Christianity, Westernization, and political and social change. A fairly liberal and progressive period in the 1870s[19] was followed by a reactionary period in the early 1880s. In 1881 the government promised political reform and started preparations for the promulgation of the Constitution in 1889 and the opening of the Diet in 1890. At the same time, however, a new emphasis was put on Confucianism and traditional values. Such conservative trends were generally antagonistic to Christianity and the political opposition. The official attitude to Christianity was negative, and the Popular Rights Movement was severely oppressed, culminating in the dissolution of the Liberal party in 1884.[20]

The oppression of the Popular Rights Movement and the political opposition was apparently closely related to the economic crisis and unrest in the early 1880s. By oppressing the Popular Rights Movement, the government stifled the grass roots modernization movement. A new policy was adopted around 1885, when the government drew attention from domestic to foreign affairs, especially to the problem of treaty revision, and started to promote a rapid modernization and Westernization from above.[21]

In supporting Westernization, Fukuzawa sought to obtain international recognition as a basis for revision of the unequal treaties. Such ideas gained wide support. As early as 1883 the government had erected in Tokyo an elaborate social hall where Western-style dances were held for the political elite and the diplomatic corps.[22] Many influential persons sent their children to Christian schools, and public opinion changed toward open support of Christianity. English was more popular than at any time before, and the government made strenuous efforts to promote the study of English.[23] Especially in 1885 and 1886, Japan seemed to be adopting wholesale, though superficially, many Western traditions, in-

Fig. 5. A public meeting ends in total disruption. Illustration from *E'iri jiyū shin-bun,* included in Miyatake Gaikotsu, *Meiji enzetsushi* [A history of Meiji ora-tory] (Tokyo, 1929). Courtesy of the main library of Doshisha University, Tokyo.

cluding some incongruous elements of Western social etiquette and fashions. Recalling the period of Westernization, a prominent Christian commented that the Japanese, in their rejection of Japanese traditions and the adoption of Western things, were "intoxicated with foolishness."[24]

The churches, of course, were greatly favored by the Westernizing trend. In spite of some reservations, it was welcomed as a great opportunity for expanded missionary work. In 1886 a mission report referred to a "most intense and wonderful enthusiasm for the study of the English language."[25] Another missionary reported enthusiastically, "Everywhere men are called for, and men who can read English! This is the cry from villages as well as towns."[26] It was certainly no coincidence that the period of rapid Westernization became a period of rapid growth for the Christian church. The intimate relationship between Westernization and Christian expansion in those years had far-reaching consequences for the relationship between Buddhism and Christianity, both in the period of Westernization and in the subsequent period of nationalism that began in the late 1880s.

CHRISTIAN EXPANSION

The interest in Christianity cannot be explained merely as a result of the trend of Westernization; there was remarkable leadership from both missionaries and Japanese Christians. The following description of the development of the churches is limited to aspects that had a particular bearing upon the relationship with Buddhism.

In spite of prohibition, hostility, and persecution in the years after 1854, a number of Japanese had become interested in Christianity; many of the hidden Christians had become integrated into the Catholic fold, and the first Protestant church among the Japanese was founded in Yokohama as early as 1872. In 1873, with the removal of the notice boards against Christianity, the number of Protestant missionaries more than doubled,[27] and increased rapidly in the following years. The treaty ports naturally served as bases for missionary activity, but after 1873 the situation was characterized by increasing activity outside the ports; and within a few years churches and Christian groups were also organized in cities, towns, and villages in the provinces. The number of Protestant Christians increased from 16 in 1872 to 1,004 in 1876 and 2,701 in 1879.[28] The decade from 1873 has been characterized as a period of "ploughing and seed-sowing,"[29] or even as "a season of progressive realization and performance."[30] Following this early phase the 1880s became an unprecedented period of "rapid growth."[31] The number of Protestant Christians had reached 5,634 in 1882; it increased nearly sixfold in the next decade, as shown in the following table:[32]

Year	Baptized	Church membership
1882	1,179	5,634
1885	3,309	10,542
1888	7,387	24,131
1891	3,513	32,334

The Christian work, initially dominated by missionaries, was more and more carried out by self-confident Japanese workers. As for the missionaries, their activity outside the ports was limited by passport regulations; passports allowing travel into the interior were granted only for "health" or for "scientific investigation." Nevertheless, missionary itineracy became one of the prominent methods of Christian propagation.[33] Many missionaries traveled regularly in the provinces, holding meetings in major cities and towns or anywhere they had contacts. Many also combined medical work or teaching positions in the provinces with propagation. For instance, within a decade after 1873, American missionaries in the Kobe-Osaka area had penetrated the entire region surrounding the two ports and had established churches or Christian communities in the prefectures of Hiroshima, Okayama, Hyogo, Fukui, Tottori, Kyoto, Shiga, Wakayama, Nara, and Mie, and in the four prefectures of the island of Shikoku.[34] Similar expansion took place in other areas.[35]

Missionary itineracy was, consequently, discussed as one of the central concerns of the General Conference of Protestant Missionaries in 1883. Even though some missionaries denounced the combination of itineracy and propagation as a "pious fraud," or simply as a "fraud," it was generally accepted that the passport system could be used to "travel at intervals through all parts of the Japanese empire and, in many ways, scatter the seed of the kingdom."[36]

Meanwhile, Japanese Christians had developed a surprisingly strong sense of responsibility, and soon carried the real burden of propagation. Because of the great number of converts with samurai background, the national church had from the very beginning a remarkable leadership, characterized by a great degree of independence, ambition, and creativity. In 1878, only five years after the notice boards against Christianity were removed, the indigenous Home Missionary Society (Nihon Kirisuto Dendō Kaisha) was founded; it was closely related to the Congregational school in Kyoto, Doshisha, and to the missionaries of the American Board. Japanese pastors and evangelists contributed to the rapid spread of Christianity in the provinces, either independently or in cooperation with itinerant missionaries. Theological students spent their summer vacations preaching in their home districts or in other places, aiming at "nothing less than the Christianising of Japan."[37] In addition, numerous Japanese colporteurs traveled all over the country, selling tracts, Bibles, and parts of the Bible.[38] A report from the Bible Society in 1883 concluded: "In no nation in modern times has the gospel made more rapid progress than in Japan."[39]

The evangelical zeal of the Christians in Japan was further intensified by a wave of revivals that began in 1883, resulting not only in numerical growth, but also bringing about a new spiritual deepening of Japanese Christianity.[40] The word "revival" became so popular that it was even taken into the Japanese language as *ribaibaru*.[41] The spiritual vigor and the expansion of the churches induced a missionary to conclude in 1884 that "the day is not far distant when the people will *flock by hundreds*, and not by tens, into the church of God."[42] Missionaries and Japanese Christians began to anticipate the day when Japan would become a Christian nation.[43]

In addition to traditional propagation, missionaries and Japanese Christians engaged in a number of ventures that made a strong impression upon the contemporary society. Many missionaries served as teachers of Western learning, including language, culture, and science. The private instruction in the homes of missionaries developed into a variety of schools, and education became one of the most promising fields of missionary work.[44] Medical missionaries introduced modern medicine, instructed Japanese physicians, trained nurses, and contributed to prison reform and social work.[45] In 1875 the Doshisha School was founded in Kyoto by Niijima Jō (Joseph Hardy Neesima, as he wrote it in English), in cooperation with American missionaries, a project that caused consternation and opposition among the Buddhists. Missionaries pioneered the field of women's education, especially in the 1880s; numerous women's schools and colleges were founded, and these played a central role in the dissemination of Christianity and Western ideas. Under the influence of missionaries or devoted American teachers a number of so-called bands of converted students of samurai background were formed in Kumamoto, Sapporo, Yokohama, and other places.[46]

Publishing and journalism were also used. In 1875 the first Christian weekly newspaper, *Shichi-ichi zappō* [Weekly miscellany] was founded in Kobe; a number of similar papers were published in the following years. In 1880 the newly founded YMCA sponsored a more serious monthly magazine, *Rikugō zasshi* [The cosmos], as a mouthpiece for Christian apologetics among the "middle and upper classes."[47] It established itself as a leading intellectual magazine in the 1880s,[48] equaled only by *Tōyō gakugei zasshi* [Journal for Eastern art and science], published by scholars at Tokyo University.[49] The apologetical skill was further demonstrated in books written by Uemura Masahisa, Yokoi (Ise) Tokio, Kozaki Hiromichi, and others.[50]

Inspired by the success of public lectures in speaking societies and political campaigns, Japanese Christians agreed in 1880 that "the time had arrived for making some kind of a public demonstration" of the Christian faith, and made bold attempts to bring their message out of churches and preaching places. They appealed to the public in great open-air meetings, or held series of apologetic lectures in public halls. So-called theater meetings were held all over the country; they were a very popular way of addressing the public, drawing large audiences in cities and towns.[51] A missionary described the situation: "The *apologetic age* is begun; no other topic now will draw the multitudes together in Japan like discussions on Christianity. The masses are appealed to as judges, and, surprised that they are of so much importance, they gladly accept the honour."[52]

The rapid expansion and confident leadership of the Christian movement in the 1870s and 1880s inevitably challenged the Buddhist world, and, hence, became an important background for the further development of Buddhist-Christian relations. For the moment the foregoing may be summarized by saying that the variety of methods used to propagate Christianity brought it out of the treaty ports, where Buddhism was less powerful, to the people in the provinces, where Buddhism had its traditional strongholds and where confrontation was more likely.

BUDDHISM AGAINST THE TIDE

The development of Buddhism after 1873 formed a sharp contrast to the successful expansion of Christianity. The Buddhist world was still trapped in a critical situation depicted in Chapter Two. Buddhism's inner weakness and the anti-Buddhist trend of the late Tokugawa and early Meiji periods had rendered Buddhism impoverished and powerless; and the government and the intellectual elite generally ignored Buddhism as an outdated superstition that could only appeal to the ignorant masses. The tacit recognition of Christianity represented another blow, and the predominant Westernizing trend intensified the Buddhist sense of crisis. Apart from a few trends that will be commented on later, Buddhism found itself working against the tide.

Officially, Buddhism maintained a certain privileged position; the government used it for disseminating the nationalistic Great Doctrine (Daikyō), referred to in Chapter Three, and employed Buddhist priests along with Shinto priests as "moral instructors."[53] The Great Doctrine was, however, dominated by Shinto; and progressive Buddhists, who welcomed the new ideas of religious freedom and separation between religion and state, wanted freedom from government supervision. Shin Buddhism was in 1875 granted permission to separate from the Academy of the Great Doctrine, and the academy itself was abolished later the same year. This opposition was a sign of renewal in Buddhism; it brought Buddhism one step toward independence and reform of its methods of propagation. On the other hand, the Buddhist understanding of religious freedom did not seem to imply any readiness to recognize Christianity on equal terms with other religions. The entire system of moral instructors, which gave the Buddhist and Shinto priests a semiofficial status and authority, was finally abandoned in 1884, and the supervision of religious affairs was transferred to the religious authorities of the respective sects. Thus the priests finally lost in people's eyes the legal authority they had assumed until then; and the change was welcomed by the Christians as a weakening of the position of Buddhism and as a preliminary step toward placing Christianity on equal footing with Buddhism and Shinto.[54]

More important than such changes in the official policy was the negative self-image held by many Buddhists in this period. This self-image was closely related to their image of Christianity. Compared to the effective propagation and confident leadership of the Christians, Buddhists felt their prospects to be rather poor.

A Buddhist anti-Christian tract published in 1881, for example, opened with the characteristic statement that "Christianity is spreading like fire on a grassy plain, so that in capital and country there is no place where it is not preached."[55] Referring to Christian statistics for 1881, the Buddhist journal *Meikyō shinshi* deplored the fact that Buddhism was "daily losing ground," in sharp contrast to the "extraordinary" Christian expansion.[56] The same journal described the critical state of Buddhism in 1882 in the following way:

> Buddhism besieged: Ten-dai shiu, without a scholar; Shin-gon shiu, neither men nor money; Zen shiu, its time is past—it hangs like a forgotten fruit; Jōdo shiu, no sect is to be seen—only a solitary [Fukuda] Giōküai; Nichiren shiu, unchanging, obstinate, proud, like a stone; Shin shiu, by flattery obtaining money, it astonishes the vulgar with its splendor.[57]

Akamatsu Renjō noted that "Buddhism was once strong, it is now weak, it may or may not revive."[58] In a public speech in 1881 Kitabatake Dōryū reportedly spoke "with eloquence and tearful pathos on the present deteriorated state of religion in Japan, the laziness of the priests, and the intrusion of Christianity."[59] In 1888 Tajima Shōji published a book in which he prophesied that Buddhism would be ruined if nothing was done to restore it. His pessimistic appraisal was accompanied by an open admiration of the competence and skill of the Christians; the activity of one dedicated Christian for the sake of civilization equaled, according to Tajima, the work of five or ten thousand Buddhist priests.[60] In 1885 Inoue Enryō lamented that all efforts to revive Buddhism merely seemed to bring about its decline and promote Christian expansion.[61] Later he described how Christianity was expanding with a vigor "like the rising sun," while the light of Buddhism was "waning like the moon in the morning sky."[62] Recalling the situation in the 1880s, Shaku Sōen wrote: "The Cross was adored and 'Amens' resounded in every city and every town of the land. An ancient Buddhist country seemed on the verge of being converted into a Christian country."[63]

The general sentiment among the rank and file priests was even more distressing. Compared with the vigorous Christian movement, the Buddhists seemed to lack moral vigor, devotion, and a living faith.[64] Some prophesied the downfall of Buddhism and the triumph of Christianity, and desertion from the Buddhist priesthood was reported in some areas.[65]

The press and public opinion were also generally negative toward Buddhism. The trend of Westernization and the political ideas advocated by the Popular Rights Movement ran counter to Buddhism. As noted earlier, Fukuzawa Yukichi and others who in the early 1880s had supported Buddhism against Christianity later denounced Buddhism and advocated the adoption of Christianity. But even Fukuzawa's support of Buddhism was pragmatic and political; it was not based on a recognition of the religious value of Buddhism and was accompanied by a scathing criticism. Fukuzawa did not believe in Buddhism or respect the priests; Buddhism, as the native religion, was only a tool for protecting the national power.[66] Thus the general impression from the 1880s is that Buddhism was in disrepute, and that the priests were in great distress.[67]

A few points, however, should be added to balance this gloomy image of Buddhism. First, even though Buddhism seemed to be working against the general trend of the times, there was a strong Buddhist current in the enlightenment movement in the 1870s, represented by such prominent Buddhists as Ōuchi Seiran, Shimaji Mokurai, Ōzu Tetsunen, Akamatsu Renjō, and others. Shimaji attempted, in the name of religious freedom, to maintain the independence of Buddhist propagation.[68] Ōuchi and others pioneered in the fields of journalism and public speaking, and also engaged in social activity.[69] A strong urge for modernization and reform came to the fore, and Buddhist delegations went to Europe and America, combining the study of new ideas with opposition to Christianity.

Second, while Buddhism had earlier been criticized from the point of view of modern science and Western thought, it tended more and more to regard these currents as allies against Christianity.[70]

Third, along with the predominant trend of Westernization, there was, especially from the beginning of the 1880s, a conservative reaction that supported Confucian virtues and traditional values against Westernization and new political ideas. Buddhism was generally well in tune with

Fig. 6. *Buttekisō* (the priests who are Buddha's enemies): "Those scandalous [priests] who admire the doctrine of Yaso [Jesus] and throw away their black robes." From Nishikata Kandō, *Buppō gyōshōka* [Buddhist songs at the morning bell] (Tokyo, 1889). Courtesy of Aoyama Gakuin University, Tokyo.

such trends, even though they did not really come into prominence until the nationalistic reaction gained force in the late 1880s and the 1890s.

Fourth, most of the statements about decay and crisis were combined with appeals for the restoration of Buddhism; that is, the negative self-image and the radical recognition of crisis went along with a growing confidence that Buddhism some day would gain sufficient strength to conquer Christianity.

CHAPTER FIVE

Christian Concern
about Buddhism

> Buddhism met the worshiping instinct of the Japanese as
> it had never been met before. It told them of something
> higher and better than the gratifications of passion and
> sense. It offered its explanation of many of the enigmas
> which beset our present life. Above all, it taught of a life
> after the death of the body, where virtue should have its
> reward and vice its desert.
>
> M. L. Gordon, Congregational missionary

BECAUSE OF THE CRITICAL CONDITION of Buddhism described in
the previous pages, most Christians did not view Buddhism as a real
rival. The threat from Western anti-Christian thought had become the
overriding concern for Christian apologetics in the 1870s and 1880s, and
Buddhism seemed to be a comparatively minor challenge. It was still
regarded as a religion of the past, powerless and bound for ruin. A characteristic statement was made by some teachers of Doshisha in 1885.

> Our Japan is a new country. The old institutions and ancient customs are fast
> dying out. . . . Buddhism is gone. Confucianism has lost its power. The tem-
> ples are left in their former grandeur; but they have very few worshipers, and
> those very few worshipers consist only of old men and old women belonging to
> the lowest classes. This is sufficient to show the impotent state of the once
> great religion of Buddha.[1]

As late as 1889 the editor of *Kirisutokyō shinbun* [The Christian]
depicted Buddhism as "a lonely castle in the midst of circling foes to
whom nothing is left but hopeless surrender," and characterized the
growing opposition to Christianity as a futile attempt to "save a waning
cause."[2]

Most references to Buddhism reveal a bias against Buddhism as the
superstitious and idolatrous religion of the masses, as we can see in the
following statements by missionaries and Japanese Christians. Japanese
religions were characterized as "a dense mass of unenlightened, besotted
heathenism."[3] Buddhism was described as a religion "full of superstitions;

its effects upon the morals of the nations is most pernicious; it is involved with false science, and modern science will cut it up root and branch; it is a system of atheism, against which the best part of human nature protests; and it leaves man to save himself."[4] "Buddhist priests have no living faith in what they teach; their morals are very low, and the religion has almost no appreciable moral power over the people."[5] A prominent Japanese Christian characterized Buddhism merely as "a bundle of lies,"[6] and a pastor argued that "the disciples of Buddhism and Shintoism are aided by the disciples of bigotry and superstition in opposing our religion."[7] With such impressions, it is not surprising that few Christians found it worthwhile to study Buddhism seriously.

On the other hand, along with this predominant tendency to ignore Buddhism, a few Christians gradually became aware of its latent power, and hence became more concerned about how to confront it. D. C. Greene suggested at an early stage that Buddhism should be studied thoroughly as a potential rival with a strong hold on the people.[8] Although Greene himself did not seem to have opportunity to engage in further studies of Buddhism,[9] a few others prepared the ground for a more penetrating understanding of Buddhism through various sorts of studies of Buddhist doctrines and practices, as well as through personal association with Buddhist priests.

J. H. DEFOREST: IDOL WORSHIP

The condemnation of idol worship was a common element in missionary preaching and activity; missionary reports and literature often included sweeping statements about "idols," "idol worship," and "idolaters."[10] The Japanese converts, most of whom were trained in Confucian traditions, shared the missionaries' aversion to "the folly of idolatry."[11] A few early tracts were particularly devoted to the refutation of idolatry. A Chinese tract directed against ancestor worship was introduced by missionaries in Nagasaki.[12] Another Chinese tract, *Byō-Shuku mondō* [A dialogue between Byō and Shuku],[13] was translated into Japanese and published by J. H. Ballagh and Okuno Masatsuna in 1874. It was a fictitious dialogue between a shrine custodian (Byō) and a Christian evangelist (Shuku), demonstrating the futility of "worshipping dried wood" and advocating the worship of the one true God. Around 1875 the medical missionary T. A. Palm, in cooperation with Oshikawa Masayoshi, published a tract with a characteristic title: *Gūzō hishinron* [Idols are not God]; it consisted of quotations from the Bible condemning idol worship.[14]

While most propaganda against idolatry was characterized by general, uninformed denunciations, one missionary, J. H. DeForest (1844–

1911), who was particularly interested in the refutation of idol worship, actually became something of an expert in the field. His activity hardly contributed to a deeper understanding of Buddhism, but at least he took popular Buddhism and folk religious practices seriously enough to devote time and energy to their study.[15] He collected and studied discarded idols, and even exported some to the United States "as a standing proof of the fact that the people of Japan are turning from idols to the living and true God."[16] He apparently found this study very interesting, as he explained in an article about *ema,* or painted votive offerings; the many hours spent in studying these and in learning the meanings of them from chatty worshippers had given him "much pleasure, as well as insight into the Japanese character."[17] The fact that DeForest later blamed himself for his unwise campaigns against idolatry makes his career of special significance.

DeForest's interest in idol worship, of course, originated from his missionary concern; he wanted to demonstrate the folly of idolatry, and he discovered that examples and illustrations of popular practices had a great appeal to the public. The widespread skepticism and ambivalent feelings among people toward priests and religious practices made idolatry an easy target for criticism, as we can see from DeForest's description of a public meeting in Okayama in 1880.

> I tell you, the second commandment makes music for an audience here. When I describe the first old woman that I saw worship an idol in Tokyo, just after I landed in Japan, and go through the motions she made before a red-painted god, it always makes a huge laugh. Then when I pretend that I am an idolater, and repeat their nonsensical prayers through my nose and clap my hands reverentially as they do, they enjoy it as much as though it were a theatre.[18]

A missionary colleague reported about another series of DeForest's "lectures to idolaters" in Osaka in 1881: "His method of contrasting religions by their natural, legitimate fruit has been very attractive, and although he has not hesitated to hold up the sins and vices and follies of heathenism in strong light, he has not failed while doing so to keep the good will of his audience." When he argued that "worshippers of idols are untruthful," he aroused some negative feelings, "but when he began to illustrate by the habits of speech of all classes, common laborers, merchants, physicians, officials, coolies, townspeople, Samurai, the fact was so apparent, and the illustrations so pat, that they had to laugh again and again."[19] The response among the audience to such lectures was described by DeForest on another occasion.

> The interest awakened was manifest by the repeated and hearty approval of the audience, and the assertions of some that, "really, if one would think, there is not a statement or teaching in the whole Buddhist religion but is loaded with

THE RICH MAN'S BISHAMON.

THE POOR MAN'S BISHAMON.

THE GAMBLER'S CHARM.

Say to the heathen from thy throne,
"I am Jehovah, God alone,"
Thy voice their idols shall confound,
And cast their altars to the ground.

DAIKOKU.

A LOAD OF IDOLS FOR THE MISSIONARY.

YEBISU

Fig. 7. "The evil of worshipping dried wood." Illustrations from one of J. H. DeForest's articles about idol worship in *Missionary Herald* (Sept. 1881), pp. 371–374. Courtesy of the Institute for the Study of the Humanities and Social Sciences at Doshisha University, Kyoto.

nonsense." Others said, "Just think of it! Here we have lived in the midst of all this our whole lives, and never opened our eyes to this folly until a foreigner comes ten thousand miles to show it to us."[20]

DeForest seemed to have a predilection for preaching about the Ten Commandments, about which he also published a series of popular tracts. The tract about the Second Commandment was entitled *Kareki o ogamu no gai* [The evil of worshipping dried wood];[21] it was, of course, directed against idol worship and sold at least 50,000 copies.[22] But other tracts also drew attention to idolatry. In his explanations about the commandment against lying, for instance, he characterized idolaters as untruthful: worshipping false gods, they will be false in other things as well, he argued. The tract about the Tenth Commandment, "The Funeral of the Seven Gods of Good Luck," maintained that "abolishing the covetous spirit" will lead to abolishing also "the gods whose worship springs from that spirit."[23]

Apart from an apparent ability to entertain his audience by imitating all sorts of people and their religious practices, the essential point of his campaign against idolatry was to demonstrate the miserable state of those peoples in the world who worshipped idols, compared to those who believed in the true God. In his tract about "the evils of worshipping dried wood" he first argued that idol worship reduced the spiritual vigor of the people. "In short," he wrote, "peoples who from old have indulged in idols have merely sunk into empty manners; and I have yet never [among these peoples] heard of such magnificent deeds as the above-mentioned [scientific and technological] inventions."[24] Then he described the close relationship between idolatry and sexual corruption: "Those peoples who are infected with idols are also infected with carnal appetite."[25] This common charge against Buddhism referred to the low moral standard of the priests, the common presence of red-light districts in the vicinity of temples, the connection between pilgrimages and prostitution, the low regard of women as merely playthings for men, and the like.[26] Finally, he argued that idolatry fostered falsehood and hypocrisy among the people; on this point he referred particularly to what he called the Buddhist priests' use of lies and other "skillful means" to make people believe in their false doctrines.[27]

Like most of the Japanese, DeForest was not really concerned about the distinctions between Buddhism, Shinto, and other religions, and he did not bother about the doctrines of Buddhism. His attitude to Buddhism was based upon his view of idol worship and his observations of popular religion and religious decay. A Buddhist funeral was, for instance, simply characterized as "the usual empty Buddhist ceremony and plenty of sake-drinking."[28] His biographer observed: "The corruption and ignorance of the Buddhist priesthood was so deeply impressed upon Mr. DeForest in those days that he never afterwards liked to use the figure of priesthood in presenting the work of Christ."[29]

This missionary who had considered it a waste of time to study a "dying Buddhism," however, gradually began to see that the hold of Buddhism on the people was more than mere superstition, and developed a new relationship with the Buddhist priests. He began to respect the intellectual ability of some of them, and was even willing to acknowledge that he could be defeated in discussion. This new awareness led him to draw lessons for himself about fair play and open-mindedness.[30] Whereas previously he had referred to Confucius, Buddha, and Jesus as "the three great men Asia had produced" only rhetorically, combining such reference with attacks on idol worship, which included Buddhism,[31] his new perspective enabled him to see Buddhism and Confucianism as part of God's preparatory work, Buddha and Confucius being "the moral prophets to fit the East for Christ."[32] Referring to the progressive development of revelation in the history of Israel, he raised the question about the divine meaning of the Japanese people: "The *a priori* conclusion was that the guiding hand of God had led the Japanese, like the Israelites, by using their environment and the borrowed or inherited elements of their religion as stepping-stones in the path to Christ."[33] Seeing God's work in the preparatory centuries, his biographer concluded, "he bowed his head and lifted his heart with a new awe, and a new understanding of the greatness and the glory of his God."[34] He refused to call the native religions "false" or to call the Japanese "heathen," because these terms to many Japanese included contempt, and he regretted bitterly his previous unwise zeal and lack of understanding. The following comment in connection with a Japanese sermon summarized his experience in a heartfelt way.

> And what a splendid unfolding of the text "I Am," making the deepest Buddhist truth of the Great Self *(Taiga)* and the Minor Self *(Shoga)* fairly shine with the Christian light of personality in God, the God of Love! Oh, if we missionaries only knew this royal road of fulfilling rather than destroying, we would have ten times the power we now have. It makes me feel how small I was twenty-five years ago when I wrote that tract, "The Evils of Worshiping Dried Wood."[35]

M. L. GORDON: SHIN BUDDHISM INAUTHENTIC

It is significant that a lecture entitled "The Religious Influence of Buddhism as an Obstacle to the Reception of the Gospel in Japan" was included in the program of the General Conference of the Protestant Missionaries in Osaka in 1883.[36] It signified a growing awareness that Buddhism was to be considered as a real obstacle; and the lecturer, the

Congregational missionary and teacher at Doshisha, M. L. Gordon (1844–1900), had for some time distinguished himself as a fervent apologist against Buddhism. He was one of the few foreigners who had devoted himself to the study of Japanese Buddhism and who had some knowledge beyond the commonplace observations about crisis and decay. Gordon's approach was scholarly, but the purpose of his study was one-sidedly apologetic.[37]

In contrast to many of his missionary colleagues, Gordon recognized the potential of Buddhism. According to his opinion, neither Shinto nor Confucianism had ever exerted "a thousandth part of the religious influence over the hearts of the Japanese" that Buddhism had. The reason, he explained, was obvious.

> Buddhism is a religion, and as a religion it has its answer to give to many of the strongest and most instinctive wants of man's nature. . . .
> Buddhism met the worshiping instinct of the Japanese as it had never been met before. It told them of something higher and better than the gratifications of passion and sense. It offered its explanation of many of the enigmas which beset our present life. Above all, it taught of a life after the death of the body, where virtue should have its reward and vice its desert.[38]

It was, therefore, according to Gordon, the obligation of the missionaries to know their opponent. "And here we are obliged to confess to a good deal of ignorance," he said. "Here is a great field for research almost untouched; at once inviting to the student and important to the missionary."[39] Although well aware of the voluminous literature and of the great differences among the Buddhist sects, he confined himself to the study of the Pure Land tradition, notably Shin Buddhism, which he regarded as "the most powerful, popular and progressive Buddhist sect in the Empire."[40] Since no authoritative study had been made about Japanese Buddhism in Western languages, he encouraged the missionaries to use the fragmentary knowledge they could pick up here and there to aid them "in the better understanding and appreciation" of the people among whom they lived.[41]

In addition to the concern for effective missionary work, Gordon was also apprehensive of the growing interest in Buddhism in the West, particularly after the publication of Edwin Arnold's *The Light of Asia* in 1879.[42] In some cases he criticized Westerners' use of Buddhism against Christianity by providing information about the real state of Japanese Buddhism.[43] He also wanted to correct the erroneous impression among some Western observers that the so-called Reformed Buddhism or Protestant Buddhism of the Shin Buddhist reformers was "a pure theism such as is taught in the Old Testament."[44]

Gordon seemed well acquainted with some Japanese sources, such as the three Pure Land sutras.[45] He further deepened his understanding through friendly intercourse with distinguished Buddhist scholars in Kyoto, including Akamatsu Renjō, the prominent Buddhist of Nishi Honganji, who, at the request of Sir E. J. Reed, had written a brief account of the Shin Buddhist doctrine.[46] Even though he seemed to respect these scholars, especially Akamatsu,[47] he told his missionary colleagues that the increased intercourse with Buddhist priests had generally "lowered rather than raised his estimation of them."[48] Finally, he was well acquainted with the Western study of comparative religion and Buddhism. He seemed to be particularly influenced by F. Max Müller in Oxford, and to a certain degree by T. W. Rhys Davids; but he also referred to such scholars as H. Oldenberg, E. Burnouf, S. Spence Hardy, J. Edkins, E. J. Eitel, and others.[49]

Gordon's studies gave him some insight into the Shin Buddhist faith. He also made some material available to others, such as his summary of the legend of Amida, including a translation of the forty-eight vows of Amida Buddha.[50] Rather than real understanding, however, his predominant concern was to prove that the Shin Buddhist doctrine was unauthentic. This was the aim of his Japanese tract, *Mida monogatari* [The story of Amida], published also in English under the title "The Doctrine of Amida Unauthentic."[51] He discussed the same issue in another booklet, *Bukkyō tanomu ni tarazu* [Buddhism is unreliable],[52] which was originally presented as a lecture in the great public hall, Meiji Kaidō, in Tokyo in 1884. At this point the critical study of Western scholars provided him with the material he needed. There was no evidence showing the existence of the doctrine of Amida until hundreds of years after the death of the Buddha; in the Buddhist literature of Ceylon and Southeast Asia there was no mention of Amida or the Western Paradise.[53] In addition, the doctrine of Shin Buddhism seemed in some respects to be exactly opposed to the teaching of the historical Buddha.

> The original teaching of Shakya, as Rhys Davids has pointed out, was that holy men are better than gods, and acknowledged no form of prayer; but here we have salvation secured by the prayer of faith. Shakya taught also the doctrine of *Nirvâna,* which is really annihilation; these Buddhists point the believer to the Peaceful Land in the West, with its myriads of pleasures, which appeal to the eye, ear, taste, and other senses. Is there not here an irreconcilable difference?[54]

His rejection of Shin Buddhism as an inauthentic deviation from original Buddhism was not primarily the result of his own studies or of missionary bias but rather reflected the consensus of Western scholars. He often referred to Max Müller as his principal witness. Max Müller's words carried special weight in Japan; he had accepted two young Shin Buddhist priests as his students and had, moreover, recently completed the translation of the *Smaller Sukhāvatī-vyūha* [The small Amida-sutra] from Sanskrit. He had found the ideas disappointing. He referred to the "silly and mischievous stories of Amitâbha and his paradise" and said that perhaps "in a lower state of civilization even such teaching has produced some kind of good. But Japan is surely ripe for better things."[55] Similar criticism was raised by Rhys Davids, whom Gordon quoted as saying that Amida, the Western Paradise, and its innumerable Bodhisattvas are "hypothetical beings, the creations of a sickly scholasticism, hollow abstractions without life or reality."[56]

As a missionary, Gordon of course did not only criticize Shin Buddhism as inadequate; he also preached Christianity; and he often did so by contrasting Christianity with Buddhism and proclaiming the superiority of the former. He found in Buddhism no adequate conception of God, only a very inadequate idea of sin and salvation, and a negative and pessimistic attitude to this world.[57] Even the Pure Land tradition, with its belief in the one Buddha and his saving grace, failed to stand comparison with the theism of the Old Testament.[58] For the sake of comparison between religions and the implicit clarification of the superiority of Christianity, Gordon regarded comparative religion as one of the most important allies of Christianity. "Its historical and comparative methods of study have brought into clearer light the differences between Christianity and other existing religions," he argued, and emphasized that "this is a *Christian* science," and "a product of Christian civilization."[59]

Gordon's use of Buddhist studies and comparative religion for apologetic purposes prevented him from a sympathetic understanding of Japanese Buddhism. His knowledge was used to refute Buddhism, and he actually engaged in quite agitated confrontations with Buddhists in Kyoto, as we shall see later. Moreover, he never seemed to revise his negative evaluation of Buddhism, as some of his colleagues did. Nevertheless, compared with the previous disregard of Buddhism among Christians, his study and activity represented some progress. At least he recognized Buddhism as a vigorous opponent with a strong hold on the Japanese people. And he did not entirely ignore the value of Buddhism, seen in the light of his Christian faith.

> And yet this doctrine of salvation through faith, so admirably suited to human weakness and sinfulness, is not all a falsehood. There is One, the evidence of whose existence, of whose infinite power and wisdom, is manifest in all nature around and within us; whose infinite love has been shown forth in the character of Jesus of Nazareth; who is able to save to the uttermost them that draw near unto God through him.[60]

Other missionaries also began to recognize that Buddhism was a potential obstacle to Christianity, and that it could no longer be ignored. For instance, J. D. Davis, Gordon's colleague at Doshisha, who untiringly maintained that the real threat against Christianity came from modern skepticism and materialism rather than from traditional religion, nevertheless stressed the need for a careful study of Buddhism, Shinto, and Confucianism.[61] In 1878 he was requested to teach metaphysics an hour a day at a school for training Shin Buddhist priests in Kyoto as a part of their apologetic study. He refused, but he promised instead to teach religion two hours a week, commenting that the Shin Buddhist faith had "nearly every doctrine of Christianity except the vicarious atonement of Christ."[62] His evaluation of Buddhism was not totally negative, even though he regarded it as a failure as a moral and religious system.[63] He was convinced that Buddhism had no strength to expand beyond the Far East, but still he expected strong resistance; according to Davis, Buddhism would make its last stand "here and now" and resort to the most desperate measures before it yielded.[64]

A similar attitude was taken by C. S. Eby, who shared Davis' apologetic concern in relation to science and skepticism.[65] His translation of *Tsurezuregusa,* a fourteenth-century collection of essays and anecdotes deeply influenced by Buddhism, indicates his interest in Japanese Buddhism.[66] It is further noteworthy that Eby in a series of six apologetic lectures in Meiji Kaidō in 1883 included one lecture about the relationship between Christianity and other religions.[67] Eby recognized "all truth as the legitimate heritage of man—the outflow from the one divine fountain," and refused to regard all other religions beside Christianity as pure falsehood. He argued that the universality of the human race, descended from a primitive pair, was demonstrated by the universality of religion and that the religious traditions had "flowed down through the ages and out into the farthermost corners of the earth." At the same time, however, he regarded the development of religion as a history of decay; and his evaluation of Buddhism, which concluded his lecture, was rather negative.

> Lofty seemed the aim of Shaka, pure was much of his teaching, vast the zeal of his disciples, wide the spread of his religion, great the extent to-day of the lands whose teeming millions count themselves his disciples. And yet, with all that can be said in its favor, history and experience show it to be, in view of the question of humanity and the progress of the human race, in religious, intellectual, and moral aspects, an impotent failure.[68]

That there had been no pure Buddhism in the world for the last two thousand years demonstrated, according to Eby, its failure as a religion. It was a failure intellectually because its "whole system of cosmology is a farce, its geography is false, its transmigration of souls is a contradiction of all sensible psychology, its condemning existence as an evil is suicidal of all hopes and inspiration for advance." And morally Buddhism had failed: "To call any purely Buddhist country now in the world, a moral country, would show an absolute ignorance of what morality means."[69]

Eby's apologetic interest in Buddhism seemed to increase in the following years, and in the end of the 1880s he was an active opponent of Buddhist lecture meetings. When Colonel H. S. Olcott of the Theosophical Society came to Tokyo in 1889, Eby held lectures to oppose his influence.[70]

Other missionaries who showed some particular interest in Buddhism were Henry Faulds[71] and J. L. Atkinson. The latter was rather critical of Japanese religions;[72] nevertheless, in 1893 he published a quite informative book about Buddhism, entitled *Prince Siddhartha, the Japanese Buddhist,* based on Japanese Buddhist sources.[73]

TAKAHASHI GORŌ: THE EMPTY DOCTRINE OF EMPTINESS

While the above-mentioned missionaries had only that fragmentary knowledge of Japanese Buddhism mentioned earlier, Takahashi Gorō (1856–1935), a uniquely talented Japanese Christian, acquired a vast amount of knowledge about Buddhist history, doctrine, and philosophy, and became the leading Christian expert on Buddhism in the 1880s. Takahashi came from a samurai family in Echigo (Niigata Prefecture), one of the Buddhist strongholds in Japan. He went to Yokohama to pursue Western studies; there he met Uemura Masahisa (1858–1925), and was introduced by him to S. R. Brown, who became his teacher. With his linguistic talent he learned English, French, and German, as well as Greek and Latin. He was baptized and cooperated for some time in the translation of the Japanese Bible. In 1880 he published *Butsudō shinron* [A new treatise on Buddhism][74] and *Shintō shinron* [A new treatise on Shinto], which, according to Uemura Masahisa, were extremely useful for Christians at that time.[75] The treatise on Buddhism provided Japanese Christians with a manual of basic Buddhist ideas; as such it was both unique and useful. On the other hand, several misunderstandings and inadequate interpretations provoked Buddhist criticism and prevented an adequate understanding of Buddhism. In the following years Takahashi wrote a number of articles about Buddhism in *Rikugō zasshi;*[76] and in 1883 he published another major work on Buddhism, entitled *Bukkyō shinkai* [A new interpretation of Buddhism], in which he responded to a Buddhist refutation of the *Butsudō shinron.*[77] Other works dealing with Buddhism were *Shoshū benran* [A compendium of religions] and *Indoshi* [A history of India],[78] both published in 1881. In addition to such studies, Takahashi published dictionaries and numerous translations of Western novels and poetry as well as books about the

Christian faith and philosophical works.[79] Although he is now primarily remembered for his extremely polemic role in the controversy about education and religion in 1893,[80] that was just one aspect of his many-sided activities. He was certainly one of the most prolific Christian writers in the 1880s, and in those years he played a central role in the Christian church as a roughshod apologist with an almost encyclopaedic knowledge and interest.

It is difficult to explain the exact reason for Takahashi's interest in Buddhism. The fact that he came from a district strongly influenced by Buddhism and that he started to write at a time when Buddhist scholars were increasing their opposition to Christianity may explain something. But primarily his interest seemed to be stimulated by the apologetic concern of an intellectual curious about the claim of various religions to represent the unsurpassed teaching; and he wanted to settle the question of religious truth through comparative studies.[81] In an article dealing with the basis of Buddhist philosophy, published in *Rikugō zasshi* in 1881, he argued that the question of truth was not yet clarified, and he encouraged his readers to "leave prejudice, forget the conventional criticism; open your minds and empty your hearts and consider thoroughly what I have written about Buddhism, compare it with other religions, and make your own impartial judgement."[82] So Takahashi purported to be fair and impartial in his evaluation of Buddhism. His approach was scholarly and much more thorough than Gordon's, but his purpose was, nevertheless, definitely apologetic.

His most thorough analysis of Buddhism is found in *Bukkyō shinkai*. In the first chapters he gave a critical review of the origin of Buddhism and of its historical development and scriptures, and indicated contradictory elements in the teaching of Buddha. He emphasized the irreconcilable differences between Theravada and Mahayana Buddhism and concluded that only Theravada represented the direct teaching of Buddha, while Mahayana was an aberration.[83] He found the essence of Buddhism primarily in the Four Noble Truths, and then in the teaching of the twelve-linked chain of causation,[84] and he stressed the pessimistic and world-negating tendency of the Buddhist teaching of impermanence.[85] In his discussion of Mahayana Buddhism he gave a lengthy review of Nagarjuna's philosophy;[86] he further exhibited an impressive knowledge of Tendai Buddhism, with its three aspects of reality or truth *(santai)*: Emptiness *(kū)*, Temporality *(ke)*, and the Middle *(chū)*, and its synthesis of these in the doctrine of True Suchness as the real essence of the Three Truths *(shinnyo jissō, chūdō jissō)*.[87]

Considering the fact that Christians in Japan still tended to ignore Buddhism as a dying religion, Takahashi's knowledge of Buddhism was really remarkable. He failed, however, to understand certain Buddhist doctrines on vital points. The doctrine of Emptiness he regarded as the basis for empty doctrines about unreal realities.[88] The ideas about Paradise, Nirvana, and Buddhas were, according to Takahashi, mere expedient means without reality. "The Buddhist Paradise is totally empty, only a name without reality," he wrote.[89] "Nirvana is just unsubstantial and empty; because Buddhism makes Emptiness its basis, it is not only very vague and inconclusive, but is totally unable to benefit the world and living beings."[90] If the existence of everything is based on ignorance and delusion, he argued, everything becomes illusive and unreal.[91] Hence Takahashi also found Buddhism unable to provide a real moral basis; its social function became negative and passive.[92] In addition to philosophical arguments, Takahashi referred to a number of ideas and practices, notably those related to the traditional Buddhist cosmology, to demonstrate that Buddhism was not only inconclusive, but even childish and superficial.[93] He was convinced that Buddhism would sooner or later be forced to abandon its present role as a religion for the secular world and return to the mountains again, that is, become a religion for monks as it was intended to be. Consequently, he did not regard Buddhism as a potential enemy of Christianity.[94]

In short, in spite of his scholarly approach and his extensive knowledge of Buddhism, Takahashi failed to give a fair picture of Buddhist philosophy, and probably strengthened the impression among Christians that Buddhism was unable to cope with matters of this world. His writings provoked several responses from Buddhist critics; however, from the Buddhist point of view his criticism was both too negative and too superficial to provide a basis for a real dialogue.[95]

Takahashi was not the only Japanese Christian who was interested in Buddhism. Apart from his own writings, *Rikugō zasshi* included a number of articles about Buddhism by such prominent Christians as Ibuka Kajinosuke, Hiraiwa Yoshiyasu, Kozaki Hiromichi, and Uemura Masahisa.[96] They were apparently familiar with both Western studies of Buddhism[97] and with Japanese traditions. Even though their evaluation of Buddhism was generally negative, the fact that so many Christians did write about Buddhism reinforces the impression that Buddhism was gradually becoming a vital concern.[98]

A. VILLION: A CATHOLIC INQUIRER

The only Roman Catholic priest who at an early stage devoted himself to serious studies of Buddhism was Father A. Villion (1843–1932) from the Paris Foreign Missionary Society (Société des Missions Étrangères). His superiors in Paris had sent him to Japan with the following instruction: "Your first duty will be to study the Buddhist religion." Recalling his first contacts with Buddhists, he commented in his autobiography that he "had seen the absolute necessity [of studying Buddhism] in order to be able to respond to the questions of these honest spirits," as he characterized the believers of Shin Buddhism.[99] One of his catechists in Kobe, Akamatsu Seiichi, had ten years earlier graduated from the Tendai Buddhist seminary of Mount Hiei outside Kyoto; his "short but very methodical" course about the Buddhist doctrine prepared Villion for the encounter with Buddhism.[100] His background enabled him to appreciate aspects of Buddhism that hardly appealed to his Protestant colleagues; he found that the ecclesiastical and liturgical traditions of Buddhism especially had much in common with Catholicism, and interpreted these as imitations of Christianity.[101]

After a few years' work in Kobe he came to Kyoto in 1879 as a teacher of French. He was bound by his promise not to teach Christianity in his capacity as a French teacher, but he felt free to preach at whatever place he made his private residence. Both impressed and discouraged by the ubiquitous influence of Buddhism and its "hosts of bonzes" in Kyoto, he decided to make Buddhism the main target of his work; the time had come, he believed, when he, with God's help, would "attack the stronghold of the Devil."[102]

In spite of his aggressive language and apologetic attitude, Villion approached Buddhism as a sincere and sympathetic student. He seemed to be somewhat familiar with Western studies of Buddhism but preferred to rely directly upon Japanese Buddhist scholars for instruction.[103] Hence he came to establish friendly relations with several of the most outstanding Buddhists in Kyoto. They taught him the essentials of their respective sects, and apparently engaged in quite lengthy discussions with him. For instance, through his friend Émile Guimet, a French manufacturer and traveler who had helped several of the Japanese Buddhist priests studying in France, he was introduced to Ugai Tetsujō, chief abbot of Chion'in and head of the powerful Jōdo sect. Ugai had distinguished himself as one of the most articulate critics of Christianity, but Villion, nevertheless, seemed to maintain a friendly relationship with him.[104] Further, the principal of the seminary of Chion'in, Kishigami Kairei, began to give him lessons in Buddhism, and for two years Villion devoted all his spare time to these studies. He also had ample opportunity to engage in discussions with the Buddhist students at the seminary, to whom he explained, among other things, the fallacy of the Buddhist cosmogony.[105] He also tried to make a similar arrangement for the study of Shin Buddhism, where he found the most profound and devout faith. He observed that Shin Buddhism outwardly seemed closest to Catholic practices, but that in other respects, it was rather like a Protestant Buddhism.[106] He was introduced to Akamatsu Renjō, who apparently was willing to give him lessons in Buddhism; however, because of the increasing tension between Buddhists and Christians, Akamatsu was not allowed by his colleagues to continue this relationship.[107]

The first years of the 1880s were characterized by a growing antagonism between Buddhist and Christians, including quite aggressive confrontations. At that time Villion had just started his studies and did not yet feel competent to contribute substantially to the struggle between the two religions; but his autobiography includes several dramatic reports about the confrontations. He never concealed his admiration for the self-confident apologetics of his Protestant colleagues, convinced that his turn would come.[108] Apart from his own studies and various kinds of contact with Buddhists, he seems to have published nothing substantial in the 1880s.[109] Later he studied the psychology of the Hossō sect with a monk at Kōfukuji in Nara; he visited Mount Minobu to study Nichiren Buddhism; he studied Shingon Buddhism at Mount Koya; and he cooperated closely with Buddhist scholars in Tokyo in publishing a major work on Japanese Buddhism.[110] He completed his lifework, *Le Bouddhisme au Japon,* in thirteen volumes, containing a total of 2,988 typewritten pages, but it was never published.[111]

It is difficult to assess the impact of Villion's activity in relation to Buddhism. The fact that his book was never published may indicate that his view was somewhat controversial and that few of his Catholic colleagues shared his concern for Buddhist studies. The final evaluation of his contribution must be based on a closer examination of his unpublished manuscripts. The impression gathered from the numerous references in his autobiography is that his understanding of Buddhism was quite similar to that of most Western observers; that is, Buddhism was interpreted from a predominantly Western theological and philosophical standpoint. It was characterized as a "magnificent pantheism."[112] He admired Buddhism as an "extraordinary effort of imagination" but regretted that it lacked the conception of a Creator. "Matter is eternally and fatally submitted to the necessary evolution of an unlimited transformation. It is the venerable Pythagoras of ancient Greece who has returned with his obsolete teachings," he wrote.[113] Furthermore, Mahayana Buddhism was regarded as a deformation of the Buddhist doctrine, resulting primarily from the influence of Nestorian Christianity; he even referred to rumors that a copy of the Gospels, transcribed by Shiran Shōnin (1173–1262), the founder of Shin Buddhism, was kept at one of the head temples of Shin Buddhism in Kyoto.[114] Hence he believed that Mahayana Buddhism could only realize its ultimate intentions in Christianity.[115]

CONCLUSION

The significance of the growing interest in Buddhism can be summarized as follows:

Fig. 8. Dispute between Christian and Buddhist priests. Illustration from Aoki Kunijirō, *Shūkyō kyōshinkai* [Religious propagation contest] (Tokyo, 1885). Courtesy of Aoyama Gakuin University, Tokyo.

The concern with Buddhism among Christians was one-sidedly apologetic. While Buddhism had previously been almost ignored, the study of Buddhism in the 1880s came from the realization that Buddhism, in spite of corruption, had a strong hold on the people and represented a spiritual power that made it a major obstacle to Christian expansion.

The Christian students of Buddhism acquired quite extensive knowledge of Buddhist doctrines and history. The information was, however, limited by traditional prejudices and misinterpretations and by apologetic concerns. On the historical level, Western Buddhist studies provided arguments that reduced Mahayana Buddhism to an inauthentic deviation from Buddha's original teaching. On the doctrinal level, Buddhism was demonstrated to be inferior to Christianity. And on the practical level, the critical state of Buddhism was used as a proof of the inadequacy of Buddhist doctrines. Even those who gradually arrived at a sympathetic attitude to Buddhism concluded that Buddhism would certainly have to yield to Christianity.

In a time when the majority of Christians and Japanese intellectuals still ignored Buddhism as a corrupt and dying religion, the study and contact described in the previous pages, however apologetic and negative, represented a significant reorientation in Christian circles. Buddhism was at least taken seriously; and in some cases the acquaintance with it led to a positive appreciation of the greatness of the old religion.[116]

CHAPTER SIX

Buddhist Concern
about Christianity

> The priests have recently bought one hundred and
> twenty copies of the New Testament and some commen-
> taries, and have put the school at work studying the
> Bible every day. What will come of it I do not know, but
> the priest who bought the books told the bookseller that
> they were bound to see what Christianity was . . .
>
> J. D. Davis, American missionary reporting
> on Buddhist activities in Kyoto

THE FAILURE of the Buddhists to crush the Christian movement in the decades after the opening of Japan was a humiliating demonstration of the weakness of Buddhism and the vigor of the intruding religion. With the official, tacit recognition of Christianity in 1873 the Buddhist opposition lost much of its vigor and motivation. The suspicion and animosity against Christianity, however, did not disappear. If the Buddhists had commanded means to check its expansion, they would certainly have used them; anti-Christian writings were published throughout the decades after 1873, and sporadic anti-Christian campaigns revealed the latent hostility of the Buddhists. Nevertheless, the character of the relationship between some Buddhists and Christians gradually changed. While the Buddhists had previously resorted to espionage and appealed for government suppression of the Christian work, after 1873 the relationship became more open. The increasing personal contact resulting from the apologetic study of Christianity even led to peaceful relationships between Buddhist and Christian adversaries. Buddhist contact with the Western world, through Buddhist priests who traveled to the West and through Western inquirers who sought contact with Japanese Buddhists, also contributed to the change.

APOLOGETICAL STUDY AND TRAVELS TO THE WEST

The new spiritual climate represented by the Japanese enlightenment movement inevitably influenced the Buddhist world. A number of progressive Buddhists identified themselves with the movement and shared its ideas about religious freedom; even though they were primarily concerned about the freedom of Buddhism and still failed to recognize Christianity on equal terms with other religions, they encountered and even cooperated with Christians who were involved in the enlightenment movement. It is, for instance, noteworthy that an influential Buddhist, Ōuchi Seiran, in 1875 founded the philanthropic organization Rakuzenkai in cooperation with such prominent Christians as Nakamura Keiu, Tsuda Sen, and the medical missionary, Henry Faulds.[1] Moreover, the interest in Western religion and culture prompted the Buddhists to send delegations to the West, a venture that had far-reaching consequences for Buddhist-Christian relations.

The first Buddhist delegation to the West left Japan in 1872, in the wake of the famous Iwakura Mission; it consisted of scholars and priests from Nishi Honganji, including such progressive leaders as Shimaji Mokurai and Akamatsu Renjō. Members of the delegation traveled to France, England, Germany, Holland, Switzerland, Italy, and Greece; Shimaji even visited the Middle East, including Jerusalem, and India on his way back.[2] A delegation from Higashi Honganji began a similar journey the same year under the leadership of Ishikawa Shuntai and Chief Abbot Ōtani Kōei, who left Japan almost secretly.[3] In the following years a number of Buddhists traveled in Europe and America, and several young priests were sent to study with Western scholars of Buddhism. The observations and contacts made during such journeys stimulated the efforts to reform and modernize Japanese Buddhism. They did not, however, much improve the relationship between Buddhism and Christianity; in fact, the Buddhist travelers were among the leading apologists against Christianity in the 1870s and 1880s.

It is quite astonishing how rapidly and to what degree the members of the first delegation to the West were able to collect material for apologetical purposes. One of the most active critics of Christianity was Shimaji Mokurai (1838–1911), who soon acquainted himself with the critical theology of Europe. He purchased books critical of orthodox Christianity, such as Ernest Renan's book about the life of Jesus and Henry Ball's *Self-Contradiction of the Bible,* which he asked a friend to translate.[4] His theological inquiry resulted in a number of essays about Christianity. In *Fukkatsu shinwa* [A new tale about the resurrection], published in 1875,[5] he characterized the doctrine of the resurrection as one of the strangest ideas in Christianity. He introduced the theory that some of the disciples of Jesus had taken his dead body to Galilee, and argued that the belief in his resurrection was based on the wild fantasies of the "madwoman," Mary of Magdala, who had previously been possessed by seven evil spirits. In other essays Shimaji rejected the idea of "coming down from heaven" as incompatible with modern science, and criticized the stories of Eden, the forbidden fruit, and original sin. In *Yasokyō issekiwa* [An evening tale about Christianity] he introduced a lengthy criticism of the biblical scriptures.[6]

Ishikawa Shuntai (1842–1931), who was a member of the second Buddhist delegation, had already distinguished himself as a fervent student of Christianity.[7] Now he fortified his arguments through contact with French scholars. In *Yasokyō himitsusetsu* [About the secret of Christianity] he introduced Voltaire and Renan as his witnesses, and argued that the teaching of Jesus was incompatible with the teaching of Moses and the Old Testament. The biblical writers had distorted the image of Jesus, and the true Jesus had been forgotten by the church.[8] In *Yawaka shōhyō* [A short criticism of Jahweh] he criticized several of the stories of the Old Testament and described the biblical God as a jealous and prejudiced sovereign. He also established in Kyoto a "translation bureau" *(honyaku-kyoku)* which, apart from promoting Buddhist and Sanskrit studies, also aimed at introducing literature about Christianity. A translation of Ernest Renan's book about Jesus was, for instance, completed, but not published.[9]

The two first Buddhists who went to the West on a long-term basis to study Buddhism were Nanjō [Nanjio] Bunyū (1849–1927) and Kasahara Kenju (1852–1883). They were sent to England by Higashi Honganji in 1876 with the express purpose of pursuing Buddhist studies. Through the Japanese consul and the dean of Westminster Abbey they were, in 1878, introduced to Professor F. Max Müller at Oxford, with whom they studied Sanskrit for several years. The relationship with Max Müller had far-reaching consequences for Buddhist studies in Japan—Nanjō became the pioneer of the modern study of Buddhism in Japan—and for the mutual relationship between Buddhists and Christians. We have already seen how Max Müller's negative evaluation of Mahayana Buddhism reinforced the missionaries' critical attitude. The missionaries were certainly aware of the apologetical motives of the Buddhists;[10] but they were hopeful that the young priests who had become Max Müller's disciples would share his beliefs.

> What will Messrs. Nanjio and Kasawara do? Will they take the advice of their teacher and on their return to Japan proclaim the very foundation doctrine of their sect a "silly and mischievous" fabrication? Or will they continue their support of a doctrine which their teacher's words and all honest investigation show to be a forgery and a fraud? We shall see.[11]

According to a missionary who visited Max Müller in the early 1880s, he hoped that his Buddhist disciples "by receiving a purer form of Buddhism would be better prepared for the ultimate reception of Christianity," and even suggested that "they were Christians in everything but the name."[12] This was certainly an overstatement by a Christian scholar who was convinced that Japan was "ripe for better things" than Shin Buddhism.[13] There are, however, several indications that Kasahara Kenju, at least, was more sympathetic to Christianity than his Japanese sponsors might have appreciated. An article written by Kasahara's teacher of English and English literature confirms the impression given by Max Müller.[14] He was impressed by Kasahara's sincerity and characterized his attitude to Christianity as "pure and innocent," that is, both ignorant and unprejudiced. The teacher had no particular intention of converting the young Buddhist, but wanted to have his reaction to the Gospels. Kasahara responded by pursuing the study of the New Testament with such zeal that he even asked to be instructed in Greek. After six months he was able to read the Gospel of John in Greek, and found, according to his teacher, a number of common points between Buddhism and Christianity. He regarded Christ as the highest expression of God; using some of the central Shin Buddhist concepts, he characterized Christ as the human revelation of the infinite light and the infinite life. Christ was a "truly superior personality"; his ethical teaching was not only blameless, but Christ himself was the perfect realization of the ideals. Moreover, Kasahara regarded Christianity as superior to Buddhism on the point of promoting the development of the individual, and he realized that the Christian doctrine of the resurrection provided a clearer hope for a future life than the doctrine of Nirvana as annihilation. It was a shame, the teacher thought, that Kasahara had died so early, before he could benefit his Buddhist brothers with his knowledge.[15]

These statements can hardly be taken at face value. With his Japanese courteousness, Kasahara may have consented to or avoided opposing his teacher's suggestions without really subscribing to them; but he would certainly have worded his evaluation of Christianity in a different way. Moreover, the teacher's conclusion does not harmonize with what Kasahara himself wrote in a major treatise published in *Meikyō ronshū* in the mid-1880s, entitled "Ikyō sōsetsu" [The foreign religion is plagiarism].[16] Because of his early death the treatise was never completed, but his suggestion that Christianity had actually plagiarized many of its central ideas from other religions hardly harmonizes with the impression given by Kasahara's teacher. On the other hand, what Kasahara actually wrote about Christianity was extremely conciliatory, without the prejudiced comments so common in Buddhist writings. He had a considerable knowledge of the New Testament and referred in detail to the discussions of the early church concerning the doctrine of God and the Trinity. In spite of the somewhat polemic title of the treatise and the fact that it was included in a collection of anti-Christian writings, it was hardly fit for apologetical purposes.[17]

A number of other students were also sent to the West and reported about Christianity and the religious situation in Western countries. In 1875 Imadate Tosui was sent to the United States,[18] and in 1881 Kitabatake Dōryū was sent to Europe. Both combined opposition to Christianity with zeal for Buddhist reform. In 1882 Fujishima Ryōon and Fujie Takutsū went to France, and Suga Ryōhō to England.[19] Fujishima had already distinguished himself as an ardent polemicist against Christianity, and the information gathered during his six or seven years' stay in France was mobilized against Christianity in the controversies in the 1890s.[20]

In Japan the apologetical study of Christianity continued. Buddhist students sought discussions with missionaries.[21] As mentioned above, J. D. Davis was asked to teach metaphysics at a Buddhist seminary in Kyoto in 1878. In 1881 M. L. Gordon reported that twenty priests of a Buddhist school had asked for permission to attend a church in order to gain knowledge with which to oppose Christianity.[22] Later it was reported that Buddhist students had bought 120 copies of the New Testament and some commentaries, and had "put the school at work studying the Bible every day."[23] Thus the study of Christianity became widespread among Buddhist priests in the 1880s, either through written sources or through personal contact with missionaries or Japanese Christians.[24]

WESTERN THOUGHT VERSUS WESTERN CHRISTIANITY

One characteristic element added to Buddhist apologetics in this period was the adoption of Western thought critical of Christianity. This had been introduced into Japan at an early stage,[25] but the Buddhist use of such trends was primarily stimulated by their travels to the West. The Buddhist travelers were delighted to discover that major currents of Western science and philosophy challenged the authority of Christianity; and they were eager to introduce to Japan literature that criticized Christianity or purported to demonstrate the conflict between religion (Christianity) and science. The criticism of Voltaire, E. Renan, and H. Ball, introduced by Shimaji Mokurai and Ishikawa Shuntai, has already been mentioned. Akamatsu Renjō was characterized by a missionary as a "Professor of Modern Infidelity" because of his efforts to introduce Western anti-Christian thought to the students of the seminary of Nishi Honganji.[26] It is outside the scope of this study to examine this trend of Western thought as such; it was generally represented by the philosophies of Comte, Mill, and Spencer, and the evolutionism of Darwin and Huxley; others who made a particular impact in Japan were Thomas Paine, John William Draper, and Robert Green Ingersoll.[27] It is, however, important to notice the differences between Buddhist and Christian reactions to the new ideas and to observe how they affected the Buddhist relationship with Christianity. It seemed to be a consensus among the Christians in Japan that the new trend of thought was the most dangerous obstacle to Christian expansion in Japan. As early as 1875 a missionary reported:

> Our worst heathenism in Japan is not Confucianism, not Buddhism, nor Shintooism, but infidelity imported from Christian lands. Before any of the Bible, save three Gospels, is published, infidel books are translated; and books full of objections to Christianity, some of them truly blasphemous in their character, are prepared and scattered broadcast through the land.[28]

Others found that "the natural heart of progressive Japan is the eager disciple of rationalistic and materialistic Europe," and argued that rather than traditional religion, the skepticism of modern Europe was the strongest opponent to Christianity in Japan.[29] Consequently, opposition to anti-Christian Western thought became the major concern for Christian apologetics, especially in the 1880s.[30]

The Buddhists, on the other hand, not only found it possible to harmonize Buddhism with the new ideas, but introduced them to the faithful, added them to their arsenal of anti-Christian arguments, and even used some of their protagonists among Japanese thinkers and scientists for Buddhist propaganda.[31] While Buddhism previously had been criticized by Christians and others for being hopelessly incompatible with modern science, now the Buddhists made use of Western science and philosophy to stigmatize Christianity. It was argued that "science has laid the Christian religion captive at its feet," thanks to the efforts of such noble men as Darwin, Huxley, Spencer, and Mill, who had "striven to shake off this horrible religion."[32] A missionary reported that some Buddhists tried to "recast their teachings, bringing them into fuller harmony with the materialistic philosophy of Europe, with which they have, even now, many points of affinity."[33] Another missionary observed that Buddhism was "capable of indirectly energizing our own sceptical literature and at least, certainly, of being highly energized by it," and suggested that Buddhism might yet "inspire with its forces the pale and lifeless cult of Western agnosticism."[34] Riding on this wave of anti-Christian ideas, the Buddhists rather naively made use of arguments that easily could be, and later were, directed against Buddhism as well.[35]

Be that as it may, the acquaintance with the anti-Christian current of Western thought stimulated the self-confidence of the Buddhists in relation to Christianity. They realized that Christianity was only one of many spiritual forces of the West and that it was challenged and threatened from many sides. Western thought furnished them with new and powerful arguments against Christianity. And they were reconfirmed in their conviction that Buddhism, in contrast to Christianity, was in complete

哲学者
耶蘇佛
法のため
に中裁
を試む

Fig. 9. The philosopher as arbitrator between Buddhist and Christian priests. Illustration from Aoki Kunijirō, *Shūkyō kyōshinkai* [Religious propagation contest] (Tokyo, 1885). Courtesy of Aoyama Gakuin University, Tokyo.

harmony with science and reason. This remained the unshakable consensus of the Buddhists in all their dealings with Christianity in the following decades.

OPENNESS TOWARD WESTERN INQUIRERS

The international contact stimulated the relationship with foreigners in Japan as well. As mentioned above, several missionaries received instruction from Buddhist scholars in Kyoto. One Buddhist especially distinguished himself as a mediator between representatives of the two religions: Akamatsu Renjō (1841–1919). He had been a member of the first Buddhist delegation to the West in 1872, and he held a high position in the hierarchy of Nishi Honganji.[36] He was an outstanding scholar and charmed his visitors with his humor, frankness, and simplicity.[37] With a good command of English and personal experience from the West he naturally became a key person for Westerners who wanted to study Buddhism. The missionaries in Japan, several of whom had frequent contact with Akamatsu, were impressed by his liberal spirit and courtesy.[38] Even though some regarded him as a "Professor of Modern Infidelity," M. L. Gordon characterized him as "this gentleman," "eminently progressive," and "a great light among his fellows."[39] In addition to missionaries, a number of foreign scholars and other visitors sought Akamatsu's guidance. Sir Edward J. Reed, who visited Japan in 1879 in order to write a book about the country, asked Akamatsu to prepare a statement in English about the doctrine of Shin Buddhism. Akamatsu then wrote a short treatise entitled "A Brief Account of 'Shinshiu,' " which became an important source for the study of Shin Buddhism; it was certainly one of the first Shin Buddhist documents ever published in English.[40] Reed characterized Shin Buddhism as an almost theistic faith; in Shin Buddhism, he wrote, "we not only have the doctrine of a saviour taught, but with it the old Christian doctrine of justification by faith likewise—but by faith, not in Jesus, but in Amita Buddha."[41] He was impressed by the energy and enterprise of Shin Buddhism and by Akamatsu himself, who had lived in Europe, "studying the Christian sects, and preparing the way for the conversion of Europe to the Shin faith."[42]

A lengthy record of a dialogue in 1876 between a French delegation and the Shin Buddhist scholars Akamatsu Renjō, Shimaji Mokurai, and Atsumi Kaien gives an interesting impression of the character of such relationships. One of the visitors was Émile Étienne Guimet, a French manufacturer who because of his travels had been commissioned by the Minister of Public Instruction to study the religions of the Far East.[43] With their Western and Christian background the visitors were interested in the characteristic differences between Shin Buddhism and Christianity.

They discussed a wide range of subjects, such as belief in a creator, Amida's power, the relationship between Japanese politics and laws and Amida Buddha, sin and delusion, prayer, forgiveness and penitence, offerings, the immortality of the soul, hell, and differences between Amida and Sakyamuni Buddha. The answers of the Buddhist scholars were polite and not really polemic, but they still expressed a firm conviction that Buddhism offered the final answers to such questions.[44]

Another traveler who published an extensive report about her encounter with Akamatsu was Isabella Bird.[45] She was a devout Christian with strong missionary concern, but she approached Buddhism as a sympathetic inquirer. Akamatsu obviously went out of his way to express his faith in a language which could be grasped by a Christian, and at the same time he indicated some of the incompatible points of the two religions. In spite of such efforts, Miss Bird found it difficult to comprehend the essential points of Akamatsu's explanations. She felt "entangled in a web of metaphysics, or lost in a chaos where nothing had form, and birth and death succeeded each other through endless eternities, life with misery for its essence, death only the portal to re-birth into new misery, and so on in interminable cycles of unsatisfying change." She was thus particularly discouraged by the doctrine of transmigration and Nirvana which left man to walk " 'in a vain show' through cycles of misery to a goal of annihilation."[46] And she concluded by wondering how Akamatsu, who had studied Christianity and the philosophies of the East and West and who was regarded as the ablest and most enlightened man in the Buddhist hierarchy, could really believe in metaphysics which had no better hope than "not to be."[47]

Such encounters were representative of the contact between foreign inquirers and progressive Buddhist scholars. The Buddhists did not conceal their Buddhist convictions or their criticism of Christianity. But their courteousness revealed a new confidence. They had a considerable knowledge of the basic Christian scriptures and doctrines. Several of them had been to the West and knew that Christianity was facing serious opposition. They knew the common questions and critical issues raised by foreigners regarding Buddhism, and they were prepared to answer, firmly convinced about the philosophical and doctrinal superiority of Buddhism. Some even envisioned Buddhist expansion in the West. They must certainly have been painfully aware of the difficulty of "translating" Buddhism into Western categories to make it relevant and meaningful even for sympathetic inquirers. On the other hand, such efforts also prepared them for the missionary work in Europe and America that began at the end of the 1880s.

BUDDHIST ARGUMENTS AGAINST CHRISTIANITY

As for the actual content of the anti-Christian propaganda in the 1880s, at least three dominant trends should be mentioned.

First, the Buddhists continued their criticism of Christian doctrines, drawing on a long tradition of apologetical studies of the Bible and of Christian doctrines. A great number of new anti-Christian writings devoted to biblical criticism were published in these years. The completion of the translation of the New Testament in 1880 and the energetic efforts of colporteurs to distribute biblical scriptures probably stimulated the Buddhists to renewed study and criticism. They failed to find new issues, however, and mainly reiterated the arguments of earlier critics.[48]

Second, the traditional charges that Christianity was a national threat gained new popularity in the early 1880s, when such criticism was stimulated and favored by a conservative trend. One of the most popular pamphlets used in the anti-Christian campaign was entitled *Yasokyō kokugairon* [Christianity a national injury].[49] It had originally been presented as a speech at a meeting held in Kyoto in June 1881 in opposition to Christian preaching services. The author, Saitō Goichirō, disavowed any personal commitment to either Buddhism or Shinto; however, "from love of country and a sincere heart" he found it necessary to warn against the inequities of Christianity. He drew special attention to what he described as two dreaded qualities of Christianity, "cruelty and rebellion" and "the seizure and robbery of other countries." Referring to ancient and modern history he further tried to demonstrate the injurious influence of Christianity, hoping to "startle these blind believers of the foreign religion in their infatuated dreams, and call the attention of the government and the people to the subject."[50] The lecture was published in various editions and spread in great numbers in connection with Buddhist campaigns.

Another type of nationalistic propaganda that gained wide popularity in these years was advocated by Sada Kaiseki (1818–1882), whose defense of the traditional Buddhist cosmology has already been mentioned.[51] A rather reactionary patriot, he agitated against all Western influence as detrimental to the Japanese nation. He explained the harmony of the Tokugawa period as a result of the absence of foreign articles, and advocated the sole use of Japanese products as a way of preventing political and social instability. In particular, he warned that the use of Western lamps would destroy the country. In the early 1880s he started a number of patriotic societies in the various districts, especially in Kyoto and the surrounding prefectures.[52] Through his campaign against foreign products and foreign influence he added a peculiar ele-

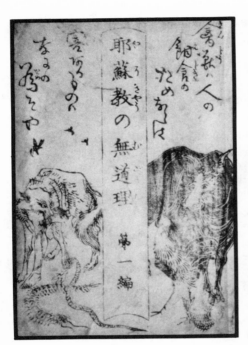

Figs. 10–13. Illustrations from Fujishima Ryōon, *Yasokyō no mudōri* [The unreasonableness of Christianity], vols. 1–3 (Kyoto, 1881). Fig. 10 illustrates the foolishness of believing in a Creator: "If animals are [created] for the sake of man, what is the purpose of harmful [animals]?" Fig. 11 depicts the story of

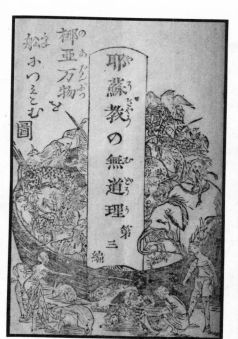

Adam and Eve and the Fall. Fig. 12 shows Noah gathering all creatures into the Ark. Fig. 13 depicts the Great Flood: "The Heavenly Lord lets the outrageous Flood come." Courtesy of the Theological Department of Doshisha University, Kyoto.

ment to the anti-Christian front. Father Villion gave a vivid description of his activity in Kyoto, comparing the "emptiness and obscenities" of Sada's oratory to the way Luther agitated the German people to abandon the papacy. According to Villion, Sada denounced Christianity as the religion of "the hairy foreigners," introducing obscene details "which one could not reproduce even in Latin." The poor Sada, however, he added maliciously, "was finally stuck in the mud"; for he came to the meetings wearing ankle-boots and a soft felt hat and carrying a parasol, all articles from Paris, and soon became the target of satirical comments from Osaka journalists.[53]

Third, the two previous types of arguments were often combined with a consistent denunciation of Christianity as incompatible with reason and modern science. Such arguments were not only used to stigmatize Christianity in educated circles, but were regarded as most effective among the common people as well. A series of pamphlets entitled *Yasokyō no mudōri* [The unreasonableness of Christianity] gives an impression of this type of popular propaganda. It was published in Kyoto in June 1881, soon after the Christians had challenged the Buddhists with public preaching services, and was written by Fujishima Ryōon, a Buddhist priest who later went to France for further studies.[54] The pamphlets repeated rather commonplace criticism, attacking unreasonable, contradictory, and cruel elements in the biblical stories of creation, of Adam and Eve, and of Noah and the Great Flood, but the simplicity of the arguments and the attached illustrations obviously appealed to the masses.[55] At least 700,000 copies of the pamphlets were distributed in connection with Buddhist campaigns.[56]

CONFRONTATIONS

The fact that Christianity after 1873 was no longer confined to the treaty ports but gradually spread to the Buddhist strongholds in the provinces inevitably resulted in more direct confrontations. This was particularly the case after the Christians, in 1880, began to hold public meetings in theaters and public halls throughout the country. The Buddhists, keenly aware that the traditional anti-Christian writings and lectures were no longer sufficient to check the Christian expansion, began to adopt quite aggressive methods, including violent obstruction of Christian work, intimidation, social pressure, and ostracism. In most cases the opposition to Christianity seemed to be spontaneous reactions against Christian expansion into new areas, nurtured by the fear of Christian encroachment upon the time-honored rights of the old religions. Such agitation was often instigated by the local Buddhist priest, sometimes under the guidance of the Buddhists' head temples in Kyoto.[57]

The Shin Buddhist leadership especially belonged to an unbroken tradition of opposition against Christianity, and tended to respond to any attempt to challenge their inherited power and privileges. It was, for instance, characteristic that the Buddhists immediately organized a movement to oppose the plans of a Christian school in Kyoto in 1875.[58] At a later stage, in 1881, they were provoked by the first Christian public preaching series in Kyoto, and engaged in protracted campaigns. Both Buddhists and Christians held mass meetings, which in many cases led to open confrontation. In Kyoto and other places Fukuzawa Yukichi and his disciples became involved in anti-Christian campaigns.[59] A Catholic observer characterized the opposition in Kyoto as "a diabolic rage," and reported that the priests had founded "associations of young braggarts, unsuccessful candidates from their seminaries and other similar sorts of students who were hired by the officials of Honganji, and started a series of speeches, or rather ridiculous diatribes composed of the old slander against Christianity. *Yaso Taiji,* 'war on the religion of Jesus!' "[60] In spite of his obvious exaggerations, his comments certainly reflected the intense animosity against Christianity. Missionaries and Japanese Christians experienced intimidations, violent assaults on person and property, and various sorts of obstruction of their work.[61]

Actually, *Yaso taiji,* or "extermination of Christianity," became one of the most popular Buddhist slogans in the years 1883–1885, rallying the Buddhist forces against the Christian enemy.[62] The Buddhist campaigns to root out Christianity were stirred by the recent revivals and church growth, but they represented more than mere spontaneous reactions;[63] they spread all over the country, supported not only by Buddhist head temples but, in some cases, even by the political authorities.[64]

It should be noticed that Christians also engaged in aggressive propaganda.[65] The Buddhist journal *Meikyō shinshi* characterized the situation in 1882 by the words "Buddhism besieged" and "Christianity attacking."[66] The Buddhists certainly adopted much more oppressive methods than the Christians; however, from their point of view, the campaigns were inevitable defense measures against the provocations of the intrusive foreign religion.

The Buddhist campaigns proved futile. They had been stirred by the resentment against Christian expansion, and they gained momentum as the government became more restrictive of movements—such as Christianity and the Popular Rights Movement—that threatened the social and political stability in the provinces. Consequently, this opposition lost much of its vigor as the official policy again changed. The renewed emphasis on Westernization, especially conspicuous after 1885, favored the cause of Christianity, and the Buddhist opposition was drowned in a new wave of Westernization. In addition, a radical change in the status of

Fig. 14. *Taiji jakensō* (the priest who is extinguishing the heretic view): "How delightful! To cut off the roots of the evil doctrine, and even let the leaves wither, from the power of the Dharma!" From Nishikata Kandō, *Buppō gyōshōka* [Buddhist songs at the morning bell] (Tokyo, 1889). Courtesy of Aoyama Gakuin University, Tokyo.

Buddhism prevented Buddhist activists from further aggression: in 1884 the government abolished *kyōdōshoku,* or the "official priesthood," not only depriving Buddhist (and Shinto) priests of their official authority as state-sponsored religious instructors, but placing Buddhism on a level more equal to Christianity.[67] The Shin Buddhist leaders in Kyoto had to admonish the faithful to accept the notifications issued by the government, condemning an appeal to violence in the struggle against Christianity.[68] While the police, for fear of public disorder, had often put restrictions on Christian meetings, the Christians were now favored by the strenuous measures of the government to prevent disorder;[69] even the word *taiji* was forbidden.[70]

The failure of the attempt to "exterminate Christianity" taught the Buddhists important lessons. They had to resign themselves to the inevitable presence of the enemy. Christianity was too vigorous to be crushed and was, moreover, supported by the Westernizing trend; and Buddhism was still too weak to mobilize the people to a successful confrontation with Christianity. At least for some time violence seemed to be counterproductive. Nevertheless, as an outburst of pent-up resentment the Buddhist campaigns revealed the latent force of the anti-Christian sentiment and foreshadowed the dramatic confrontations between the two religions in the 1890s.

CONCLUSION

The Buddhist concern about Christianity in the 1870s and 1880s represented a continuation of earlier trends. The increasing knowledge of Western Christianity and the anti-Christian currents of Western thought, resulting from the direct contact with the West, added a number of new arguments to the anti-Christian propaganda and strengthened Buddhist confidence. In most cases the narrowly apologetical concern hindered real understanding; the Buddhists searched for the weak points and aimed at the refutation of Christianity. The successful expansion of Christianity intensified the animosity, and its presence in the provincial strongholds of Buddhism inevitably led to direct confrontations.

On the other hand, a new type of relationship developed between a few Buddhists and Christians. The courteousness and tolerance shown by several Buddhist leaders toward Western inquirers, missionaries, scholars, and other travelers signified a growing awareness that Christianity could not be conquered through aggression alone. Contact and personal friendship with a number of Christians removed some of the emotional barriers between the two religions. In addition, it is significant that the Buddhists referred to above belonged to the progressive parties of their respective sects. They were painfully aware of the crisis of Buddhism in Japan, and saw the Christian expansion as a real threat. But as zealous reformers they were also stimulated by the challenge from Christianity and believed that the situation would change as soon as their reforms were adopted. This combination of reform zeal and increasing confidence vis-à-vis Christianity contributed to more friendly attitudes and in various ways prepared for open dialogue.

CHAPTER SEVEN

The Nationalistic Reaction and Buddhist Reform Movements

> A union of all those who wish to protect our land and religion from the contempt of the foreigner.
>
> Buddhist patriotic slogan

THE REMAINDER of this study will deal with the decade from 1889 to 1899. That is, twice as many pages are devoted to the development of Buddhist-Christian relations in this period than to the four previous decades. The reason is obvious: never before had such dramatic confrontations and radical changes in the relationship between the two religions occurred. Most of the attitudes and types of contact depicted in the previous pages can be observed also in the 1890s, but during this decade they were more intense and on a larger scale; the confrontations were more violent and the mutual recognition more unreserved. So the 1890s can be regarded as the conclusion of almost four decades of development in Buddhist-Christian relations.

THE NATIONALISTIC REACTION AND THE SEARCH FOR A JAPANESE IDENTITY

The year 1889 symbolized the end of an epoch of rapid Westernization and Christian expansion. The Constitution guaranteed the long-cherished freedom of religious belief; but contrary to expectations, the churches entered a period of hardship, persecution, and retarded growth. The trend toward Westernization in the mid-1880s, which had brought about an almost wholesale rejection of Japanese traditions, was inevitably followed by a nationalistic reaction favorable to Buddhism and indigenous religions and disastrous to Christianity. The reaction had been prepared from the early 1880s; it gained momentum in connection with the failure of the treaty negotiations in 1887 and 1889, and it soon became so strong that the democratic development represented by the promulgation of the Constitution in 1889 and the opening of the Diet in 1890 failed to create the expected results. The pendulum went to the other extreme: Western traditions, ideas of freedom and popular rights, Christianity, and the English language lost their attraction; and popular attention now focused on the preservation of Japanese traditions or the search for a true national identity, often accompanied by an emotional rejection of all elements that endangered the national polity.

A number of other trends also influenced the intellectual climate of the period. The industrial growth of the 1890s, stimulated by the Sino-Japanese War (1894–1895), brought about a number of social problems. Religious and intellectual leaders became more aware of social issues; there was a growing interest in socialism, especially in Christian circles. Socialism was studied and the first socialist party was eventually founded in 1901. The intellectual climate gradually became more open, but also more uprooted. Japanese intellectuals searched for a new identity in the tension between Japanese and Western morality and modes of thought. Liberal theology and Unitarianism challenged and confused the churches. The literary world underwent radical changes, influenced by romanticism, individualism, naturalism, and other trends, anticipating the acute feeling of "agony" so characteristic of the first years of the twentieth century. They will be examined later, insofar as they influenced Buddhist-Christian relations.

None of these trends, however, exerted an influence comparable to that of nationalism, which remained the focus of Buddhist-Christian relations in the 1890s. It is of particular interest that nationalism not only was the main source of Buddhist aggression against Christianity, but also eventually enabled Buddhists and Christians to engage in dialogue and peaceful cooperation.

The nationalistic reaction and the political changes in the years around 1890 stimulated Buddhists toward both reform and anti-Christian attitudes. Representative Buddhist movements and their protagonists contributed to the reaction. It should be emphasized that the nationalistic reaction itself was not created by Buddhists, and would certainly have arisen naturally and inevitably without Buddhist support.[1] Most Buddhists, however, supported the reaction when it came and benefited from its emphasis on Japanese traditions rather than foreign and Christian ideas. Moreover, several Buddhists were actively involved in the reaction, adding to it a distinct religious fervor and strengthening its anti-Christian tendency.

INOUE ENRYŌ AND BUDDHIST RENEWAL

Inoue Enryō (1858–1919) established himself as one of the most articulate Buddhist apologists and anti-Christian propagandists with his book *Haja shinron* [A new refutation of the evil religion], published in 1885,[2] the year that marked the start of his work for Buddhist reform.[3] In this and many other of his numerous books[4] he combined the struggle for Buddhist renewal with the refutation of Christianity. In 1886–1887 he published *Shinri kinshin* [The guiding principle of truth] in three volumes,[5] with the subtitles "Should Christianity Be Refuted on the Theoretical Level?" "Should Christianity Be Refuted on the Practical Level?" and "On Buddhism as the Religion that Satisfies both Intellect and Emotion." In 1887 he published *Bukkyō katsuron* [On the renewal of Buddhism] in four volumes.[6] Apart from the introductory volume, which advocated the need of Buddhist reform, one volume was devoted to the refutation of Christianity, the next aimed at a positive demonstration of the truth of Buddhism, and the last was devoted to Buddhist apologetics.

As a Buddhist apologist Inoue constantly found himself caught in the tension between Eastern and Western thought, Buddhism and Christianity. He was the first son of a Buddhist priest from Niigata Prefecture, belonging to the Ōtani sect of Jōdo Shin Buddhism. In his youth, however, he seemed to find both Buddhism and Confucianism inadequate, and in 1873 he turned to Western learning.[7] He entered Nagaoka School of Western Learning in 1874 in order to pursue Western studies, but later, in 1877, enrolled as a student of a Buddhist school in Kyoto. He seemed to be temporarily attracted to Christianity;[8] however, according to his own description, he "gradually understood what was not true in Christianity and proved the fallacies in Confucianism. Only the teachings of Buddhism agreed for the most part with philosophical truth."[9] In 1882 he studied philosophy at Tokyo University; in cooperation with friends and colleagues, such as Katō Hiroyuki, Hara Tanzan, Shimaji Mokurai, Kitabatake Dōryū, and Ōuchi Seiran, he founded in 1884 the philosophical society Tetsugakkai and in 1886 the journal *Tetsugaku zasshi* [Journal of philosophy]. In 1887 he founded his own school of philosophy, called Tetsugakkan, a center of learning that later developed into the present Tōyō University. He also founded a publishing company, Tetsugaku Shoin, which especially in the 1890s published numerous anti-Christian books.

As the names of all these activities and institutions indicate, philosophy *(tetsugaku)* was Inoue's central concern. It should be noted, however, that philosophy never became an isolated theoretical discipline; it provided him with concepts and tools that he applied to the concrete needs of the contemporary society. He was well acquainted with Western philosophy and had a considerable knowledge of Christian doctrine and history, and was thus well equipped for his attack on Christianity.

Two important factors seemed to be decisive for Inoue's work for Buddhist renewal. First, he was extremely pessimistic about Buddhism's ability to withstand the growing influence of Christianity in the mid-1880s. He deplored the fact that all efforts to revive Buddhism rather seemed to accelerate its decay and promote Christianity: "When one in one's heart prays for the ruin of Christianity, one seems to promote its expansion."[10] Even years of strenuous efforts for Buddhist renewal seemed to be in vain.[11] While Christianity expanded with an energy like the rising sun, he wrote, the light of Buddhism was waning like the morning moon.[12] He regarded contemporary Buddhism, as it was "practiced by the masses and transmitted by ignorant priests," as a barbarous religion, full of evil practices, and bound to decay.[13]

Second, Inoue was anticipating a radical transformation of Japanese society in connection with the promulgation of the Constitution in 1889 and the opening of the Diet in 1890. He seemed to favor the changes; but he found the Buddhist world totally unprepared for the new situation and challenged it to wake up from its slumber. Without a total renewal of Buddhism, Inoue argued, the political changes would only benefit Christianity while Buddhism would helplessly decline.[14]

In sum, the crisis of Buddhism in the 1880s and the anticipation of a political change that would threaten Buddhism and favor Christianity supplied the background for Inoue's effort to rejuvenate Buddhism. Three aspects of his work seem to be of special relevance in this connection.

THE PHILOSOPHICAL LEVEL

With Inoue's philosophical interest it was quite natural that his main activity had a philosophical character. His refutation of Christianity was based on the firm conviction that Buddhist philosophy was superior to the Christian doctrine. In *Haja shinron* and in the first volumes of *Shinri kinshin* and *Bukkyō katsuron honron* he devoted most of the space to detailed demonstrations of the irrationality of Christianity. In the two former books his argument was developed in twelve chapters, in which he discussed the cosmocentric world-view of Christianity, the idea that man is head of creation, the problem of free will, good and evil, the omnipotence of God, beginning and end of time and space, different types of theism, the criterion of truth, doctrinal changes, the idea that the East is without (true) religion, and the origin of man. His criticism of Christianity was rather traditional, but it revealed his extensive knowledge of Christian traditions and Western philosophy. In spite of a somewhat pedantic and detailed analysis and a predilection for diagrams and enumerations, his knowledge was expressed with conviction and clarity. In this way he strengthened the Buddhist feeling that even though Christianity was powerful, it was inferior on the level of philosophy and doctrine.

> If one looks at the world of religions through a philosopher's eyes, he can easily see that objective truth lies within the realm of Buddhism. Christian truth is biased and incomplete. Compared to Buddhist truth, it is like the tip end of a hair or a shadowy echo. Ah, how clear is Buddhist truth, how obscure that of Christianity, similar to the dimming of the stars before the moon's brilliance. Ah, how complete the truth of Buddhism, how partial that of Christianity, similar to the insignificance of rivers as they enter the sea. How can I even discuss the two religions on the same day?[15]

THE PRACTICAL LEVEL

In spite of his philosophical bent Inoue was convinced that the outcome of the struggle between Buddhism and Christianity would be settled on the practical level.[16] Hence the practical refutation of Christianity became the central concern of the second volume of *Shinri kinshin,* where he advocated the necessity of Buddhist participation in society. According to Inoue, the success of Buddhism was not merely a question of effective propagation, but depended upon whether or not Buddhism actually benefited the people *(minri)* and the state *(kokueki).* He went on to discuss five specific fields of Buddhist concern in this context: the level of international relations, politics, morality, education, and, more generally, the responsibility to promote enlightenment and religious reform. True apologetics could not be accomplished on the theoretical level, he wrote, but was to be realized in actual society.[17]

While Inoue had no doubts about the superiority of Buddhism on the philosophical level, he seemed pessimistic about the future prospects of Buddhism in society. He feared that Christianity would benefit from the political and social changes at the expense of Buddhism. Further, since he was convinced that the increasing power of Christianity would have negative consequences for the Japanese nation, he became increasingly concerned with the question of nationalism.

NATIONALISM

In Inoue's thinking nationalism was not merely added as an extra element beside philosophical arguments and social and political issues. Nationalism was one of the basic components of his philosophical thinking. He coined a new compound word to express the inseparable unity of nationalism and philosophy, *gokoku airi,* which literally means "protection of the nation and love of reason." As we have seen, the combination of nationalism and Buddhist apologetics was a deep-rooted tradition that had followed Buddhism since its introduction into Japan; Inoue went further and attempted to establish a theoretical basis for a synthesis of nationalism and philosophy.[18]

Hence Inoue's philosophical and practical refutation of Christianity became organically related to his characteristic Japanese nationalism. In a time of rapid Westernization and Christian expansion he was convinced that Japanese independence depended upon the preservation of traditional Japanese ideas and values. And Buddhism was in his view indispensable as the spiritual backbone that supported the Japanese people. Buddhism was inseparably related to Japanese history and was a unique expression of the national culture, while Christianity as a foreign religion endangered the Japanese nation. A religious change in the direction of Christianity would, according to Inoue, subvert the entire Eastern civilization. He had already expressed such ideas in *Haja shinron* in 1885,[19] but he began to emphasize them more strongly. In 1888 he was one of the promoters of *Nihonjin* [The Japanese], a new magazine that soon established itself as one of the leading advocates of a characteristic *Nihon-shugi*, or "Japanism."

Inoue's nationalistic and anti-Christian attitudes, however, did not imply exclusionism or total rejection of Western influence. Actually, his philosophy was deeply influenced by Hegelianism; and during his travel to Europe and America in 1889 he expressed his sympathy with Western nationalism. In Western countries he found support and inspiration for his view that protection of "a characteristic Japanese learning" was indispensable for national independence, history, literature, and religion. He thus wanted to develop his school of philosophy into a "University of Japanism," where Japanese independence, although "assisted by the sciences of the West," should be founded on Japanese learning.[20]

Furthermore, Inoue was not a fanatic anti-Christian. He took part in anti-Christian preaching,[21] engaged in a campaign against the public recognition of Christianity in 1889,[22] and wrote forceful philosophical refutations of Christianity; but he seemed to avoid emotional confrontations. Even during the controversy about religion (Christianity) and education in 1893, when most Buddhists were enraged by the Christian attacks on Inoue Tetsujirō, Inoue Enryō limited himself to a rather abstract discussion about the relationship between religion and education, and did not directly attack the Christians.[23] He emphasized that even though he had to denounce Christianity for its philosophical irrationality, he had a deep appreciation of the person of Christ; Christ was his "brother" and "spiritual friend" whom he respected and loved. He even argued that the Buddhist-Christian controversy should not influence social relations, but should be conducted with kindness and courteousness.[24] He also admitted that he always listened respectfully whenever he entered a Christian church,[25] and regarded Buddhists and Christians as people who, from the religious point of view, were seeking the same goal, and hence should live in brotherhood and friendship. Even though Christianity was inferior, he was convinced that it could be integrated into Buddhism as an "expedient means" *(hōben)* in man's search for truth.[26]

In sum, Inoue Enryō's search for Buddhist renewal offered a philosophical basis for the refutation of Christianity. He found practical issues more important for the struggle between Buddhism and Christianity than theoretical reflections. Buddhism was regarded as the undisputable basis for Japanese independence. In spite of his anti-Christian tendency, however, he was not an exclusionist. Others drew more radical conclusions.

SEIKYŌSHA AND *NIHONJIN*

Nihonjin has already been mentioned as a journal that contributed to the nationalistic renewal in the late 1880s. The first issue was published in April 1888 as an organ of the Seikyōsha (literally, Association of Politics and Religion), an association that had been founded earlier the same year to provide an alternative to the rapid Westernization of Japan. One of the central concerns was to prepare Japan for the fatal choice of its future course, including religion, morality, education, art, politics, and the economic system.[27] *Nihonjin* denounced the one-sided Westernization and advocated protection of the national characteristics, and was extremely critical of Christianity. The journal obviously met a need, and soon established itself as the intellectual rival of the popular Christian *Kokumin no tomo* [The people's friend].[28]

Seikyōsha and *Nihonjin* were not based on Buddhist principles, and the promoters represented a variety of standpoints. The main leader, Miyake Setsurei, stood for a philosophy that seemed to harmonize Eastern thought, notably Taoist philosophy, with the philosophy of Schopenhauer and Hartmann.[29] Most of the members were less concerned with religion than with nationalism.[30] Several Buddhists however—including Inoue Enryō, Shimaji Mokurai, and Tatsumi Kojirō—were members of the group and wrote regularly in *Nihonjin*. The purely Buddhist press hardly reached beyond Buddhist circles, and *Nihonjin* was, therefore, an important channel for advocating Buddhist views on social and political issues. The Buddhist writers in *Nihonjin* naturally emphasized Buddhism as the "main element of all the main elements that characterize a Japanese as a Japanese."[31] It goes without saying that they strengthened the anti-Christian tendency of the journal. In this respect they easily cooperated with people whose philosophical standpoint was antireligious and therefore anti-Christian. It was generally not until a later stage that such antireligious ideas also included Buddhism as a target for criticism.

As indicated in the case of Inoue Enryō above, the circle around Seikyōsha and *Nihonjin* was not narrowly nationalistic. It was opposed to Western capitalism and imperialism, which were becoming burning issues in the East, but such concerns were also shared by many Christians.[32] Ultimately it was a question of how to protect Japan and the Orient; and the nationalist concern expressed in *Nihonjin* in principle did not represent a morbid chauvinism or antiforeign exclusionism. Miyake Setsurei could allow himself to be extremely critical of the Japanese, whom he characterized as "mendacious, evil, and ugly."[33] The emphasis on the national characteristics was rather what *Japan Weekly Mail* characterized as a natural and inevitable reaction to a wholesale adoption of foreign civilization, including a "wholesale sacrifice of [the Japanese] individuality."[34]

Some new trends were discernable, however, especially among the Buddhist members of the group. As the time of the new Constitution drew near, they seemed to feel increasingly uncomfortable about the future. In an article on January 3, 1889, Tatsumi Kojirō advocated Buddhist support of Count Gotō Shōjiro and his conservative party, Daidō Danketsu. Tatsumi had previously supported the official recognition of Christianity, hoping that this would challenge and stimulate Buddhist propagation;[35] now he argued that the political changes would throw the Buddhists into confusion and the Christians would take advantage of the new situation. If the Christians managed to accomplish their goal, he warned, the eight million gods of Japan would disappear, and Japan would become the land of the one God of the Christians. Like a chain reaction the Imperial Household would lose its dignity, the vitality of the state would vanish, and Japanese independence would be lost. Appealing to the thirty-nine million Japanese (Buddhist) citizens to abandon interior strife and unify against Christianity, he advised them to use their overwhelming political influence to secure Buddhist power in the Diet.[36]

Similar ideas were advocated by another association, Sonnō Hōbutsu Daidōdan (The Great Association for Revering the Emperor and Worshipping the Buddha), which soon developed oppressive methods against the Christians. The details of this association will be discussed below, but it is significant that the Buddhists who had been active in Seikyōsha and *Nihonjin* were among the promoters of the new association. Their positive emphasis on national characteristics thus entailed a potential exclusionism and antiforeign element that was blatantly expressed in Sonnō Hōbutsu Daidōdan.

It is also noteworthy that several Buddhists who had earlier been recognized for their liberal attitudes, in these later years supported a policy

that was hardly consistent with their liberal background. Shimaji Mokurai, for example, had distinguished himself in the early Meiji period by
his successful work for religious freedom, that is, the independence of
Buddhism from Shinto dominance and state interference. He went to
Europe as early as 1872, and, returning by Jerusalem, was the first Buddhist in modern times to visit the holy land of the Christians. He had certainly never concealed his critical view of Christianity, and he had not
been willing to recognize Christianity on equal terms with Buddhism, yet
he represented a liberal spirit of "civilization and enlightenment." Instead
of drawing the logical conclusions from his ideas, in the 1880s he
appealed to the authority of the state for the protection of Buddhism at
the expense of Christianity. Together with Inoue Enryō and Ōuchi
Seiran, another champion of liberal Buddhist views, he claimed that,
while Buddhism should be officially recognized as the national religion,
Christianity should be excluded from such privileges.[37] He also supported the attempt to exclude Christians from all important positions in
the political, educational, and financial world, by linking Buddhism to
the dignity of the Imperial Household, in opposition to Christianity.[38]

SONNŌ HŌBUTSU DAIDŌDAN

With the establishment of Sonnō Hōbutsu Daidōdan the potential exclusionism and aggressive anti-Christian character of Buddhist nationalism
became manifest and was developed into a concrete strategy. Religious
strife was politicized in a fatal way, apparently with public sanction of
prominent Buddhists, and the violent methods of political struggle found
a way into the sphere of religion.

Daidōdan was founded by Ōuchi Seiran in January 1889, in cooperation with his closest associate, Saji Jitsunen, who later joined the Unitarians. Other promoters were Inoue Enryō, Shimaji Mokurai, Ashitsu
Jitsuzen, Maeda Eun, Tatsumi Kojirō, and Katō Eshō.[39] The general
purpose expressed in the name of the association was further defined in
its prospectus.

> This Association is formed for the purpose of maintaining the majesty of our
> Emperor and the truth of the doctrine of Buddha—a union of all those who
> wish to protect our land and religion from the contempt of the foreigner.
> Those who unite with us are expected to avoid everything that would lessen
> the honour and reverence due to His Imperial Majesty or the influence of the
> Buddhist doctrine.[40]

The background of the association was generally the same as we have
observed in the previous pages: a reaction against the one-sided Westernization and the growing power of Christianity, understood as expressions

of "the contempt of the foreigner." The destructive elements of Westernization and Christian propagation were, however, exaggerated to the
extreme, so the reaction inevitably became the more extreme. Ōuchi
described Christianity as a "dreadful religion" which, in cooperation
with Western powers, tended to destroy the national history of other peoples, including their traditions, social order, and rulers, before it finally
took the land.[41] According to Ōuchi, the Christians regarded the adoption of the new Constitution and the National Diet as the collapse of the
old Japan and the beginning of the new Japan, which was to be established under Christian leadership. Against Christianity and republican
ideas he appealed to loyalty to the Emperor and to faith in Buddhism.[42]
Tatsumi Kojirō argued that the very perpetuation of the Japanese race
was at stake; the blood lineage, represented by the Emperor, and the spiritual lineage, represented by Buddhism, could be preserved only through
a state religion that advocated both *sonnō,* "revering the Emperor," and
hōbutsu, "worshipping the Buddha."[43] A drawing in the first issue of
Daidō shinpō expressed dramatically the anti-Christian zeal of the association: A crowd of people marching under the slogan, "Revere the
Emperor! Worship the Buddha!" is driving away a handful of Christians
who are crushed under a cross on the ground.[44]

What distinguished Daidōdan from other Buddhist organizations was
not only that its reaction was more extreme than other representative
movements, but also that its concrete strategy of social and political
action went far beyond the realm of merely religious strife.

> For instance, in selecting our representatives to the national parliament, to
> provincial assemblies, to town councils, or local offices, in the distribution of
> all honours, in appointing school-teachers, officials of societies and business
> companies, etc., we pledge ourselves carefully to exclude all who are disloyal
> to our Emperor or untrue to Buddhism by believing in the foreign religion
> called Christianity. . . . Give us your hand; we shall then all stand together
> and add to the strength and life of our *Yamato-damashii* (Spirit of Old
> Japan).[45]

The purpose was not to create a new political party but to call upon
the Japanese people to exclude Christians from all positions in the political world as well as from important sections of the educational and
financial worlds. Several Buddhists favored cooperation with Daidō
Danketsu, a political association of former leaders from the Liberal party
(Jiyūtō) and the Progressive party (Kaishintō) respectively, under the
leadership of Count Gotō Shōjirō. The party gave some attention to
political and economic reforms, but it was characterized by its anti-Western standpoint and its criticism of the government for its obsequiousness
before the Western powers.[46] Tatsumi Kojirō's support of the party has
already been mentioned; several other Buddhists claimed that Sonnō

Fig. 15. A group of Christians is driven away by a crowd of people marching under the slogan *Sonnō hōbutsu,* "Revere the Emperor! Worship the Buddha!" one of the most powerful slogans in the years after 1889. Illustration from *Daidō shinpō,* no. 1 (March 11, 1889), p. 17. Courtesy of Kandadera, Tokyo, whose collection of material on Meiji Buddhist history is now at Shidō Bunko, Keio Gijuku University, Tokyo.

Hōbutsu Daidōdan and Daidō Danketsu represented the same *daidō,* "agreement on the vital points" of nationalism, and that the party deserved support for its attempts to realize these aims on the political level.[47] In positive terms, Sonnō Hōbutsu Daidōdan wanted to mobilize the 130,000 Buddhist priests in political activity and to motivate people to vote for Buddhist representatives; if there were no appropriate Buddhist candidate, the Buddhist priests were even urged to leave the priesthood to run for election.[48]

Daidōdan launched campaigns all over the country and spread rapidly in the provinces, notably in places where Shin Buddhism was strong.[49] Christians criticized the association as a "monster" that greatly hindered Christian propagation in the provinces, and reports referred to innumerable intrusions of mobs into Christian preaching places.[50] According to Yoshida Kyūichi, there was little difference between the activity of Daidōdan members and that of Minoda Kakunen, one of the most aggressive anti-Christian agitators.[51] Buddhist temples, supposed to be "Dharma-castles," became organs for political campaign and anti-Christian activity.[52] The temporary suspension by the government of one of Daidōdan's journals, *Daidō shinshi,* because it disturbed public peace indicates the aggressiveness of the agitation that followed its activity.[53]

In spite of support from several prominent Buddhists, Daidōdan was harshly criticized in the press. *Chōya shinbun,* which was generally favorable to Buddhism, criticized it for not limiting religious strife to the realm of religion, and indicated the possible antiforeign implications of its activity.[54] Others were more critical and accused Buddhism of taking advantage of the reactionary mood of the time, endeavoring to "rekindle the embers of a faint faith by connecting the dignity of the Throne with the permanence of SHAKKA'S [*sic*] doctrine."[55] *Hōchi shinbun* denounced "the slanderous diatribes against Christianity" and the political agitation of the Buddhists; even if they succeeded in getting a number of representatives in the Diet, "could they hope to propagate Buddhism and defeat Christianity by a vote of the Diet, or by the aid of political interference? . . . If measures of that kind are relied on, the future of Buddhism is indeed in a perilous condition."[56] *Nichi-nichi shinbun* regarded the combination of political and religious motives as an expression of one of the worst features of the West, "hateful in the extreme." It also found it absurd that Buddhists regarded their religion as a safeguard to the honor of the Emperor. "Buddhism declines," it stated, "but the influence of the EMPEROR increases continually." Those who advised "the expulsion of Christianity in order to maintain the majesty of the EMPEROR, will be like monkeys who climb to the loftiest tree-tops and are rewarded by a sudden fall."[57]

The Christians denounced Daidōdan as a "monster." *Kirisutokyō shinbun* referred to the "outrageous Sonnō Hōbutsu Daidōdan," and found its mixture of religion and politics a regrettable adoption of Western political traditions.[58] It was further characterized as another effort in a series of experiments to "save a waning cause," a futile attempt to "try anything to save what is left." "But the attempt to attach themselves to the EMPEROR, as if His Majesty, too, were in similar straits, is comical. Where is there a Japanese who does not honour the EMPEROR?"[59] The argument that the Christians did not honor the Emperor, however, soon proved to be more serious than the Christian writer seemed to recognize.

Even though Daidōdan created serious problems for Christian politicians and managed to add severe blows to Christian expansion in the provinces, it was generally a failure.[60] Its activities failed to make an impact on the first general election for the Diet, on July 1, 1890, when several Christians were successfully elected.[61] Ōuchi, who ran for a seat himself, was defeated, and Daidōdan publicly apologized for its failure.[62] In the second general election in 1892, none of the Buddhist representatives who had previously abandoned the priesthood to engage in political life were re-elected, and leading Buddhists warned against direct Buddhist participation in political life.[63]

In short, Daidōdan intensified the animosity between Buddhists and Christians by combining Buddhist apologetics with political struggle. Even though its strategy failed, the politicization of the Buddhist-Christian controversy introduced a new stage in the relationship between the two religions, as violence increasingly dominated the political climate of this period.

OTHER MOVEMENTS

In addition to the few representative persons and organizations that have been introduced to demonstrate the close connection between Buddhist renewal and anti-Christian nationalism, a great number of Buddhist associations were established in these years, a sign that Buddhism was gaining strength and was responding vigorously to Christian expansion.[64] *Japan Evangelist* characterized the tendency in the following way:

> Decided opposition to Christianity seems to be the great watchword of the numerous Buddhist associations. When one reads the proceedings of the Temperance Societies, Young Men's Buddhist Associations, Young Women's Buddhist Association, Associations of Buddhists, Summer Schools, Schools for the Poor, Lecture Associations, and so on to the end, the question arises, why this stirring of dead men's bones? And whence this desire to spread the truth? And why this morbid patriotism?[65]

Apart from the sarcastic remarks about the "stirring of dead men's bones," it seems that the Christian journalist rightly pointed out the characteristic combination of patriotism, missionary zeal, and "decided opposition to Christianity." These associations cannot be examined in detail here, but a few general trends will be mentioned.

BUDDHIST COOPERATION

One of the characteristic features of Buddhist activity was the emphasis on cooperation among the different Buddhist sects. As we have seen, such cooperation had been established in the early Meiji period when the violent movement to "exterminate Buddhism" and the challenge from Christianity had united the Buddhists into a common front for apologetics and anti-Christian activity. In a similar way Buddhist cooperation was strengthened at the end of the 1880s. It is significant that the Buddhist organizations referred to above were not limited to one particular sect, but worked beyond denominational structures. People such as Inoue Enryō, Ōuchi Seiran, and other Buddhist activists who were campaigning against Christianity all over the country took pride in cooperating with temples and Buddhist associations regardless of their denominations. The various Buddhist sects or Buddhist temples in a district often united in their struggle against Christianity.[66]

On the official level the cooperation was organized as a Conference of Chief Abbots of Buddhist Sects (Bukkyō Kakushū Kanchō Kaigi). The first conference was convened in Tokyo June 12–14, 1890; during this time another organization, the Association of Buddhist Sects (Bukkyō Kakushū Kyōkai), was established to promote Buddhist expansion through peaceful cooperation. A number of other organizations and conferences with a similar purpose were also organized in this period.[67] The second All-Japan Meeting of Buddhists (Zenkoku Bukkyōsha Daikonwakai) met in Nagoya April 20–23, 1891, gathering approximately 160 representatives from all over Japan. It passed a resolution against allowing Christians to be buried in Buddhist cemeteries and voted to form an alliance against the scheduled residence of foreigners in the interior of Japan.[68] The third meeting, now called the All-Japan Buddhist Meeting (Zenkoku Bukkyō Daikonwakai), met in Kyoto April 8–10, 1892. It deplored the fact that the reaction against Christianity, which for a while had reached the "extreme point of excitement" and had seemed to "retrieve years of declining fortune," had come to a standstill; and it appealed for renewed action against Christianity.[69]

This front against Christianity seemed to be an essential part of most Buddhist cooperation. In Kyoto a Buddhist university was planned to neutralize the influence of the Christian school, Doshisha.[70] A Buddhist hospital, named Hakuaikan (The Hall of Universal Love), and other projects were also planned as countermeasures against Christianity.[71] In connection with the World's Parliament of Religions in 1893, Buddhist cooperation was advocated to create a united front in the Buddhist world mission.[72] In spite of such efforts, the discord between the different Buddhist groups and sects seemed to be a constant problem, especially because of the sectarian emphasis of Nichiren Buddhism.[73]

COOPERATION WITH NON-BUDDHIST MOVEMENTS

As the anti-Christian nationalism among the Buddhists was generally a part of a broad popular reaction, it was natural that Buddhists also supported and cooperated with groups and individuals who, under other circumstances, hardly would be regarded as partners. The reaction was not concerned with doctrinal issues, but aimed at preserving national traditions; and Japanese Buddhists supported whoever defended the cause of nationalism against Christianity. In spite of recent Shinto suppression and traditional Confucian criticism of Buddhism, the Buddhists generally identified themselves with Shinto and Confucianism, regarding the three religions as the three Great Ways of Japan. Sonnō Hōbutsu Daidōdan actively defended the Shinto belief in the eight million Gods of Japan.[74] As we have seen, Seikyōsha and its journal, *Nihonjin,* included people with a variety of religious attitudes.[75] Another association, the Greater Japan Association for the Great Way of the National Doctrine (Dai Nihon Kokkyō Daidōsha), advocated the unification of the three Great Ways—Shinto, Confucianism, and Buddhism—into a national religion. Shinto was thought to represent the national polity *(kokutai),* Confucianism state affairs *(keisei),* and Buddhism spiritual deliverance *(gedatsu).*[76] The founder, Kawai Kiyomaru, was a Shinto priest, and the general character of the association seemed closest to Shinto nationalism; but it was also supported by Buddhists, and its idea of religious unification was combined with opposition to Christianity.[77] One of the active supporters of the association was Torio Tokuan (Koyata), a prominent politician, philosopher, and Buddhist layman who advocated Buddhist atheism.[78] As early as 1884 he had started the patriotic Association for the Defense of the Country (Gokoku Kyōkai) as an organ to oppose the Western influence and the Popular Rights Movement; he was broadly supported by people who held reactionary views.[79]

Seen from this point of view, Buddhist nationalism was hardly distinguishable from the general wave of anti-Western and anti-Christian reaction, in spite of its Buddhist overtones. It is a general impression that the reaction was not based on genuinely Buddhist concerns; it was rather a result of the fact that Japanese Buddhism had identified itself with the conservative trend in social and political thought. On the basis of nationalism, cooperation was possible even with groups that were potentially critical of Buddhism.

INTERNATIONAL CONTACT

The contact with Buddhists on the international level developed rapidly toward the end of the 1880s. Japanese Buddhists established contacts with the Theosophical Society, which was regarded as an effective means of Buddhist expansion in the West.[80] The Society for Communication with Western Buddhists (Ōbei Bukkyō Tsūshinkai) was founded in 1887; it was later reorganized as the Buddhist Propagation Society (Kaigai Senkyōkai, literally Overseas Missionary Society), under the leadership of Akamatsu Renjō.[81] Its purpose was to propagate Buddhism in the West, through missionaries and publications.[82] A branch office was established in London in 1890, and a journal was published, entitled *Bijou of Asia* [Ajia no hōshu].[83]

The contact with overseas Buddhists did not diminish the nationalistic sentiments of Japanese Buddhists, but rather supported and strengthened them in their rejection of Westernization and Christianity. Colonel Henry Steele Olcott, president of the Theosophical Society, was invited to Japan in the winter of 1888–1889, and again in 1893. He traveled all over Japan and preached in temples and schools. In addition to his appeal for renewal and unification of Buddhism, his addresses often included anti-Christian propaganda, and he tended to emphasize the decreasing influence of Christianity in the West.[84] Another Western Buddhist, C. Pfoundes, also supported Japanese Buddhists against Christianity. He had first come to Japan in the 1860s as an officer in the British navy and remained for about twelve years, of which he reportedly spent seven or eight years in Buddhist temples. As an admirer of the ancient Japanese civilization and of Buddhism, he had dedicated much of his time to lecturing on Buddhism in the United States (1876–1878) and in England (1878–1893).[85] He served as secretary of the London branch of the Buddhist Propagation Society and came to Japan again in 1893 at the invitation of his Buddhist friends.[86] In his many meetings he appealed to the national sentiment and attacked Christian missionaries for slighting Buddhism and despising Japan as a barbarian country.[87] Both Olcott and Pfoundes left Japan after controversies with their Japanese sponsors.[88]

LAY BUDDHIST PARTICIPATION

One characteristic feature of Buddhist movements in this period was the activity of lay Buddhists, especially the so-called *koji*, who had received a sort of ordination without being priests.[89] They were usually fervent Buddhists who had been trained under one or several masters and who devoted themselves to Buddhist propagation and similar activities. Takada Dōken envisioned the ideal Buddhist *koji* as a sort of "lay Bodhisattva" who had not yet reached the state of liberation, but whose mind was already seeking the Great Way.[90] Shaku Unshō, Fukuda Gyōkai, Hara Tanzan, and Shimaji Mokurai, especially, gathered many such lay Buddhist disciples.[91] The period around 1890 was characterized by a particular zeal in *koji* activity.

Two of the most prominent lay Buddhists in this period, Ōuchi Seiran and Torio Tokuan, who have already been introduced as key persons in the anti-Christian movement, were *koji*, and put more emphasis on lay activities than on priestly functions. Several others of the most ardent Buddhist reformers and anti-Christian propagators were also *koji*, including Mekata Sakae, who combined patriotism and Buddhist apologetics;[92] Ohara Masao and Minoda Kakunen; and a number of other Buddhist activists. Several *koji* were also active politicians, functioning as Buddhist apologists in conservative circles.[93] The activities of the Buddhist *koji* became so widespread that the Buddhist journal *Meikyō shinshi* finally found it necessary to denounce the "fake Buddhists and fake patriots" who overran the country, making their living on anti-Christian campaigns and assuming the title of *koji* and similar titles.[94] Inoue Enryō was also a lay Buddhist, but not a *koji*.

YOUTH PARTICIPATION

The participation of youth was becoming a conspicuous element in the Buddhist movements in the late 1880s. The first Japanese YMCA had been founded in 1880, and had made a considerable contribution to the rapid growth of the Christian church in the following decade. A few years later the Buddhists started to organize similar Young Men's Buddhist Associations. Especially around 1890 numerous such associations were established at various schools and universities. With their reform zeal and critical attitudes to the corrupt state of established Buddhism, some of these associations developed positive relations to Christian groups;[95] but most of the Buddhist youth associations combined the zeal for renewal with strong patriotic and anti-Christian sentiments. An editorial in *Reichikai zasshi* expressed such a view in a characteristic way: The youth associations were expected not only to promote Buddhist renewal, but to strengthen the opposition against Christianity; they hated Christianity as an evil force in Japan, and their knowledge of Western science and philosophy would enable them to see through the unreasonableness of the Christian doctrine.[96] The Greater Japan Buddhist Youth Association (Dai Nihon Bukkyō Seinenkai) was formally founded in 1894, competing with the Christians by imitating their popular summer seminars and celebrating Buddha's birthday on April 8, as an alternative to Christmas.[97]

CHAPTER EIGHT

Political and Ideological Issues

Only God can be worshipped; but all people, the living
and the dead, should be objects of obeisance.

From *Kirisutokyō shinbun* [The Christian]

THE EXAMINATION of some representative Buddhist movements and
their protagonists in the previous chapter has revealed the close connection between Buddhist renewal and anti-Christian nationalism. The aim
of the present chapter is to show how closely the Buddhist reaction was
related to the political and ideological trends of the period. A few conspicuous aspects will be particularly emphasized, such as international
relations, represented by the problem of treaty revision; the political system, represented by the Constitution and the Diet; and the whole question of national identity and educational policy, symbolized by the Imperial Rescript on Education, the so-called incidents of lese majesty, and the
controversy about religion and education. These issues will be treated
separately for the sake of convenience; it should, however, be stressed
that they were all closely related and, especially from the point of view of
Buddhist-Christian relations, must be seen as aspects of one continuous
development.

THE PROBLEM OF TREATY REVISION

The unequal treaties, forced upon Japan by the Western powers from the
middle of the century, had since the very beginning been a cause of
resentment among the Japanese. The humiliating terms of the treaties
and the failure to revise them inevitably influenced Japanese sentiments
toward the West, and toward Christianity as the supposed religion of the
West. Especially in the 1880s the negotiations about treaty revision had

serious consequences. As indicated above, Japanese intellectual and political leaders had increasingly stressed Westernization as a means to prove that Japan had reached the cultural level of the West and thus "deserved" to be treated as a civilized country. The official policy of Westernization was generally favorable to Christianity. It was even argued that Christianity should be the future religion of Japan; adoption of Christianity would facilitate the Western recognition of Japan on equal terms with the Western nations, and thus prepare the revision of the unjust treaties.[1] Just as Christianity was favored in anticipation of treaty revision, however, the failure of the treaty negotiations in 1887 and 1889 created a heated anti-Western atmosphere that dealt a heavy blow to Christianity.[2] As the proposed treaties included concessions that seemed favorable to Christian work, the missionaries were openly charged with responsibility for the failure of the negotiations.[3] Christian meetings lost much of their attraction; the enrollment in Christian schools decreased drastically around 1889; and Christian work generally experienced serious setbacks as a result of the crisis in treaty negotiations.[4]

Actually, Christians in Japan had neither supported the treaties nor opposed their revision. As early as 1884 the Osaka and Kobe Missionary Association had called for a revision of the treaties and for the abolishment of extraterritoriality,[5] and the same position was reaffirmed in 1890.[6] In September the same year, Japanese Christians held prayer meetings for equal treaties, and even issued a memorial to the Queen of England about the problem.[7] Some Buddhists ridiculed such Christian initiatives,[8] while others recognized their positive intentions.[9] Be that as it may, the popular agitation in connection with the treaty negotiations tended to turn against Christianity, a sentiment that was shared by the Buddhists.

As for the Buddhists, the alleged responsibility of the Christians for the delay of treaty revision was less important than another problem: A clause in the proposed treaties would open the way for "mixed residence," that is, freedom for foreign residence, travel, and trade in the interior of Japan. The Buddhists feared that this would eventually favor Christianity by opening the way for foreign mission in the Buddhist strongholds in the interior. It is thus characteristic that when the leader of the Conservative party, Viscount Torio, endeavored to enlist Buddhist sympathies in the anti-treaty-revision cause in 1889, he argued that mixed residence would lead to "an inundation of Christian propagandists, to the no small injury of Buddhism." The Buddhists eventually decided to "keep their hands out of the mess,"[10] but there is no doubt that this aspect of the treaty negotiations was a burning issue for the Buddhist community. As we shall see later, the problem of interior residence of foreigners and the related problem of public recognition of Buddhism at the cost of Christianity remained a central concern for Buddhists throughout the 1890s.

THE CONSTITUTION AND THE DIET

The Meiji Constitution, which had been prepared in various ways since 1881, was promulgated on February 11, 1889. The Constitution incorporated a whole range of conflicting ideas and introduced a new political system, including the national Diet. The following examination will focus on three areas that particularly influenced Buddhist-Christian relations: (1) The Constitution confirmed the absolute sovereignty of the Emperor; (2) it guaranteed the freedom of religion; and (3) it introduced a new political system based on popular, though limited, franchise.

THE SOVEREIGNTY OF THE EMPEROR

The Constitution was drafted on the assumption that the Emperor would be the axis of the new constitutional order. It confirmed the rule of the Imperial household as eternal, and the Emperor as sacred and inviolable, representing a dynasty that had reigned in an unbroken line of descent from ages past. Moreover, the Constitution was presented as an imperial grant, a gift of a benevolent and charitable Emperor to the people of his country. In other words, the Constitution was not based on the Western idea that the sovereignty resides with the people; all sovereignty was united in the person of the Emperor.[11]

Even though certain popular rights were introduced—such as freedom of religion, freedom of speech and publication, freedom of assembly and association, liberty of residence, rights to property, and due process of law—they were hedged about with such phrases as "except in cases provided for in law," or "within limits not prejudicial to peace and order."[12] Even more important than the various limitations of popular rights is the fact that these were not based on an idea about universal human rights, but were understood as benevolent and charitable grants of a sovereign Emperor.

The implications of the idea of the Emperor's sovereignty were not understood at once, either by Buddhists or by Christians; but they gradually became apparent in the following years. Actually, the whole series of incidents referred to in the following pages, such as the problems related to the Imperial Rescript on Education and the required obeisance to the Emperor, the alleged incidents of lese majesty by Uchimura Kanzō and others, and the conflict about religion and education, were all intimately related to the sovereignty of the Emperor. The Constitution, which was supposed to introduce democratic rights, proved to be a "bulwark for the conservatives rather than for the radicals."[13]

From one point of view, the Constitution implied a hidden criticism of Buddhism. According to Itō Hirobumi, the leading thinker behind the Constitution, the axis of the new constitutional order could not be found in the traditional religions of Japan. In Europe the constitutional system was based on a thousand years of tradition, and religion (Christianity) had penetrated and unified the people. "In Japan, however," Itō wrote, "the power of religion is weak and cannot at all become the axis of the state. Even though Buddhism once exerted a strong influence, unifying all classes of the people, it is now already about to decline." Likewise Shinto, qua religion, failed to provide a spiritual unification, even though it expounded the precepts of the ancestors. Hence only the Imperial household could be the axis of the Japanese people.[14]

The Buddhists, however, did not apprehend this implicit distrust of Buddhism and never seemed to question the role of the Imperial household as the focus of identity, or "axis," of the Japanese people. They merely maintained their traditional uncritical combination of political and religious loyalty[15] and engaged in further attacks on Christianity when the potential conflict between Christianity and the idea about the absolute sovereignty of the Emperor surfaced in the following years.

FREEDOM OF RELIGION

While the emphasis on the Emperor's sovereignty had fatal consequences for the Christian church and its relation to Buddhism, another aspect of the Constitution caught the immediate attention of both Buddhists and Christians, the guarantee of religious freedom in Article 28 of the Constitution: "Japanese subjects shall, within limits not prejudicial to peace and order, and not antagonistic to their duties as subjects, enjoy freedom of religious belief."[16]

The question of religious freedom had been a continuous problem for Christians. The notice boards against Christianity had been removed in 1873, but no official document had declared that Christianity was recognized. Several drafted laws and regulations had suggested freedom for the Christian faith, and since the end of the 1870s the press had repeatedly advocated the freedom of religion as a natural right. In 1878 several prominent Christians had appealed to the Ministry of Home Affairs for freedom of faith. Ten years later, in 1888, another group of Christians presented a written petition to the Senate (Genrōin) concerning public recognition of Christianity; the petition had stirred much discussion in the press, but no official reaction was given at that time.[17] Article 28 of the Constitution was, therefore, generally understood as an official recognition of Christianity; and those who still opposed Christianity had apparently lost their legal basis.[18] The churches welcomed the new Constitution with thanksgiving services and prayer meetings all over

the country on the day of its promulgation.[19] The German missionaries .
Spinner and Schmiedel extended a letter of thanks to the Emperor,
through Count Ōkuma, for the public recognition of Christianity.[20] In
Tokyo a joint meeting of the Christian churches was held in the Kōsei
Building where the hall was decorated all over with red lamps and green-
ery. The front wall was decorated with the words "Freedom of Religion"
and "Long Live the Emperor!" On the side wall the whole of Article 28
was written. It was also read aloud during the service, and prayers and
addresses drew attention to the new situation of the church. A picture of
the rising sun in the front of the hall suggested that the Constitution
introduced a new day for the Christian church. It was characterized as a
"Second Restoration," an "unprecedented happening," or "the basis for
the new Japan."[21]

The immediate Buddhist reaction generally seemed to support the
view that the Constitution introduced an official permission for the practice of Christianity instead of the previous tacit approval.[22] The new religious policy of the government was further substantiated by the fact that
the chief abbots of the powerful Shin Buddhist head temples in Kyoto
and other Buddhist dignitaries, who expected to be present at the promulgation ceremony of the Constitution, were not invited. From the point
of view of the government, this was in accordance with the policy of separation between politics and religion, but the Buddhists resented the decision as an obvious expression of their loss of status.[23]

The Buddhists, therefore, soon began to question the meaning of religious freedom, and some even advocated political sanctions. It was, for
instance, argued that the Constitution would not be valid until the Diet
had been convened the following year, and that the interval of one year
would provide them with ample opportunity to engage in political suppression of Christianity.[24] The most common argument, however, was to
criticize the Christians for failing to take account of the obvious limitations of Article 28, expressed in the words, "within limits not prejudicial
to peace and order, and not antagonistic to their duties as subjects." The
Buddhists emphasized these conditional clauses so strongly that they generally concluded that Christians did not enjoy the freedom of religious
faith defined in the Constitution. For instance, it was argued that the
Christian "superstition" in a "prejudiced God" naturally prejudiced
Christians against the creeds of the Emperor and the Japanese people,
and thus created disharmony in their relations to family and neighbors;[25]
that if Christianity caused religious strife, it was the duty of the political
authorities to intervene;[26] that Christianity exercised destructive influence on the state and was incompatible with loyalty to the Emperor.[27]
Such arguments resulted in a strategy designed to make Buddhism a
national religion or "state-recognized religion," while Christianity, on the

other hand, would merely be tolerated as a private religious institution, provided it did not disturb peace and order or hinder its members from performing their duties as subjects.[28]

It should be mentioned that the Buddhists were not alone in their emphasis on the limitations of religious freedom. To a certain degree they were supported by official comments on the problem.[29] And further, while public opinion around 1889 supported the view that Article 28 was a public recognition of Christianity, the development in the following years put more emphasis on the conditional character of this recognition. As we shall see, the conflict between Christianity and the national polity eventually became so acerbated that Article 28 failed to provide the necessary guarantee for religious freedom.

ELECTION AND THE DIET

The year 1890 was regarded by Japanese Buddhists as a fatal and crucial year, in which the future of Buddhism would be decided. The first general election was held on July 1, 1890, and the Diet was convened on November 25 the same year. Inoue Enryō's apprehensions about the political changes have already been mentioned, and Buddhists generally shared his feelings that this was the "dawn" when the unrealistic dreams would vanish and the true colors of reality appear. What mattered now was real power to engage in the desperate struggle in the political arena.[30]

The result was not merely that a religious element was added to the political strife. A further consequence was that the religious world was fatally influenced by the atmosphere of the political world, which had become increasingly violent. The political fervor became so strong among Buddhists that Buddhist leaders began to worry about its negative consequences within their own camp. The first Conference of Buddhist Chief Abbots in 1890 took up the problem of political and social disruption as one of the central issues, and appealed to Buddhist priests to keep aloof from politics and to avoid using temples for political meetings; the priests in the provinces especially were admonished to do their utmost to establish harmony.[31]

The warnings of Buddhist leaders as well as public criticism in the press seemed to be in vain.[32] Buddhist priests opened their temples for political agitation and supported various political parties, attacking others as "Christian" parties. In the provinces especially, political campaigns often seemed like Buddhist meetings. In Niigata Prefecture, for instance, the local Progressive party (Kaishintō) tried to defeat the Christian candidate by employing more than ten Buddhist and Shinto priests to oppose his candidacy. In Kyushu, on the other hand, the Kaishintō was attacked as a "Christian" party;[33] and in Nagano Prefecture it was denounced as an "enemy of Buddhism" because of alleged Christian influence.[34]

The political world of Japan in these years was marred by increasing violence, including political assassination.[35] A conspicuous role was played by the so-called *sōshi,* who not only engaged in political struggle, but also were employed by Buddhists to obstruct Christian work. *Sōshi* are usually referred to as "hired thugs," "political bullies," "hooligans,"[36] or somewhat more accurately as "political rowdies . . . some of whom were merely hired ruffians, others of a better sort but given to violence under pretentious names."[37] *Japan Weekly Mail* suggested the somewhat awkward, but fairly accurate, translation, "physical-force men."[38] *Sōshi,* however, were not merely young and violent political agitators. They were of samurai descent, and had thus more than the ordinary amount of education. *Jiji shinpō* described them as a uniquely Japanese product; just as Russia had her nihilists and Germany her socialists, Japan had her *sōshi.* The difference was that *sōshi* did not have a political platform of their own; some were conservatives, some radicals, and some liberals. It was argued that the *sōshi* possessed "just enough knowledge to be dangerous, and just enough gentility to be useless as a bread-winner, while the hereditary qualities of [their] class render[ed them] reckless and violent where personal peril [was] in question."[39] Alienated from society, they acted out their frustrations on the political scene.[40] Some of the *sōshi* seemed to be idealists with "disinterested patriotism and public spirit," but generally they were denounced as a "lawless mob," "degraded and mercenary," and thus willing to be hired by various political groups.[41]

The *sōshi* had played a prominent role in connection with the struggle for treaty revision. In 1887 they had forced their advice on leading politicians and used such aggressive methods that the Peace Preservation Ordinance had to be issued.[42] In 1889 again, *sōshi* had been used by both supporters and opponents of treaty revision; and the leader of the negotiations, Count Ōkuma, was seriously hurt, apparently attacked by a *sōshi.* According to *Nichi-nichi shinbun,* the confusion in the political world was "beyond description." In the last half of 1889 "party strife daily became more and more violent, until men began to think that the struggle of parties was a curse to the country."[43] In spite of public criticism, political parties began to employ *sōshi* as weapons of defense and offense.[44]

Inevitably, then, the political campaigns for the first Diet election were quite violent. *Japan Weekly Mail* remarked sarcastically that the election campaign was not marked "by a spirit quite as law-abiding as the general demeanour of the Japanese people has led us to expect," and referred to "bribery, physical violence, quarrels between relatives and friends, and other evil incidents."[45] Such violence increased further, and the second election to the Diet, on February 15, 1892, turned out to be the bloodiest election in Japanese history. The official figures listed 25 killed and 388 wounded in melees between the police, *sōshi,* and politicians.[46]

It is difficult to assess exactly at which point the Buddhists started to employ *sōshi* against Christians. At a later stage the use of *sōshi* seemed to be a generally recognized fact, and Buddhist journals referred to the *sōshi* as representatives of a respectable spiritual tradition.[47] Even though no definite evidence is available, the direct use of *sōshi* by Buddhists probably began as a result of the politicization of the religious struggle before the first general election in 1890.

In spite of strong opposition the election proved to be quite successful from the Christian point of view;[48] and the opening of the Diet on November 25, 1890, was celebrated with thanksgiving and prayer meetings in churches all over the country, similar to the celebration of the promulgation of the Constitution in 1889.[49] At one of the great Christian conventions in the beginning of the 1880s the hope had been voiced that the first Diet be opened with "prayer to the One, true God."[50] That dream was not realized, but the Christian churches certainly saw the Diet as an expression of a new age of Christian expansion, and they responded with prayer and praise.

In short, the political changes around 1889–1890 introduced a situation that was of great concern to Buddhists as well as Christians. The Buddhists had anticipated the change with uncertainty and fear; keenly aware that they were unprepared, they expected the Christians to benefit from the new situation. The Christians, on their side, regarded the political changes as signs of a new age, a new Restoration that would pave the way for the Christianization of Japan. At the same time, however, several trends seemed to lead in the opposite direction. Even though Christians could now enjoy freedom of religion and were quite successful in their political activities, the Christian church was entering a period of oppression, persecution, and retarded growth. On the other hand, the Buddhists, who were dismayed by the new situation and generally failed to materialize their political ambitions, nevertheless entered a period when they felt that they were finally starting to regain what they had lost to Christianity in the previous decades.

THE IMPERIAL RESCRIPT ON EDUCATION AND INCIDENTS OF LESE MAJESTY

The ambiguities and inherent contradictions in the development sketched above were especially exposed in the field of education, which became increasingly problematic for Christians. The Christian church had a long experience at all levels of educational work in Japan; Christian education was the object of admiration, envy, and criticism. Especially in the wake of the rapid Westernization in the 1880s a great number of Christian schools had been established, emphasizing women's education, foreign language and history, and Christianity. The so-called Mission Schools were generally regarded as the main agent of Westernization and were inevitably hit by the nationalistic reaction; the number of students decreased drastically, and many schools had to close.[51] Apart from the various pressures against Christian schools, Christian teachers and students in other schools also encountered numerous problems in the 1890s.

CONSERVATIVE TRENDS AND POTENTIAL CONFLICTS

The problems were not merely a result of an emotional reaction to Westernization but were closely related to a steady conservative development in the educational world that started in the early 1880s. After 1886 the elementary school system was avowedly dedicated to the training of the moral and patriotic individual. Education was not "for the sake of the pupils but for the sake of the country." Tokyo University was designated "Imperial" and was expected to teach the arts and sciences essential to the state. Particular attention was paid to teacher training, and the students were required to live in dormitories under military-type discipline. *Yōgaku kōyō* [Principles of instruction for youth], written by the Confucian moralist Motoda Eifū, emphasized national principles and was adopted as the commentary for the newly established program of education. A dominating German influence went in the same direction. The educational system combined modern teaching of scientific knowledge with a strong nationalistic spirit. The Imperial Rescript on Education, issued in October 1890, represented the final sanction of traditional Confucian virtues, loyalty and filial piety.[52] Along with the Constitution the rescript became one of the fundamental documents of modern Japan, and the object of deep reverence. The practice of sending portraits of the Emperor to schools to be used as objects of reverence had already been established; and soon various schools directed that ceremonies be held to commemorate the rescript.[53] In many cases the picture of the Emperor and the rescript were actually treated like religious objects. In some places incense and rice cakes were offered; in other places they were enshrined in Shinto shrines erected in schools for this purpose.[54] In the countryside especially there seemed to be confusion whether they should be worshipped according to Shinto or Buddhist ritual.[55]

With the emphasis on the sovereignty of the Emperor and the virtues of loyalty and filial piety, the foundation was laid for several years of intense attacks on Christianity. The criticism did not provide new arguments, compared to the nationalistic reaction already described, but the focus of the reaction gradually moved from political to educational issues. The rescript became one of the crucial issues, being a characteristic expression of the national polity, and, allegedly, being incompatible with Christianity.

Christian schools had repeatedly been attacked for their lack of respect for religious and national festivals. Doshisha, Meiji Gakuin, and Kanazawa Jogakkō, for example, were criticized for refusing to give the students holidays at the time of Shinto festivals or on the Emperor's birthday.[56] The consensus, however, seemed to be that Japanese Christians at least celebrated the Emperor's birthday quite patriotically, with prayer meetings and cheers,[57] and that they were not particularly critical of the Rescript on Education and shared the common reverence for the Emperor.[58] The previously mentioned comment in *Kirisutokyō shinbun* was characteristic: "Where is there a Japanese who does not honour the EMPEROR?"[59] The real issue for the Christians was not whether or not they should revere the Emperor and the rescript, but how the reverence should be expressed. Ultimately it became a question about the relationship between obeisance and religious worship.

Meiji Christianity was characterized by a strict rejection of all sorts of idol worship. It was thus difficult for Japanese Christians to find an easy solution when participation in non-Christian religious ceremonies was required. The problem was thoroughly discussed in an article in *Kirisutokyō shinbun* in 1890. Responding to a letter from a worried Christian student in Miyagi, who had requested guidelines for the correct attitude to worship of the picture of the Emperor and worship in the Shinto shrine of Miyagi, the paper solved the problem by distinguishing between religious worship *(reihai, hai-suru)* and formal obeisance *(keirei)*. Only God should be worshipped, it was argued, while all people, the living and the dead, should be objects of reverence.[60] Even though a viable solution was thus suggested to the painful problem, reality was much more complicated. The article was, for instance, criticized by Buddhists as an example of the evil influence of Christianity,[61] and Christians were scrutinized by the suspicious eyes of people who wanted to expose the basic conflict between Christian faith, and loyalty and filial piety.

THE UCHIMURA INCIDENT

The most famous incident in this connection, which dramatically revealed the potential conflict between Christianity and the national polity, was the so-called Uchimura Kanzō incident of lese majesty. Uchimura was a part-time teacher at the First Higher Middle School in Tokyo. The school had already held a ceremony to celebrate the newly issued Imperial Rescript of Education on the Emperor's birthday on November 3, 1890. On December 25, however, the school had received a special copy of the rescript with the Emperor's personal signature, as a special favor granted to the seven higher middle schools in Japan.[62] Hence a new ceremony was held on January 9, 1891, to commemorate the rescript and the Imperial signature attached to it. The ceremony was characterized by a strong patriotic spirit,[63] and included the reading of the rescript, followed by a ceremony in which all teachers and students were required to make obeisance to the rescript and the sacred signature of the Emperor. The teachers and students approached the rescript in groups of five to pay obeisance. According to Uchimura himself, they were supposed to make a deep bow before the rescript in the same way as Japanese bow their heads in front of the tablets of the ancestors.[64] Standing in front of the rescript he read it reverently, but he hesitated to express an attitude of religious worship. He just bowed slightly and returned solemnly to his place.[65] Uchimura did not intend to express any disrespect; he merely refused to take part in what he regarded as religious worship of the rescript or the Emperor's signature. He had never criticized the rescript, and he emphasized later that its purpose was to be practiced in real life, not to be worshipped. From the school's point of view, the problem was not that he had failed to express respect, but that his obeisance had been insufficient. Nevertheless, Uchimura's behavior was generally regarded as a blatant expression of irreverence. Several of his colleagues denounced him as a traitor, and the students were enraged. He was criticized for "defiling the sacred place of ceremony," and was requested to repeat the obeisance in a proper way. After conferring with Christian friends and colleagues he agreed to repeat the obeisance, making the distinction between obeisance and religious worship.[66] Because of severe illness, however, his Christian colleague, Kimura Shunkichi, actually performed the ceremony as his representative on January 29. The day after, on January 30, his friends wrote a letter of explanation in Uchimura's name and sent it to numerous newspapers and journals. It expressed his deep respect for the rescript and referred to his effort to teach the students its spirit; further, it apologized for Uchimura's insufficient respect to the rescript during the ceremony and indicated his willingness to make proper obeisance.[67] Thus the problem could have been solved; but the day after, another letter was written to the school principal, expressing Uchimura's intention to resign, and he was released from his position. Uchimura, or rather his friends, referred to his illness as the reason for his decision, but his resignation was generally considered a result of the severe criticism he had encountered.[68]

Uchimura's so-called lese majesty thus originated as a minor incident, but it turned out to be one of the major issues in the anti-Christian propaganda. Uchimura was, in fact, a man of strong patriotic sentiment; he was critical of missionaries and of many Western ideas, and emphasized the national traditions.[69] As a teacher at the First Higher Middle School he had also become popular because, instead of teaching English through difficult and remote Western literature, he used the English translation of Itō Hirobumi's comments on the Japanese Constitution as a textbook.[70] His famous motto based on the two J's, "Japan and Jesus," was also a characteristic expression of his patriotic spirit.[71] Because the facts about the so-called lese majesty were greatly distorted and exaggerated, however, Uchimura came to be regarded as a national traitor, a prototype of the disloyal Christian, representing a faith that was incompatible with the national polity expressed in the Imperial Rescript on Education.

As the discussion developed, several Christians responded by defending Uchimura, in the press and through various meetings.[72] At a meeting in Ikisaka Church in Tokyo on February 4, 1891, the speaker, who spoke about Christianity and nationalism, defended Uchimura by referring to the problem of idol worship in the Roman Empire. The meeting was disrupted by shouts and threats about killing the Christians and expelling the foreigners. The editor of *Yomiuri shinbun* happened to be present, and the news about the disturbance thus spread all over the country.[73] A similar meeting in Sendai was also disrupted by the angry audience.[74] In the end of February five prominent Christians published an open letter, defending Uchimura and criticizing the custom of worshipping "a piece of paper on which the Imperial Rescript is printed." The letter recognized the political etiquette towards sovereigns, but argued that it was contrary to the religious freedom guaranteed in the Constitution to expect religious worship of the Emperor as if he were a God; actually, death would be preferable to Emperor worship, it proclaimed. Finally, it was argued that the religious element should be deleted from all ceremonies in which the entire nation was supposed to participate.[75] The strongest support of Uchimura came from Uemura Masahisa, one of the five, who was the editor of *Fukuin shūhō*. Uemura referred to the persecution of Christians in the Roman Empire. At the present time there was no persecution of Christians by punishment and torture as in the early church, he wrote, but Christians still had to obey their conscience against the current opinion, unreasonable blackmail, criticism, and oppressive regulations.[76] The government responded by immediately banning the publication of the magazine.[77]

The defense of Uchimura from the Christian side and the attacks from others indicated that there was more at stake than the mere question of Uchimura's conduct. The discussion soon developed from personal attacks on the individual Christian, Uchimura Kanzō, to more general attacks on Christianity.[78] In the following years the Uchimura lese majesty affair became one of the most popular and powerful arguments used against Christianity. Several other similar incidents were added to the arguments, but the Uchimura incident was remembered as the case of lese majesty par excellence.

The Uchimura incident was closely related to the dominating trend in the educational world, where the nationalistic sentiment was extremely strong, nurtured through a decade of conservative development. The Buddhists engaged actively in the debate, but did not play any decisive role. The incident generally affirmed them in their previous attitudes toward Christianity, and, moreover, furnished them with effective arguments against the Christians. Uemura Masahisa, who regarded the incident as a minor happening that would soon disappear like ripples in the water, referred somewhat sarcastically to "foolish Shinto priests and crafty Buddhist priests" who used the incident to attack Christianity in the name of patriotism.[79]

In a study of Buddhist attitudes toward the Uchimura incident, Yoshida Kyūichi has made a thorough analysis of articles in twenty-one representative Buddhist journals and newspapers. According to Yoshida, the first Buddhist comment on the incident appeared in *Mitsugon kyōhō* on January 25, 1891, sixteen days after the incident. In an article entitled "Worship of a Piece of Paper Is Contrary to the Christian Doctrine," the journal reported that the Christian "Professor" Uchimura Kanzō had refused to worship the picture of the Emperor and forbidden Christians to worship a piece of paper. Later the same journal reported that Uchimura had declared that he would not pay obeisance to "objects without spirit," such as Imperial Rescripts, the Ise Shrine, or the Palace Sanctuary; and the journal concluded that Christianity was contrary to the national polity. Thus the Buddhist journal introduced some of the characteristic exaggerations and distortions that marred the debate about Uchimura, and that also became the basis for other Buddhist criticism. That Uchimura was not a professor but a part-time lecturer was a minor mistake. He had refused to take part in religious worship of the rescript, but he had neither referred to it as a "mere piece of paper" nor intended to demonstrate irreverence; and it was a total misunderstanding that he had refused to bow to the picture of the Emperor or generally refused to pay respect to sacred objects, as the criticism alleged.[80] One Buddhist journal reported that Uchimura had even refused to attend the ceremony of reading the Imperial Rescript.[81] Similar misunderstandings were reported frequently in other Buddhist journals, strengthening the Buddhist bias against Uchimura. The prominent Buddhist leader, Shimaji Mokurai, who in his struggle for religious freedom in the early Meiji period had been criticized for attitudes similar to Uchimura's, now denounced Uchimura's conduct, interpreting it as the result of a lack of love and respect for the Emperor.[82] Such misunderstandings and exaggerations were found not only in the Buddhist press but in the popular press as well.[83]

But the Buddhists consistently based their criticism on the most negative reports and made few efforts to distinguish between facts and distortions.[84] The facts of the incident seemed less important to the Buddhists than what they regarded as Uchimura's basic standpoint. Their reaction was predominantly opportunistic and was characterized by an emotional anti-Christian tendency. A few Buddhists revealed a certain understanding of Christianity, or sympathy with Uchimura, or discussed the incident fairly dispassionately; but there was not a single example of Buddhist defense of Uchimura.[85] While the Christians, after the first intense discussions, tended to ignore the whole issue, Uchimura's name itself and the words "incident of lese majesty" *(fukei jiken)* became familiar elements of the Buddhist agitation against Christianity in the 1890s.

OTHER INCIDENTS

An incident that aroused sentiments similar to the Uchimura case happened in Kumamoto on January 11, 1892. During the installation ceremony of the new principal of the Christian school, Kumamoto Eigakkō, one of the teachers, Okumura Teijirō, gave an address as the representative of the school. He characterized the educational policy of the school as neither "Japanism," nor "Asianism," nor "Westernism," but the principle of universal love, which would foster world citizens. The emphasis on universalism rather than nationalism had characterized the school since the previous principal, Ebina Danjō; nevertheless, Okumura was immediately attacked as being in conflict with the spirit of the Imperial Rescript of Education. On January 25 the governor of Kumamoto Prefecture demanded that Okumura be fired. The school was divided over the issue, and one group of teachers established another school; however, both schools were closed the following year.[86]

The incident was commented on in several Buddhist journals and newspapers. The Buddhists generally criticized the incident in the same way as they had done in the Uchimura case, regarding it as another expression of the inevitable conflict between Christianity and the national polity. In this case, too, the argument was one-sidedly emotional.[87] On the other hand, when the governor of Kumamoto in June the same year instructed that teachers who became Christians would be "summarily dealt with"[88] and made efforts to prevent individual Christians from keeping their faith, several Buddhists endorsed the Christian protest. In this case they did not see the issue as a question about Christianity versus the rescript but as a question about the religious freedom of the individual.[89]

Apart from such incidents, which became major problems, numerous other minor acts of lese majesty were reported in the Buddhist press. The common criticisms that Christian schools failed to celebrate religious and national holidays, or hesitated to pay respect to Shinto shrines, to the picture of the Emperor, or to the Rescript on Education, have already been mentioned. Again and again Christians, notably pastors and teachers, were accused of making irreverent utterances about the Emperor, saying that only God is sacred, or failing to show due respect to the picture of the Emperor or to the Rescript on Education.[90] Such a case was even reported from San Francisco, where a Christian youth had declined to take part in what he called "idol worship" of the picture of the Emperor.[91] The mood of the Buddhists was characteristically expressed in *Shimei yoka,* which warned that incidents like Uchimura's lese majesty could happen anywhere, worrying lest "traitors and conspirators would come forth in great numbers."[92]

In addition to incidents that allegedly revealed a lack of patriotic sentiment, Buddhist journals seemed to have a predilection for reporting incidents that defamed the Christians in various ways, such as accusing them of misconduct or crimes.[93] According to Christian critics, *Kakuyū hōchi,* a newspaper that supported Buddhism against Christianity, specialized in such defaming reports.[94] A book entitled *The Japanese Bride,* written by the Japanese pastor Tamura Naomi, was also denounced in much the same way as the above-mentioned affairs. The book included a scathing criticism of the role of women in Japan. Critics argued that Tamura had thus demonstrated that he was not only in conflict with traditional views on women; writing the book in English, he had even betrayed his country by revealing their shame to foreigners.[95] It may seem a trifling incident, but it stirred a heated emotional argument and was frequently commented on and criticized in Buddhist journals.[96]

The cases of so-called lese majesty and other forms of irreverence tended to stir up emotional arguments and uncritical denunciations of the Christians. The validity of some of the incidents was dubious; some of them may even have been fabricated by the Buddhists.[97] More important than finding out to what degree the numerous reports were based on actual facts is noting how central such incidents became in Buddhist-Christian relations. The incidents described above were dramatic expressions of the suspicion and animosity that separated Buddhists and Christians in those years, reaching a climax in the controversy about religion and education.

INOUE TETSUJIRŌ AND THE CONTROVERSY ABOUT EDUCATION AND RELIGION

The so-called conflict between education and religion is often referred to as an incident that occurred in 1893, caused by the writings of Inoue Tetsujirō.[98] This is correct to a certain degree. In the middle of January

1893, Inoue began to publish a series of articles entitled "The Conflict between Education and Religion." It was published in the educational journal *Kyōiku jiron* and simultaneously in a number of other journals and newspapers.[99] The articles were then collected and published as a book in April the same year.[100] Inoue thus stirred a heated discussion about his central concern: the incompatibility of Christianity and the Imperial Rescript on Education. To a great extent the discussion developed as a bitter conflict between Inoue and his supporters, including the Buddhists, on the one side, and a united Christian front on the other. Even the Orthodox Archbishop Nicolai threatened to take legal proceedings against Inoue.[101] The most humiliating attack on Inoue came from the Christian scholar Takahashi Gorō; and the discussion eventually turned out to be a confrontation between Inoue and Takahashi. The book was finally prohibited as a cause of disturbance of public order.[102] Thus the controversy became one of the most important conflicts between Christianity and the nationalistic reaction in the 1890s.

It would, however, be misleading to regard the conflict as an isolated incident that occurred in 1893. It was intimately related to the incidents examined in the previous pages and could rather be seen as the conclusion to several years of continuous conflict. Inoue himself had for several years repeatedly expressed his view on the conflict between Christianity and the national polity. His critical attitude toward Christianity was expressed as early as 1883, in *Rinri shinsetsu* [A new essay on ethics].[103] In 1889 he had published *Naichi zakkyoron* [About mixed residence], warning against foreign residence in the interior of Japan. The presence of foreigners would, according to Inoue, open Japan for the destructive influence of Christianity.[104] In the new edition, entitled *Naichi zakkyo zokuron* [About mixed residence, continued], published in 1891, he referred especially to the Uchimura incident, denouncing monotheism as "oppressive" and "threatening," and incompatible with loyalty and filial piety.[105] He also declared that mixed residence would result in the defeat and destruction of Buddhism and Shinto.[106] His criticism of Christianity was further clarified in an article entitled "The Relation Between the Imperial Household and Religion" and in an interview entitled "The Conflict between the State and Christianity," published in *Kyōiku jiron* in January 1891 and November 1892, respectively.[107] Several Christians responded to the latter, and a heated discussion developed. The articles Inoue began to publish in January 1893, entitled "The Conflict Between Education and Religion," were a continuation of the previous discussion, which was now reaching its climax.

A closer look at Inoue's articles also reveals that, rather than introducing a new conflict, Inoue was using familiar arguments, and to a great extent based his criticism on the above-mentioned incidents of alleged lese majesty. A recognized scholar, Inoue naturally became a rallying force in the anti-Christian movement. The articles were not characterized by scholarly thoroughness. They did not present a systematic criticism of Christianity; they rather appealed because they included most of the popular arguments against Christianity, functioning as a sort of conclusion and summary of years of discussion.

Inoue's main point was to demonstrate that Christianity was incompatible with the Imperial Rescript on Education. Inoue rejected the viewpoint that the Christians were not against the rescript but merely refused to worship it as a superficial excuse. He noted that, in contrast to Buddhists, Confucians, and Shintoists, only the Christians had had problems with the rescript, and he explained this as the inevitable result of a basic conflict with the very spirit of the rescript.[108] Commenting on Uchimura's act of lese majesty, he declared that Christian monotheism, with its rejection of any supreme authority apart from God, was the main cause of the conflict.[109] He further justified his criticism by mentioning numerous examples of incidents of alleged lese majesty by Christians, generally based on reports in the press. In addition to Christian monotheism, Inoue also criticized the Christian lack of nationalism, referring to the above-mentioned conflict at Kumamoto Eigakkō and other similar incidents.[110] He found that Christianity was opposed to patriotism in the West also, and he rejected the common view that Christianity had caused the strength of the European countries.[111] He questioned the idea that Jesus had been patriotic,[112] and concluded that Christianity could not be harmonized with the spirit of the rescript.[113] In the above-mentioned interview in *Kyōiku jiron* in November 1892, he had already summarized similar views in four points: (1) The Rescript on Education taught loyalty and patriotism, while Christianity was unpatriotic; (2) while Christianity emphasized the future life, the rescript was concerned about the present life; (3) the Christian teaching of indiscriminate love failed to pay due attention to filial piety; and (4) Christianity failed to teach the virtue of loyalty.[114]

Space does not allow a detailed account of the Christian response to Inoue's attack. Among the numerous Christians who engaged in the debate with great vigor and confidence were Honda Yōichi, Yokoi Tokio, Ōnishi Hajime, Motora Yūjirō, Uchimura Kanzō, Uemura Masahisa, and Takahashi Gorō. They rejected Inoue's charges and demonstrated in various ways that even though Christianity emphasized spiritual life, it made an important contribution to social and moral life and was an indispensable element for the future of the Japanese nation.[115] The Christian writers made a considerable impact, and even the Buddhist-oriented *Chōya shinbun* expressed admiration for the active response of the Christians, in contrast to the Buddhist tendency to depend upon others' attack on Christianity.[116]

In order to see how the Inoue controversy influenced Buddhist-Christian relations we have to consider Inoue's attitude to Christianity and to Buddhism; further, the Buddhist response to Inoue's attack on Christianity; and, finally, the Christian reaction to the Buddhist support of Inoue.

Inoue was obviously prejudiced against Christianity. His emotional rejection of Christianity as a foreign element was combined with a consistent criticism of the Christian doctrines of monotheism and universal love, and was directed against what he regarded as acts of irreverence resulting from such doctrines. At the same time, however, he maintained friendly relations with some Christians. When, for instance, the validity of his argument was questioned, he asked his Christian friend Yokoi Tokio to investigate the cases of lese majesty. Yokoi declared Inoue's charges as groundless and erroneous, and his explanation was included as an appendix in Inoue's book. Inoue conceded that his information had been based on journals and newspapers and hence might be misleading, but he was not willing to change his view on Christianity.[117] At a later stage he indicated that his criticism had influenced the Christians in a positive way, strengthening the trend toward Japanization of Christianity.[118]

Inoue's relation to Buddhism was more complex. Even though he was regarded by the Buddhists as their spokesman against the Christians, he never declared himself a Buddhist. His thinking was less influenced by Buddhist ideas and categories than by German philosophy, evolutionism, and Confucianism. He recognized the value of Buddhist philosophy, and advocated that Buddhism should absorb Western philosophy in order to oppose the progress of Christianity. His positive evaluation of Buddhism was partly a consequence of what he regarded as its ability to identify itself with the national polity; as a "polytheistic" religion it could recognize Shintoism and the divinity of the Emperor, in contrast to Christianity.[119] On the other hand, he was also critical of Buddhism. He regarded Buddhist philosophy as superior to Christianity, but found its pessimistic and world-negating tendency incompatible with the spirit of the Rescript on Education. Finally, his attack on Christianity was not based on Buddhist ideas. Rather than using Buddhist or religious arguments, he argued from the standpoint of education, nationalism, and the national polity.[120] This was indicated by the only Buddhist critic of Inoue, Furukawa Rōsen, who argued that the real opponents of Christianity in this connection were not the Buddhists, but those who advocated the absolute sovereignty of the state, the Confucians, those who were irreligious in secular matters, and those who advocated egotism in contrast to universal love.[121]

In spite of Inoue's ambivalent relation to Buddhism, his writings created an enthusiastic response among the Buddhists, who supported him wholeheartedly. At least fifteen Buddhist journals and newspapers published Inoue's articles about the conflict between education and religion.[122] The book was published in April, but some Buddhists had apparently ordered two thousand copies in advance.[123] Inoue became the undisputed ally of Buddhism against Christianity.[124] Buddhist journals reported about his "conquest of Christianity,"[125] "the total defeat of Christianity,"[126] and further described the "fear and consternation" among the Christians after Inoue's "magnificent essay."[127]

Even though Inoue had referred to the conflict between education and religion, the discussion became to a great extent a controversy between Buddhism and Christianity. It is characteristic that one of the collections of material about the controversy, consisting of 226 selections from books and articles, included 145 selections concerned with the conflict between Buddhism and Christianity.[128] This aspect of the controversy became even more conspicuous after Takahashi Gorō attacked Inoue in several articles in *Kokumin no tomo,* which were soon collected and published in a book entitled *Hai-gitetsugakuron* [Refutation of the false philosophy]. Takahashi had distinguished himself in the 1880s as a roughshod apologist, and had engaged in quite extensive studies of Buddhism.[129] His attack on Inoue was full of abusive language and cutting remarks about his qualifications as a scholar, combined with sarcastic references to his relation to Buddhism. Takahashi denounced Inoue as a "fake philosopher" and a "prostitute of learning" who used his position as a teacher of comparative religion to favor Buddhism and attack Christianity. He described the poor moral power and the world-negating tendency of Buddhism as incompatible with the Rescript on Education and further questioned Inoue's understanding of Buddhism.[130] While Inoue had praised Buddhism for its polytheism and its ability to adapt to Japan, Takahashi regarded this as an expression of Buddhist decay and loss of identity. He thus questioned Inoue's philosophical spirit, wondering whether he was worthy of his position as professor at the Imperial University, and also denounced his "shameless" response to his "Buddhist clients."[131]

Takahashi's attack aroused a storm of protest in Buddhist circles, where support of Inoue was accompanied by an equally unanimous denunciation of Takahashi and Christianity. A characteristic expression of the Buddhist resentment is found in Urasato Rōen's *Yasokyō no kiki* [The crisis of Christianity],[132] originally published as articles in *Chōya shinbun.*[133] On the book cover was a drawing of a broken cross, symbolizing the defeat of Christianity. The support of Inoue was accompanied by even more abusive language against Takahashi than Takahashi had used against Inoue.[134] The defeat of Christianity in the controversy was described in five stages: (1) the period of consternation, caused by the attack from the great scholar; (2) the period of defense; (3) the period of personal attack, represented by Takahashi; (4) the period of defamation; and (5) the period of despair. A similar description is found in *Meikyō shinshi,* where the five stages of the controversy were characterized as consternation, personal attack and slander, false defense, deception, and disruption.[135] The same aggressive tone is found in another book, *Yaso-kyō no matsuro* [The end of Christianity], written by Fujishima Ryōon. Fujishima had already distinguished himself as an aggressive anti-Christian propagator; in the early 1880s he had published a series of pamphlets entitled *Yasokyō no mudōri* [The unreasonableness of Christianity], which had been distributed or sold in more than 700,000 copies. He had studied Western philosophy in Paris from 1882 to 1889, and was especially interested in the relationship between church and state in Europe.[136] Now again he exhibited his apologetic talent by supporting Inoue and deeming Christianity to have reached total defeat and stagnation.

Among other Buddhist books related to the controversy were Inoue Enryō's *Kyōiku shūkyō kankeiron* [About the relationship between education and religion] and *Chūkō katsuron* [About the renewal of loyalty and filial piety] and Murakami Senshō's *Bukkyō chūkōhen* [Buddhist loyalty and filial piety].[137] Inoue Enryō criticized Christianity in a rather academic way, without engaging too actively in the actual controversy; Murakami Senshō wrote a detailed historical study in which he admitted that both Buddhism and Christianity advocated universal love.[138] On the other hand, he also argued that, while Buddhism had introduced the idea of loyalty and filial piety in Japan, the Christian doctrine lacked this spirit.[139] Nakanishi Ushio, a Buddhist who was attracted to Unitarianism, wrote *Kyōiku shukyō shōtotsu dan'an* [The last word about the conflict between education and religion], declaring that Christianity was opposed to the Rescript on Education and the national polity. At the same time he expressed his hope that the Japanization of Christianity would lead it in the direction of Buddhism. In *Sekai sanseiron* [The three sages of the world], written in the same year, he admitted that both Buddhism and Christianity represented universalism, in contrast to Confucian nationalism; however, he still argued that Buddhism, in contrast to Christianity, fostered a patriotic spirit.[140] Generally, it could be said that no Buddhist anti-Christian book was written in 1893 without being affected, directly or indirectly, by the Inoue controversy.

In a detailed survey of the Buddhist press, Yoshida Kyūichi has demonstrated how deeply the Buddhists were involved in the conflict; their support of Inoue was accompanied by an almost unanimous emotional denunciation of Christianity.[141] The only Buddhist who, according to Yoshida, gave a somewhat impartial account of the controversy was

Fig. 16. The broken cross illustrating Urasato Rōen's *Yasokyō no kiki* [The crisis of
Christianity] (Tokyo, 1893) expresses the
aggressive tone of Buddhist polemics in the
1890s. Courtesy of Aoyama Gakuin University, Tokyo.

Fig. 17. Victorious Buddhists expel Chris-
tian crusaders from the stronghold of
Nagoya. Front cover of Umehara Kitarō,
Butsu-Ya zessen: Yaso daihaiboku [A Bud-
dhist-Christian battle of tongues: The great
defeat of Christianity] (Nagoya, 1892).
Courtesy of Aoyama Gakuin University,
Tokyo.

Furukawa Rōsen (Isamu), who wrote in the reform Buddhist journal, *Bukkyō*. Furukawa was only twenty-two years old, a student at the Imperial University, and one of the pioneers of the so-called New Buddhism.[142] In contrast to other Buddhists, he admitted that even though Christianity deviated from the Imperial Rescript on Education, it was not opposed to it and did not represent an evil influence in Japan.[143]

The Buddhist involvement in the controversy also influenced the evaluation of Buddhism among Christians. The strong response of the Christians clearly indicates that Inoue's attack was felt as a blow to the Christian church.[144] On the other hand, they certainly did not feel the controversy to be a defeat, as the Buddhists generally declared. They rather regarded the Buddhist identification with Inoue as pure opportunism which demonstrated the decay of Buddhism; how could the Buddhists support Inoue's criticism that some of the basic Christian doctrines were in conflict with the Rescript on Education as long as Buddhism included similar doctrines? A French missionary, Father Ligneul, reported as a widespread opinion that the controversy represented the final battle of Buddhism.[145] Others suggested that the "mob" that served as Inoue's "lantern-bearers" later would turn their weapons against Buddhism as well.[146] A number of Christian critics argued that the pessimistic and world-negating doctrines of Buddhism were much less beneficial to society than Christianity and that Buddhism represented the same kind of universalism as that for which Christianity was denounced. Even though few engaged in such a fierce personal attack as Takahashi Gorō, they supported his biting criticism of Inoue and the Buddhists; and several even used the same humiliating words, characterizing Inoue as a "prostitute of learning" because of his badly founded and opportunistic appeal to the national sentiment.[147] *Kirisutokyō shinbun* held that, rather than Christianity, it was the "Buddhist superstition of the lower classes" and the "corrupt Buddhist faith" that was in conflict with education.[148] And in *Nihon hyōron* Uemura Masahisa characterized the lack of concern for moral education among Buddhist and Shinto priests as "a disgrace for the state."[149]

It is difficult to evaluate the outcome of the controversy. While educational circles naturally tended to support Inoue,[150] his ideas were not so influential among other intellectuals.[151] Both Buddhists and Christians claimed victory, but gradually the controversy lost its attraction. The Buddhists became more concerned with a positive demonstration of the Buddhist doctrine,[152] and suggested that anti-Christian activity based on nationalism was less important than the positive propagation of Buddhist faith.[153] The Christians finally managed to demonstrate their supreme patriotic spirit in connection with the Sino-Japanese War; the traditional arguments lost their power and were not used for a while.[154]

CONCLUSION

The Inoue controversy has already been characterized as a conclusion to several years of conflict. The examination of several important incidents, ranging from the problem of treaty revision at the end of the 1880s to the Inoue controversy in 1893, has revealed that the confrontation between Buddhists and Christians changed its character from a political struggle to a conflict about educational policy. The basic issues remained very much the same, but the area of conflict shifted: In 1889–1890 the Buddhist concern was to exclude Christians from the political world; in 1893 it seemed more important to deprive them of their position in the educational and intellectual world. The development was part of a reactionary movement, the reaction against Westernization and the attempt to lay a strong national foundation for the Japanese state. The reaction brought about a stronger self-confidence among the Buddhists; they became more powerful and their propaganda had stronger appeal.

On the other hand, the nationalistic mood and the anti-Christian agitation did not cause renewal in the sense that Buddhism became better prepared to face the challenges of a society in rapid transformation. The new power and self-confidence did not become creative forces, limited as they were by a basic reactionary tendency. Buddhism identified itself with the reaction against Christianity and Westernization, but it did not contribute new ideas or new approaches. The lack of Buddhist creativity was indicated in connection with the Inoue controversy by the generally pro-Buddhist newspaper *Chōya shinbun,* which criticized the Buddhist tendency to identify passively with those who attacked Christianity, even depending upon an "outsider" like Inoue.

> As Christianity is the public enemy of Buddhism they rejoice when somebody appears to reject Christianity. However, when somebody appears in order to reject the one who rejected Christianity, they immediately become distressed. Then they immediately rejoice again when they discover somebody who denounces the one who denounced the one who rejected Christianity.[155]

Because of its reactionary character and lack of creativity, Buddhism was fighting in retreat. In spite of fervent political activity, the Buddhists failed to create a political front, and lost their seats in the Diet. Even though they engaged in heavy attacks against Christian influence in the educational world, there, too, they failed to establish their position. Educational authorities maintained their anti-Christian policy, but at the same time Buddhism became a target of their criticism.[156]

CHAPTER NINE

Anti-Christian Campaigns

> The hardships [of the Christians] have reached an extreme, and even for the casual observer it is a pitiable sight.
>
> Comment in the Buddhist journal *Bukkyō shinundō*

THE FOREGOING EXAMINATION of Buddhist movements and some central ideological controversies has shown how closely Buddhist renewal was related to the anti-Western and anti-Christian reaction. Apart from references to the public discussion in newspapers, journals, and books, however, we do not yet have a clear picture of the actual confrontation between Buddhists and Christians. Under what circumstances did they clash with each other? The aim of this chapter is, therefore, to survey anti-Christian campaigns as concrete manifestations of the conflict. I have elsewhere described in great detail how the confrontation took place in Kyoto, Nagoya, and in two rural areas, the regions of Hokuriku and Nankai;[1] but here I shall limit myself to a more general examination of such campaigns, based on more than two hundred reported incidents of disturbance or persecution in the years 1889–1894. In addition to material from the areas covered in the above-mentioned study, information will be included from other parts of the country as well. The material covers 44 of Japan's 46 urban and rural prefectures, and includes 15 cases from 1889, 46 from 1890, 26 from 1891, 43 from 1892, 38 from 1893, and 41 from 1894—in all 209 cases.

Some initial comments have to be made concerning the character of the material and the sources of information. The material includes a great variety of information, from short general remarks about Buddhist campaigns to long reports that include details about time, place, persons, and happenings. Some of the material gives general information and refers sweepingly to numerous incidents or to disturbances that had lasted for a long time; in other cases a wealth of information is provided about one single incident. Thus one "case" can refer to numerous incidents over a long period or just to one single happening, depending upon the type of information available. In most cases the source is a Christian journal, such as *Fukuin shūhō/Fukuin shinpō* or *Kirisutokyō shinbun,* or historical records and studies of local churches. Unfortunately, Buddhist journals have rather sparse information about anti-Christian campaigns. Quite a few cases are based on Yoshida Kyūichi's detailed account in *Nihon kindai Bukkyōshi kenkyū* [Studies in modern Buddhist history], many of which I have not been able to check with other sources.[2] Thus it is not possible to make any accurate statistical analysis based on the 209 cases; the numbers referred to in the following should be understood against this background and not misinterpreted as exact statistical material. Some characteristic tendencies are, nevertheless, clearly discernable.

THE GENERAL BACKGROUND

From one point of view the Buddhist anti-Christian campaigns merely represented a continuation of the opposition we have observed throughout the entire Meiji period. The frequency and aggressiveness of Buddhist campaigns, however, increased drastically after 1889, and the years 1889–1894 mark the dramatic peak of hostilities. The background of the campaigns can be summarized as follows:

First, in most cases the anti-Christian activity was directly related to obvious signs of Christian expansion. The 1890s are properly characterized as a period of retarded growth and inner weakness in several churches; however, this does not mean that Christians in Japan lost their evangelical zeal. Even in the 1890s they expected Japan to become a Christian nation within a few years. Missionaries and Japanese evangelists expanded their work and made strenuous efforts to penetrate to every nook and corner of the country. In addition to the work of the established missions and churches, new missionary societies arrived and started work in new areas or enforced the work in other areas.[3]

It is, therefore, characteristic that whenever the reason for anti-Christian activity is indicated (127 cases), the reason given almost unanimously (125 cases) refers directly to obvious signs of Christian expansion. In 50 cases the background seemed to be various forms of Christian public meetings in theaters or churches, drawing audiences of from less than a hundred up to several thousand people; another 50 cases refer to other sorts of new Christian initiative, such as active propagation, the presence of a resident evangelist, or the building or dedication of churches and preaching places; a number of other signs of Christian expansion are also mentioned, such as an increase in the number of seekers or baptisms. In this connection it is interesting to notice that only 13 cases indicate that the anti-Christian activity was related to direct criticism of Buddhism, offensive utterances, or other provocative actions against Buddhism.

We have already seen that the Christian expansion in Buddhist-dominated areas inevitably was regarded as a one-sided provocation, threatening and destructive in its character. Hence it is somewhat misleading to talk merely about Buddhist anti-Christian campaigns. From the Buddhist point of view, such campaigns were provoked by unjustifiable intrusions by Christian propagators. On the other hand, it should be emphasized that few Christians consciously wanted to challenge Buddhism. They realized its strong influence on the uneducated masses, but they did not consider it a real rival contending for the spiritual leadership of the "new" Japan; when Buddhism would lose its power was just a question of time and intellectual development.[4]

Second, along with the deep-rooted feeling of crisis that had developed under the threat from Christianity, a new confidence was developing among the Buddhists. Buddhist activists were generally convinced of Buddhism's doctrinal superiority over Christianity and were eager to defeat whoever dared challenge their conviction.[5]

Third, in addition to the Buddhist renewal, the nationalistic reaction with its anti-Western character became extremely useful for Buddhist anti-Christian activity. The Buddhists have often been criticized for their opportunistic use of this reaction in their opposition to Christianity. This is not quite fair; in spite of obvious opportunistic elements, it was not a new idea for the Buddhists to denounce Christianity as detrimental to national security and traditions. The Buddhists had persistently made use of such arguments since the opening of the country. What made the situation different in the 1890s was that their charges were finally supported by a wave of nationalism, and hence could be used as effective weapons against Christianity. Among various elements that enabled the Buddhists to organize more effective and persistent opposition, a number of trends have already been mentioned, such as cooperation between Buddhist sects, new organizations, the activity of traveling speakers and Buddhist laymen, youth participation, and international contact.[6]

METHODS USED AGAINST THE CHRISTIANS

The material indicates clearly which methods were most popular in the opposition against Christianity. The 209 cases of confrontations include 63 cases of anti-Christian meetings and 90 cases of disturbance of Christian meetings and worship services. A great number of cases refer to other forms of social pressure as well.

ANTI-CHRISTIAN MEETINGS

The consistent trend of anti-Christian propaganda increased drastically toward the end of the 1880s. Traveling Buddhist priests and laymen penetrated the country with their lectures and sermons, combining Buddhist apologetics with zealous refutation of Christianity. Anti-Christian propaganda tended to become the main focus of Buddhist preaching.

Such anti-Christian meetings were often called *haja enzetsukai,* or *bakuja enzetsukai,* "meetings for refutation of the evil religion," or were designated by the classical term *haja kenshō,* "refuting errors and demonstrating the truth." Representing an old Buddhist tradition, *haja kenshō* did not necessarily have to be as aggressive as the term seems to indicate;[7] threatened by the expansion of Christianity, however, Buddhism often turned to desperate efforts to malign and repudiate it. A variety of popular expressions in connection with anti-Christian meetings emphasize their aggressive tendency: *gekyō bokumetsu,* "extermination of the alien religion," *gedō bokumetsu,* "extermination of the heresy," *Yaso taiji,* "extermination of Christianity," *jakyō taiji,* "extermination of the evil religion," *Yasokyō fumitsubushi,* "crushing of Christianity," *Yasokyō shōmetsu,* "annihilation of Christianity," and the like. In 4 cases Buddhist meetings aimed at the "extermination of Christianity and Tenrikyo,"[8] a combined effort to suppress two new and vigorous movements that threatened Buddhism. The material includes 14 cases in which Buddhist meetings were held as a direct response to Christian public meetings.

The Christians generally referred to such meetings as "the usual abuse and slander" of Christianity, or similar expressions,[9] and seldom paid attention to what was actually said by the Buddhists. The common trend of the speeches was to denounce the pernicious influence of Christianity and to stigmatize the Christians as traitors. The Christians dismissed such propaganda as stereotyped and reactionary slander and interpreted the methods of the Buddhists as expressions of an outdated faith, hopelessly condemned to self-destruction. At the same time, however, it was obvious that the meetings exerted a strong influence and, especially in the provinces, stirred up further opposition and often resulted in violent obstruction of Christian work.[10] Prominent Buddhists gradually seemed to agree that the aggressive anti-Christian propaganda was without lasting effect, or even counter-productive; especially after 1894, they began to emphasize the importance of a more positive Buddhist propagation.[11]

Even though the Christians repudiated the Buddhist anti-Christian propaganda as "the usual abuse and slander," it was probably less stereotyped than the Christian reporters generally acknowledged. The doctrinal refutation of Christianity drew on a long tradition and seemed to be quite common also in the 1890s. The point was naturally to demonstrate the foolishness of Christian doctrines and the superiority of Buddhism. Such doctrinal refutation revealed a deep-rooted emotional aversion to Christianity, but it was nevertheless often based on quite extensive studies of the Bible and Christian doctrines and history and on personal contact with Christians.[12] Hence it was quite natural that comparative studies of Buddhism and Christianity became popular. Such comparisons did not aim at an objective analysis of the two religions but were prepared to defeat the other religion. The trend is found in numerous publications, such as *Butsu-Ya hikakuron* [Comparison of Buddhism and Christianity], *Shūkyō yūretsuron* [Merits and demerits of religions], *Butsu-Ya yūshō reppaiben* [Distinguishing between merits and demerits of Buddhism and Christianity], and *Bukkyō to Yasokyō shinkō kajō* [Buddhist and Christian articles of faith].[13] Sometimes the comparison was made in a more dramatic way, described as a wrestling tournament between the two sumo wrestlers Shakagatake and Yasogawa, that is Sakyamuni and Jesus, or as a court trial where Jesus was sued by Buddha for alleged libel.[14] In spite of their popular character, such pamphlets often included quite complicated doctrinal arguments, indicating that doctrinal refutation continued to be one of the central concerns of anti-Christian propaganda.[15]

Along with the doctrinal refutation of Christianity, the Buddhists had a long tradition of criticizing the destructive character of Christianity. This trend became increasingly popular; especially after 1889, political and nationalistic issues tended to dominate, notably through the activity of such an organization as Sonnō Hōbutsu Daidōdan. In fact, a considerable number of Buddhist public meetings around 1890 were almost like political meetings. As we have seen, Buddhist priests opened their temples for political parties, or were even hired by political parties to attack opposing parties as allegedly Christian. The material about Buddhist meetings includes few direct expressions of anti-Christian propagation on the basis of nationalistic and political issues; however, a great part of what the Christians merely rejected as "the usual abuse and slander" must have been of such a character.[16]

DISTURBANCES OF CHRISTIAN MEETINGS

As Buddhist opposition was closely related to obvious signs of Christian expansion, it was almost inevitable that all sorts of Christian meetings were disturbed. The material includes 90 cases of such disturbance, which was apparently one of the most popular methods of Buddhist opposition. A great variety of expressions was reported, from spontaneous jeering to serious rioting and destruction of houses.

The most widespread disturbance (67 of 90 cases) seemed to be various efforts to obstruct and interrupt the speaker, such as jeering and yelling, asking questions, clapping hands and stamping feet, using wooden clappers or other noisy instruments to drown out the speaker, shouting out all manner of abuse and slander, or threatening to beat and kill the Christians. The Buddhist priests seemed to have a predilection for raising questions in order to start a discussion and thus get an opportunity for refutation of Christianity instead of a one-sided Christian message; such questioning is reported in 27 cases. The Christians preferred to refuse all such discussion, claiming that it would only end in total confusion and defamation of the Christians, a standpoint that was supported by bitter experience.[17]

In several cases such disturbance was serious enough to force the Christians to cancel the meeting. In other cases the disturbance was accompanied by more violent behavior, where church furniture and equipment were destroyed. It seemed most popular to start smashing lamps and then to destroy sliding doors, windows, chairs, signboards, doors, and fences; the material includes 27 cases of such destruction of furniture and equipment. In serious cases the rioting included efforts to destroy the whole building, pulling down pillars, destroying the roof, or even setting fire to the house. The most serious cases of such destruction were reported from Akita Prefecture in 1889, Fukui Prefecture in 1890, Ishikawa Prefecture in 1892, and Yamaguchi Prefecture in 1894.[18]

Another quite common harassment, which often went along with such destruction, was throwing of stones and rubble, reported in 27 cases. It was especially popular to smash lamps and windows with stones, but the Christians also became the target and were sometimes seriously injured. Beating and similar violence was quite common, and numerous Christian preachers and lay people suffered such harassment on their way to and from Christian meetings.[19]

It is almost impossible to give an accurate account of the dynamics behind the disturbance of Christian meetings. The material tends to refer merely to "the mob" (gumin, ganmin, gunshū), "hooligans" and "ruffians" (buraikan, akkan), and sōshi; in some cases it refers somewhat more accurately to day laborers, fishermen, poor people, ricksha-coolies, or outcaste people. But usually the Buddhist priests were designated as the real source of action, whether fighting openly or creating trouble behind the scenes. The priests were criticized for employing sōshi, hiring people to start disturbances, or just instigating the crowd.[20] It is, in fact, difficult to imagine such disturbances without the background of a rather intense Buddhist agitation. Christianity was certainly unfamiliar and was met with suspicion and animosity by most people, and political agitation was sometimes raised against Christians; but only the Buddhist priests seemed to be sufficiently organized and motivated to oppose Christianity effectively. Fearing that Christianity would destroy both their spiritual monopoly and their economic basis, they responded with violence.

Fig. 18. A Buddhist vision of the final defeat of Christianity. Illustration from Ohara Masao, *Bukkyō daishōri Yasokyō daihaiboku: Butsu-Ya katsumondō* [The great victory of Buddhism and the great defeat of Christianity: An actual Buddhist-Christian dispute] (Osaka, 1889). Courtesy of the main library of Doshisha University, Kyoto.

BUDDHIST-CHRISTIAN DISCUSSIONS

Apart from spontaneous attempts of Buddhist priests to interrupt Christian meetings and start discussions, there were numerous cases of actual Buddhist-Christian discussions, on both the private and the public level.

One of the most common types of such discussion seemed to be the result of private visits to the residence of the Christian evangelist, pastor, or visiting preacher. A traveling evangelist who held meetings all over Fukui Prefecture in 1892 reported that he was visited almost daily by Buddhist priests who interrogated him.[21] He did not comment on the content of the interviews, but other material suggests that the main purpose of such encounters was to defeat the Christians in discussion, make them abandon their faith, or at least give up preaching. In this connection intimidation might have been common as well. A book entitled *Butsu-Ya kessen* [The bloody battle between Buddhism and Christianity] reports on the confrontations between the Buddhist activist Minoda Kakunen and five foreign missionaries. Minoda was introduced as *bakuja senmonka,* a "specialist on the refutation of Christianity."[22] Such private encounters did not seem to include any violence, in contrast to many of his confrontations with Christians in public meetings. In private discussions the doctrinal refutation of Christianity became more important than the nationalistic agitation, which tended to appeal to the more vulgar sentiments of the crowds. The discussions, nevertheless, aimed at the destruction of Christianity.[23] The time was not yet ripe for sympathetic and peaceful dialogues.

Public discussions between Buddhists and Christians were less common than the private encounters, for obvious reasons.[24] Confrontations in Kyoto and Nagoya are described in books with such characteristic titles as *Bukkyō daishōri Yasokyō daihaiboku: Butsu-Ya katsumondō* [The great victory of Buddhism and the great defeat of Christianity: an actual Buddhist-Christian dispute] and *Butsu-Ya zessen: Yaso daihaiboku* [A Buddhist-Christian battle of tongues: the great defeat of Christianity].[25] Such discussions were usually the result of Buddhist pressure and were considered by the Buddhists to be an effective method of anti-Christian propaganda. With a large audience it was easier to arouse anti-Christian sentiments through emotional references to nationalistic issues. A great amount of courage and self-confidence was required by the Christians who dared to take part in such discussions; they often ended in total confusion, giving the Buddhists a sense of victory. For instance, an Orthodox priest who agreed to give a lecture about Christianity in a temple in Kakunodate in Akita Prefecture in 1889 discovered immediately that the purpose of the meeting was to make an assault on the Christians. He managed to leave the temple in time, but three days later the chapel was burned down and he had to escape during the night.[26] A Protestant evangelist was, in spite of protest forced to take part in a Buddhist-Christian discussion in the village of Yumura in northern Hyogo Prefecture in 1892. The meeting ended with the Buddhists claiming victory and expelling the Christians from the district.[27] The only discussion reported as successful from a Christian point of view was held in the village of Hashimoto at the foot of Mount Koya in 1893.[28]

SOCIAL PRESSURE AND OSTRACISM

In a traditional community where social harmony was a central concern, Christianity was naturally opposed as dangerous and destructive. While other religions and religious practices coexisted in an established harmony, Christianity came as an intruder, overturning the rules and disrupting the harmony. The natural response of the community was to defend itself by excluding the intruder through social sanctions.

As one of the fundamental units in Japanese society, the household would usually find it intolerable to accept Christian faith among its individual members. Buddhism was established in Japan as the religion of the household; as long as the head of the household was against Christianity, it was extremely difficult for individual members to withstand the pressure. Even though the records have little direct information about such pressure, it was probably one of the main factors that kept people away from contact with Christian work.[29] A classic example of family pressure was reported from a fishing village in Shizuoka Prefecture, probably some time in the 1890s. A poor fisherman explained in a meeting how opposition from his elder brother prevented him from making open profession and being baptized.

> "What," he says, "give up your temple for this foreign superstition—the temple on the register of which the names of our ancestors have been inscribed from time immemorial, where we and our family have always worshipped—forsake the priest who has performed so many ministrations for us!" These are arguments that appeal with terrible force to one living in a little village community and with innate ideas of respect and reverence for the ties and obligations of family life.[30]

In many cases severance of family ties was advocated as a proper sanction against obstinate Christian family members.[31]

If the household was unable to keep its members from contact with Christianity, the neighborhood and local community took over, often under the leadership of the Buddhist priest. A characteristic example was reported from Kusatsu in Shiga Prefecture, where Buddhist priests from all the temples in the area gathered to discuss the appropriate measures against the influence of Christianity. Their first step was to visit all the

一家中宗教のあらそひ

Fig. 19. Religious struggle in the household. Illustration from Aoki Kunijirō, *Shūkyō kyōshinkai* [Religious propagation contest] (Tokyo, 1885). Courtesy of Aoyama Gakuin University, Tokyo.

Christian seekers individually, admonishing or threatening them to change their minds, or making their parents take responsibility for controlling them. If they still refused to obey, other methods would be adopted to prevent them from attending Christian meetings, such as arranging urgent business at the time of such meetings.[32]

In addition to the popular contempt of Christianity and various forms of spontaneous pressure from family, temple, and local community, the Christians also suffered organized ostracism. In some places the Buddhist priests made people sign contracts that they would never become Christians.[33] In other places oppression from the community and fear of being dismissed from one's office were quoted as causes of trouble.[34] A characteristic example of organized ostracism was reported from the village of Chitose in northern Tama in Kanagawa Prefecture, where the Buddhist priest had his parishioners form an alliance against the Christians. All links were to be severed with those who disobeyed, as the Christians were guilty of creating disorder in the village and disharmony in the parish. The few Christians appealed both to the village headman and to the police station in Fuchu, but both regarded the case as being beyond their authority and did nothing about it.[35] In the village of Sakashita in Omi in Shiga Prefecture, a Buddhist organization made the villagers make a covenant with four clauses: (1) Christians shall be ostracized; (2) Christians shall be deprived of their former rights in the common forests; (3) Christians shall not be admitted into our houses nor will we enter theirs. If it is necessary to transact any business with them, we will stand outside of their houses while talking with them; (4) We will prevent the Christians from working in the mountains. We will not turn aside for them when we meet them upon the street.[36] The fact that an almost identical covenant was made against Orthodox Christians in a village in Mie Prefecture[37] may indicate that such covenants were quite widespread, instigated by the Buddhist headquarters in Kyoto.

More than anyone else the Christian evangelists and preachers were hit by the various forms of ostracism. The most effective way to exclude Christian influence in new places was simply to refuse to give lodging to preachers or to lend houses or suitable places for meetings; the material includes 23 such cases. Sometimes the refusal was a spontaneous result of the popular aversion to Christianity, or fear that Christian work would lead to disorder and riots; but in several cases it was obviously the result of Buddhist pressure or intimidation. To prevent the Christian evangelist from remaining in a place, even if he had a lodging, it was quite common to organize a sellers' boycott (the material includes 6 such cases), making the whole village or town refuse to sell food and other necessary goods or to render him any services, even to draw water from the well.

As the trend in the educational world became more critical of Christianity, it was inevitable that the Christians felt the pressure there as well. Christian students and the children of Christians were harassed at school by teachers or fellow pupils, and Christian teachers came under pressure from colleagues and parents, and sometimes from local authorities.[38]

Christians were also refused burial in the Buddhist graveyard, even though the law gave the Christians the right to be buried in the family grave.[39] Such methods hit the Japanese Christians with great force, as they naturally maintained their emotional connection with the family grave, and wanted to be cared for after death. Family pressure was thus easily combined with the problem of burial site, as in the above-mentioned case of the fisherman from Shizuoka: "The next objection, brought by some of Omura's friends, is one which will sound singular to Christian ears. 'Very well,' they say, 'go on, become a Christian, and then see what will happen to you when you die!' " The question, of course, referred to the problem of who should take care of his grave, visit it with offerings and incense. "In place of the trim, well-kept temple ground, a solitary dishonoured grave on some lonely hillside is what awaits the Christian dead."[40]

With this background it is possible to imagine the pressure upon Japanese Christians, especially in the towns and villages of the rural areas. It was observed that "in many of the smaller towns the Christians are for the most part settlers there, and not from the original inhabitants of the place."[41] This was an almost inevitable result of the circumstances described above.

GOVERNMENT AND LOCAL AUTHORITIES

It is quite puzzling that the most aggressive wave of Buddhist anti-Christian activity came after the Constitution had guaranteed freedom of religion. The Buddhists justified their activity by emphasizing the conditional character of such freedom, expressed in the words, "within limits not prejudicial to peace and order, and not antagonistic to their duties as subjects," and concluded that Christianity failed to qualify for religious freedom. The government also stressed these limitations,[42] yet adhered to the Constitution and guaranteed support against religious oppression and discrimination. When, for instance, the governor of Fukuoka Prefecture instructed that teachers who became Christians should be "summarily dealt with," he was reprimanded by the Ministry of Education and the Ministry of Home Affairs.[43] Likewise, the Ministry of Home Affairs responded to missionary complaints about the persecution in Tsuruga by dismissing the responsible policemen for failing to control the riots.[44]

On the local level, however, the official policy of religious freedom was not always respected. We have already observed cases in which governors engaged in activity against the Christians; and educational authorities especially seemed to favor anti-Christian tendencies.[45]

Among the local authorities no one became so much involved in the confrontations between Buddhists and Christians as the police. The police generally adhered strictly to their main function, to maintain public order, and the Christians trusted them as the loyal servants of the law. They did not hesitate to ask for police protection against disturbance; and the police, who often regarded the "purity" of Buddhism and Buddhist priests with skepticism, seemed to do their utmost to restore order in meetings, protect Christians, dispel crowds, arrest people who became violent, and in many cases to dissolve meetings when the commotion became too serious. Even though they sometimes were unable to master the situation, there is no evidence that the Christians ever suspected them of supporting rioting Buddhists.[46] Even in the case when two policemen were dismissed as a result of a missionary's complaint, the local Christians actually commended the police for their loyal work.[47] The police, after all, were among the strongest stabilizing forces against Buddhist aggression and local harassment.

EXTENT AND RESULTS OF PERSECUTION

The fact that the material used for this examination includes 44 of Japan's 46 rural and urban prefectures indicates that Buddhist persecution of Christianity was a nationwide phenomenon. The primary concern of the Buddhists was to check the expansion of Christianity in new places; and their campaigns naturally spread all over Japan as Christian work expanded into new areas and fortified its position in the provincial cities, towns, and villages. In spite of violent opposition in such major cities as Nagoya and Kyoto, and some incidents in other cities, the anti-Christian campaigns were strongest and most frequent in the rural areas. But there also Buddhist opposition varied in intensity and tenacity, as I have demonstrated in a comparison of Buddhist campaigns in two different regions.[48] In the Buddhist-dominated Hokuriku region on the Japan Sea coast the campaigns were extraordinarily strong, consistent, and protracted, and to a great extent managed to suppress the Christian movement. In the Nankai region, comprising the Wakayama Prefecture and the island of Shikoku, which was characterized by weaker Buddhist influence and more open attitudes to new ideas, the opposition to Christianity was more temporary, and without lasting results. It is noteworthy that areas with a strong influence of Shin Buddhism mustered the most effective and aggressive opposition, not only in the Hokuriku region but also in the prefectures of Shiga, Gifu, Aichi (including Nagoya), Mie, Kyoto and northern Hyogo, and Hiroshima. In other places, too, where

the Buddhist opposition was particularly strong it was often related to
the influence of Shin Buddhism. Examples include the city of Takada in
Tochigi Prefecture, which was a stronghold of the Takada sect of Shin
Buddhism,[49] and the town of Hagi in Yamaguchi Prefecture, where the
churches for years were flooded by waves of violent persecution because
of the influence of a major Shin Buddhist branch temple *(betsuin).*[50] In
some districts the campaigns were said to be the result of cooperation
between the Buddhist sects, or stirred by the agitation of particular sects,
such as Nichiren Buddhism in Chiba Prefecture,[51] Shingon Buddhism in
Wakayama Prefecture,[52] and Zen Buddhism in Fukui Prefecture[53] and in
Kamakura.[54] Most of the opposition of these Buddhist sects, however,
seemed rather arbitrary and temporary. Only Shin Buddhism had sufficient vitality and influence to mobilize the people to a consistent and protracted opposition to Christianity.

As for the duration of the anti-Christian campaigns, the most intense
and consistent opposition took place in the years from 1889 to 1894.[55]
This does not mean that the campaigns were limited to those years.
Numerous incidents took place during the 1880s; and even though the
most aggressive campaigns disappeared after the Sino-Japanese War, the
anti-Christian propaganda continued in the provinces, with occasional
outbursts of violence.[56] As we shall see in the next chapter, the problems
of "mixed residence" and the struggle for "state Buddhism" induced the
Buddhists to engage in energetic anti-Christian activity until the turn of
the century.

It is not easy to evaluate the effects of the anti-Christian campaigns.
The Christian reporters naturally emphasized elements that seemed
favorable to the Christian church, while the Buddhists usually referred to
signs of Buddhist success. One of the most common conclusions of the
reports in the Christian press was that the Buddhist campaigns, in spite
of the painful trials inflicted upon the Christians, ultimately benefited the
Christian work. It was argued that the faith and dedication of the Christians were strengthened; Christian propagation was stimulated; and people's interest in and curiosity about Christianity were increased, resulting
in large audiences and an increasing number of seekers. There is no reason to doubt that the Buddhist campaigns in many cases actually were
counter-productive, turning people's attention to Christianity and pro-
voking antipathy and criticism against Buddhism. On the other hand, in
some cases such views were hardly more than stereotyped conclusions or
hopeful prayers that the outdated and aggressive methods of the Buddhists would eventually prove to be "suicidal" or "self-destructive."[57] In
many places the apparently "suicidal" campaigns of the Buddhists resulted in serious setbacks for the Christians. Apart from the general animosity against Christianity, which must have been a serious impediment to

expansion, in many places Christian evangelism was checked in the very beginning, particularly in the Hokuriku region. In some cases the Buddhist campaigns lasted until the Christian faith was completely eradicated.[58] The Buddhist opposition to Christian expansion thus became one of the main reasons why a period of intense and dedicated Christian propagation was also a period of retarded growth.

CHAPTER TEN

Opposition to Equal Status of Religions

> To defend Buddhism by rejecting every one, whether
> official or layman, who unjustly tries to hinder the pros-
> perity of Buddhism.
>
> Buddhist guidelines for opposition to Christianity

AS WE HAVE SEEN, the Buddhist development around 1890 was characterized by reform zeal and nationalistic fervor. The Buddhists advocated their faith as the basic element of "Japaneseness," identifying Buddhism with the national polity and engaging in political activity designed
to exclude the Christian element in society. In the present chapter the
various threads from the development around 1890 will be gathered
together; and we shall see how the discussion reached its conclusion
around the turn of the century, concentrated on two main issues: the
problem of so-called mixed residence and the question of whether or not
Buddhism should obtain the position of "state religion" or "state-recognized religion."[1]

Both issues were closely related to the problem of treaty revision. The
Buddhist concern in both issues was obviously to prevent Christianity
from obtaining a status that would facilitate further expansion. In this
process the mainstream of Japanese Buddhism revealed in all clarity its
identification with the Japanese state, affirming the absolute sovereignty
of the Emperor and providing a spiritual support for the burgeoning Japanese imperialism.

MIXED RESIDENCE

While the support of Christianity and Westernization had been regarded
as important means toward facilitating treaty revision in the mid-1880s,
the anti-Western reaction naturally questioned the role of Christianity,

and designated the foreign faith as a national threat. The anti-Western mood resulted in strong opposition to mixed residence. This was one of the concessions made in the draft treaties, according to which the interior of Japan would be opened for foreign residence, travel, and trade, in return for the abolition of the hated consular jurisdiction over foreigners (extraterritoriality).

According to the old treaties, foreigners were supposed to reside in the limited foreign settlements in the treaty ports; they were not allowed to travel in the interior, except for health reasons or for the sake of scientific research. The government issued special passports for such travel, which had been used quite liberally; many missionaries combined travel with extensive evangelism. But still the activities of the foreigners were limited, and travel restrictions could be strictly enforced if necessary.[2]

One of the main reasons for the collapse of the treaty negotiations in 1887 and 1889 was that the fear of the consequences of mixed residence became stronger than the indignation against extraterritoriality. The reaction revealed a peculiar mixture of national pride and a sense of inferiority toward the Westerners. The new treaties were finally concluded with England on July 16, 1894, soon followed by the United States and other Western powers, to come into force as of July 17, 1899. The problem of mixed residence remained an urgent concern for the Buddhists until the treaties were enforced. The discussion generally developed in three stages: (1) opposition to the idea of mixed residence, until about 1894; (2) preparation for mixed residence, until 1899; and (3) the discovery in 1899 that mixed residence, in fact, created only minor problems.

OPPOSITION

The most widely read polemic on mixed residence was probably an essay by Inoue Tetsujirō, entitled *Naichi zakkyoron* [About mixed residence], written in Berlin in 1889.[3] Inoue, who depended heavily on Spencerian theory, argued that the inflexible principle of the survival of the fittest would make the Japanese lose the competition with the "superior races" of Western countries. In his chapter on "Treaty Revision and Self-Determination," Kenneth B. Pyle summarizes some of Inoue's concerns as follows:

"Japanese," he wrote, "are generally inferior to Westerners in intelligence, financial power, physique, and all else." The superiority of the Westerner was evident not only from his greater stature but also from his more highly developed cranium. The shape of the Westerner's head was indicative of a superior intellect. Japanese, he said, were not equal to Westerners in either intricate analysis or profound generalization. Westerners also had a self-assurance and a spirit of independence that Japanese lacked: "We stand before Westerners exposing our weak and inferior civilization; it is rare that we can hold our heads high and peer down on other races as they do."[4]

Admitting the supposed inferiority of the Japanese, Inoue feared that foreign capitalists would dominate Japanese commerce and monopolize the most valuable land, or even gain control of the government and destroy the unity of Japan. "History showed Inoue that more than cultural unity would be lost; racial destruction was the inevitable result of close contact between superior and inferior races."[5] Mixed residence was premature, Inoue argued, and the existing treaties should be maintained, in spite of their humiliating clauses, until the Japanese were prepared to compete with the foreigners on equal terms.

Inoue expressed a popular sentiment, and his view was widely supported by Japanese Buddhists, who were apprehensive of the consequences of mixed residence. As the revised treaties, moreover, seemed favorable to Christianity, it was not surprising that the Buddhists opposed the new trend. To jeopardize the negotiations in 1889, conservative politicians appealed to the Buddhist opinion, claiming that the consequence of mixed residence would be an "inundation of Christian propagandists, to the no small injury of Buddhism"; but the priests of Nishi Honganji eventually decided to "keep their hands out of the mess" and avoid political campaigns against the treaties.[6] A similar stand was taken by Higashi Honganji in 1894, before the final conclusion of the treaties.[7] The Buddhists, however, shared the negative attitude to mixed residence. According to *Reichikai zasshi,* there existed five great threats to Buddhism: Christianity, marriage with foreigners, the republican system (generally associated with Christianity), foreign settlement outside the concessions, and Christian schools.[8] The All-Japan Meeting of Buddhists, which was held in Nagoya in April 1891, decided to organize an alliance against mixed residence.[9] All over the country Buddhist agitators warned against it as an extremely dangerous phenomenon in a time when the Japanese were spiritually weak, referring particularly to the danger of increasing missionary activity.[10]

PREPARATION FOR MIXED RESIDENCE

The most vigorous reaction to the problem of mixed residence came after the treaties had been concluded in 1894. The Sino-Japanese War diverted the interest for a while, but in 1896 and 1897 prominent groups within the Buddhist establishment began to worry about the consequences of foreign activity in the interior after the enforcement of the treaties in July 1899.

Consternation. The most vociferous reaction came from those who exaggerated the consequences of mixed residence. They anticipated that

Buddhism would become involved in a fatal struggle for existence, and believed that the foreigners would "make their way into the interior of Japan without a moment's delay" and thus make a great impact on the "unsurpassed national polity" of Japan.[11] Christian foreign missionary societies were expected to take advantage of the new situation and use their financial resources to attract supporters, distributing cheap literature and medicine, building schools and offering cheap education for poor children, and using other devices to draw people into the Christian church. The West would try to "colonize" Japan, it was explained; Christianity would be used to deprive the people of its spirit, before the country would finally be taken by military force. Hence the churches should be regarded as "traps," and Christian charity as a "bait."[12]

The background of this consternation was an almost desperate recognition of the weakness of Buddhism and an exaggerated fear of the power of Christianity. The natural consequence was to launch a campaign to warn against Christianity and to prepare the Buddhist population for the inevitable confrontation with foreigners. Thus "preparation for mixed residence" *(naichi zakkyo junbi)* became the rallying point for many Buddhists. Numerous organizations were founded with the express purpose of preparing for mixed residence, such as the Great Apologetical Association for the Preparation of Mixed Residence (Zakkyo Junbi Gohō Daidōdan), founded in Kyoto in 1897; the Society for the Preparation of Mixed Residence (Naichi Zakkyo Junbikai), founded in Nagoya the same year; the Apologetical Society for the Preparation of Mixed Residence (Zakkyo Junbi Gohōkai), founded in Osaka in 1898; and the Buddhist Apologetical Association for the Preparation of Mixed Residence (Zakkyo Junbi Bukkyō Gohōdan), founded in 1898. Buddhist journals and newspapers published articles about the problems, and numerous pamphlets and books were also published.[13]

According to many Buddhists, one of the basic problems in connection with mixed residence was the insufficient awareness in the people of what it meant to be Japanese. Without a strong sense of national identity and Buddhist consciousness, the national spirit would be destroyed; hence it was necessary to enlighten the people about their Buddhist and national heritage.[14] Rather than a positive elucidation of this heritage, however, the propaganda was still dominated by exaggerated warnings against Christianity and the destructive consequences of mixed residence.

One of the most active Buddhist propagators in this connection was Katō Taiichirō (Totsudō), who wrote numerous articles and pamphlets with detailed instructions for Buddhists on how to deal with mixed residence. He expressed a rather commonplace patriotism, according to which he contrasted Buddhism and Christianity in their relation to the Imperial Rescript on Education, patriotism, the Japanese spirit, and the national polity.[15] He compared mixed residence to including a stranger with widely different manners and traditions into one's family, with the inherent emotional problems and religious conflicts. Referring to recent religious strife between Christians and Muslims in Crete and Turkey, he predicted that emotional and religious conflicts in connection with mixed residence would lead to international conflicts between Buddhist and Christian nations.[16]

The aggressive mood among Buddhists who anticipated a fatal struggle between Buddhists and Christians in the interior of Japan was expressed in a manual for Buddhist-Christian confrontation written by Takada Dōken, editor of the conservative Buddhist newspaper *Tsūzoku Bukkyō shinbun*. The book was entitled *Naichi zakkyo Butsu-Ya mondō* [Mixed residence: a Buddhist-Christian dispute],[17] and consisted of a series of provocative fictional interrogations of a foreign missionary, a foreign lay Christian, a Japanese pastor, and a Japanese lay Christian. The interrogations were characterized by a strong nationalistic sentiment and an overwhelming sense of inferiority toward Christianity. The author described its effective methods of propagation, its charitable work and educational institutions, its kindness, its worship where "beautiful women play the organ," and its efficient pastors who seemed more clever than the Buddhist priests. The specter of colonialism was also raised against the missionary, who was forced to answer why he came to Japan, and where the money came from. When he innocently acknowledged that he was in Japan for the same reason as the Japanese sent missionaries to Taiwan, he was suddenly trapped by the Buddhist: Japanese Buddhists were working in Taiwan because it was regarded as Japanese territory; the avowal that missionaries were in Japan for the same reason implied that the missionary societies actually regarded Japan as the territory of the foreign countries. The further discussions purported to disclose how the foreign Christians despised Japan, and Japanese Christians were designated as traitors and insurgents. In sum, the traditional arguments against Christianity as incompatible with the national polity were mobilized; Christianity was "absolutely unpatriotic" and, "according to the express provisions of the Constitution," it should not be granted freedom.[18]

Several of the repressive methods that had been used against Christians at the beginning of the 1890s, such as ostracism and disturbance of Christian meetings, were used again in these years.[19] Thus the preparation for mixed residence brought about a radical deterioration of Buddhist-Christian relations. The Buddhist journal *Dentō* characterized the relations in 1899 in the following words: "Even though the Christians usually relate to the Buddhists with a gentle look, the Buddhists continually face the Christians with an angry look."[20]

Reform Zeal. A more moderate reaction came from Buddhists who, even though they anticipated mixed residence with a certain apprehension, tended to regard the new situation as an incentive to Buddhist reform. Inoue Enryō is a characteristic representative of this attitude. As he had before advocated Buddhist reform in order to cope with the political changes in 1889–1890,[21] he now emphasized that Buddhism had to prepare itself for the decisive battle with Christianity. Victory would not be obtained through such traditional weapons as propagation of Buddhist doctrines, he said, but would rather depend on whether or not Buddhists were able to compete with the Christians on the practical level; Buddhism would succeed only if people felt the need of Buddhism in society. In this connection Inoue was primarily thinking in terms of charitable work.[22] While many Buddhists looked at Christian charity with a sense of powerlessness and resignation, Inoue challenged the Buddhists to outdo the Christians precisely in the field of charitable work, such as by reforming the education of Buddhist priests and by establishing charity hospitals, orphanages, reformatories, and charitable schools and universities with low fees for common people. He envisioned a modern Buddhism that could compete with Christianity on an equal level, leaving the judgement about prosperity or decay to the people. His hope was certainly that if Buddhism served the society and the state, its indispensable value would be recognized.[23] Many prominent Buddhists shared Inoue's views.[24]

Inoue's response to mixed residence and the challenge from Christian charitable work did not involve any original or creative ideas; it was hardly more than a reaction to the social activity of the Christians and aimed at neutralizing the Christian influence by copying and, it was hoped, surpassing the Christian activities. It was, nevertheless, a positive response that contributed to the modernization of Buddhism and also revealed a certain confidence vis-à-vis Christianity.[25]

Buddhist Self-Confidence. Inoue's emphasis on Buddhist reform was combined with a careful optimism that the outcome of the Buddhist-Christian struggle would be favorable to Buddhism.[26] A stronger confidence naturally resulted in a positive attitude to mixed residence. Ōuchi Seiran, for instance, who had been a forceful anti-Christian activist in the beginning of the decade, expressed his view on mixed residence poetically by describing how the autumn shower failed to change the color of the pine tree; that is, Christianity would never be able to affect Buddhism and the national polity.[27] Ōuchi, in fact, had little to say about the problem, even when he was asked to lecture on it. He just compared it to the preparation for guests. As nobody allowed himself to receive guests with a dirty house or in a nightgown, the Japanese had to prepare themselves for mixed residence by ridding themselves of shameful habits, he said. He acknowledged the zeal and dedication of Christianity, but he was confident that Buddhism would prevail.[28]

Another Buddhist who had raised harsh criticism against Christianity in the 1880s and the 1890s, Fujishima Ryōon, now denounced the antiforeign propaganda as an effort to "rekindle the dead embers of seclusionism and exclusionism." Such propaganda would, according to Fujishima, merely affirm the foreigners in their impression that the remains of the "purely Oriental conservatism" were not yet washed away. As a Buddhist well acquainted with Western history, he argued that no people changed religion as a consequence of foreign residence in the country; moreover, he explained, the interior of Japan was still so inconvenient that few foreigners would actually want to reside there. Instead of attacking Christianity as an evil religion as before, Buddhists should receive the foreigners kindly as guests. And rather than worrying about mixed residence, Japanese Buddhists should take a step ahead and engage in overseas missionary work, and especially support the Japanese government in its colonial expansion.[29]

ENFORCEMENT OF MIXED RESIDENCE

When the new treaties were finally implemented in July 1899, even the most pessimistic Buddhists were relieved to discover that they had exaggerated the consequences of mixed residence. There was, in fact, nothing to be afraid of; unexpectedly few foreigners entered Japan, and Christianity did not prosper.[30] Thus the issue suddenly lost its relevance.

The opposition to Christian influence nevertheless still continued. For another issue had not yet been settled: Should Christianity be recognized officially on an equal level with Buddhism?

THE PROBLEM OF "STATE-RECOGNIZED RELIGION"

When the Constitution guaranteed freedom of religion in 1889, the Buddhists attempted to obtain a special status for Buddhism as "state-recognized religion." While Christians, supported by public opinion, regarded the paragraph on religious freedom as an official recognition (kōnin) of Christianity, Buddhists argued that, even though the Constitution included an official permission (kōkyo) for the practice of Christianity instead of the previous tacit approval (mokunin), it did not imply an official recognition on an equal level with Buddhism; Christianity, they maintained, should merely be regarded as a "private religious association" (shikyōkai).[31]

The issue of state recognition, though brought to the fore by the Constitution, has to be understood against the background of similar discussions in the 1880s. At that time the growing influence and prestige of

Christianity began to challenge the traditional view among Buddhists that their religion was the national religion. In 1884 Fukuzawa Yukichi abandoned his support of Buddhism and began to advocate the adoption of Christianity as a means towards facilitating Western recognition of Japan.

> The adoption of Western religion, along with institutions and customs, is the only means by which the social colour can become so assimilated as to remove this bar to intercourse and this cause of opposition. . . .
>
> Looked at from this point, it would appear that we ought to adopt a religion which, prevailing in Europe and America, exerts so considerable an influence over human affairs and social intercourse, so that our country may become a part of Christendom, presenting the same social appearance as Western powers, and sharing with them the advantages and disadvantages of their civilisation.[32]

In the wake of the rapid Westernization in the mid-1880s the adoption of Christianity as the state religion seemed quite acceptable, and Fukuzawa was supported by many intellectuals and politicians.[33] It was even reported that some went so far as to urge that the Emperor receive baptism so that Japan might at once be counted as a Christian nation.[34] As we have seen, the Christian expansion was so rapid in the 1880s that the Buddhists feared that Buddhism would be extinguished, while the Christians envisioned Christianity as the future religion of Japan. Thus the Buddhist claim to represent the national religion was seriously questioned.

The anti-Western reaction toward the end of the 1880s again strengthened the Buddhist position, and encouraged Buddhist leaders to assert their traditional "rights." In May 1889 the chief abbots of the major Buddhist sects signed a petition to the Ministry of Home Affairs, demanding a system of "state-recognized religion." The petition was reportedly drafted by Fujishima Ryōon, who had returned from several years of study in France, with firsthand knowledge of the relation between church and state in Western countries. Rather than state religion he and his colleagues preferred a system according to which only the religions that complied with certain conditions could qualify for state recognition. It was suggested that a religion should have a history of at least a hundred years of propagation in Japan and have more than 100,000 members. If a religion had fewer than 100,000 members but more than two hundred years' history, or less than a hundred years' history but more than one million members, it could still qualify for recognition. In any case, religions that depended on foreign countries and received orders or support from abroad should be excluded. The conditions were obviously directed against Christianity, and the conclusion was simply that only Buddhism qualified for state recognition.[35] The idea was supported by such influential Buddhists as Shimaji Mokurai and Inoue Enryō.[36] Inoue Enryō, for instance, argued in 1889 that state recognition of Buddhism was necessary for national independence and the permanency of the Imperial household.[37]

One of the Buddhists' main arguments was that Buddhism was actually functioning as a state-recognized religion. In contrast to Christianity, Buddhism and Shinto were under the jurisdiction of the Bureau of Shrines and Temples of the Ministry of Home Affairs, receiving government supervision and protection.[38] Apart from Article 28 of the Constitution, the government had never issued a systematic law concerning religions, and thus there was no legal standard for dealing with Christianity on the official level in matters of education, police affairs, or court ceremonies.[39]

In 1893, in conjunction with the treaty negotiations, the Ministry of Home Affairs began to prepare a religious law common to Shinto, Buddhism, and Christianity. As late as 1898 it was not yet settled whether or not Christianity legally should be treated with the status of a recognized religion.[40] By then, the Buddhists had again intensified their campaigns against the recognition of Christianity. In 1897 they drafted a proposition that would have given Buddhism a privileged position; in 1898 they requested the Ministry of Home Affairs to include such clauses in the bill concerning religion. Their expectations, however, were betrayed. The bill as proposed gave the government a legal basis for extensive control of religious organizations and teachers of religion, and, furthermore, implied an official recognition of Christianity by virtue of the proposed regulations. The Buddhists, consequently, decided to oppose the bill, and made the Conference of Chief Abbots of Buddhist Sects the center of their activity; numerous other organizations were also founded to oppose the bill and promote state recognition of Buddhism.[41]

The Buddhist protest was not only directed against the loss of traditional privileges; it also criticized clauses that deprived the chief abbots of their authority to decide internal governance and religious matters and instead allowed the government to interfere in religious matters without granting Buddhism any privileged status: "Christianity as a minority is put on a par with Buddhism, which represents the majority. Buddhism is subject to interference which Christianity should be subject to, and Christianity has obtained the same privileges that should be held by Buddhism."[42]

The "prison chaplain question" especially incited the Buddhists to fervent activity. On September 4, 1898, the warden of Sugamo Prison dismissed two of the three Buddhist priests who had served as chaplains and appointed a Christian chaplain, Tomeoka Kōzuke. This sparked a violent opposition from the Buddhists, who referred to September 4 as a "disastrous day." They regarded the decision as an open violation of their privileges and an oppression of the Buddhist faith of the 1,800 prisoners. Moreover, they argued, by appointing a Christian to such a position the government illegally treated Christianity as a state-recognized religion.[43]

The first organized protest came from the Greater Japan Buddhist Youth Association (Dai Nihon Bukkyō Seinenkai), under the leadership of Chikazumi Jōkan, but it was not the only organization to protest. Among the Buddhist sects, the Ōtani Sect of Shin Buddhism was most active.[44] In October more than five hundred concerned Buddhists gathered in Kyoto and founded the National Alliance of Buddhists (Bukkyōto Kokumin Dōmeikai), which soon established branches all over the country. The purpose of the alliance was to "manifest the original character of Buddhism, and through its influence first strengthen the unity of the people, and then adopt means to promote national prosperity and to contribute to the independence of the nation and the enlightenment of society."[45] The protection of Buddhism was among its central concerns, as it was expressed in several of the guidelines of the Alliance:

> to induce the Government to establish a system of state recognition of religion
>
> to urge the Government to clarify speedily its treatment of non-recognized religions[46]
>
> to persuade the Government to take the state-recognized religion under its protection, subjecting it at the same time to strict supervision . . .
>
> to defend Buddhism by rejecting everyone, whether official or layman, who unjustly tries to hinder the prosperity of Buddhism[47]

Thus the Sugamo Prison chaplaincy incident added abundant fuel to the fight for Buddhist privileges. *Yomiuri shinbun* described the situation in a review of the year 1899.

> The prison chaplain question, which had grown hot enough to reach flash point toward the close of last year, burst forth into full blaze with the new year. It furnished an opportunity to the advocates of a "state-recognised religion" to force to a definite issue the question of the relation between state and religion. Among the various schemes that were started in this connection, the polemists of the Higashi Hongwanji school issued a new magazine as their mouth-piece, while at the same time canvassing the provincial towns. Influential Buddhists of other denominations gradually fell into line and for nearly a year now, with the exception of a few radicals and of those who habitually keep themselves aloof from such wrangles they have all kept on talking on this politico-religious problem.[48]

Even though the Ministry of Home Affairs approved of placing Buddhism and Christianity on the same footing in the chaplaincy incident, the Buddhists won a partial victory—the warden was removed to another prison and the Christian chaplain resigned his position.[49] The incident was not an isolated case, but was just one important expression of a continuous effort on the part of the Buddhists to keep Christians out of key positions in Japanese society, especially in politics, education, the military, and other public work.

In April 1899 the so-called Alliance for the Realization of a System of State-recognized Religion (Kōninkyō Seido Kisei Dōmeikai) was founded in Chion'in in Kyoto. A similar Alliance for the Realization of the Protection of Buddhism (Bukkyō Hogo Kisei Dōmeikai) was also founded by representatives of seven Buddhist sects.[50] In December 1899 and January 1900 more than 760,000 people signed a petition for state recognition of Buddhism, to be submitted to both houses of the Diet. In February 1900 the proposed bill concerning religion, which had been amended to a certain degree, was finally defeated in the House of Peers.[51]

Meanwhile, the unified front of the Buddhists was gradually breaking down, especially after the enforcement of the revised treaties in July 1899. The powerful Honganji sect of Shin Buddhism criticized the effort to obtain state recognition, supported the new bill, and eventually withdrew from the Conference of Chief Abbots. The following criticism was voiced in its journal, *Dendō shinshi.*

> Those who cry for state religion or request state recognition of Buddhism are not aiming at finding a peaceful way out of their problems, . . . To turn exclusively to politicians from the extremely corrupted secular world, making all sorts of movements to demand protection, means nothing but increasingly subjecting the life of religion to certain destruction.[52]

Thus the two most influential Buddhist sects were in disagreement over the issue; the Honganji sect supported the bill, while the Ōtani sect led the agitation against it. It was commonly believed and openly charged by a group within the Ōtani sect that its head temple spent large sums of money in bribing members of the House of Peers in order to prevent the passage of the bill.[53] Even though it was defeated, subsequent ordinances from the Ministry of Home Affairs legalized a system that was almost identical with the provisions of the rejected bill. The implicit government control of religions was somewhat contradictory to the principle of religious freedom, but Christianity was at least treated on an equal basis with Buddhism and Shinto.[54]

Referring critically to these efforts to affirm Buddhist privileges and to hamper the Christian movement, Kashiwabara Yūsen concludes that this trend was generally in accord with the way Buddhism had functioned under the feudal system of the Tokugawa period. After a somewhat liberal stage in the early Meiji period, the development since the end of the

1880s had increasingly induced the Buddhists toward identification with the Japanese state; Buddhism was to a great extent functioning as a religious support of the development toward political absolutism and imperialism.[55] The new laws and ordinances put an end to Buddhist attempts to obtain privileges at the cost of Christianity; Buddhism lost some of its autonomy, and all religious bodies were submitted to government control. In spite of opposition on the part of many Buddhists, the Buddhist identification with the Japanese state was strengthened; on the other hand, Christianity was also expected to play a more prominent role in the service of the state. This was realized after the turn of the century as Buddhists and Christians engaged in what could be called the "establishment dialogue," that is, a common effort of religious leaders to provide a spiritual support of the government.[56] Of course, this was not only the result of legal and political changes; the basis for cooperation had already been laid through a series of drastic changes within the Buddhist and Christian communities.[57]

THE FAILURE OF BUDDHIST OPPOSITION

In spite of some successful attempts to oppress Christianity and check its expansion in the 1890s, the Buddhist opposition described in this and the foregoing chapters must be characterized as a failure. At the turn of the century the Buddhists had lost most of their traditional privileges; they were no longer favored by the exaggerated anti-Western and anti-Christian sentiment that characterized the years around 1890. And the Christians were prepared to regain what they had lost during the decade of retarded growth. I shall not here try to explain the reasons for the failure, but rather conclude the examination of the Buddhist-Christian struggle by indicating the shaky foundation of the Buddhist opposition to Christianity.

We have seen in great detail that the conflict was based on a more or less express fear of Christian expansion, coinciding with a deep-rooted crisis within Buddhism and accompanied by apprehensions that Buddhism was bound for destruction. Thus the conflict to a great extent became a struggle for existence—a struggle for the right to free expansion of Christianity on the one side and a struggle for the traditional power and privileges of Buddhism on the other. Ultimately, both religions claimed the right to lay the foundations for the spiritual uplifting of the nation.

Missionaries and Japanese Christians generally identified Christianity with development and Westernization, and envisioned a "new Japan," dominated by Western ideas. They regarded Buddhism as an outdated faith of the ignorant masses, which would disappear together with the

old society. The Buddhists, on the other hand, tended to identify themselves with the "old Japan," including traditional Japanese values, morality, and political ideas. These gave them effective weapons at times of
strong nationalistic sentiments. The nationalistic reaction from the late
1880s thus came as a great relief to the Buddhist world. Such arguments,
however, lost their power when the wave of exaggerated nationalism
receded. As we shall see later, the fact that the patriotic spirit of the
Christians finally was recognized also undermined the Buddhist arguments that Christianity was subversive.

More problematic, from a genuinely Buddhist viewpoint, was that the
nationalistic propaganda was not based on Buddhist ideas as such, but
rather was in conflict with basic Buddhist doctrines. The doctrinal refutation of Christianity drew on a long tradition of studies, and expressed,
in spite of its narrow-mindedness, a genuine Buddhist concern. But this
often yielded to slander and emotional criticism of Christianity as incompatible with the national polity. Buddhism was harmonized with current
ideas in a way which to a great extent distorted Buddhist thought. This
was not a new phenomenon, as we have seen in the initial chapters, but
in the 1890s it became the main thrust of Buddhist propaganda.

The distortion was especially obvious in the central issues of the Buddhist-Christian conflict, questions concerning nationalism, loyalty to the
Emperor and the state, filial piety, and social morality.[58] The Christian
ideas of monotheism, universalism, universal love, and faith in the kingdom of God were all stigmatized as incompatible with the duties of loyal
and filial Japanese. In many cases it was, in fact, Christians who found it
necessary to remind the Buddhists that Buddhism also stood for universalism rather than nationalism; that the Buddhist doctrine of universal
compassion was more central than its ideas of nationalism, loyalty, and
filial piety; and that detachment rather than secular concerns was a vital
aspect of Buddhism.[59]

It was thus obvious that the Buddhist opposition to Christianity in the
1890s, rather than being motivated by genuinely Buddhist concerns, had
become a struggle for power and traditional privileges. The Buddhist
establishment shared the values of traditionally minded Japanese, Shintoists, Confucians, and conservative politicians. They favored a return to
the past, or entrenched themselves in the old positions, and were unable
to encounter Christianity in a creative way.[60]

Against this background it was not surprising that a new generation of
Buddhist reformers found it necessary to combine their search for a true
Buddhism with a radical rejection of what was then considered traditional Buddhism, and with an attempt to find a new and creative
approach to Christianity.

CHAPTER ELEVEN

The New Christianity

> We should believe in Christianity as Japanese, study the-
> ology as Japanese, propagate Christianity as Japanese.
> . . . We should hold up Christianity with the right hand
> and stretch down the left hand to grasp the forty million
> [Japanese] brethren.
>
> Yokoi Tokio, Japanese Christian leader

IN THE MIDST of the conflict and aggression described above, some new trends[1] gradually gained momentum and created more tolerant attitudes between Buddhists and Christians. The purpose of the following chapters is to trace the origin of these trends and uncover some of the dynamics that made rapprochement possible. The conclusion will not be anticipated here, but it is worth keeping in mind that the new relationship to a great extent was related to the same nationalistic reaction that affected Buddhist-Christian relations in such a negative way.

CHRISTIAN PATRIOTISM

In the wake of the nationalistic reaction, it had become a popular dogma that Christianity was unpatriotic and incompatible with the national polity, and throughout the 1890s the Christians were criticized as potential traitors and insurgents. Such criticism, however, was never accepted by the Christians, who rather claimed that their faith had enabled them to serve society more effectively as true patriots.[2] Behind such opposite views there was a basic difference in the Buddhist and Christian understanding of the state.

BUDDHIST NATIONALISM AND CHRISTIAN PATRIOTISM

It is impossible here to deal substantially with the differences between Buddhist and Christian concepts of nationalism and the state; only a few points will be mentioned in order to clarify why it was so difficult for Buddhists and conservative Japanese to recognize Christian patriotism.

First, Buddhist nationalism represented a rather unreflecting traditional identification with the state. Buddhism had been introduced into Japan from above and was, from the beginning, closely related to the state; Buddhism served as a spiritual and ritual guarantee for the state and received state protection and supervision. One of the important roles of classical Japanese Buddhism was expressed in the term *chingo kokka,* "to pacify and protect the nation" by the power of the Buddha or religious prayers.[3] At the same time Buddhist morality was generally identified with Confucian concepts of social relations; loyalty and filial piety were emphasized as the main virtues. More than two centuries of state protection and supervision during the Tokugawa period had made Buddhism passive and powerless and had strengthened its identification with the regime. After a short period of crisis following the Meiji Restoration, the Buddhist establishment transferred its allegiance to the new authorities.[4]

The Buddhists conceived of the state in a rather unsophisticated way as the "state household" *(kokka)* with a clearly defined hierarchy of authority, obligations, and rights. Buddhist nationalism consisted primarily in identifying itself with such a state *(kokka-shugi),* and Buddhism regarded itself as "state Buddhism" *(kokkateki Bukkyō,* or *kokka Bukkyō).*[5] In popular terms, Buddhism was regarded as the cement needed between the bricks in the house of the state.[6]

In contrast to Buddhism, Japanese Christians had a much more sophisticated understanding of the state and the role of religion in society. The majority of Christians and the entire Christian leadership in the Meiji period came from samurai background; they were trained in Confucian traditions, and thus regarded themselves as an intellectual elite with great responsibility for the welfare of the nation. While the Confucian influence in Buddhism inclined the Buddhists toward a passive acceptance of feudal ideas, the Confucian training of the Christians stimulated them toward an active, progressive role in society. Their Christian faith, however, had changed their priorities; even such traditional virtues as loyalty and filial piety were not any more of ultimate value.[7] Their sense of loyalty toward the Meiji government was weak. Many Christians came from domains that had been loyal to the Tokugawa regime, and they were thus somewhat estranged from the political establishment.[8] Moreover, their Protestant faith and their acquaintance with Western thought had furnished them with a new vision for the future, described by a prominent Christian, Kozaki Hiromichi, as the "age of the *new Japan* or the age of *reform*."[9] A characteristic expression of such an attitude is found in his *Seikyō shinron* [A new treatise on religion and politics], written in 1886.

> Truly today our country is being reborn; it is a day of the creation of a new Japan and can be said to be an unprecedented period of great reform. . . . This reform, by destroying the old Japan and creating the new, is not different from destroying an old established house and erecting on its site a newly-designed house from old and new timbers. . . . Truly, this renovation is not just the renewal of Imperial Rule, but should be called the renovation of the State, or the reform of society. . . . We ourselves are products of this great reform. . . . Oh, would that today were the time when our country, casting off from the port of old Japan, set sail for the new Japan.[10]

This passionate vision of the new Japan was undoubtedly born out of the patriotic spirit of the Christians, but Buddhists perceived it as subversive and dangerous. According to the Christians, the role of the state was limited to creating public order and granting freedom to citizens; compared to the individual citizen, the state was of secondary importance and should not be idolized. Rather than "nationalism" (*kokka-shugi*) they seemed to prefer the term "nationality" (*kokumin-shugi*), which emphasized the people (*kokumin*) rather than the state. "The people" was defined by Kozaki as "a moral structure of people who, from top to bottom of society, are aware of their role as citizens."[11] In short, Christian patriotism identified itself neither with the past nor with the state, as Buddhist nationalism had tended to do, but rather with the future and with the people.

Second, while Buddhist nationalism emphasized the concern for the Japanese state and the priority of national loyalties, the Christians combined patriotism with a strong emphasis on universal principles and the supremacy of faith in God, in addition to open support of Western ideas. Even though a number of prominent Christians skillfully and convincingly argued that the patriotic spirit of the Christians was manifested in society, where Christians in action demonstrated the patriotic virtues others were just talking about, the conservatives did not seem to be convinced.[12] From the point of view of most Buddhists, Christian universalism was ultimately incompatible with nationalism.

Third, the close relationship among Japanese Christians, missionaries, and Western nations gave abundant material for the criticism that the Christians not only professed a foreign faith, but depended on foreign support and advice and would, if necessary, abandon their national identity. Thus, it was charged, the ultimate loyalties of the Christians were not with the Japanese state, but with foreign missionaries and foreign powers, or with the kingdom of God.

In sum, Buddhist nationalism and Christian patriotism seemed incompatible, even though both were concerned about the welfare of the Japanese nation. They were not totally contradictory, but they were revolving around different axes and they followed different orbits. Several changes, however, gradually brought the two worlds closer together.

THE NATIONALISTIC REACTION AND CHURCH INDEPENDENCE

The fact that Christianity had benefited from the tide of Westernization and encountered severe setbacks as the tide receded did not imply that Japanese Christians had identified themselves completely with the West and resented the reaction. One of the most outspoken critics of the West was Tokutomi Sohō (Iichirō), editor of the Christian journal, *Kokumin no tomo*. In a scathing criticism of Western colonialism he wrote in his *Shōrai no Nihon* [The future Japan] in 1887:

> The present day world is one in which civilized people tyrannically destroy savage peoples. . . . The European countries stand at the very pinnacle of violence and base themselves on the doctrine of force. . . . India, alas, has been destroyed, Annam has been destroyed, Burma will be next. The remaining countries will be independent in name only. . . . What is the outlook for Persia? For China? Korea? And even Japan? The future will be extremely critical. This, I feel, is unbearable.[13]

Tokutomi's criticism of the West was supported by an increasing number of Christians who had awakened from their illusions about the West as God's own country. Uchimura Kanzō's encounter with the United States in 1884 is a characteristic expression of such a shocking discovery: "My idea of the Christian America was lofty, religious, Puritanic," he wrote. "I dreamed of its templed hills, and rocks that rang with hymns and praises." He had been told about "worship" of money and about race prejudice, but he could not believe such things were true about the country he regarded as "a *Holy Land*." His conclusion, however, left little room for doubt.

> Is this the civilization we were taught by missionaries to accept as an evidence of the superiority of Christian Religion over other religions? With what shamefacedness did they declare unto us that the religion which made Europe and America must surely be the religion from on high? If it was Christianity that made the so-called Christendom of to-day, let Heaven's eternal curse rest upon it! Peace is the last thing we can find in Christendom. Turmoils, complexities, insane asylums, penitentiaries, poor-houses! . . . One thing I shall never do in the future: I shall never defend Christianity upon its being the religion of Europe and America.[14]

According to Cary, "It became the fashion among those who went to America or England to pay special attention to the defects of those countries."[15] Matsumura Kaiseki recalled how he and other Christian leaders changed from "worship of Westerners" or Western things to a new national awareness that eventually caused problems with some of the missionaries.[16] Even though they generally rejected the xenophobic and anti-Christian trend as irrational and prejudiced, they criticized one-sided Westernization and supported the preservation of the national essence. It is characteristic that Kozaki Hiromichi, in the above-mentioned essay on nationality, welcomed the nationalistic reaction, with its emphasis on the national essence, Japanism, and the national polity, as important for strengthening the sense of being a people.[17] Yokoi Tokio recalled the "German-style wedding ceremonies, American-style Sundays, Western food, and Western clothing." Western language allied itself with Christianity and spread in all directions, he wrote, and explained how the need of missionaries had been closely related to the fact that they could teach English.[18]

Thus the nationalistic reaction among Japanese Christians was not only expressed as a critical attitude to the West and a new appreciation of Japanese traditions, but in many cases it complicated the relationship with foreign missionaries and missionary societies and stimulated the liberation from missionary dominance. According to Cary, "Much was said and written derogatory to the missionaries; and some preachers, especially the younger men, seemed to think that in addresses before unbelievers it would help them to win favour if they showed their independence of the foreign teachers by speaking in disparagement of them."[19]

In some cases the missionaries were even urged to leave the work in the other fields to the Japanese ministry, and rather go "into the interior and even to the Loochoo Islands," as one of the pastors said.[20] According to a missionary report, the Japanese Christians were "stung by the charge that they were servile 'lantern-bearers' and 'sandal-carriers' of foreigners."[21] Another missionary indicated that the missionaries might have to leave Japan, after which the Japanese Christians—Protestant, Catholic, and Orthodox—would perhaps be brought into harmony "under the magic of that cry, *Japan for the Japanese,* and *a Japanese Christianity for Japan.*"[22]

A great number of mission schools had to be closed as a result of the cooling off of the zeal for Westernization. Criticism was raised also within Christian circles that the schools stimulated a foreign spirit among their pupils rather than fostering Japanese attitudes.[23] Uchimura Kanzō and Matsumura Kaiseki resigned their positions in Hokuetsu Gakkan in Niigata in 1889 and 1891 after friction with the missionary staff. Doshisha had similar problems.[24] The principal of Kumamoto Eigakkō was reported to have developed an antimissionary spirit; he discharged the missionary teachers and finally declared the school to be nonreligious.[25]

The reaction against Western dominance also stimulated Japanese Christians to establish independent organizations and to avoid financial dependence on missionary societies. The trend had been obvious already in the 1880s when self-confident Japanese Christians, often stimulated by the missionaries, argued that Christian propagation had to be carried out by Japanese and supported by Japanese.[26] The trend was radically strengthened in the early 1890s when the Congregational Church (Kumiai Kyōkai), particularly, emphasized its financial and spiritual independence.[27]

The Buddhists certainly took notice of the critical attitudes to Western influence and the new sense of independence in the Japanese churches.[28] It was, however, hard to believe that the Christians had completely abandoned the foreign spirit of Christianity. The new trends had to be substantiated by further changes within the churches in order to gain credibility.

PATRIOTIC BEHAVIOR

Christian patriotism was not easily recognized, in spite of the creative role of Christians in social and moral development, because they failed to adhere to what was considered patriotic behavior. One common criticism, for instance, was that Christian schools neglected Japanese traditions, refusing to observe national and religious holidays apart from Sundays and Christian holidays, or even forbidding students to participate in Shinto festivals or to celebrate the Emperor's birthday.[29] In his recollections of his student days, Tokutomi Sohō wrote about Doshisha as "a completely American school. There was no recess for national holidays. The Japanese flag was not flown. There were no banzais for the Emperor. Saturday was a holiday and Sunday was a day for hearing sermons."[30]

A gradual change, however, occurred among Japanese Christians. Among the reforms Uchimura Kanzō introduced in Hokuetsu Gakkan in 1889 was the attempt to abandon the compulsory morning prayer, to introduce Japanese holidays, and to study the Analects of Confucius along with the Bible.[31] As a result of criticism, the Emperor's birthday was celebrated with prayer meetings and cheers both in mission schools and in local churches. Meiji Gakuin began to give its students free time on the days of the spring and autumn festivals of the Meiji Shrine.[32] The celebrations and prayer meetings in the Christian churches in connection with the promulgation of the Constitution in 1889 and the opening of the Diet in 1890 were also obvious expressions of patriotism.[33] In 1892–1893 Doshisha rejected charges of neglect of Japanese holidays as ill-founded slander. Even though the Christians were still criticized for insufficient reverence for the Emperor, it seemed to be an established practice that they paid obeisance to his picture and to the Imperial Rescript on Education and other objects of reverence.[34] As we shall see in more detail below, the trend was strengthened by the Sino-Japanese War in 1894–1895. The Shinto journal *Kyōrin* observed that in the past Christianity "made its believers worship the cross but now it seeks to propagate its faith through worshipping the image of our Emperor."[35] A similar observation was made by the Buddhist journal *Hansei zasshi,* which regarded the new nationalistic trend among the Christians as a recognition that it was necessary to "kneel reverently in front of the idol of the State."[36] Doshisha, which had often been suspected for its foreign spirit and Christian principles, expressed its patriotic spirit in the following promises to the Kyoto Government in 1896:

1. The moral education of the Doshisha Ordinary Middle School will be founded upon the Imperial Educational Rescript. . . . It will seek to inculcate an earnest spirit of loyalty and filial obedience by which the people shall each honour his own ancestors and shall reverence the spirits of the Imperial Ancestors. . . .

2. On the National Holidays the pupils will be called together, the Imperial Educational Rescript will be read to them, and they will be carefully instructed as to the Imperial will, or taught of the great virtues and illustrious deeds of past Emperors, or of the lives and teachings of the ancient sages; or other addresses suitable to the National Holidays may be given them in order to cultivate a spirit of loyalty to the Emperor and of love to the country. This is the purpose which we hope to carry into practice.

3. In the graduation and like exercises in the Doshisha ordinary Middle School religious exercises will not, of course, be held, but there will be an effort to deeply impress the students with the precepts of the Imperial Educational Rescript.[37]

It may also be noted in this connection that Article Three in the Constitution of Doshisha, which emphasized Christianity as "the foundation of the moral education" of the school, after 1898 was no longer applicable to the departments of Doshisha except the Theological School. According to Cary, this was the result of "the nationalistic spirit and an extremely liberal theology."[38]

Thus the dominant trend within the Japanese churches adapted itself to the patriotic atmosphere and accepted the popular expressions of loyalty and patriotism. More than anything else, however, the Sino-Japanese War gave the Christians an opportunity to demonstrate their fervent patriotic spirit.

THE SINO-JAPANESE WAR

The Sino-Japanese War (1894–1895) was almost unanimously supported by Japanese Christians. The Christian press abounded in enthusiastic reports about the war and about Christian activity in connection with the war. *Japan Evangelist* characterized the year 1894 as "the most brilliant year of our history."

> When the year 1894 dawned upon this Land of the Rising Sun, probably no one dreamt of the brilliant events that were so near at hand. . . . The government established over the seized portions of China is better and kinder than Chinese rule itself has been. This is conduct which is really Christian in principle, . . . "Greater Japan" is the watch-word today—greater in aspiration, greater in influence, greater through the propagation of our Japanese spirit.[39]

Probably no religious group in Japan responded as spontaneously to the war as the Christian churches. Immediately after the war was declared, a number of prominent Christians gathered under the leadership of the Methodist pastor Honda Yōichi and decided to support the war "under the banner of the Gospel," providing medical help for soldiers and relief for families who suffered from poverty as a result of the war.[40] Famous pastors and educators, such as Honda Yōichi, Harada Tasuku, Ebina Danjō, Iwamoto Yoshiharu, and Matsumura Kaiseki, were dispatched all over Japan to collect funds and enlist nurses for the work among the soldiers.[41] The patriotic Association of Christian Comrades (Kirisutokyōto Dōshikai) was founded, with its main work in Hiroshima, the military headquarters. Branches of the association and similar patriotic Christian societies were established all over the country.[42] The churches sponsored public meetings featuring the war, often accompanied by stereopticon shows about their activity at the front. They donated warm clothes, sweets, literature, and Bibles to the soldiers; they started "self-denial donations," sent volunteers to the front, held prayer meetings for the soldiers, or gathered at the station every time a group of soldiers was sent off to the front.[43] While it had been complicated for Christian officers and soldiers to express their Christian faith, the Vice-Minister of War now gave permission for Christians to visit all the garrisons in Japan in order to supply the men with copies of the Gospels. Five prominent pastors, including Honda Yōichi and Miyakawa Tsuneteru, were sent to the front as chaplains, recognized by the military authorities under the official designation "comforters" *(imonshi)*.[44] Cary gives the following description of the situation:

> The most favourable opportunity for work was among the sick and wounded soldiers in the hospitals. Missionaries joined with Japanese Christians in carrying books, papers, pictures, flowers, and other things to the patients, who were glad for anything that would relieve the monotony of the hours. Those in charge of the hospitals welcomed such ministrations and gave the missionary ladies freedom to visit all parts of the hospitals and to converse with the patients. Some of the hospitals were under the care of the Red Cross Society.

This had become very popular in Japan. Most of the prominent citizens of the country were members, and a large force of nurses had received training under its auspices. Though not a Christian society, its symbol was significant of the fact that its principles of charity to be shown to friend and foe alike had come from the teaching of Him who had died upon the Cross. When it was remembered that not many years before the Japanese had trampled upon the cross as the sign of a hated religion, it was very suggestive to see it now becoming an honoured symbol.[45]

The almost unanimous support of the war among Japanese Christians was emphasized by the fact that even the Japanese Society of Friends (Quakers), for whom pacifism had been a central concern, supported the war by allowing its members to join the army. When the American Friends criticized their Japanese colleagues and expelled four students from their school for abandoning pacifism, they were accused of failing to combine love of one's fellow men with love of one's country. The conflict finally ended with a split within the Society of Friends, and the American Quakers withdrew their support of the Japanese work of the society.[46]

The patriotic fervor of the Christians naturally made a great impact on public opinion. It was written with reference to Doshisha that "if there existed any real doubt of the entire compatibility of Christianity and patriotism, all the semblance of ground for doubt has been swept away by the enthusiasm shown at every stage in the Chino-Japanese [sic] war."[47] *Japan Evangelist* commented with satisfaction that Christian work advanced "along with the brilliant victories of the war."[48] Even though reports from some districts referred to stagnation in Christian work as the interest of people was diverted to the war,[49] the general trend was characterized by a growing sympathy with Christianity which facilitated the work.[50]

The Buddhists also expressed admiration for the strenuous efforts of the Christians, and gradually engaged in the work among the soldiers.[51] Because of their slow and rather passive response, however, they were often criticized for poor patriotic spirit, as it was expressed at an early stage of the war: "The black-robed priests who make their livelihood on the State under the cloak of compassion and universal love, what are they doing now? Have the 200,000 Buddhist priests already entered the sleep of death, unable to wake up even if their ears are pierced by the approaching war-cry of the demons?"[52]

Thus the Sino-Japanese War introduced major changes in the popular evaluation of Christianity. Christianity was widely recognized for its fervent patriotism, while Buddhism, which had been scathingly critical of the unpatriotic spirit of Christianity, became the target of such criticism.

The international development in connection with the Sino-Japanese

War also made Japanese Christians more aware of their Oriental heritage. When Japan, in spite of the victory and the consequent Treaty of Shimonoseki (April 17, 1895), was forced by Russian-German-French diplomatic intervention to give up the Liaotung peninsula, the Japanese resentment naturally was quite strong. The intervention has been characterized as "a national humiliation" and "one of the most tragic chapters in the history of modern Japan."[53] The fact that the Triple Alliance represented "Christian nations" also suggested religious implications of the conflict. A Buddhist journal commented:

> The well-known fact that William II. of Germany painted a caricature depicting the alliance of Western nations against the East and sent it to Nicholas II. of Russia, shows that the religious phase of the Eastern Problem is attracting the attention of the world. Leaving political questions to statesmen, it behooves us as religionists to take cognizance of this fact and study our proper course of action.[54]

The "religious phase of the Eastern Problem" induced Japanese Christians to react against Western Christianity by expressing their religious solidarity with the East. An editorial in *Jogaku zasshi,* entitled "The Problem of the Religious East," argued, for instance, that in the present international situation Japanese Christians should identify themselves with Eastern religions against the Christianity of the West.[55]

IDENTIFICATION WITH THE NATIONAL POLITY

Such changes introduced a new epoch in the relations between Christianity and the state and between Buddhism and Christianity. It was reported by a contemporary observer that while previously pastors and lay Christians both had been "obstinacy itself, with many edges" or "stubbornly incorruptible in character, lacking versatility, and phlegmatic in social intercourse with relatives," now they had become "very able to adapt themselves to the circumstances." Sumiya Mikio comments on the change by concluding: "Thus the Christian church, which had been extremely combative against the Japanese social establishment, in this period lost its critical power and its ability to struggle and gradually compromised with the Japanese society."[56]

The most extreme change was perhaps represented by Tokutomi Sohō, who abandoned his radical democratic ideas expressed in the so-called *heimin-shugi,* that is "democratism," "populism," or, literally translated, "common people-ism,"[57] and instead began to advocate an extreme imperialism, emphasizing military expansion and the supreme authority of the state.[58] Tokutomi was, of course, not quite representative of Christian attitudes, and had not even in his democratic period identified himself with the Christian church. More representative changes occurred within the Christian leadership in relation to the Imperial household and the state. The concern now was not merely to demonstrate that Christianity was beneficial for the welfare of the people or that Christian faith was not in conflict with the national polity, but to advocate positive identification with the national polity and to acknowledge the sovereignty of the state. From the educational point of view, Matsumura Kaiseki stressed that moral education had to be "State education," fostering "loyalty, patriotism, and service to the State." Honda Yōichi praised the patriotic spirit of the soldier who dedicated himself to the country as a pure sacrifice, "just as the officiating priest offers the sacrifice on the *kamidana* [Shinto altar]." Miyakawa Tsuneteru, who was the son of a Shinto priest, argued that even though Christianity stood for equality in human rights, he would devote himself to loyal service if anything should happen to the Emperor. He refused to regard Shinto as a religion, but appreciated it as a worship of the Imperial ancestors and those who had served the country. With his emphasis on loyalty and patriotism he was, according to Suzuki Norihisa, a "typical Christian pastor of the modern Japan."[59] A similar view was held by Hiraiwa Yoshiyasu, who claimed that Christianity could be harmonized with the national polity. He also regarded Shinto as a neutral state ritual, and concluded that Christians could pay obeisance both to the picture of the Emperor and to the Great Shrine of Ise.[60]

Thus *Hansei zasshi* was not quite off the point when it described how the Christians had begun to "kneel reverently in front of the idol of the State."[61] Sumiya Mikio concludes that while Christians before had seen the development of the people as the basis for the development of the state, now they tended to emphasize the development of the state as a basis for the development of the people. The previous idea of nationality, with its emphasis on the people, was more and more dominated by the idea of state supremacy.[62]

Some critics warned against the change among the Christians as a superficial and opportunistic adaptation,[63] but the general opinion appreciated the new image of Christianity, regarding its assimilation into the national polity as the basis for recognition and cooperation.[64] A fairly neutral observer described the adaptation of Christianity as a question of survival; in the struggle for existence the species unable to adjust themselves to the circumstances would be extinguished.[65] A Christian historian like Sumiya regards the change as a fatal compromise, resulting from the weakness of the church and introducing a new epoch in which Christianity disappeared from the foreground of Japanese society.[66] Be that as it may, Christian patriotism brought about a new climate which promoted Buddhist-Christian cooperation, emphasized the spiritual solidarity with the East, and enabled both religions to "entrench themselves in the same citadel of nationalism,"[67] as it was expressed in an editorial in the Buddhist *Sōtō kyōhō*. This trend had already been evident for several years in the theological world.

THE NEW THEOLOGY

Several major changes in the theological world gradually influenced Buddhist-Christian relations in Japan. The changes were partly the result of a development within the Japanese churches, closely related to the patriotic reaction and expressed as a demand for a Japanese theology, but they were also stimulated by outside influences, notably by liberal theology and Unitarianism.

JAPANIZATION

The nationalistic reaction in the Japanese churches was expressed on the theological level as a clamorous demand for a "Japanization of Christianity" or a "Japanese theology."[68] The demand for Japanization was not merely a result of the anti-Western reaction, but sprang out of a deep concern for Christian propagation. The stagnation of Christian work around 1890 had disclosed the unfortunate identification of Christianity and Westernism; the demand for Japanization, consequently, entailed a de-Westernization of Christianity. The Christianization of Japan had to be carried out through a Japanization of Christianity.

Regarding such a change, Yokoi Tokio, representing a dominant trend within the Japanese churches, wrote in 1890 that the first act of Christian propagation was over. All varieties of Western Christianity had been introduced, from Episcopal high-church piety to the simplicity of the Friends. "Actually, the present Christian church is just like a foreign colony," he wrote; and the natural consequence was to reject the theological dominance of the West. Christianity had to "lay off the Western clothes" and wear a Japanese dress. Yokoi explained how theology, rituals, and customs had changed through the ages, according to time and circumstances; as there was a Greek theology, a Roman theology, and a German theology, now a genuinely Japanese theology had to abandon the foreign traditions in order to resume the essence of Christianity.[69] One of the results of the rejection of Western models was a radical attempt to simplify or abandon traditional confessions and creeds and to substitute for them shorter declarations of faith.[70] An enthusiastic American observer wrote in this connection: "Vigorously has the Christian consciousness of Japan cast off the sectarian and provincial creeds of merely English-speaking Christendom. Refusing the swaddling-bands of the Scotch, Yankee, and Anglican phases of the faith, it has sought the simplicity that is in Christ. . . . They with the Bible in hand choose the shortest path to Christ."[71]

More important than the rejection of Western theology, however, was the positive program of Japanization, which introduced new attitudes to the indigenous traditions. Yokoi Tokio compared Christianity to a tree; Japanese Christians should receive the sunshine, rain, and dew of Christianity from above, but at the same time be rooted in the soil of Japanese customs and manners: "We should believe in Christianity as Japanese, study theology as Japanese, propagate Christianity as Japanese. . . . We should hold up Christianity with the right hand and stretch down the left hand to grasp the forty million [Japanese] brethren."[72] While Western Christianity had developed on the basis of Greek literature and Roman jurisprudence, Japanese Christianity should "stand on Confucian and Buddhist civilization."[73] Yokoi was, however, extremely critical of the actual state of Buddhism and Confucianism, and concluded that "Buddhism is already corrupted and cannot recover" and that "Confucianism has declined and will never be able again to take the moral leadership in our country."[74] He contrasted the Christian ideal of life with the "dead scholasticism of the Confucianist teachers, or the gorgeous rites and unintelligible ceremonies of the Buddhist priests."[75] As we shall see, with many of his colleagues he was convinced that Christianity inherited and fulfilled the best in the indigenous traditions and had to develop in intimate contact with these. Similar views were expressed by Matsumura Kaiseki, who claimed that Japanese Christianity should be "largely modified by Buddhist and Confucian ideas."[76] Matsumura characterized himself as a "Confucian Christian," and gradually developed a religiosity that harmonized Christianity and other religions, with special emphasis on Confucian Wang Yang-ming philosophy.[77] The samurai background of the Christian leaders facilitated the assimilation of Confucian ideas into Christianity. After the Sino-Japanese War especially, Confucian ideas were adapted and advocated in the form of a Christian Bushido spirituality.[78] Worth mentioning in this context also is Ebina Danjō's attempt to develop a "Shinto Christianity," that is, a Christian spirituality that inherited and developed the best in Shintoism.[79]

The renewed interest in Japanese traditions also resulted in a growing appreciation of Buddhism. This was partly expressed as a recognition of Buddhism as an indispensable part of the Japanese culture, as suggested in the writings of Yokoi and Matsumura, or as an interest in the life of Sakyamuni Buddha, or the Buddhist masters of Japan. We have already seen how Western Buddhist studies were used as critical weapons against Japanese Buddhism;[80] but in the wake of the nationalistic reaction Christians also began to study Buddhism, stimulated by a genuine interest to learn about the spiritual roots of the Japanese people. Instruction in Buddhism was introduced in several Christian schools;[81] the growing number of articles and studies about Buddhism written by Christians in the

1890s is also a clear indication of such concern.[82] The Buddhist journal *Bukkyō shinundō* referred to this interest in 1890 with the following somewhat sarcastic comment:

> Even if it is under false pretences, the Christians give Sakyamuni the name of one who has discovered the truth. Whenever they preach about Christ, they unfailingly bring along their explanation of Sakyamuni as well, just as a parvenu strives to have social intercourse with men of rank, and avoids the contempt of others by concealing his own identity. The Buddhists are as uncompromising as ever, rejecting Jesus and not even letting him serve in a subordinate position, just as men of good birth detest outlaws.[83]

In some cases the interest in Buddhism led to a conscious effort to harmonize Christianity with Buddhist spirituality. This was even recognized as a specific theological current, characterized as Tōyō-ha, "The Oriental school," and was primarily expressed by a group related to *Jogaku zasshi*. In some cases it was also referred to as a "Buddhist Christianity"[84] or "Zen-flavored Christianity."[85] The most articulate advocates of such a Christian spirituality were Togawa Yasuie, who was characterized as a "Buddhist Christian," and Iwamoto Yoshiharu; both were said to stand for an "elegant Zen-like simplicity."[86]

The interest in Zen was perhaps not surprising, considering that Christians of samurai background, acquainted with Bushido, were not entirely unfamiliar with Zen spirituality. A detailed account of such a Christian rediscovery of meditation was recorded in *Jogaku zasshi* in 1892. The writer, Hoshino Tenchi (1862–1950), describes how, after a lapse of many years, he resumed the practice of Zen meditation under the guidance of Zen Master Dōkan in Kenshōji, a temple in Kamakura. He writes about his struggle with the *kōan* usually called "Jōshu's Mu," his interviews with the Master, and how he finally received a sort of Buddhist lay ordination as *koji*. "Even though I am a disciple of the illustrious Christ, I asked to be accepted as a Buddhist disciple and practice Zen," he wrote, arguing that it was possible for one who had "received the crown of Jesus" to have a Buddhist name as well. The practice of Zen was then warmly recommended to Christians, and particularly to pastors.[87] This was not a unique phenomenon, and did not seem to involve great problems, either among Buddhists or Christians.[88] A few years later, in 1898, another Christian, Yoshida Seitarō, who later distinguished himself as a prominent pastor, received three years of Zen training in Tenryūji, a famous temple in Kyoto, because he was "called by God" to do so.[89]

It is noteworthy that this Christian interest in Buddhism developed at a time when the relationship between the two religions was at its most aggressive stage and when Buddhism, moreover, according to the consensus of intellectual Japanese, was extremely corrupted. With their critical view of the actual state of Buddhism, it was natural that the Christians directed their interest in Buddhism toward the historical Buddha, famous Buddhist masters, Buddhist philosophy, or Zen Buddhism, which tended to keep aloof from the direct confrontation with Christianity.

It is left to our imagination to guess what the theological consequences of the program of Japanization would have been if the demand for a Japanese theology had developed at a time when the Buddhist-Christian relationship was more positive. One of the results might have been a more thorough application of Buddhist modes of thought in Christian theology.

LIBERAL THEOLOGY

The term "liberal theology"[90] is somewhat diffuse, but will be used about the theological development in Japan that was particularly influenced from two sources: American liberal theology, represented especially by the Congregational Andover Theological Seminary, and German liberal theology, represented by the so-called Tübingen school. Unitarianism and Universalism, which were often associated with liberal theology, will be treated separately. The aim of the following review is not to make a general analysis of liberal theology in Japan but to examine how it influenced the understanding of revelation and religion and how it affected Buddhist-Christian relations.

In spite of strenuous efforts of American missionaries to protect their Japanese colleagues from the influence of liberal trends, the new ideas were introduced toward the end of the 1880s, and soon made a decisive impact on Japanese churches. According to Cary, Western books and magazines were most important for the introduction of liberal theology, strongly supported by personal contact with liberal circles through visits and studies, primarily in the United States. It was noted that Japanese theologians who went abroad, "even when supported by help gained through the mediation of missionaries, took more interest in seeking interviews with noted advocates of new opinions than in pursuing their studies in the schools to which they had been sent"; and they returned as advocates of the new theology.[91] German liberal theology was introduced primarily by the missionaries of the so-called liberal mission, the Evangelical Protestant Missionary Society (Der allgemeine evangelisch-protestantische Missionsverein), which was based in Germany and Switzerland.

The Evangelical Protestant Missionary Society had been founded in 1884 by the Swiss pastor Ernst Buss, who wanted liberal Christianity to engage in missionary work on a declared liberal basis.[92] The mission stood for toleration toward other religions, and cooperated in India with

Brahmo Samaj, a syncretistic movement that aimed at the unification of Christianity and Hinduism.[93] The first missionary to Japan, Wilfred Spinner, who arrived in Kyoto in September 1885, had originally planned to go to India; he had studied Sanskrit and visited Max Müller in London, where he had also met his Japanese disciples, probably Nanjō Bunyū and Kasahara Kenju.[94] Thus Spinner himself, as well as Otto Schmiedel, who arrived in 1887, and several others of his colleagues were particularly interested in the study of comparative religion. The journal *Shinri* [Truth], which was published from 1889,[95] became an important channel for liberal ideas. In a characteristic way the mission advocated "reconciliation of Christianity with the modern view of the world by striving after an up-to-date expression of the eternal truth of the simple Gospel of Jesus, adapted at the same time to the particular needs of the Japanese."[96]

An article in the first issue of *Shinri* argued that truth was not a monopoly of the Christian faith, but was found in "innumerable ways." The study of philology, ethnology, and comparative religion had revealed that elements of truth were contained in every religion. In contrast to Unitarianism, however, the article never questioned the uniqueness of the Christian faith; strict loyalty to the Christian doctrine was emphasized, and Christianity was consistently held up as the culmination of religious development. The role of Christian mission was, according to *Shinri,* to stimulate the development of the Japanese people from polytheistic religion toward monotheism and the highest moral religion, Christianity.[97]

With this basic attitude, both the missionaries and their Japanese associates naturally regarded the study of religion as an important means for harmonizing Christianity with Japanese traditions. At the same time it was also regarded as a tool for Christian propagation, as it revealed "the vulnerable spots of the enemy." The study of religion was not regarded as a threat, but rather as an ally that provided a scientific demonstration of the superiority of Christianity.[98] German liberal theology thus combined the recognition of the positive value of other religions with an active missionary spirit and a critical view of many religious practices. Spinner criticized Buddhism, for instance, for its pessimistic world-view.[99] In a dialogue with the Buddhist activist Minoda Kakunen, he said that Buddha and other philosophers were propagating "the teaching of God," but in contrast to Christ they had a "poor knowledge of God." Minoda naturally reacted negatively and found Spinner's Christianity "weird," wondering whether it was really Christianity.[100] In spite of some confusion among Buddhists about the real character of German liberal theology, the effort to allot a positive role to the religious evolution of humankind generally facilitated the development of harmonious relations between the two religions.

Apart from the associates of the German and Swiss "liberal mission," Japanese Christians did not initially support the liberal ideas. Uemura Masahisa and Kozaki Hiromichi, who cooperated with Spinner in the beginning, found his attitudes vague and discontinued the cooperation in 1887 when they realized the character of his theology.[101] In a lecture on the inspiration of the Bible two years later, however, Kozaki introduced elements of the "higher criticism," a happening that is often referred to as the beginning of the liberal period of the Japanese churches.[102] Kozaki's views were criticized, but soon after liberal ideas were readily accepted and advocated by some of the most prominent Japanese Christians, such as Kanamori Tsūrin, Yokoi Tokio, Ōnishi Hajime, and Ebina Danjō.

Significantly, many of the protagonists of liberal theology were among the most fervent supporters of Japanization. The causal relationship is somewhat vague; did liberal theology facilitate Japanization, or vice versa? A clear-cut answer can hardly be given; it suffices to observe that the program of Japanization and the rejection of Western theology were combined with the rapid acceptance of Western liberal theology. This dual trend was observed and supported by Ōnishi Hajime as early as 1890;[103] and Yokoi Tokio commented that liberal theology was welcomed by the Japanese as a means to establish theological independence.[104] A closer look at Japanese theology in the early 1890s reveals that in spite of a clamorous program of Japanization, aiming at modifying Christianity to Buddhist and Confucian ideas, the actual theological content was thoroughly molded by liberal ideas. On the other hand, liberal theology introduced some basic attitudes that facilitated recognition and assimilation of other religious traditions.

With Yokoi Tokio as the main reference we shall see how Japanese liberal theology, along with the program of Japanization, introduced new attitudes toward other religions.[105] Yokoi shared the contemporary belief in evolution, and applied it with great optimism to the field of religion. He envisioned the development and improvement of the imported Western Christianity, and argued that its encounter with Japan introduced a new stage which would bring contemporary Christianity back to the original apostolic faith.[106] This process would include both an assimilation of national traditions and a rejection of the evil elements in religious practices and traditional theology. Characteristic also is his optimistic belief in the inherent goodness of the human mind; religion was conceived as the sympathetic response of man's conscience and deepest aspirations.[107] He shared the common concern of liberal theologians to harmonize and adapt Christianity to the modern spirit and to traditional Japanese values.

Yokoi advocated consistently that the central concern in Christianity was not doctrines, asceticism, worship, or rituals, but religious and ethical life.[108] Theology would change according to various circumstances, but apostolic Christianity stood for the "unchangeable fact of religion,"[109] the most simple, ordinary, unique Way" of benevolence and love *(jin* or *jin'ai).*[110] The ultimate meaning of religion was to "abandon selfishness and practice the Way of benevolence, and quietly entrust one's life to Heaven" and to "return to the most simple and humble mind."[111]

With his weakening of the doctrinal aspect of Christianity and his emphasis on benevolence and love, moral and religious life, Yokoi inevitably had to acknowledge similar ideas in other religions,[112] and that the true light had also enlightened the hearts of Socrates, Sakyamuni, and Confucius who, with the sages of all ages, had grasped the ultimate meaning of religion.[113] On the other hand, he maintained his belief in the superiority of Christianity and the uniqueness of Christ. The difference between religions was not primarily to be found on the theoretical or doctrinal level; it was not a difference in their essential character, but in degree. All religions contained revealed truth, but only Christianity represented the highest development. As Moses had guided his people toward Christ, Buddha and Confucius were also leading toward him. Expressed in poetical language, other religions were like stars shining in the night, while Christianity was like the bright autumn moon.[114] Yokoi was thus convinced about the uniqueness of Christ, describing him as the "perfect man," the unsurpassed "embodiment of benevolence and love." He acknowledged that other religions knew the ideals; but Christ manifested in his life directly the unsophisticated way of man, and was still working as a great influence and inspiration in the world.[115] Truth was revealed partially in other religions, while Christianity was based on the historic fact of Jesus in whom God's heart had been revealed. Being a true man in his words and deeds, his life was an expression of the words and deeds of God; in him God and man became one.[116] On this point Yokoi criticized the Unitarians with whom he was often associated; too concerned with a complicated philosophy, according to his opinion, they failed to see the simplicity of Christian life, revealed as a historic fact in the life of Jesus.[117] With a variety of expressions Yokoi thus maintained the uniqueness of Christianity. He concluded that Christianity was the "way of salvation" coming from God, while other religions were "ways of [spiritual] cultivation" based on human efforts. "Christianity comes from Heaven and belongs to Heaven; other religions come from the earth and belong to the earth."[118]

In spite of Yokoi's personal style and some expressions that reveal Confucian and, perhaps, Buddhist influence,[119] he hardly produced more than a Japanese variety of a common pattern of liberal theology. As such he is not particularly interesting. As representative of Japanese theology in the 1890s, however, he stood for a movement that in a significant way laid the theological foundation for a reconciliation with the indigenous traditions.

In short, the positive contribution of liberal theology was, in this context, its attempt to recognize Japanese traditions and assimilate them into a comprehensive understanding of Christian faith. It can be questioned whether or not his attempt was successful; but liberal theology was certainly a significant factor for establishing a Japanese Christian identity and a positive relationship to other religions. On the other hand, some of the negative elements should not be forgotten. The criticism of orthodox Christianity contributed to the cooling off of faith, and thus drained the churches of both personnel and vitality; many, including some of the protagonists of liberal theology, eventually left the church. And it facilitated compromise with reactionary forces, introducing an active support of nationalism and of the burgeoning Japanese imperialism.[120]

UNITARIANISM

Unitarianism was officially introduced into Japan in 1887, with the arrival of Arthur May Knapp, who was sent by the American Unitarian Association.[121] Rather than calling himself a missionary, Knapp preferred to be regarded as an "envoy" or "ambassador" who had come to "express the sympathy of the Unitarians of America for progressive religious movements in Japan, and give all necessary information to the leaders of religious thought and action in that country."[122] At that time the Unitarian principles were already quite well known in Japan. Unitarianism had been unofficially introduced in the 1870s, in a translation of *Chambers's Encyclopaedia*.[123] The first advocate of Unitarian principles was probably Yano Fumio, a disciple of Fukuzawa Yukichi and editor of the prestigious newspaper *Yūbin hōchi shinbun*. He introduced Unitarianism in various publications in 1886, suggesting that Japan needed such a moral religion, and advocating the adoption of Unitarianism as state religion.[124] The Unitarian mission was the result of urgent invitations sent by prominent Japanese leaders, and was from the very beginning met with sympathy and interest in intellectual circles.[125] Both Yano and Fukuzawa played vital roles in preparing for the arrival of Knapp in 1887. Fukuzawa's son, Ichitarō, attended Knapp's farewell party in Boston, and wrote later that Japan had to choose between a totally reformed Buddhism or Christianity, indicating that Unitarianism would be the best choice.[126] Fukuzawa Yukichi supported the Unitarians in many ways, for example, through personal friendship with Knapp and by giving Knapp and other American and British Unitarians opportunities to teach at his school, Keiō Gijuku. In addition to Fukuzawa and Yano, a number of prominent scholars and leaders lent their support to Unitarianism; among this group of supporters were Katō Hiroyuki, Toyama Masakazu,

Nakamura Keiu, Kaneko Kentarō, and Sugiura Jūgō.[127] As we shall see later, a number of Buddhists also welcomed Unitarianism.[128]

Knapp left Japan permanently as early as 1890, but the Unitarian mission had been firmly established by then. It was continued under the leadership of Clay MacCauley, who arrived in Japan in 1889, accompanied by Kanda Saichirō, who became one of the Japanese leaders of Unitarianism. The work was supported by various foreign teachers of Keiō Gijuku, but most of them left after a short time.[129] A number of Japanese Christians, mainly of Congregational background, were also associated with the work, and so were several Buddhists.

In 1890 the Unitarians began to publish a journal with the sectarian name *Yuniterian* [Unitarian], which was changed to *Shūkyō* [Religion] in 1891. With their growing influence they gradually dominated the prestigious journal *Rikugō zasshi,* which in 1898 finally was merged with *Shūkyō* and published by the Unitarians. Emphasizing education, they held courses on religion, ethics, and social science. In 1891 the courses were organized as the School of Liberal Theology (Jiyū Shingakkō), later renamed the School for Advanced Learning (Senshin Gakuin). The school was closed in 1895, but for a few years it made a great impact on religious and intellectual circles, under the leadership of Ōnishi Hajime as dean and Kishimoto Nobuta as secretary. The Unitarian influence was further advanced through lectures at the headquarters, in a hall called Unity Hall (Yuiitsukan); through a publishing department; and through the so-called Post Office Mission, which specialized in propagation through correspondence.[130]

After a few years of successful expansion, during which Unitarianism exercised a great influence in intellectual circles, it gradually entered a period of stagnation. Clay MacCauley left Japan in 1900, and the work continued under the leadership of Kanda Saichirō and Saiji Jitsunen.[131] By 1910 the Unitarian Association had lost its attraction; it never again exercised any influence worth mentioning. In spite of the short duration of the Unitarian influence, however, it played a vital role in Buddhist-Christian relations in the 1890s. The aim of the following examination is to present some of the basic characteristics of Unitarianism in Japan, including its doctrinal profile and its attitude to other religions and to orthodox Christianity; and further to describe its actual relations with Buddhist groups and individuals.

"The Sympathy of Religions." Before his departure from Boston in 1887 Arthur May Knapp made a characteristic statement about the purpose of his travel to Japan: "We come not to convert but to confer."[132] The idea was further elaborated on various occasions in Japan, where Knapp and his colleagues consistently emphasized that their purpose differed from the aims of other missionary societies.

The errand of Unitarianism to Japan is based upon the now familiar idea of the sympathy of religions. With the conviction that we are messengers of distinctive and valuable truths which have not been emphasized, and that, in return, there is much in your faith and life which to our harm we have not emphasized, receive us not as theological propagandists, but as messengers of the new gospel of human brotherhood in the religious life of man.[133]

Knapp refused to regard other religions as false in contrast to Christianity as the truth, and he did not want to use "an offensive word like 'heathen.' " The aim of the mission was not to obtain converts, but to expand friendship, he said, not to "swallow up" other religions, but to "study them and express sympathy with them."[134] That Knapp's attitude was representative can be seen from Clay MacCauley's record of Unitarian viewpoints.

Rev. H. W. Hawkes, the earnest English volunteer to our work, describes the Unitarian aim in these words;—"We seek to build broader foundations than creed or sect; to demonstrate reason in religion, science in theology, and all things in God. This is grander than any denominational triumph." Rev. W. I. Lawrance, whose devoted and all too brief service in the Mission is well remembered in Tokyo, wrote that "our work in Japan marks a new departure in missions." We "bear the simple gospel of fellowship, and character. We not only acknowledge with frankness, but accept with gratitude, all that is true and uplifting in the faiths already there. We hold up to them pure theism and the deep-rooted optimism of Christianity. Our method is based on the sympathy of religions." Also, that my own declarations in the establishment of the Mission may appear as part of this record, I recall this passage from a published answer to an inquiry made to me by a Buddhist priest: "Unitarianism has not come to Japan to destroy, but to fulfil. Unitarianism is here to set men free, or rather to help the free minds of Japan to set all minds free; and to hasten the coming in the world, as far as may be, of the sublime empire of love and righteousness, which will at last make of Humanity a true Brotherhood under the care of the infinite and eternal God, our Father."[135]

Knapp summarized his aims in three points: (1) to study the religious situation among the intellectual class of Japan, (2) to introduce American liberal ideas to the intellectuals, and (3) to show these a form of Christianity that harmonizes with liberal ideas and as far as possible obtain their cooperation.[136] These aims reveal the limitation of the Unitarian idea of the sympathy of religions and religious cooperation. Even though Unitarianism was important for the development of the study of religion and religious cooperation in Japan, Knapp was not concerned about the study of Japanese religions as such, but was mainly interested in "the religious situation among the intellectual class," that is, liberal religious trends that could be stimulated and challenged by Unitarianism. As for religious cooperation, he was primarily interested in cooperation with "progressive religious movements"; the point was "to discover, to encourage and to co-operate with any religious association or group of persons, or with individuals, irrespective of form of religious sect or personal belief, that might wish to know of the mature and advanced thought in Christendom about man's higher, or spiritual problems or interests."[137] Thus the Unitarian idea of the sympathy of religions was limited to sympathetic trends in other religions. The sympathy was accompanied by an obvious disdain of old-fashioned religion, which was characterized as "superstition or traditional dogmas" or "the ancient sage and priestlore imported from India and China."[138] In the words of Clay MacCauley, Unitarianism should be "a movement springing out of Christianity, which seeks to become the representative religious force of the present age."[139] The sympathy of religions was a part of this program.

Rejection of Orthodox Christianity. The Unitarian emphasis on the sympathy of religions went along with an extremely critical attitude to orthodox forms of Christianity. The Unitarian doctrine emphasized a radical monotheism and rejected traditional trinitarian Christianity: Christ was regarded merely as a man, honored as the "superior teacher" who guides man in his religious progress; but he was not divine and was not to be the object of worship. A number of other traditional orthodox doctrines were also rejected, such as the doctrine of original sin and man's total depravity, the doctrine of atonement, hell, and the infallibility of the Bible.[140]

Several of the doctrines rejected by Unitarianism had been the main targets of Buddhist polemics, and it was quite natural for Buddhists to sympathize with the rejection of these in the name of reason.[141] Moreover, the negation of the divinity of Christ enabled the Unitarians to recognize other religious prophets and masters on an equal level with Christ. According to MacCauley, the law of love was "taught and shown in the lives of the Christ and his fellow-prophets."[142] It was thus quite natural that Buddha's birthday was celebrated on April 8, in keeping with a tradition that had recently been revived by Buddhist youth, with lectures and speeches at the Unitarian Unity Hall.[143] According to some Buddhists, the monotheistic faith in God as creator was the only point that distinguished Unitarianism from Buddhism.[144]

The Unitarian views were introduced into Japan at a time when traditional dogmas were losing ground. Clay MacCauley described the decay of orthodox doctrines as "signs of promise" in Japan.[145] Not only was orthodox theology attacked, but traditional missionary work and methods were denounced as well, and the Unitarian activity was hence felt as a painful betrayal of traditional Christianity. A German "liberal" missionary noted that it seemed as if Unitarianism was "more friendly to Buddhists than to Christians"; an observer who later joined Unitarianism wrote, "Strange to say, the Unitarianism of Japan shows a strong sympathy towards Buddhism, while it shows a strong hostile feeling towards its brother sects of Christianity."[146] Defending orthodox Christianity, Takahashi Gorō observed critically that Buddhists supported Unitarianism because it had "the negative benefit of neutralizing the evil effects of Christianity" and commented that Unitarianism had become "the spearhead of Buddhist attack" on orthodox Christianity.[147] Against such views the Unitarians stressed that Unitarianism was not in opposition to true Christianity, but "definitely against orthodox Christianity."[148]

The tolerant and inclusive character of Unitarian relations to other faiths, in addition to its attempt to dissociate itself from orthodox Christianity and traditional missionary methods, naturally facilitated the acceptance of Unitarianism among the Japanese public, and especially among the intellectuals.

The Religion of the "Modern Spirit." More important than the rejection of orthodox views was the impact some of the Unitarian principles and doctrines made in religious circles; in many cases they were regarded as the very basis of liberal religion. The Unitarian principles were defined positively in three points, representing basis, method, and purpose: (1) Unitarianism is not based upon the authority of tradition but on rational and scientific truth; (2) its method is free inquiry; (3) its purpose is to promote the highest moral development of the individual and of society.[149] Some further comments will help us to recognize the influence of these principles in religious circles in the 1890s.

The Unitarian representatives in Japan emphasized untiringly the rational and scientific basis of religious faith. According to MacCauley, they wanted to attract "men freed from superstition or traditional dogmas," but they did not claim Unitarianism to be "the only religious movement that works by rational and scientific methods, or accepts for religious use the results of these methods." Among the religious movements influenced by the "modern spirit," however, only Unitarianism had "submitted itself without reserve to the direction of this 'spirit.' " Rejecting both agnostic utilitarianism and orthodox Christianity, he argued that "Rationalized Religion only can really serve the Japanese people." Other characteristic expressions have already been mentioned, such as "reason in religion, science in theology, and all things in God," and "pure theism and the deep-rooted optimism of Christianity." MacCauley summarized the Unitarian understanding of "pure religion" in the following way:

By "pure religion" therefore Unitarians mean: (1) worship of God as infinite and eternal Source, Power, Life, Guide, and Ruler of the Universe; (2) following the life exemplified by the world's spiritual teachers, saints, and benefactors, among whom we reverence Jesus Christ as Leader; (3) obedience to moral law, however made known; (4) endeavor to realize a perfect Brotherhood of Mankind; (5) cherishing a hope of immortal life.[150]

The basic method of Unitarianism, defined as free inquiry, involved a critical examination of doctrinal traditions and scriptures; everything opposed to reason and scientific knowledge was to be rejected. The emphasis on free inquiry naturally appealed to intellectual circles, strengthened critical and liberal trends within the churches, and made a great impact in Buddhist circles as well.

As for moral development, the emphasis seemed to be put equally on both "moral" and "development." Morality was regarded as the central expression of religious life, and the contemporary belief in evolution inclined Unitarianism toward an optimistic expectation of the moral development of mankind. God was seen as the one whose "infinite power, wisdom, and compassion guides the universe through the process of natural development." Human beings were the children of God because they represented "the noblest result of development," and Christ was the "supreme teacher" who contributed to the religious development of mankind.[151] Rejecting orthodox views on man's total depravity, Knapp wanted to base Unitarianism on "the scientific truth about the evolution and development of man."[152]

The Unitarian movement regarded itself as a central force in the moral development on the individual as well as on the social level. The Unitarian journal, Shūkyō, was published in order to advance "the welfare of the people of Japan, by making known to them the best and most practical results of social sciences in the largest comprehension of the term, . . . that it may emphasize the conclusions of the profoundest ethical research." The School for Advanced Learning was described as an institution in which "faculty and students could seek a true Theology and the fundamental principles of Morality and of Social Order."[153]

With its emphasis on reason, free inquiry, and moral development, and with its critical attitude to "all effete ideas and doctrines,"[154] Unitarianism had little understanding of the emotional aspects of religion. It tended to be one-sidedly intellectual and philosophical, and hardly appealed outside the limited circle of intellectuals and scholars. In many cases Unitarianism was not even regarded as a religion, or it was described as a "religion of philosophers."[155] This was a period, however, when many Buddhist intellectuals were searching for new approaches in order to reform Buddhism; and a number of them were attracted to Unitarianism exactly because it programmatically and consistently wanted to submit itself to the "modern spirit."

Unitarianism and Buddhism. With their emphasis on dialogue and cooperation with progressive religious movements in Japan, the Unitarian representatives were naturally interested in establishing a positive relationship with Buddhism. In an article in *Yuniterian* in 1890, entitled "Similarity and Divergence between Unitarianism and Buddhism," Arthur May Knapp stated that while Unitarianism was in sympathy with orthodox Christianity in moral questions, intellectually it was much closer to Buddhism. Even though Unitarianism was unrelated to Buddhism in its origin, "the old faith of the East" and "the new faith of the West" were spiritually "brothers of the same family" and should help each other intellectually and spiritually.[156]

Without too keen a critical sense Knapp enumerated five points of similarity between Unitarianism and Buddhism: (1) In contrast to traditional belief in creation as a historical fact, both Unitarianism and Buddhism conceived of creation as a continuous process without beginning or end. (2) In contrast to the orthodox Christian belief in man's soul as something given to man at birth, Unitarianism and Buddhism regarded the soul or the spirit as something eternal, as a part of God. (3) Both Unitarianism and Buddhism were based on the principle of recompense or *karma*. (4) While both Unitarians and Buddhists honored their founders as teachers of divine life, neither regarded them as absolute, as there were Buddhas apart from Sakyamuni and children of God apart from the Christ. (5) Neither Buddhism nor Unitarianism was based on old traditions or tales, but on human reason and natural principles.[157] Knapp then enumerated what he regarded as the major differences: (1) Unitarianism represented a scientific faith in God, while the Buddhist idea of God was based on ancient philosophy;[158] (2) Buddhism was pessimistic and emphasized the dark side of life, while Unitarianism stressed the bright side of human life; (3) Unitarianism was optimistic in its emphasis on vigorous activity in the world, while Buddhism was pessimistic and passive; (4) in contrast to Buddhism, Unitarianism was a belief in the constant progress and development according to natural laws. Against this background, Knapp argued that Unitarianism could challenge Buddhism, stimulate a development toward a more affirmative and active role in the present world, and thus renew the power and influence of Buddhism.[159]

Responding to Knapp's views, Takahashi Gorō criticized the ill-advised "alliance between Unitarianism and Buddhism," alleging that the Unitarians were "flattering and fawning upon the Buddhists, doubting, appealing, begging, and praying, asking for pity, and soliciting for patronage." He especially questioned Knapp's hope for a compromise between Buddhist atheism and Christian monotheism, indicating that Knapp lacked a basic understanding of Buddhist principles.[160] Knapp replied that he had never envisioned a Unitarian "alliance" with Buddhism, but merely wanted to express his sympathy with Buddhism; he further argued that his view was shared by Yokoi Tokio, who held that Christianity must "stand on Confucian and Buddhist civilization."[161]

On the other side, many Buddhists responded positively to Knapp's approach,[162] partly because, as we have seen, Unitarianism, rather than being regarded as a Christian denomination, was seen as a representative of the "modern spirit" which threatened traditional Christianity and stimulated progressive ideas. In an article entitled "Unitarianism and the Indigenous Religions of Our Country," Unitarianism was described as "dew and rain from heaven" which could stimulate reform and renewal of Shinto, Confucianism, and Buddhism.[163] Another article referred to the several hundred potential Buddhist reformers in Japan and suggested the pioneer role of Unitarianism by greeting its representatives as "our guides."[164] According to MacCauley, the name "Unitarian" was "attached to religious liberals, whatever their sectarian associations, . . . A Christian, a Buddhist, a Shintoist, a Confucian, need but make himself now a prophet of the new day for the mind and soul, to receive, sooner or later, the name we bear."[165]

The Buddhists not only sympathized with Unitarian principles; a number of them were actually closely associated with the Unitarian movement and even became members of the Unitarian Association. MacCauley reported that among thirty-two students enrolled in the School of Advanced Learning in one year, seventeen were Buddhist priests, "belonging to the enlarging liberal parties in the sects; all the students men of mature years, who will occupy places of greater or less prominence in education, in letters, or in the Church hereafter."[166]

Two of the most prominent Buddhist reformers, Ōuchi Seiran and Nakanishi Ushio, were closely associated with Unitarianism; Ōuchi was a lecturer at the Unitarian School of Advanced Learning, and contributed frequently to *Yuniterian,* later *Shūkyō;* Nakanishi even worked as editor of the journal, in addition to lecturing.[167] Ōuchi stressed that he could not accept the monotheistic belief of Unitarianism,[168] but Nakanishi argued that Unitarianism and Buddhism were basically identical. Referring to pantheistic tendencies in Unitarianism, he concluded that the Unitarian ideas would be fulfilled in Buddhism.[169] Hirai Kinzō, who was described by MacCauley as a leader among the progressive Buddhists as well as "one of Japan's most ardent and influential Unitarians,"[170] even proclaimed that he believed in "the existence of God."[171] From the Unitarian point of view, the Buddhist reformers were regarded as "Buddhist Theists," or they were said to represent an "optimistic pantheism" that would reach its fulfillment in "rationalized Christianity," or in the "larger faith and life" of Unitarianism.[172] The Buddhist reformers, however, never abandoned their basic Buddhist standpoint, but rather adapted Unitarian principles to their Buddhist ideas. Thus the close relationship between Unitarianism and Buddhism developed on a somewhat vague basis of concord and harmony which changed into discord and disruption of relationships when the differences were finally brought to light.

Before the problematic relationship between Unitarianism and Buddhism is further commented on, a brief account should be made of the activity of Saji Jitsunen (1856–?), who was a noteworthy example of a Buddhist-Unitarian compromise. Without abandoning his Buddhist ideas, Saji was active as a Unitarian leader and propagator for nearly two decades. He was the second son of a Buddhist priest belonging to the Ōtani sect of Shin Buddhism, and became a priest to carry on the family tradition after his brother died. He was educated and trained at the school of the head temple, Higashi Honganji, and worked there until 1883, when he decided to propagate Buddhism independently. The decision was influenced by Ōuchi Seiran, whom he had met in 1882. In close cooperation with Ōuchi he engaged in Buddhist propagation all over the country. According to Saji himself, he and Ōuchi were recognized as the two most prominent Buddhist speakers in Japan at that time.[173] His activity included a rather harsh criticism of Christianity.[174] He refused to regard Jesus as even a sage, denoting him as far inferior not only to the Buddha, but to Confucius and Mencius. He also denounced the Christians for calling Buddhism "idol worship," even though Christianity itself often deteriorated to "idol worship" of the trinity, the angels, Mary, or the cross.[175] When Ōuchi in 1889 founded Sonnō Hōbutsu Daidōdan in order to oppose Christianity, Saji was one of the promoters, and worked as secretary of the association. He also worked at the Buddhist Higher Normal School in Tokyo, a school supported by various Buddhist sects.[176] When the school was closed around 1890 because of lack of support, he returned to his home in the province of Harima, the present Hyogo Prefecture, but abandoned the priestly work of his temple and became, according to himself, a *rōnin,* that is, a free man without any master, a term originally used for masterless samurai. He then started a journal that specialized in publishing lectures delivered at the Higher Normal School, a work that gave him a good income until it was concluded in August 1892. Exactly at that time he was urged by Clay MacCauley, through Kanda Saichirō, to work for the Unitarian Association. He accepted the offer, and began seventeen years of active work for Unitarianism.[177]

Saji's relation to Christianity and Unitarianism, however, had started before he entered the Unitarian Association in 1892. He had always had a low regard for orthodox Christianity and recalled later with embarrassment the missionary books about Buddhism and the aggressive conflict between Doshisha students and young Shin Buddhist priests in Kyoto around 1883–1884. He found the struggle superficial, lacking in mutual respect and knowledge. To increase his own knowledge of Christianity he had approached the Orthodox Church in 1882 and asked to be enrolled in its seminary as a student. He was refused on the grounds that the theological education aimed at priesthood, but he was allowed to study the Orthodox faith privately with a priest. According to Saji himself, he pursued the study of Christianity in order to find out whether it was as superficial as his Buddhist colleagues said. This finally led him to Unitarianism, which he knew was somewhat different from "commonplace Christianity," and he was deeply impressed when, in 1889, he was introduced to Knapp and MacCauley, with Kanda Saichirō as interpreter. Hearing about their frank rejection of traditional dogmas, and, further, about the Unitarian principles of rationality, free inquiry, and moral progress, he felt that for the first time he had been able to harmonize faith and reason. After that he attended Unitarian meetings quite frequently, in spite of some criticism from Buddhist circles. He even agreed to become a member of the organizing committee of the Unitarian Association in 1889, well aware that his fame as a Buddhist propagator would be used by the Unitarians for their own purposes. Thus when Saji was employed by the Unitarian Association in 1892, he had already been acquainted with Unitarian circles for three years.[178]

In a time of increasing animosity between Christianity and Buddhism it was not surprising that the Buddhists resented Saji's "defection" from Buddhist propagation. Saji himself argued that it was merely a nominal transfer from Buddhism to Unitarianism and that he had not abandoned his Buddhist faith. His move was, nevertheless, denounced as "high treason," and the priests from Higashi Honganji in particular slandered him as "a devil" or "a heretic." He was harassed and persecuted in various ways, and even attacked by a group of young Buddhists who beat him with clubs. It was rumored that he had become "a lanternbearer for the Unitarians" for the sake of money and fame, a charge he repeatedly rejected.[179]

Saji's main duty was to lecture in the Unitarian theological school, teaching religion—especially Buddhism and Confucianism—ethics, philosophy, and sociology. Further, he alone was in charge of the weekly Sunday lectures which, according to himself, became increasingly popular; in a few years the attendance increased from 20–30 to 150–200. It should be mentioned in this context that Saji for a period around 1899 invited a number of famous orators, Buddhist and Shinto priests, and educators to lecture and thus give his audience a wider perspective on religion, ethics, and philosophy.[180] He was also in sympathy with socialist ideas, and opened the Unity Hall for study meetings about socialism, to which such people as Kōtoku Shūsui, Sakai Toshihiko, Murai Tomoyoshi, and Abe Isoo gathered.[181] This relationship was broken after a while because of disagreements about financial matters. Saji served for many years as president of the Unitarian Association, and shared the leadership with Kanda Saichirō when MacCauley left Japan in 1900. In 1909 Saji left the association because of a conflict with Kanda.[182]

Saji maintained that his work for Unitarianism did not imply a break with his Buddhist faith. Even though he criticized orthodox Buddhism, denouncing it for its destructive influence on the nation and finding it incompatible with reason,[183] he was deeply influenced by Buddhist thinking. In his lectures he referred frequently to Buddhism and Confucianism; Christian ideas seemed rather peripheral.[184] His religious view was characterized by a radical rationalism, according to which differences between Buddhism and Christianity became insignificant. The point was not whether religious devotion was directed toward Amida Buddha or God, Sakyamuni or Jesus, he said, but whether it stimulated the development toward a perfect morality.[185] Saji's religion could thus be characterized as Unitarianism with Buddhist coloring, or Buddhism influenced by Unitarianism.

A closer look at Saji's religious outlook reveals that, in spite of his Buddhist background and Unitarian ideas, the religious element was more insignificant than for many of his Unitarian colleagues. He called for a development from "religious religion," which he identified with doctrinal faith and superstition, toward an "ethical religion," in which traditional religious elements would disappear.[186] When it came to social problems, Saji found it irrelevant to ask about monotheism, atheism, pantheism, and other doctrinal differences. "There is no time for engaging in arid theoretical struggles. Any religion or sect will do. . . . I earnestly desire that all religions will unite in order to work for the sake of these social problems."[187] Thus, in Saji's "Buddhist" Unitarianism the religious elements were of secondary importance; his real concerns were social and political issues.

Returning to the problems involved in the relationship between Buddhism and Unitarianism, it should be noted that the contact between Buddhists and Unitarians was also accompanied by an inherent tension. From the very outset Knapp and his colleagues had maintained that the purpose of religious cooperation was to stimulate progressive trends within Buddhism, and they obviously expected a development toward "rationalized Christianity." In spite of a radical relativization of the role of Christ, they still regarded Christ as the supreme realization of man's religious ideals.[188] Unitarianism was the only genuine Christianity, called to solve the problems of modern Japan. MacCauley expected an increasing struggle between Buddhism and Christianity about the religious leadership of Japan. He also hoped that the effort of other Christians in Japan to "win the nation to a true theism" would bring about "the permanent solution of the problem of religion in the far East."

> The greater conflict of Buddhism with Christianity is yet to come. Evidently Buddhism shows rapid renewal of strength. . . . If, then, Christianity, voicing man's faith in the eternal Fatherhood of God, showing forth the universal Brotherhood of Mankind, and supporting hope in eternal life for each human soul, is placed over against Buddhism, telling of man's despair before "the evil of conscious existence," searching for an "enlightenment" by which eternal unconsciousness for each human mind is gained, it is hardly to be doubted, though the followers of both the Christ and the Buddha show their faiths daily in justice, mercy, love, and piety, that the cause of the Christian will triumph. Christian faith, sustained by man's enlarging knowledge, we may be confident, will ultimately bear the victory in "the Mikado's land."[189]

Comparing the above quotation with the view of the "Buddhist" Unitarians who found in Unitarianism a preparatory stage for the development toward Buddhism, the latent tension between "Buddhist" and "Christian" Unitarians stands out in relief. The ambiguous character of Unitarianism had enabled a number of Buddhists to become members of the Unitarian Association or to advocate Unitarian principles, but the gradual clarification of the basically Christian character of Unitarianism became problematic for the Buddhist members. Among others, Nakanishi Ushio withdrew his membership in 1895, explaining that he had entered the Unitarian Association because he regarded Unitarianism as a basis for a future religious unification. When he finally understood that Unitarianism was merely one stage in the evolution of orthodox Christianity, the inevitable conclusion was that he, as a Buddhist, would have to give up his membership. MacCauley responded by distinguishing between "Unitarian believers" *(Yuniterian kyōto)* and "Unitarian sympathizers" *(Yuniterian kyōyū,* literally, "friends of Unitarianism"), indicating that the Buddhists were welcome as "sympathizers." Nakanishi agreed to continue to teach at the School for Advanced Learning, but he resigned his position as editor of *Shūkyō*.[190] According to *Dentō,* he eventually resigned from the school as well; and Ōuchi Seiran, who had also been closely associated with Unitarianism, refused to fill the vacancy.[191]

Along with the growing tension and conflict with Buddhists who had been closely associated with Unitarianism, even stronger criticism was raised by Buddhists who resented the vague character of Unitarianism and its claim to be the representative religious force of the modern age. A critic said in a discussion with Knapp that Unitarianism was superficial and opportunistic, and "as slippery as an eel."[192] A Buddhist journal wrote: "Unitarianism is most to be feared, because, while it is near to Buddhism in objecting to Christ's deity, and in its sympathy with the idea of evolution in Humanity, it is still but Christianity colored by science. Already Orthodox Christianity fears it, and now it has begun to encroach upon the Buddhist field."[193]

Thus the effort to initiate dialogue and cooperation with Buddhism on the basis of the harmony of religions was far more complicated than the Unitarians had imagined. In spite of such problems and apprehensions among many Buddhists that the Unitarians were encroaching upon the Buddhist field, however, there is no doubt that Unitarianism made a major contribution to the development of friendly relations between Buddhists and Christians in the 1890s. Its contribution to the study of comparative religion, and the close relationship between Unitarianism and the New Buddhism will be examined below.

CHAPTER TWELVE

The New Buddhism

Buddhists, be bold! The Buddhists of the Meiji period should not cause the suppuration of the tumor for fear of the short pain of operation!

Furukawa Rōsen, Buddhist reformer

THE BUDDHIST WORLD went through a period of upheaval and radical change in the 1890s. Even though the dominant trend of Buddhism identified itself with the nationalistic reaction and sought to restore the power and influence of Buddhism by appealing to traditional privileges, a number of Buddhists understood that a simple return to the past would not do. They realized that traditional Buddhism had neither been able to conquer Christianity nor to cope with the new situation; they started to reexamine traditional attitudes and practices, and searched for new approaches to the rapidly changing Japanese society. In the following examination of the search for a new mode of Buddhism, special attention will be given to the Christian influence on Buddhist ideas of reform; and some additional material will be included about a few progressive reformers and reform movements for whom the relations to Christianity became a conspicuous factor in their attempt to reform Buddhism.

THE CONCEPT OF A NEW BUDDHISM

The term "New Buddhism" (shin Bukkyō) is often reserved as an epithet for the radical Buddhism of Furukawa Rōsen and his supporters and successors, who propagated their ideas about a New Buddhism mainly in the journals Bukkyō [Buddhism] and Shin Bukkyō [The New Buddhism]. Even though Furukawa became the unchallenged leader of a whole generation of progressive Buddhists, however, the concept of a New Buddhism was not created by Furukawa; it was in general use before he began to advocate his own ideas. The concept will be used more generally as an epithet for various Buddhist movements that, from the late 1880s, advocated a radical reformation of traditional Buddhism and introduced a more or less critical relationship to the Buddhist establishment, the so-called Old Buddhism. Because these movements were dominated by young and restless Buddhist reformers, they were often just referred to as "the young Buddhists" *(seinen Bukkyōto).*[1]

The reform zeal of the young Buddhists cannot be explained as merely a natural concern for renewal of traditional Buddhism; both the concept and the program of the New Buddhism must be understood against the background of the sixteenth century Protestant Reformation, or rather, the popular image of the Reformation in Japan. Popular Japanese terms for Roman Catholicism and Protestantism are *kyū-kyō* and *shin-kyō,* that is, the "Old Doctrine" and the "New Doctrine."[2] And it was not just coincidental that Japanese Buddhists adopted a similar set of terms, *kyū Bukkyō* and *shin Bukkyō,* "Old Buddhism" and "New Buddhism," when they advocated the need for a Buddhist reformation.[3]

The intimate relationship between the Reformation and Buddhist reform movements was quite obvious in the writings of the first advocates of a New Buddhism, Mizutani Jinkai in his *Shin Bukkyō* [The new Buddhism] in 1888 and Nakanishi Ushio in *Shūkyō kakumeiron* [On religious revolution] in 1889 and *Shin Bukkyōron* [On the new Buddhism] in 1892.[4] Mizutani (1836–1896) was a highly respected priest belonging to Tendai Buddhism. He criticized Buddhist decay and advocated the moral and spiritual reform of Buddhism, and was hence called a "Japanese Luther." Referring to Luther's indomitable spirit and self-sacrificing work for the sake of a reformation of the Roman Catholic "Old Doctrine," one of Mizutani's associates wrote: "Now, as we carefully observe the condition of Buddhism in our country, it not only resembles the former Roman Catholicism, but its abuses are even more serious. Thus I am always lamenting that if no Luther appears in Buddhism now, its future can only be bound for destruction." However, he wrote, the "Buddhist Luther," Mizutani Jinkai, had appeared to save Buddhism from decay and annihilation.[5]

Nakanishi Ushio (1859–1930) also regarded the New Buddhism as a reform similar to the Reformation. While Mizutani, in spite of his preaching about the New Buddhism, stood for rather traditional views, Nakanishi attempted to relate Buddhism to modern ideas and wanted to find a place for Buddhism in the evolutionary history of humankind. He was critical of orthodox Christianity, but he regarded the Reformation as one of the central events in the religious evolution. A whole chapter of *Shūkyō kakumeiron* was devoted to a discussion of the Reformation, which became the model and central reference point for his ideas of Buddhist reform. As the Reformation proclaimed the "New Doctrine" in opposition to the evils of the Catholic "Old Doctrine," Nakanishi claimed that the New Buddhism would be built upon the ruins of the old.[6]

Protestantism also influenced other aspects of the Buddhist reform movements. Preliminarily, it can be concluded that the very concept of a New Buddhism was formed by the popular image of the Reformation, the model for a religious renewal that involved a radical rejection of the old.

CHRISTIANITY AS CHALLENGE AND MODEL

Buddhist reform movements at the end of the 1880s and in the 1890s were characterized by a deep sense of crisis. Apprehensions about Christian expansion were combined with a desperate feeling of Buddhist decay and powerlessness. The immediate reaction was to appeal to nationalistic sentiments in order to resist the threatening presence of Christianity. The sense of crisis, however, did not lead exclusively to anti-Christian attitudes. Or rather, the reform zeal that accompanied the realization of Buddhist decay and Christian strength often included a hesitating or grudging recognition that Christianity was a real challenge. A writer in the Buddhist journal *Shimei yoka* suggested, for instance, that rather than regarding Christianity as the enemy of Buddhism, Buddhists should acknowledge their debt of gratitude to Christianity as a "stimulant" for a corrupt Buddhism.[7] Such a positive attitude was not yet common in the late 1880s when the article was written, but few, if any, representative Buddhists failed to realize that Christianity could only be defeated if Buddhism responded actively to the moral and spiritual challenge of Christianity.

One of the most dramatic appeals about Buddhist decay appeared in a book entitled *Bukkyō metsubōron* [The ruin of Buddhism], written by the lay Buddhist *koji* Tajima Shōji. The book was a passionate "prophecy" about the ruin of Buddhism in "the age of the latter Dharma," and depicted how Buddhism was struggling amidst "the tornado of development," "the torrential rain of philosophy," and "the rough waves of Christianity."[8] The author had previously distinguished himself as an articulate critic of Christianity;[9] and his purpose now was not to attack Buddhism, but to arouse the resentment of the Buddhist priests against corruption and decay and thus make them surpass the Christian ministers.[10] Despite his critical attitude toward Christianity, he admired the activity of the Christians, which he contrasted with the ignorance and moral corruption of the Buddhist priests. The activity of one dedicated Christian for the sake of civilization equalled, according to Tajima, the work of five or ten thousand Buddhist priests. In addition to such praise of the Japanese

Christians, he also allowed himself to point out the similarity between Christianity and Pure Land Buddhism. "Christianity is the Shin Buddhism of the West; Shin Buddhism is the Christianity of the East," he said, and suggested that the two religions would be the main contenders for the religious leadership of the East.[11]

Other Buddhists expressed similar views on reform. Inoue Enryō realized in the mid-1880s that Christianity was expanding with an energy like the rising sun, while the light of Buddhism was waning like the morning moon. According to Inoue, the Buddhist priests were poor, passive, and emasculated; years of efforts seemed to be in vain and rather to promote Christian expansion.[12] Ashitsu Jitsuzen deplored the fact that the attempt to expose the ugliness of Christianity had only revealed its beauty, while, on the other hand, Buddhist efforts to demonstrate "the dimple of Buddhism" merely revealed "its pockmarks."[13] Kitabatake Dōryū described the corruption of Buddhism as a result of the ignorance and illiteracy of the priests, and had a strong sense of humiliation in relation to the foreign (Christian) countries.[14] Shaku Sōen expressed his pessimism in the following way:

> See the Buddhist priests. They are busying themselves with the preservation of their temples, and with efforts to raise them to higher rank; they eat meat and have wives; they are eager for fame, and some of them pride themselves on a smattering of Western science. Some, instead of trying to cultivate the faith of their believers, seek for Government patronage, and others think their duty discharged if they read the scriptures, offer prayers and bury the dead. Some are like dogs wagging their tails before money, and others are as cunning as foxes in deceiving the ignorant. Can such characters become efficient forces in the new movement of Buddhism? Buddhism has not had a great man for a long time, and if no one arises at the present juncture, there is almost no hope for the revival of this great religion.[15]

Shaku Sōen was thoroughly convinced about the superiority of Buddhism, but still recognized that "as to practical activity" Christianity excelled Buddhism.[16]

These Buddhists were all moderate reformers loyal to the Buddhist establishment; and their views were representative of a realization that became a sort of consensus among sensitive Buddhists in the 1890s: Christianity was not only a threatening enemy to be destroyed by all means, but it posed a real challenge to a corrupted Buddhism; Christianity could only be defeated through a radical moral and spiritual reform of Buddhism. The sense of crisis thus entailed a certain appreciation of Christianity. In many cases it was merely a hesitating recognition, hardly more than rhetoric to awaken Buddhism from its slumber. It is, however, also possible to discern an increasing tendency in Buddhist circles to imitate Christian activities. Christianity became not only a challenge, but a model.

It seemed to be a common conclusion in Buddhist circles that Buddhism was superior on the doctrinal level but that Christianity could offer guidance concerning methods of propagation, charity, education, and organization. In the words of Shaku Sōen, they should learn from Christians "the necessity of coming into contact with the people."[17] The situation was summarized by Cary in the following way:

> The more progressive priests had . . . imitated the methods adopted by Christians. They had established schools for boys and girls, summer schools, philanthropic societies, Young Men's Buddhist Associations, and other organisations. One magazine now published an article entitled "Learn from Christianity," in which the activity of the Christians, their readiness to adapt themselves to the national situation, and their spirit of devotion to principles rather than to money, were held up as worthy of imitation. Other magazines urged that the spirit and methods of the Christians be more generally copied. Though Buddhism as a system had given but little honour to women, it was now urged that they were well fitted to spread the tenets of their faith, and they were exhorted to speak of religion in their homes, to organise women's societies, and to establish kindergartens, girls' schools, and schools for nurses.[18]

Among all Christian activities charitable work had a special attraction among Japanese Buddhists, creating a sense of powerlessness and envy, but also zeal. With its feudal and Confucian ideas about society the Buddhists were less prepared than the Christians to grasp the social problems in a rapidly changing society, and they tended to depend on Christian models for social work.[19] Charity was regarded as the unique prerogative of the Christians, and the Buddhists were generally satisfied with the idea that the Christian influence would be limited through an increasing activity on the part of the Buddhists. Inoue Enryō, as we have seen, hoped to outdo the Christians by copying their educational institutions, hospitals, and reformatories. Shaku Sōen, likewise, argued that the Buddhists should resist the practical superiority of Christianity and establish "poorschools, charity hospitals, and reformatories, organize work among soldiers and criminals, correct the corruptions of society, and engage in active work in every department of life."[20] *Japan Evangelist* commented in 1895 that it would be completely mistaken to regard Buddhism as a fossil any more: "Remarkably sensitive is Japanese Buddhism to the world-movements, especially in the religious sphere. It is thoroughly alive to the fact that one of the most excellent features of Christianity is its wide-spread deeds of charity."[21] A Buddhist observer described the tendency in the following way: "What is presently being done of charitable work in society is for the most part due to the influence of Christianity."[22]

At one point Christianity challenged Buddhism also on the doctrinal level. Liberal theology, Unitarianism, and the Western historical study of Buddhism introduced methods and ideas that gradually faced Buddhism with a number of new problems and led to a critical reexamination of the basis of Buddhist faith. The consequences of the new quest will be discussed in the examination of more radical Buddhist reform movements below, but it is noteworthy that the need of doctrinal reexamination was felt among moderate reformers as well. As a consequence, the attention was gradually drawn away from a one-sidedly negative denunciation of Christianity toward a more positive attempt to demonstrate the authenticity of Mahayana Buddhism. From the end of 1893 especially, Buddhist priests and scholars seemed to become more philosophical and expository; the emphasis gradually changed from *haja,* "refutation of errors," to *kenshō,* "manifestation of the truth."[23]

PROGRESSIVE REFORMERS AND REFORM MOVEMENTS

The Christian influence on Buddhist reform movements was in many cases the result of an indirect challenge; the Buddhists, realizing that reform was needed if they were to cope with the expanding work of the Christians, applied methods and ideas they had learned from them. In a number of cases, however, the search for renewal led to direct contact with Christianity, as we shall see in the following examination of some progressive reformers and reform movements.

HANSEIKAI

One of the most active movements directed against the moral and spiritual decay of Buddhism was begun by the temperance association, Hanseikai (The Temperance Association).[24] It was formally founded on April 6, 1886, by Sakurai Gichō, Takakusu Junjirō, and other concerned students at the Normal School of Nishi Honganji. According to Sakurai, the reputation of the students was extremely bad in the city, since they "at all times entered the red-light districts, drinking sake and singing noisily, indulging in quarrels and having rough manners."[25] Hanseikai aimed at a total renewal of the moral standard of the students; the use of "wine, spirits, and strong drink which tempt men to sin,"[26] was regarded as the main cause of moral decay and social problems. Along with temperance as the key to a "pure life,"[27] the association emphasized proper and moral conduct, continence, and courtesy.[28]

The journal of the association, *Hanseikai zasshi* (English title, *The Temperance*) was published from 1887.[29] Apart from advocating the basic principle of temperance, it also began to voice the need of other reforms; it questioned the world-negating type of Buddhism; it responded to criticism from Christians by advocating equal rights for women as a Buddhist virtue;[30] and it supported propagation among young people and rescue work among prostitutes.[31]

Hanseikai was supported by the leadership of Nishi Honganji, and seemed to bring about a great change among the Buddhist students.[32] After five years the membership passed ten thousand and included, in addition to the founders, a number of prominent Buddhists, such as Shimaji Mokurai, Akamatsu Renjō, Inoue Enryō, Murakami Senshō, and Furukawa Rōsen.[33] According to *Bukkyō,* Hanseikai became the pioneer of Buddhist reform in the decade after its start in 1886; what was new or progressive in the Buddhist world had either been started by Hanseikai or influenced by Hanseikai; furthermore, most of the so-called New Buddhists were at some time members of the association. In 1895 the membership had increased to almost twenty thousand.[34]

Hanseikai was, especially in the beginning, critical of Christianity. Recalling his years in Kyoto when Hanseikai was founded, Furukawa Rōsen characterized the period as a time of Westernization when Christianity reached the peak of prosperity and the Buddhists were weeping at the sad state of Buddhism: "The students folded their arms in resentment and roused up in order to defend Buddhism."[35] Japanese Christians were denounced as slaves of the foreigners; they were undermining the Japanese spirit, changing "noble Japanese into Englishmen," and thus making Japan like "a second India."[36] The members further engaged in a dedicated work for Buddhist propagation in the West, and supported overseas Buddhists through the Buddhist Correspondence Society, later reorganized as the Buddhist Propagation Society. For a short time around 1890 the editor of *Hanseikai zasshi,* Sakurai Gichō, also published the English journal *Bijou of Asia,* and in 1898–1899 an English edition of *Hansei zasshi,* entitled *The Hansei Zasshi,* with 4,000 subscribers.[37] The overseas expansion and the missionary zeal of the members were seen as a sign that the period of Christian expansion was passed and the time of Buddhist resurrection had arrived.[38]

On the other hand, in spite of missionary zeal and critical attitudes to Christianity, the activity of Hanseikai was deeply influenced by Christianity. Temperance was advocated on the basis of Buddhist precepts; but the movement was inspired by Western temperance movements, and every issue included reports from overseas temperance societies. The lectures by Mrs. Mary Clemmer Leavitt, who had come from America in 1886 as the representative of the Woman's Christian Temperance Union, had especially aroused the interest in temperance among Christians as well as members of other religions.[39] The foundation of Hanseikai in 1886 may well have been stimulated by Mrs. Leavitt's lectures. It was puzzling to the Buddhist reformers that temperance was so strongly supported in Christian countries, even though there was no Christian commandment concerning abstinence from alcohol, while, on the other hand, the Buddhist world was so negative to temperance, in spite of the unmistakable precepts.[40] Along with temperance, other Puritan ideals also stimulated the members of Hanseikai, such as the emphasis on "pure life," strict moral codes, and reform.[41] An article in *Hanseikai zasshi* in 1890 advocated programmatically that the urgent task of Buddhist reform was to foster "democratic," "pure," and "persevering" "Japanese Puritans" on the basis of the "gospel of Buddha."[42] The idea of overseas mission was greatly stimulated by the missionary activity of the Christians, and the journal carried frequent reports on Christian activity in various parts of the world.

The international outlook and the stimulation from Christian activities made it difficult for the members of Hanseikai to maintain a negative attitude to Christianity or the West. Takakusu Junjirō, who had been one of the founders, even married a Christian woman from Kobe.[43] In 1888, a time when the anti-Christian and anti-Western mood prevailed among Japanese Buddhists, the editor of *Hanseikai zasshi* advocated the need of learning from the West about the administration, activities, and discipline of the churches, and of emphasizing both propagation and social work.[44] In 1893 *Hansei zasshi* was fairly unbiased in its evaluation of the controversy about education and religion (Christianity),[45] and supported the World's Parliament of Religions.[46] Inspired by the spirit of the Parliament it even suggested that a similar Parliament should be convened in Japan, and supported the first Buddhist-Christian Conference in Japan in 1896.[47] It welcomed the Salvation Army when its work was begun in Japan in 1895.[48] When the journal in 1896 was moved to Tokyo, it soon developed into a broadly oriented Buddhist cultural journal. It introduced itself as the "most widely read Journal of Japanese Religions,"[49] and featured articles by such outstanding writers in the intellectual and literary world as Tsubouchi Shōyō, Kunikida Doppo, Masaoka Shiki, Kōda Rohan, Shimazaki Tōson, and Anesaki Masaharu.[50] At the end of the 1890s it consistently criticized the Buddhist efforts to oppose mixed residence and to establish Buddhism as state religion or state-recognized religion; tolerance was held up against antiforeign and anti-Christian sentiments; instead of fearing Christianity, it was argued, the Buddhists should rather be confident about the final victory of Buddhism.[51] The liberal trend was completed when the journal in 1899 was retitled *Chūō kōron* [The central review], establishing itself as a progressive cultural journal.

In short, as the first representative association of young Buddhist reformers, Hanseikai exercised a decisive influence on the various New Buddhist movements. It began as a "Society for the propagation of 'Buddha's Doctrines, Teetotalism,' and 'High Morality,' in accordance with the principles of Buddha,"[52] and was characterized by a strong anti-Christian spirit. Since Christianity to a great extent became both a challenge and a model, however, the attitude to Christianity gradually changed. After a while Hanseikai came to stand for a religious tolerance that in a characteristic way was combined with reform zeal and missionary fervor.

NAKANISHI USHIO AND UNITARIANISM

Nakanishi Ushio has already been mentioned as a "Unitarian" Buddhist. Some additional comments are needed in order to evaluate his role in the New Buddhist movement, especially with regard to Christianity. As a prolific writer, Nakanishi managed at an early stage to clarify his view on the New Buddhism and its relation to Christianity; and thus he anticipated some of the ideas and attitudes that characterized later advocates of the New Buddhism.

As a staunch advocate of "the great law of evolution," Nakanishi interpreted the history of religion as a continuous evolutionary process, leading from polytheism via monotheism toward pantheism.[53] Christianity was, according to Nakanishi, characterized by the sharp distinction between God and the universe. God was regarded as the origin of the universe, but he could not be identified with the universe itself. In Western thought, however, Nakanishi found a basically pantheistic trend which conceived God's essence as identical with the universe. He further claimed that the contemporary religious development was bringing about a radical transition from the period of monotheism to the period of pantheism. The progress of science was, according to Nakanishi, destroying the monotheistic faith, and was thus paving the way for pantheism. Even though modern theology tried to come to terms with evolutionism and science, it would be impossible without a transformation of monotheism into pantheism. Instead of the Christian expectations about conquering Buddhism, he predicted that Buddhism would replace Christianity as the unifying religion of the twentieth century.

In this connection Nakanishi had great expectations toward Unitarianism, which, he hoped, would play an important role in the religious evolution of mankind as a mediator between Buddhism and Christianity. Unitarianism, which was throwing orthodox Christianity into confusion, was thus promoting the transition from Christianity to Buddhism.[54] At the same time it was facilitating the transition toward pantheism by breaking down the traditional distinctions between monotheism and pantheism.[55] Nakanishi suggested, for instance, that the Unitarian view of God as the "absolute, infinite Being" (*zettai mugen no sonzai*) or the "Source of all things in the Universe" (*uchū banyū no hongen*) could be harmonized with the more profound Buddhist realization of Thusness (*shinnyo*) as "the absolute, infinite pure Spirit" (*zettai mugen no junrei*).[56] Further, he suggested that the Buddhist idea of the inherent Buddha-nature of all sentient beings was expressed in the Christian idea that "the evolution of all things are fulfilled in Christ" or that "the contradictions in the universe are reconciled in Christ."[57]

Nakanishi not only regarded Unitarianism as a mediator between monotheism and pantheism, but also applied its principles to Buddhist reform. He was convinced that traditional Buddhism was "stagnated, corrupted, and had lost its true essence."[58] "In the old Buddhism the true character of Buddhism is mixed with bigotry, prejudice, carnal desires, decay, ostentation, blind belief, hypocrisy, and other evils born out of human weakness and social conditions." He further characterized traditional Buddhism by a number of contrasts that clearly indicated the direction of his criticism: The old Buddhism was conservative, aristocratic, materialistic, scholarly, individualistic, doctrinal, and based on delusions; in contrast to this, the New Buddhism was progressive, democratic, and spiritual; it emphasized faith, and it was social, historical, and based on reason.[59] Nakanishi was early acquainted with Unitarianism, and the above ideas about the New Buddhism, written in 1889, may have been inspired by Unitarianism.[60] When in 1893 he wrote *Shin Bukkyōron* [On the New Buddhism] in order to develop his ideas in more positive terms, the Unitarian influence was more conspicuous. Among new elements were, for instance, a strong emphasis on the optimistic character of the New Buddhism, in contrast to the world-negating tendency of traditional Buddhism. He gave absolute priority to "free investigation" (*jiyū tōkyū*), which was the main catchword of the Unitarians; he described faith as the "unique life" of religion, and he advocated the need of changing the method of interpretation in order to unify not only Buddhism, but all religions of the world.[61]

As mentioned before, Nakanishi cooperated with Unitarians in Japan. It was possible for him to be a high-ranking member of the Unitarian Association and to dedicate himself to Unitarian activity because he regarded the Unitarian principles, and not its Christian doctrines, as the basis for the unification of Buddhism and Christianity. When he terminated his membership, it was not because he abandoned the Unitarian principles, but because he realized that his Buddhist interpretation of Unitarianism was rejected by the leadership of the Unitarian Association. Their emphasis on the Christian character of Unitarianism was, according to Nakanishi, misguided, and contradicted the natural religious evolution from monotheism toward pantheism. If Christianity was given priority, he argued, the ultimate unification of Buddhism and Christianity would fail, or would at best be an attempt to deepen and complement Christianity with Buddhist ideas.[62]

After the break with the Unitarian Association, Nakanishi did not seem to be much concerned with Unitarianism. Thirty years later he still maintained his basic rejection of the Christian doctrines, stressing that the Orient would save the present civilization, and quoting the following words of Jesus as representing the spirit of the Oriental civilization: "Blessed are the poor in spirit: for theirs is the Kingdom of Heaven."[63]

FURUKAWA RŌSEN AND "THE AGE OF DOUBT"

Furukawa Rōsen (1871–1899)[64] managed, in spite of his early death at the age of twenty-eight, to establish himself as the unchallenged leader of a whole generation of young Buddhist reformers. A critical spirit and a brilliant writer, his influence went far beyond the narrow circle of progressive Buddhists, primarily through the journal he edited from 1894, *Bukkyō,* but also through others' journals, such as *Hanseikai zasshi/ Hansei zasshi, Zenshū, Chūō kōron,* and others.

Critical Tolerance of Christianity. Furukawa Rōsen was born in Wakayama in 1871 and grew up in a temple belonging to the Honganji sect of Shin Buddhism.[65] The Buddhist influence in his childhood was strong, and when, in 1886, at the age of fifteen, he entered the newly established Normal School of Nishi Honganji in Kyoto, he soon distinguished himself as a skillful advocate of Buddhism in speech and writing. His activities in those years were characterized by his resentment against Buddhist corruption and Christian expansion.[66] He was among the founders of Hanseikai in 1886, and he engaged in fervent activity for the moral and spiritual reform of Buddhism. Further, he wanted to diminish the influence of Christianity in the East through Buddhist propagation. Such ideas were expressed in the first issue of *Hanseikai zasshi* in August 1887, when he reminded Japanese Buddhists about their responsibility for guiding the Korean civilization.[67] He also supported the work for Buddhist mission in the West, convinced that the period of Christian expansion would be replaced by Buddhist resurgence.[68] When he moved to Tokyo in 1889, he soon engaged in efforts to publicize a scandal at the Christian Women's School.

With such a critical attitude toward Christianity it was rather surprising that he, after having attended various schools, entered the Christian Meiji Gakuin in September 1889, a time when Christian schools were facing serious problems all over Japan. According to his friend Sugimura Jūō, he did this "with the intention of spying on Christians from within."[69] He left Meiji Gakuin in April 1890, after only seven months, but the experience must certainly have changed his attitudes toward Christianity. Sugimura characterized the changes in the following way:

> Once he was inside and had contact with Christians day in day out he realized that the Christians could not be rejected indiscriminately, and gradually

cultivated a tolerant attitude. He, who in the beginning entered as an enemy, finally left as a good friend. The liberal and tolerant ideas about the Christians he maintained throughout his life were primarily conceived at this time.[70]

This did not mean that Furukawa abandoned his critical attitude to Christianity. His tolerance of Christianity was combined with a persistent conviction that it would be defeated. For instance, he could discuss the prospects of Buddhism and Christianity in rather belligerent language, describing how the Buddhist and Christian "armies" defended their ground. He maintained his strong resentment against Westernization and Christian expansion, and expressed his satisfaction at the anti-Christian reaction. Finding signs of renewal and decay among Buddhists as well as Christians, he concluded that Buddhism would ultimately win the battle and become the unifying religious force in the world.[71]

Furukawa's unique contribution to the controversy about education and religion in 1893 has been mentioned above. He was the only Buddhist who gave an unbiased and independent evaluation of the conflict and who criticized the Buddhists for making Inoue Tetsujirō their spokesman against Christianity. His plea for tolerance, however, was not based on any sympathy with Christianity; it included a scathing criticism of Christianity which, according to Furukawa, was an illusion based on vain dreams: "While the time is near when the general trend of the twentieth century will banish it [Christianity] from the civilized world and, further, welcome the great light of the Buddhist truth, from now on it is really a delusion to try to spread the scraps of Christianity in our country, the inner citadel of Buddhism."[72]

At the same time it should be noticed that his rejection of Christianity was also combined with sincere friendship with and admiration of individual Christians. A beautiful evidence of such affections is his description of his relationship with a Christian woman, named Yabu Isoko, who died from tuberculosis in 1898, the year before he himself died. In spite of her Christian faith, he discovered in Isoko a spiritual friend who was able to appreciate the greatness of Buddhism, especially Zen. "She was embracing Christianity without being stained by its corrupt customs," he wrote. "Even though she did not believe in Buddhism, she was a truly religious person who had the real taste of it."[73]

"The Age of Doubt" and Unitarianism. Furukawa had contributed actively to the work for Buddhist reform since he entered the Normal School of Nishi Honganji in 1886; however, the search for a New Buddhism entered a new stage when, in January 1894, he published an article entitled "Kaigijidai ni ireri" [Entering the age of doubt] in *Bukkyō*.[74] Here he described the intellectual evolution of humankind as a continual development through three stages: the "age of dogmatism" *(dokudan*

jidai) was followed by the destructive "age of doubt" *(kaigi jidai),* leading to a constructive synthesis of the two in the "age of criticism" *(hihyō jidai).*[75] The age of criticism would, according to Furukawa, develop into a new age of dogmatism, different from previous dogmatism, and the process would continue. He found the pattern in philosophy and religion as well as on the individual level.

Furukawa's concern was not to formulate a general philosophy of intellectual evolution but to diagnose the situation of contemporary Buddhism and call for a bold departure from the age of dogmatism into the age of doubt. According to Furukawa, the Buddhists were far behind the Christians on this point. Protestant Christianity in Japan had in the beginning been characterized by its dogmatic belief in the infallibility of the Bible and the absolute truth of Christianity, refusing to see truth in anything else. The age of dogmatism, however, had been replaced by the age of doubt, which in recent years had resulted in great confusion and numerous defections from Christianity. Now, he argued, Christianity was already about to enter the age of criticism, searching for a constructive synthesis[76] of the over-confident dogmatism and the extreme doubt in the previous stages. The period of criticism was characterized by new methods of interpretation that allowed Christians to accept the good and abandon the unacceptable elements of Christianity. On this point Furukawa was, of course, referring to the theological development described in the previous chapter, notably to Unitarianism, which advocated the three principles of rational faith, free investigation, and moral development.

In contrast to Christianity, Buddhism was, according to Furukawa, just in the process of leaving the age of dogmatism and reluctantly entering the age of doubt. The dogmatic belief in Buddhism as the unsurpassed truth, the scientific religion, and the highest morality was being replaced by serious doubts about the inner contradictions and failures in the historical development of Buddhism. The crucial question in this connection was, of course, the widespread criticism that Mahayana Buddhism was an inauthentic deviation from Buddha's teaching. This and similar problems were creating a great bewilderment among Buddhists, introducing the age of doubt also in the Buddhist world. Instead of despairing, Furukawa claimed that doubt was necessary in order to reach the stage of criticism. Buddhism would eventually enter a new period of affirmation, a new age of dogmatism, different from before. In contrast to the conservative Buddhists who recoiled from doubt and criticism as destructive, and merely wanted to return to the old dogmatism, Furukawa characterized the progressive Buddhists as pioneers who let themselves be carried away "into the raging waves of society, sacrificing themselves by suffering all sorts of hardships on behalf of their brethren, in order to make the great ship of Buddhism reach the other shore of peace and happiness."[77] He concluded by exhorting his Buddhist friends and critics: "Buddhists, be bold! The Buddhists living in the Meiji period should not cause the suppuration of the tumor for fear of the short pain of operation!"[78]

Furukawa's essay, written in consultation with his close associates, Nishiyori Ichiriki and Sugimura Jūō, became a manifesto of the New Buddhism. *Bukkyō* became the mouthpiece of progressive Buddhists, and the year 1894 was designated as the decisive stage toward the great Buddhist reform.[79] Further, in December 1894 a new association called Keiikai[80] was founded by Furukawa and a number of his associates. Keiikai emphasized the two principles of "free investigation" (*jiyū tōkyū*) and "progressive reform" (*shinshū*)[81] as the warp and woof of the association. The prospectus further declared: "This Association is a union of those who believe in Buddhism as the highest and greatest religion and who want to propagate Buddhism and universally spread its blessings to all humanity, regarding freedom of investigation and toleration of religious sects as its basic policy."[82] In a characteristic way Keiikai and *Bukkyō*, which became its organ, combined the conviction of the superiority of Buddhism with progressive ideas about critical self-examination, free investigation, and religious tolerance.

Among the most conspicuous features of the new development were the critical study of Buddhist history and the increasingly critical evaluation of contemporary Buddhism. Murakami Senshō distinguished himself as the pioneer of the historical study of Buddhism in Japan; in cooperation with Sakaino Kōyō and Washio Junkei he founded, in 1894, a new journal for the historical study of Buddhism, called *Bukkyō shirin*. Nishiyori Ichiriki also made outstanding contributions to such studies.[83] They were all closely associated with Furukawa's movement; confronting the difficult problems concerning the authenticity of Mahayana Buddhism, they laid the foundation for the historical-critical study of Buddhism in Japan.

Such studies inevitably brought the decay of contemporary Buddhism into relief. In his search for the original Buddhism Furukawa found that Japanese Buddhism was hardly preferable to Catholicism or orthodox Protestantism; hence he denounced the "so-called Buddhism" of those who based their authority on tradition; in his view, they were superstitious, opposed free investigation as heresy, and neglected the present world in their concern for the next.[84] Furukawa himself managed somehow to maintain his relationship with the Buddhist establishment. The failure of reform in the Ōtani sect of Shin Buddhism, however, undermined the hope for reform of traditional Buddhism,[85] and several of his associates became so negative in their criticism that a break finally became inevitable.[86]

In contrast to the negative evaluation of traditional Buddhism, Furukawa and his associates were strongly influenced by Unitarianism. Furukawa himself repeatedly acknowledged its influence;[87] and the basic principles advocated by Furukawa were mostly inherited from Unitarianism, notably the rejection of dogmatism, the optimistic affirmation of the present world,[88] and the emphasis on free investigation, reform, and religious tolerance.

Furukawa's wholehearted support of Unitarian principles, however, did not signify an acceptance of its Christian elements. He clarified his view on Unitarianism in a number of articles, and consistently criticized it for establishing itself as a Christian sect. For instance, in an essay on Unitarianism in *Bukkyō* in April 1894,[89] he supported Unitarian principles and also commended Unitarianism for its attempt to criticize and transform orthodox Christianity; but he still refused to recognize Unitarianism as a satisfactory religion. The "common faith" of Unitarianism, expressed in its seven basic doctrinal statements was, according to Furukawa, thoroughly molded by Christian ideas. He especially criticized its view of God and man as a serious limitation. While in Buddhism all sentient beings had Buddha-nature and were destined for Buddhahood, in Christianity man as the child of God was not equal to God and could never become God. With such limitations Unitarianism could never become a perfect religion. What he found valuable in Unitarianism was not its "positive faith," but its "negative doubt," that is, its destructive role as a critic of religion. Hence, he argued, Unitarianism should abandon its Christian background and stop representing itself as a religion; instead of following "the policy of befriending distant states and antagonizing neighbors," that is, instead of having friendly relations with other religions and attacking orthodox Christianity, Unitarianism should become "irregular troops," attacking old dogmatism and evils in all religions equally.[90] If Unitarianism hesitated to leave its religious pedestal, Furukawa proclaimed, the Buddhists would develop their principles one step further and transform Unitarianism into Buddhism.

As early as in 1891 he had suggested that Japan would become the "great distillation place" where Christianity would be transformed into Unitarianism, and further into Buddhism. This New Christianity, transformed by Buddhism, would then spread to the West, and Buddhism would unify the world.[91] In another article about "Unitarianism, the New Buddhism, and Zen," written in *Zenshū* in November 1895,[92] he suggested that the Zen boom after the Sino-Japanese War signified that Zen, understood as the basis of all Buddhism, was taking over the previous role of Unitarianism. He acknowledged that a number of Buddhists had become Unitarians in recent years, but he was convinced that they would return to Buddhism. For Buddhism not only included the negative and critical aspects of Unitarian principles, but was a perfect religion without all the Christian limitations of the Unitarian doctrines.

BUDDHIST PURITANISM

The disappointment with traditional Buddhism finally resulted in a break between the young Buddhist reformers and the Buddhist establishment. Because of the increasingly radical editorials by Sakaino Kōyō (1871–1933) in *Bukkyō*, Keiikai withdrew its support from the journal, and the society was eventually dissolved in 1899.[93] Furukawa Rōsen himself was fatally ill and died in November 1899; Nishiyori Ichiriki returned to the country, and several other members devoted themselves to other activities.[94] *Bukkyō* was published until 1902, but another organization had already taken over its role as the main agent for the New Buddhists. Its name was Bukkyō Seito Dōshikai (Association of Buddhist Puritans); it was founded in February 1899.[95] It represented the most consistent effort to propagate and organize the New Buddhism as a radical alternative to traditional Buddhism. Its journal, published from July 1900, was quite appropriately called *Shin Bukkyō* [The New Buddhism], and the name of the association was in 1903 changed to Shin Bukkyōto Dōshikai (Association of New Buddhists).[96]

Even though several of Furukawa's associates withdrew from active participation, the new association was recruited from the circle around Furukawa, and represented a continuation of the trends already depicted in the foregoing pages. The most conspicuous period of activity of Dōshikai belongs to the first decade of the twentieth century;[97] however, since Dōshikai was founded in 1899, and represented the conclusive development of the New Buddhism of the 1890s, it is natural to include here a short description of some of its concerns that had a particular bearing on Buddhist-Christian relations.

First, the name of the association proclaimed the Puritan character of the movement. The traditional term for Puritanism was *seikyō,* and for Puritans *seikyōto,* not *seito,* but the reference to Puritanism was unmistakable. Puritanism was promoted as a spirituality that brought about the "new pure light of faith and morality."[98] In his recollections of the ten-year history of Dōshikai, Sakaino Kōyō explained that the term "Puritan" was adopted because "only the English Puritans, with their emphasis on saving the present moral corruption, could sufficiently arouse the sense of austerity."[99] Another Puritan influence was its effort to "purify" religion from unessential elements and to restore faith in its purity; Dōshikai denounced both inherited superstition and government protection and interference, and maintained that religion should be "pure and innocent" *(seijō keppaku)*, depending exclusively on the power of religious faith. Consequently, Dōshikai rejected all efforts to obtain a privileged status for Buddhism as state religion or state-recognized religion.[100]

Second, Dōshikai represented a clear-cut break with the so-called Old Buddhism, bringing the earlier tension to its inevitable conclusion. The Manifesto of the association, published in the first issue of *Shin Bukkyō*, proclaimed the New Buddhism against the dark background of Buddhist decay.

> There are temples; there are priests. They chant sutras; they preach. Ten thousands of believers surround them, shed tears of adoration in magnificent temple halls, and show their reverence for the robes of embroidered brocade. If this is to be called Buddhism, it is without doubt the corrupted, routine Old Buddhism. They know how to worship wooden statues and pictures of Buddha. They know how to worship in front of the priests and listen to their sermons. They know how to cling to the biased views of the individual sects and not to be inferior to each other. They know well how to chant *nenbutsu* and *daimoku* with their mouths and how to hold the rosaries and sutras with their hands. Have they not already lost the life of faith? If such things should really be called Buddhism, it is undoubtedly the moribund, formalistic Old Buddhism.[101]

Referring to various types of prayers and superstitious practices, traditional Buddhism was further denounced as the "superstitious Old Buddhism," the "world-negating Old Buddhism," or the "utopian Old Buddhism." "We are already advocating the cause of the New Buddhism, and our attitude to these forms of Old Buddhism is self-evident. The New Buddhists are necessarily opposed to the Old Buddhists; or, perhaps, not opposed, but rather wanting to save them from their delusions." Even though the New Buddhists maintained that they were not exclusively aiming at the destruction of the Old Buddhism, they were hardly counting on a reform of the present structures of priesthood and temples; they had already "deliberately severed the relations with the Old Buddhism."[102]

Such attitudes naturally led to the denunciation of the New Buddhists by the Buddhist establishment. According to Sakaino, the members of Dōshikai were regarded as destructive elements and detested like snakes.[103] They were not allowed to hold their meetings in Buddhist temples; fearing the reaction of the Buddhist establishment, the Dōshikai members in the beginning worked half secretly.[104]

Third, in contrast to the break with traditional Buddhism, Dōshikai was characterized by a quite positive relationship to Christianity, particularly to Unitarianism. The Manifesto of the New Buddhists even alluded to a unification of the two religions: "The unification of Buddhism and

Christianity is also one of our ideals, one of our hopes."[105] Among the leaders of Dōshikai, Sakaino Kōyō especially had a positive relationship to Christianity. His positive evaluation of Christianity can partly be explained by his background. Coming from Miyagi Prefecture he went to a Catholic primary school in Sendai, a city where the Christian influence was particularly strong. He established close relations with several Christians in Sendai, and reportedly felt more friendly toward Christians than Buddhists. His mother and younger brother and sister actually became Christians, understanding Christianity from the background of Confucian Wang Yang-ming philosophy. The encounter with Buddhism at a Buddhist school in Sendai, and later at Tetsugakkan, turned Sakaino into a dedicated Buddhist. For the rest of his life, however, he was said to maintain a "smell of Christianity."[106] Another Dōshikai leader, Sugimura Jūō, had previously been closely associated with the Unitarians.[107] The fact that a number of prominent Christians were interviewed along with Buddhists in a series of interviews in *Shin Bukkyō* concerning the future of religion expresses the confidence in Christianity among Dōshikai leaders. The journalist even confided that while the Buddhists tended to be negative, he was impressed by the positive response of the Christians.[108]

As we have seen in the earlier phases of the New Buddhism, however, the relationship with Christianity was primarily conceived in terms of interaction with Unitarianism. The six basic principles of Dōshikai revealed a dominant Unitarian influence; in a characteristic way the call for reform was combined with a strong emphasis on free investigation and the rejection of superstitious traditions.

1. We regard a sound Buddhist faith as our basic principle.
2. We will promote and spread sound faith, knowledge, and morality, and work for the radical reform of society.
3. We advocate free investigation of Buddhism and other religions.
4. We anticipate the extermination of all superstition.
5. We do not recognize the necessity of preserving traditional religious systems and ceremonies.
6. We reject all sorts of political protection and interference.[109]

Commenting on the meaning of "sound faith" Sakaino argued that faith should be intellectual, but also esteem the emotional aspects; further, faith should be this-worldly, optimitic, active, and ethical.[110] The New Buddhism was conceived as a Buddhism for the rational, common-sense middle class, in contrast to traditional Buddhism, which was regarded either as an aristocratic pastime or lower-class superstition.[111] Thus the New Buddhism made an attempt to appeal to the middle class, which had previously been neglected by Buddhism and was greatly influenced by Christianity.[112]

The Unitarian journal *Rikugō zasshi* declared that the principles of Dōshikai were identical with the Unitarian principles, and concluded: "We do not hesitate to call Bukkyō Seito Dōshikai 'Unitarianism' within Buddhism."[113] Inoue Enryō feared that the Puritan influence and the cooperation with Unitarianism could be misunderstood as a "Christianization of the New Buddhism." The New Buddhism was, according to Inoue, theoretical, destructive, and had a "smell of Christianity." It failed to maintain its independence and yielded to the Unitarians; the New Buddhism was conceived "not as a guest of Unitarianism, but as a parasite; not as a relative of Unitarianism, but as a foster child."[114]

Against this background it was not surprising that several Dōshikai members and Unitarians envisioned a unification of the two as the final stage toward the formation of a new religion. On April 7, 1901, a number of representatives of the two associations met in the Unitarian Unity Hall and decided to hold a great conference in the autumn to realize the unification of the two movements. According to *Rikugō zasshi*, "Unitarianism and [Bukkyō] Seito Dōshikai were the signs of a new religion in Japan. We hope that some day the two will come together in one great union and reform the religious world in our country."[115] *Chūō kōron* referred to the agreement as a "remarkable happening in the religious history of Meiji," and commented that a group of the Unitarians were "Buddhist Christians," while the majority of the members of Bukkyō Seito Dōshikai were "Christian Buddhists."[116]

The planned conference was never held. As a result of the meeting in April, however, Dōshikai was allowed to use Unity Hall for its meetings totally free of cost, a practice that lasted for more than ten years. *Rikugō zasshi* characterized this as a major contribution to the development of Buddhism, and added: "Unity Hall is from now on not only the center of the Unitarian movement, but will become the place of expansion for the sound and original religious philosophy of Seito Dōshikai."[117]

Both the Unitarians and the New Buddhists seemed to agree that the only common problem still unsolved was the inherent tension between Christian monotheism and Buddhist pantheism. But several Dōshikai members were more optimistic about rapprochement than earlier New Buddhists had been. Sakaino argued, for instance, that the complete unification of Buddhism and Christianity would be realized when the emotional side of religion, represented by monotheism, and the intellectual side, represented by pantheism, were unified. A stronger emphasis on the emotional elements in Buddhism on the one hand, and a philosophical interpretation of Christianity on the other, could contribute toward such a rapprochement, he declared.[118] An editorial in *Shin Bukkyō* suggested in a similar way that Buddhism and Christianity were approaching each other from opposite sides; in the historical development of Buddhism there were reminiscences of or precognitions of a "personal reality" *(jinkakuteki jitsuzai)*, and Christianity was gradually developing pantheistic tendencies.[119]

Even though such a recognition of monotheism facilitated the rapprochement between Buddhism and Christianity, it was only a limited recognition. Monotheism had, from the Buddhist point of view, merely a relative value as an expression of the emotional side of religion; ultimately it was a question of unification on the basis of pantheism.[120] This basic standpoint of the New Buddhists corresponded to a similar but opposite attitude among the Unitarians, who considered monotheism as the ultimate basis for unification. Consequently, when the Unitarian representative, Clay MacCauley, in 1910 again asserted the specific Christian character of Unitarianism, several members left the Unitarian Association, and the relationship between Unitarianism and the New Buddhism gradually lost significance.[121]

CHAPTER THIRTEEN

Comparative Religion
and Buddhist Studies

> Believing or not believing, the essential point is to regard
> all religions impartially and place them in the wrestling
> ring where the fittest will survive.
>
> Kishimoto Nobuta, pioneer in the study of
> comparative religion in Japan

THE FOUNDATION of a scientific study of Eastern religion was laid in
the first half of the nineteenth century; and in the latter part of the century a number of scholars did a pioneer work of editing and translating
Pali and Sanskrit texts and engaging in various sorts of comparative studies of language, culture, mythology, and religion. A number of missionary scholars also contributed to the study of comparative religion; and it
was only natural that it gradually influenced theology and missionary
thinking. As the Japanese Buddhists in the 1870s began to develop contacts with Western scholars, they soon became acquainted with and challenged by comparative religion, and notably Western studies of Buddhism. The purpose of this chapter is to trace the influence of such
studies on Buddhist-Christian relations in Japan.

COMPARATIVE RELIGION AND APOLOGETICS

One of the most influential scholars in this field was undoubtedly Friedrich Max Müller (1823–1900), who in 1868 became professor of comparative grammar at Oxford. His major contribution was in the field of
Indic studies, where he was a "singularly dominating figure" during the
latter half of the nineteenth century.[1] He did not regard himself as an
expert in Buddhist studies and referred to himself merely as a "humble
gleaner,"[2] yet he wrote important essays on Buddhism, translated the
Dhammapada (1869), and distinguished himself as the editor of the
monumental work *The Sacred Books of the East*. He also introduced the
term "science of religion" in 1867,[3] and laid the foundation for the study

of comparative religion in such books as *Introduction to the Science of Religion* (1873), *The Origin and Growth of Religions* (1878), and numerous other essays and books.[4] His comparative approach was characterized by distinct ideas about religious evolution from primitive stages toward nonphysical and nonhuman conceptions of the divine. Even though his ideas are now mostly obsolete,[5] he made a great impact in the scholarly world; and his ideas carried great weight also in Japan. His influence was, in fact, particularly strong in Japan, probably because two of his disciples were Buddhist priests, sent from Higashi Honganji in Kyoto to pursue the study of Sanskrit and Buddhism. One of the students, Kasahara Kenju, died in 1883, soon after his return to Japan; but the other, Nanjō [Nanjio] Bunyū, became an internationally recognized scholar.[6]

Another major contribution to Buddhist studies was made by T. W. Rhys Davids (1843–1922). He published his *Manual of Buddhism* in 1878 and founded the Pali Text Society in 1881, introducing Buddhist Pali texts and translations to the West.[7] Other scholars who deserve mention in this context include Monier Monier-Williams in England, Hermann Oldenberg in Germany, Sylvian Lévi and Eugène Burnouf in France, Henry Clarke Warren in the United States, and a number of missionary scholars, such as R. Spence Hardy, Joseph Edkins, Ernest John Eitel, James Legge, and Timothy Richard.[8] The individual who stirred the greatest interest in Buddhism in the West was probably Sir Edwin Arnold (1832–1904), whose great poem about the Buddha, *The Light of Asia: The Great Renunciation,* achieved a phenomenal success. It was published in 1879, and had already been published in more than thirty editions when the text was revised in 1885; it was reportedly even more widely read in the United States than in England.[9] The poem was published in Japanese in 1890.[10]

Through the work of such pioneers Buddhism was gradually appreciated in the West. In spite of the sympathetic attitude to other religions held by many of the above-mentioned scholars, however, the comparative approach was characterized by a rather rigid understanding of religious values and a deep-rooted belief in evolutionary processes.[11] W. Brede Kristensen characterized the trend of comparing religions as an attempt to make it possible to "determine which religions were lower and which were higher. And most important, could not the comparative approach clearly demonstrate the superiority of Christianity?"[12] This tendency was not only found among missionaries and theologians, whose apologetic concern was obvious,[13] but was shared by most of the Westerners interested in the study of comparative religion.

It is also significant that even the scholars who had a sympathetic understanding of the teaching of Buddha tended to be deeply critical of

Mahayana Buddhism, which they regarded as a corruption of Buddhism. T. W. Rhys Davids, for instance, expressed his sympathy with Buddha's teaching in the following way: "Buddhist or not Buddhist, I have examined every one of the great religious systems of the world, and in none of them have I found anything to surpass, in beauty and comprehensiveness, the Noble Eightfold Path of the Buddha. I am content to shape my life according to that Path."[14] At the same time he rejected the ideas of Pure Land Buddhism as "the creations of a sickly scholasticism, hollow abstractions without life or reality."[15] Max Müller's evaluation of Pure Land Buddhism was equally negative.[16] In spite of apprehensions among some Christians that comparative religion and the translation of *The Sacred Books of the East* would injure the missionary cause, such studies were generally supported as effective tools for Christian propagation: "The study of comparative religion is sure to work good to the cause of truth. When the daylight shines into the musty, fusty temples; when the idols are dragged forth into the sun's rays; when the old records and sacred books are turned over, their power will be gone and their folly will appear."[17] Max Müller, Rhys Davids, Legge, Eitel, and Edkins were characterized as Christians whose work "will furnish a new link in the chain of evidences of Christianity." "Place the selectest of the doctrines of heathendom over against the teachings of Christianity, the imperfections of heathenism are at once apparent, just as a straight-edge reveals the inequalities of a crooked surface."[18] Such a view was generally shared by Christians in Japan,[19] who monopolized comparative religion as a "Christian science."[20] And no less an authority than Max Müller became the principal witness, testifying about Christianity as the most exalted religion of the world.

The missionaries of the German Evangelical Protestant Missionary Society had been strongly influenced by Western scholarship in comparative religion, and introduced a liberal appreciation of other religions. But they never questioned the unique position of Christianity; comparative religion became a tool for Christian propagation; it was seen as a scientific demonstration of the superiority of Christianity.[21] The Unitarians went further in their recognition of other religions; they did not want to "convert but to confer," and they consistently emphasized the principle of the harmony of religions. Also in this case, however, openness was combined with a firm conviction about the final victory of Christianity; and Clay MacCauley concluded confidently that "comparative religion shows the superiority of Christianity."[22]

In this way Western studies of comparative religion and Buddhism supported missionaries and Japanese Christians in their propagation. Comparative religion became, so to speak, a "scientific" evidence of the unique position of Christianity. Their knowledge of Buddhism and other religions certainly increased, but this was mainly used to demonstrate their limitations and fallacies.

The fact that Japanese Buddhists at an early stage sent promising students to the West to pursue the scientific study of Buddhism suggests that Western scholarship posed a great challenge to traditional Buddhist learning. According to Suzuki Norihisa, Nanjō Bunyū and Kasahara Kenju were the first Japanese who, as students of Max Müller from 1878, became acquainted with what may safely be called the science of religion.[23] Perhaps inspired by Nanjō, Ishikawa Shuntai acknowledged in 1884 that the study of religions was a valuable approach: "While I am personally a believer of the Shinshū sect, I acknowledge the value of conducting my discussion here from a point of view beyond my own religious commitments, namely, from the standpoint of the science of religion *(science de religion)*."[24]

In spite of an early recognition of the more objective approach, the Buddhist interest in Western scholarship was dominated by apologetic concerns. We have seen before that the Buddhist students in Europe combined their Buddhist and Sanskrit studies with extensive studies of Christianity and Western thought. The apologetic concern, however, reduced most studies of Christianity to superficial denunciations or mere enumerations of contrasts between Buddhism and Christianity. There were few traces of a sympathetic study of other religions, as the Western study of comparative religion at least purported to be.

One effect of the international contacts and the acquaintance with Western scholarship was the gradual realization that the Western interest in comparative religion and Buddhist studies could undermine the traditional claim of Christians that their religion was unique, or superior to other religions; it was even hoped that this would eventually prepare the ground for Buddhist expansion in the West.[25] In contrast to Western scholars, Japanese Buddhists began to appreciate comparative religion as a demonstration of the superiority of Buddhism.[26]

Lectures in comparative religion were introduced in Japan as early as 1887, in the Department of Theology at Doshisha and in the Buddhist Tetsugakkan, founded by Inoue Enryō. Similar lectures were offered in the Christian Meiji Women's School in 1889, and probably the same year in the Protestant Seminary of the General Evangelical Church and the Tokyo San'ichi Seminary of the Episcopal Church. A course was offered in the Tokyo Imperial University in 1889, but probably not realized until Inoue Tetsujirō started his lectures on "Comparative Religion and Oriental Philosophy" in 1891.[27] The fact that the Buddhists had great expectations about Inoue's lectures indicates that comparative religion, even in the purely academic field, had not yet reached beyond partisan interests and was still used as a tool for religious polemics.[28]

BEYOND APOLOGETICS

Along with such partisan interests among Buddhists and Christians, there was, however, a growing awareness that comparative religion introduced an alternative way, leading to a truth beyond the traditional orthodoxy of the established religions. Western scholars of Buddhism tended to maintain their adherence to Christianity, but they were often willing to regard Buddhism as an equal or even superior doctrine. Max Müller emphasized the similarities between Buddhism and Christianity, and suggested Buddhist influences on Christianity.[29] By writing about Christ as *The Light of the World* after he had published *The Light of Asia,* Edwin Arnold indicated that Christ was superior to Buddha; but in many ways Arnold seemed to be closer to Buddhism than to Christianity.[30] Referring to the development in the United States, Joseph M. Kitagawa suggests that the interest in the World's Parliament of Religions in 1893 was closely related to "the religious and philosophical inquiry into the possibility of the unity of all religions." The history of religions was regarded as neutral in the conflict between Christianity and other religions; religious liberalism stressed the continuity of Christianity with other religions and preferred the philosophical to the theological approach to the subject of religion.[31] A characteristic representative of this view in the United States was Paul Carus, who combined Buddhist convictions with a sympathetic understanding of Christianity. He believed in the purifying role of comparative religions: "For the sake of purifying our conception of religion, there is no better method than a study of comparative religion; and in comparative religion there is nothing more fruitful than a tracing of the analogies and contrasts that obtain between Buddhism and Christianity."[32]

THE WORLD'S PARLIAMENT OF RELIGIONS

The most tangible and impressive manifestation of the new climate of religious sympathy was undoubtedly the World's Parliament of Religions, held in connection with the World Fair in Chicago in 1893.[33] Because of its impact in Japan, I include an examination of those aspects of the parliament that had particular bearing upon Buddhist-Christian relations in Japan.

The main purpose of the Parliament of Religions was, apart from bringing "the leading representatives of the great Historic Religions" together in conference, to demonstrate what and how many important truths the various religions hold and teach in common; to promote and deepen the spirit of human brotherhood among people of diverse faiths;

and in various ways to unite and support religions in their confrontation with the great problems of the present age.[34]

The parliament became a magnificent demonstration of the power of religion and of harmony between different faiths. For the first time in history representatives of all the major religions were gathered under the same roof in peaceful conference. The Columbian Hall was packed with people; an estimated total attendance of nearly 150,000 persons listened eagerly to messages from religious leaders from all over the world.[35] The official record of the parliament defined its spirit by referring to an inscription on a temple in Kashmir, quoted by Tennyson: "O God, in every temple I see people that see thee, and in every language I hear spoken, people praise thee."[36] The president of the parliament concluded his opening address by saying, "This day the sun of a new era of religious peace and progress rises over the world, dispelling the dark clouds of sectarian strife. . . . IT IS THE BROTHERHOOD OF RELIGIONS."[37] In short, the idea of "the sympathy of religions" seemed to permeate the whole atmosphere.[38] The parliament made a great impression on the delegates and contributed to the change of climate among different religions.[39]

The Buddhist delegates from Japan apparently shared the mood of reconciliation and harmony. The delegation consisted of four prominent Buddhist priests as official delegates, assisted by three translators who also contributed with addresses, and, in addition, a Buddhist layman who represented Nichiren Buddhism.[40] Most of them returned with strong impressions of the parliament. It was widely reported and commented on in Japan, in the form of speeches, articles, and books.[41] It had been preceded by intense discussions in Buddhist journals and newspapers; preparatory committees and money-raising campaigns were organized; and a large number of meetings were held both before and after the parliament to introduce it to the Buddhist public.[42] In addition to the general emphasis on tolerance, Buddhist reports also supported religious cooperation as a means to solve common social and political problems;[43] they emphasized the need of a common front against materialism and irreligion[44] and maintained that religions had to find a solution to the tension between science and religion.[45] Finally, the study of comparative religion was introduced as a way to demonstrate that truth was found in all religions.[46]

This impression was affirmed by Christian observers who felt that the parliament had contributed to a greater tolerance among Japanese Buddhists.

The effect of the World's Parliament of Religions has been very great in Japan. Many Buddhist priests attended the parliament, and became well acquainted with the truths of all religions. They returned with the conviction that it was not wise for them to consume their energies in narrow-minded hostility to Christianity, but that the work before them was to teach and emphasize in a positive way the truths of their own religion.[47]

These impressions must, however, be supplemented by a few observations that modify the official image of reconciliation and harmony. Behind the surface of religious sympathy, cooperation, and common fronts against common enemies, there existed a profound discord between the Western, generally Christian, and the Eastern, Buddhist and Hindu, delegates. At an early stage of preparation Buddhist observers had argued that the idea of religious unification tended to serve apologetical purposes, and suggested that the real issue of the parliament was which religion was going to assume sovereignty?[48]

There is no doubt that the parliament was promoted by Christians whose general ideas were molded by Christian and Western traditions.[49] Religion was defined in terms of theism and immortality,[50] or in terms of the Fatherhood of God and the Brotherhood of Man.[51] The motto of the parliament was "Have we not all one Father? Hath not one God created us?"[52] The preface of the official report expresses eloquently the expectations of the sponsors: "It is believed that the Oriental reader will discover in these volumes the source and strength of that simple faith in Divine Fatherhood and Human Brotherhood, which, embodied in an Asiatic Peasant who was the Son of God and made divinely potent through Him, is clasping the globe with bands of heavenly light."[53] It is also characteristic that the hymns and prayers used throughout the parliament were one-sidedly taken from Christian traditions;[54] the sponsors apparently failed to discover that the Buddhists refused to participate in such ceremonies.[55] According to the official report of the parliament, it was obvious that, along with the idea of greater religious unity, it "did emphasize and illustrate the great Evangelical claim that the historic Christ is divine, the sufficient and only saviour of mankind."[56] An almost unanimous testimony of the Christian delegates concluded that the parliament marked "a new era of Christian triumph."[57]

The Christian delegates from Japan shared this general conviction. M. L. Gordon attempted to demonstrate why Buddhism was not the final religion.[58] Kozaki Hiromichi described Buddhism as a religion for the "ignorant and inferior classes" in Japan, and found it "beyond doubt" that it was merely a question of time before Japan would become a Christian nation.[59] And Kishimoto Nobuta claimed that "Christianity will survive and become the future religion" of Japan.[60] Similar views were expressed by P. Goro Kaburagi: "the teaching of Jesus Christ is the rising sun in Japan";[61] and Matsuyama Takayoshi: "Christianity alone can satisfy our every demand."[62] The affirmation of Christianity as the absolute religion was often accompanied by a liberal belief in evolution and progress. Kishimoto Nobuta, for instance, explained the superiority of Christianity in the perspective of the struggle for existence and the survival of the fittest: Religion will survive irreligion; Christianity will survive the other religions; and the Christianity of Japan will survive Catholic and Protestant Christianity.[63]

The atmosphere of Christian self-assertion and triumph did not pass unnoticed by the Buddhists.[64] But they drew different conclusions and, not without reason, interpreted their contribution as a successful expression of Buddhist progress. They soon discovered that their presence at the parliament challenged many Christians, a conclusion that corresponded to apprehensions among some Christians who feared that the parliament offered non-Christian religions an undeserved opportunity for propaganda.[65] The Buddhists effectively distributed thousands of pamphlets, prepared by Buddhists from Japan and Ceylon for the purpose of propagation,[66] and they were continually surrounded by curious and eager inquirers.[67] They were also able to hold meetings for interested people, and after the parliament they traveled in the United States, propagating Buddhism in various places.[68]

The four official Buddhist delegates from Japan appealed as a picturesque element, impressive as they were in their colorful robes.[69] Their addresses, however, could hardly appeal; they were traditional and heavy, and were read by representatives, since the delegates themselves did not know English.[70] Only two Buddhists managed to communicate meaningfully: the captivating personality of the Ceylonese Buddhist, Dharmapala,[71] and the eloquent Buddhist layman, Hirai Ryūge Kinzō, from Japan. The latter made a bold attack on the role of Christianity in Japan, characterizing it as a history of "foreign devastation under the guise of religion," and was met with a tremendous emotional response: "Loud applause followed many of his declarations, and a thousand cries of 'Shame' were heard when he pointed to the wrongs which his countrymen had suffered through the practices of false Christianity."[72] Against Christian missions he advocated a "synthetic religion," in which Buddhism and Christianity could be harmonized.[73]

The Japanese Buddhists did not hesitate to proclaim that the parliament was a unique breakthrough for Buddhist mission. The Buddhist presence was characterized as "an epoch-making, unprecedented happening, unheard-of in history."[74] It was felt that the situation was ripe for "Buddhism in Japan in the Far East to turn the wheel of Dharma in America in the Far West."[75] At the dawn of the twentieth century Bud-

dhism was appearing at the scene of world culture spreading the unfathomable light and compassion of the Buddha.[76] A representative Buddhist
journal concluded that the parliament was "the most brilliant fact in the
history of Buddhism."[77]

Intimately related to this sense of mission was the evaluation of the
parliament as an expression of Christian weakness. The parliament was
described by a Buddhist delegate as a call for other faiths to help a
stagnated Christianity deal with the problems it was unable to solve
itself.[78] Furthermore, the comparative study of religion, which Christians hitherto had tried to monopolize for their own apologetical purposes, was now applied as a method of depriving Christianity of its arro-
gant status as the supreme religion. Some Japanese Buddhists actually
interpreted the Christian interest in comparative religion as a sign of
decay.[79] In the parliament Christians had to meet other faiths on an equal
level, and the notion of Christian superiority was broken down. "Thus,"
it was concluded, "we cannot but say that Christianity in the meeting lost
more than it obtained."[80] Against this background, it was only natural
that the Buddhist delegates declared the encounter at the parliament as a
"peaceful war," in which Buddhism "had won the greatest victories and
the greatest honor."[81]

Such observations make it somewhat dubious whether the Parliament
of Religions can be described as a part of the development in Japan
beyond apologetics. It is perhaps symptomatic that there is no indication
that Buddhist and Christian delegates from Japan ever actually met each
other in Chicago. They subscribed to the general spirit of tolerance and
engaged in peaceful dialogue with representatives of other faiths, but the
mutual distrust between the two religions in Japan still seemed to be an
obstacle against a meaningful encounter.

Nevertheless, in spite of obvious apologetical concerns, the parliament
also pointed beyond apologetics. The atmosphere of religious sympathy,
with all its limitations, made an impact on the participants. We have
already noticed that Japanese Christians sensed a greater tolerance
among Buddhists as one of its effects; and the spirit of sympathy was supported by a growing number of liberally minded Japanese Christians. It
should also be added that, especially among the Buddhists, the self-assertion and missionary zeal had paradoxical implications, expressing a new
confidence that enabled them to confront Christianity in a more adequate way than before. Christianity was no longer felt so much as a
threat, and it was easier to meet on equal terms. Finally, directly and
indirectly the parliament paved the way for the first public conference of
Buddhists and Christians in Japan, in 1896. Without the inspiration
from Chicago and the experience of peaceful encounter the conference of
1896 would certainly not have been possible at such an early stage.[82]

JAPANESE DEVELOPMENTS

Particularly after the Sino-Japanese War (1894–1895) the new trend of unbiased study gained momentum. Religious liberals began to search for a religiosity beyond the narrow confines of traditional Buddhism and Christianity. Two scholars distinguished themselves as pioneers of comparative religion: Kishimoto Nobuta and Anesaki Masaharu; the former was a Christian and the latter a Buddhist, but both devoted themselves to religious tolerance and unity.

Kishimoto Nobuta (1866–1928) was a Congregational Christian who had been engaged in fervent evangelism as a theological student at Doshisha, from which he graduated in 1887. In 1890 he entered the Divinity School at Harvard University, where he probably attended George Foot Moore's lectures on the history of religion. He studied philosophy of religion, comparative religion, Sanskrit, and Pali, and graduated in 1893. He attended the World's Parliament of Religions and, returning to Japan the same year, he taught the science of religion at Tokyo Senmon College (the present Waseda University) and the Universalist Theological Seminary. His lectures at Tokyo Senmon College were published as a series of articles in *Shūkyō* and, in 1895, as a booklet entitled *Shūkyō no hikakuteki kenkyū* [The comparative study of religion].[83] Kishimoto claimed that comparative religion should be analytical, historical, and comparative. He emphasized impartiality: "It is of secondary importance whether or not one believes in religion. . . . Anyway, believing or unbelieving, the essential point is to regard all religions impartially and place them in the wrestling ring where the fittest will survive."[84] From this point of view, he criticized the partisan use of comparative religion, a tendency that he seemed to find especially among his fellow Christians. "For instance," he wrote, "one does not study comparative religion in order to defend Christianity; moreover, it is completely mistaken to study the science of religion in order to attack Buddhism. [The purpose of] the science of religion is neither to attack nor to defend a certain religion, but only to study religion as a reality."[85] Since the various religious traditions of Asia, including Christianity and Buddhism, had been preserved in Japan, this was, according to Kishimoto, the most suitable place for the study of comparative religion. In Japan various religions had coexisted in harmony; and the Japanese had a peculiar ability to integrate different traditions; so Japan was, according to Kishimoto, the appropriate place for the birth of a new, perfect religion, Japan's special contribution to the world.[86]

Kishimoto's activities in the 1890s were closely related to Unitarianism. He frequently advocated his ideas in the Unitarian journal, *Shūkyō*, as well as in *Rikugō zasshi* when the two journals were merged in 1898.

A number of his essays on comparative religion in *Shūkyō* and *Rikugō zasshi* were in 1899 compiled into a book entitled *Shūkyō kenkyū* [The study of religion], where his views on the classification, origin, and evaluation of religions were systematically developed. He defined religion as "the adoration, respect, and obedience of man, with his limited knowledge and power, toward the great Source of all things, the Providence of the universe."[87] Deeply concerned about the future of religion, he suggested that the future religion must be scientific, moral, philosophical, universal, and idealistic, emphasizing both social and individual reform.[88]

Even though it was remarked that his discussion of religious progress was essentially a "defense of Unitarian dogma,"[89] Kishimoto's role as a pioneer of comparative religion and promoter of liberal attitudes and religious cooperation cannot be denied.[90]

Anesaki Masaharu (1873–1949) exercised for almost half a century a great influence in the field of comparative religion, Buddhist studies, and the study of Christianity in Japan, both as professor of the science of religion at Tokyo Imperial University and as a prolific writer. His *History of Japanese Religions*[91] is still used as a standard work. After he graduated from the Imperial University in 1896, at the age of twenty-three, his influence as a scholar of religion increased rapidly. From the very beginning he was a consistent advocate of religious tolerance and cooperation, combined with a fine critical sense. With Kishimoto Nobuta he founded the first Japanese Society for the Study of Comparative Religion.[92] The main part of his lifework, however, belongs to the twentieth century, and his contribution in the initial period, in the 1890s, was hardly comparable to that of his senior colleague, Kishimoto Nobuta.

In sum, the Western study of comparative religion and of Buddhism was mainly introduced into Japan as part of Christian or Buddhist apologetics. Rather than promoting friendly relations, it provided material for mutual struggle. The World's Parliament of Religions provided a stimulus toward greater tolerance, but it was not until the middle of the 1890s that comparative religion began to be practiced as a strictly scholarly discipline relatively independent from secondary apologetical and sectarian purposes. From that time it became an important element in the development toward religious toleration and cooperation.

CHAPTER FOURTEEN

The Adventure
of Dialogue

> The age of blind obedience and suppression has already
> passed, and the age of gentleman-like criticism and
> study is about to come. How can gentlemen who al-
> ready once have talked cheerfully with each other in the
> same hall, and, moreover, had a photo taken together,
> once more start to abuse and slander each other?
>
> Comment in *Rikugō zasshi* in 1896

THE FIRST BUDDHIST-CHRISTIAN CONFERENCE

WE HAVE in the previous chapters observed two contradictory trends in Buddhist-Christian relations. One trend was characterized by mutual suspicion and a violent Buddhist opposition to Christianity; even though the most aggressive persecution subsided around the time of the Sino-Japanese War, dominant groups within the Buddhist establishment continued their anti-Christian activities until the turn of the century. Another trend, dominated by liberal Buddhists and Christians, emphasized the need for mutual recognition and respect, and paved the way for more tolerant attitudes. In this process some individual Buddhists and Christians had established friendly contacts and even various forms of cooperation; but until 1896 few of them had ever met each other in dialogue. It was therefore considered an unprecedented adventure when forty-two Buddhists and Christians met in the villa of Viscount Matsudaira in Tokyo on September 26, 1896.[1] Because the meeting was the first organized Buddhist-Christian dialogue on a public level, with symbolic meaning far beyond the actual happening, it deserves particular attention. The following pages will include a description of the meeting and its immediate background, a sketch of the various models of interfaith relationships represented, and a few considerations of the implications of the meeting.

The meeting was officially called the Conference of Religionists (Shū-kyōsha Kondankai), but it was generally referred to as the Buddhist-Christian Conference (Butsu-Ya Ryōkyō Kondankai). Since it was primarily a meeting of Buddhists and Christians, this more informal designation will be used here. The conference was organized as a social gathering for exchange of opinions *(kondankai)*, and was the result of weeks and months of intense discussions in various journals and newspapers, especially in the sponsoring journal, *Nihon shūkyō*.[2]

The discussion was prompted by a questionnaire concerning the future of religion in Japan, published by *Nihon shūkyō* in May 1896. Intellectual and religious leaders were asked to respond to six questions, giving special attention to the choice of a future religion.[3] In spite of the increasing emphasis on tolerance, this was still a touchy issue. Religious journals abounded in comparative reports about the strengths of the two religions, indicating the universal implications of the religious development in Japan. It was a popular idea to interpret the geographical location of Japan as the meeting place between East and West. As Buddhism had gradually penetrated eastward from India, via China and Korea, to Japan, Christianity had proceeded the opposite direction, from Palestine and Asia Minor, through Europe and America, and had finally reached Japan, where the stage was set for the decisive encounter between the two religions.[4] The urgency of the problem was emotionally emphasized by the fact that the turn of the century was drawing near, bringing about a new era, before which many thought the fatal struggle between the two religions would be settled. A characteristic example of such a comparison of strength before the new age is found in an essay by Inoue Enryō, who described the confrontation between Buddhism and Christianity as a world-wide wrestling tournament between East and West. In spite of his attempt to give an objective account of the two sides, one can still discern the burning question behind his thinking: Who is going to win?[5]

With this background the questionnaire concerning the future religion naturally aroused strong emotions. A number of prominent intellectuals filed their reactions, and religious journals added their comments.[6] The discussion soon changed character, however, as it sparked off a proposal by Shaku Sōen, head of the Rinzai sect and chief abbot of Enkakuji, the famous Zen monastery in Kamakura. Responding to the questionnaire, he argued that the question was too important to be dealt with in a superficial way: "Before deciding this great problem, I would like to arrange a conference of both Buddhists and Christians from the whole country; let them meet in a hall and have a friendly talk with each other. What is your opinion?"[7] This proposal became the concrete starting point of the Buddhist-Christian Conference.

It is significant that Sōen limited himself to Buddhism and Christianity as partners in the proposed meeting. He had elsewhere suggested that the two religions were now equal adversaries, the only "true religions" in Japan.[8] The old established Buddhism and the old European Christianity were both unfit for the modern Japan; the real question concerned the new Buddhism and the new Christianity: "Which will prevail over the other?"[9] Obviously two somewhat contradictory concerns were present in his mind: on the one hand, his apprehensions about the outcome of the struggle between the two religions; on the other hand, his hope for future cooperation.

Even though it was not a new idea,[10] Sōen's proposal created a sensation in religious circles. Many conservative Buddhists and Christians feared that such a conference would only aim at a vague synthesis of the two religions;[11] and the traditional animosity and mutual suspicion were still so strong that the respective religious communities were divided in their opinions about the advisability of such a meeting.[12] A considerable amount of courage was obviously needed to realize the plans.

In addition to Shaku Sōen, the promoter on the Buddhist side was Ōuchi Seiran, who has already been introduced as an effective anti-Christian propagator and one of the most prominent Buddhist laymen in the Meiji period. The organizers on the Christian side were Iwamoto Yoshiharu, a prominent educator, head of the Meiji Women's College, and editor of the women's magazine, *Jogaku zasshi;* and Togawa Yasuie (Zanka), who had distinguished himself as pastor, poet, and literary critic.[13]

Since the Buddhist-Christian Conference was prepared amid a storm of protest, criticism, and ridicule on the one side, and support and applause on the other, it was inevitable that the participants had mixed feelings about the venture. The tense atmosphere was described by a Buddhist participant, who referred to the unstable and threatening weather as an indication of the mood. Heavy layers of dark clouds, showers of rain, and a whistling autumn wind gave him a sense of uncertainty: "Would it be gloomy or bright?" He himself had strongly disapproved of the whole project when he received the invitation, and could not understand how two of the most respected Buddhist leaders of the Meiji era could engage in such an illusive scheme: "What problems do they have since they put their signature beside and make a common cause with Christians whom they naturally regard with antagonism and suspicion?" Would it not be a vain effort to cooperate with people who failed to recognize any Lord beside God, and whose faith inevitably had resulted in continuous incidents of lese majesty? He acknowledged that both Buddhists and Christians were concerned about the national morality; but it seemed completely futile to cooperate with Christians who advocated universalism while the Buddhists themselves stood for nationalism and hence were in conflict on the basic standpoint.[14]

With the background of such skepticism, one can easily imagine the uneasiness and excitement in the big hall of Viscount Matsudaira's villa, where prominent members of all denominations had come together. They were seated according to their respective faith, the Buddhists on the one side and the Christians on the other.

> On the left side [were] Christians such as Matsumura, Yokoi, Ōnishi, Ebina, Iwamoto, Togawa, and Amishima [Tsunashima]; on the right side Buddhists such as Shimada, Takatsu, Ōuchi, Maeshima, Shaku [Sōen], and Murakami. They were sitting formally on the floor facing each other, leaving the impression that they were staging again the old play of separation according to faith and life. . . . After all, it was a great spectacle of the Meiji era.
> The time had come when the former enemies were sitting side by side in the same hall. Since no one had yet opened his mouth and expressed his feelings, however, it was difficult to predict the result, just as the weather was unpredictable. Would it be gloomy or bright? That was the reason why the whole place was in total silence.[15]

This description may be slightly exaggerated, since all participants, at least in principle, were in favor of friendly relations between the two religions. On the other hand, the simple fact that people who for years had been involved in mutual struggle now for the first time met each other face to face seemed almost miraculous, and must have created a very peculiar atmosphere.[16]

The meeting opened with a greeting by one of the Christian promoters, Togawa Yasuie, who briefly presented the purpose of the meeting, stressing mutual knowledge through actual encounter, search for cooperation in social work, and the need to avoid emotional conflict.[17]

Then Ōuchi Seiran rose and described how he, more than twenty years before, had engaged in philanthropic work; in cooperation with such ardent Christians as Tsuda Sen, Nakamura Keiu, and Kishida Ginkō[18] he had founded the philanthropic organization Rakuzenkai. Later he had cooperated with Tsuda Sen in an educational project for the blind and dumb. Even though Buddhism and Christianity seemed to be as irreconcilable as oil and water, he himself had found a basis for cooperation in the Lotus Sutra, according to which the Bodhisattva Kannon (Avalokitesvara) appears in thirty-two different forms for the sake of the salvation of all sentient beings: "To those who must be saved in the Body of Brahma, he appears as Brahma and preaches to them the Law. . . . To those who must be saved in the body of Mahesvara, he appears as Mahesvara and preaches to them the Law."[19] Following the Lotus, Ōuchi argued that the Christian God should be understood in the light of the Indian deities. If, in the time of Sakyamuni, there had been people who worshipped a god called God, he said, there would certainly have been a passage in the Lotus Sutra saying that for those who must be saved in the body of God, Kannon appears as God and preaches the Dharma. Thus integrating

Christianity into Buddhism, even characterizing Jesus as a Great Bodhisattva, Ōuchi found no basic difference between the two faiths.

The only remaining problem, according to Ōuchi, was the strong foreign spirit of many Christians. That was the reason why, some years before, he had started the movement that advocated "reverence for the Emperor and worship of the Buddha," agitating all over the country against Christianity as a national injury. "So there are probably some of the participants present who at that time were slandered as traitors and heretics," he said, emphasizing the "joyful fact" that he who had previously denounced Christians as traitors had become one of the organizers of the meeting and could meet so many Japanized Christians face to face.[20] At the same time, however, he spelled out the consequences for Christians who again betrayed the great principle of reverence for the Emperor. In such cases he would even expect the Christian participants to join hands with the Buddhists to attack and punish the disloyal Christians.

By advocating cooperation "for the sake of the Emperor, for the sake of the Empire,"[21] Ōuchi set the tone of the meeting in his twenty minutes' speech. A Buddhist observer commented that his address that day was quite extraordinary; and the Buddhist participants "were extremely anxious about whether or not the Christians would subscribe to his arguments, and eagerly waited for the response."[22]

There was obviously no need for worry. After a short silence, Yokoi Tokio, famous for his liberal theology and Japanized Christianity, responded positively, saying that the incidents of lese majesty had been based on misunderstandings. Disregarding what had been done, he said, all religionists should now join hands to promote the dignity of Japan.[23] He described the spirit of purity and beauty as a gift of Buddhism, and emphasized the role of Buddhism for the development of Japanese religion and culture. Especially in a time when the tide of materialism was flowing over Japan, it was necessary to infuse interest in Buddhism into Japan, adapt it to Western methods, and enhance the glory of Japan in the world. He also argued that Christianity after some years would become assimilated into Japanese customs, add a new element, and thus benefit the people.[24]

Shaku Sōen, who had originally proposed the meeting, rejected prejudices on both sides, and also the antitraditional prejudice that made people search for a new religion beyond established Buddhism and Christianity. The emotional barriers should be broken down for the benefit of society. He did not expect any total union of Buddhism and Christianity, but he argued that believers of the two religions should cooperate about matters they agreed about, and work independently where they differed. He believed that "the universal great truth" was hidden in both religions, and saw it as the duty of religionists to have boundless compassion; for Christian love and Buddhist compassion were basically the same: "If Sakyamuni from India and Jesus from Judea had been together in the hall and shaken hands today, Kashapa would certainly have laughed with a faint smile, as he did in the past, when the Buddha lifted the lotus."[25]

Sōen did not expect any solutions on the theoretical level, where Buddhism and Christianity seemed incompatible; but on the practical level compassion should be realized as Buddhists and Christians together engaged in philanthropic work. Arguing that Buddhists could regard Christ as an incarnate Bodhisattva *(Bosatsu no gongen)* or as the future Bodhisattva Maitreya, and, further, that Buddha had been worshipped by Christians as a saint under the name of Josaphat,[26] he pleaded for mutual recognition.

Shibata Reiichi, a Shinto participant, was an outsider in the predominantly Buddhist-Christian encounter. He had been included because of his support of religious tolerance. He had, in fact, proposed a meeting of all religions of the world as early as 1881[27] and had been a member of the Japanese delegation to the World's Parliament of Religions in Chicago in 1893. Shibata referred to the remarkable spiritual power that enabled Japan to assimilate all the virtues of foreign countries and to integrate them into a genuinely Japanese spirituality. If he could create man anew, he said, he would make Buddhist imperturbability the bones, strengthen him with the flesh of Confucian morality, let the blood of Christian universal benevolence circulate through his veins, and make Shinto his brain.[28]

Ebina Danjō, pastor of the Congregational Church (Kumiai Kyōkai) had come all the way from Kobe by boat to attend the meeting. He admitted that he had always wanted to meet such prominent Buddhists as Shaku Sōen, Murakami Senshō, and Ōuchi Seiran, whom he knew by reading. In order to guide the world Japan needed a Great Spirit, fostered by the power of religion, he maintained. Under the spiritual power of nationalism the different religions could be reconciled, mature, and develop, and finally become a universal religion leading the whole world.[29]

Murakami Senshō, one of the leading Buddhist historians, who had been very critical of Christianity,[30] emphasized the differences between Buddhism and Christianity. Yet he maintained that they should cooperate whenever it was possible, for the sake of the progress of humankind and for the sake of their own religion.[31]

Matsumura Kaiseki, a Congregational pastor who in recent years had won fame as a YMCA lecturer, described the division between conservative and progressive Christians. Among the progressive participants in the meeting, he characterized Togawa Yasuie as a "Buddhist Christian,"

Ebina Danjō as a "Shinto Christian," and himself as a "Confucian Christian." In a very emotional speech he expressed his resentment against the decay of the political and religious leadership of the country and advocated a religious unification for the sake of the renewal of the nation.[32] Foreign nations had been destroyed by enmity between different religions, but Japanese nationality had a transforming power, he argued. As Buddhism and Confucianism were Japanized, so the enmity between Buddhism and Christianity would be transformed toward a "happy reunion."[33]

In this way one after another of the participants stood up and in brief seven-minute addresses unanimously shared the joy of meeting for the first time; even though doctrines differed, at the point of love and compassion they could open their hearts, join hands, and plan for the future of society.[34]

Just one of the speakers broke the pattern. In an extremely witty and unconventional speech Oda Tokunō[35] described how problematic the meeting was from the point of view of Buddhist propagation. It is no problem for scholars, he said, but the common people cannot understand. If Ōuchi had preached in the countryside in the same way as he spoke earlier in the meeting, he would have aroused a great commotion, he said. Those who were engaged in the propagation of Buddhism would have to continue to denounce Christianity as an evil religion. He himself would be compelled to make for the countryside again and continue his slander of Christianity. "I hope you won't be enraged at me, thinking that Oda Tokunō, in spite of attending this meeting, again stages that sort of detestable action," he concluded, making the whole audience laugh.[36]

Oda's point was a reminder that the relationship between Buddhists and Christians was still characterized by suspicion and animosity. And the following speaker, the Christian philosopher Ōnishi Hajime, immediately retorted that the Christians were prepared to defend their faith.[37] But the very fact that Buddhists and Christians were able to laugh at a problem that for decades had created suspicion and hatred was in itself a sign of a new age.

The meeting continued with another nine addresses, representing slight variations of the above-mentioned themes. The session was concluded by Takashima Gayuemon, a Confucian diviner, who advocated the necessity of including the Christian God in the Japanese pantheon and thus adapting Christianity to Japan.[38]

After three hours of addresses by seventeen of the participants, they all proceeded to the garden to take a commemorative photograph, an inevitable Japanese custom, to keep for the future a remembrance of the "people who for more than a decade had rejected each other," as *Kirisutokyō shinbun* commented.[39] During the more informal dinner—without alcohol, as expected by religious reformers of that time—both Buddhists and Christians again had to prove their ability to compromise. For the strict Buddhists it was a meal outside the ordinary schedule; since the planned vegetarian meal proved to be terribly expensive, only the two Zen Buddhists, Shaku Sōen and Imagawa Yūzen, got vegetarian food. The Christians, on the other hand, had to refrain from the habitual common prayer before the meal.[40]

In the relaxed atmosphere the participants joked with each other and enjoyed themselves to the full. The following conversation took place as Ōuchi Seiran told Ebina Danjō how he the previous year had attempted to obstruct Ebina's meetings in the town of Mihara in the present Hiroshima Prefecture.

> "At *that* time I was defeated," Ebina said scratching his head, "since nobody came to my meetings." And Ōuchi [commented]: "At *that* time, in *that* place, I was perhaps saying that a traitor named Ebina had come to town. But from *now* on there ought to be nothing like that any more. As for this, too, however, let us just not forget the two characters, *son-nō* [revere the Emperor]!"[41]

The participants felt that they had experienced something unheard of in the history of Japan, initiating a great period in the field of religion.[42] *Rikugō zasshi* wrote that the conference

> signifies that the age of blind obedience and suppression has already passed, and the age of gentleman-like criticism and study is about to come. How can gentlemen who already once have talked cheerfully with each other in the same hall, and, moreover, had a photo taken together, once more start to abuse and slander each other?[43]

Before the meeting ended at eight o'clock in the evening, it was decided to continue with biannual meetings every spring and autumn. When the participants left the villa of Viscount Matsudaira, the clouded weather had cleared and the bright autumn moon was reflected in the harbor of Shinagawa, as if it was giving expression to the delighted mood of the meeting: the dark clouds of uncertainty and doubt had been dispelled.[44]

MODELS OF INTERFAITH RELATIONSHIPS

In spite of the superficial contact established at the Buddhist-Christian Conference, one can easily discern among the participants a whole range of attitudes concerning the opposite faith. Their opinions were often confusing and inconsistent, but they reflected models of interfaith relationships that not only survived the initial stage of contact but still to a great extent seem to characterize Buddhist-Christian relations. For the sake of clarity, I shall focus on three areas of relationships: (1) ideas concerning tolerance and coexistence, (2) ideas about practical cooperation, and (3) the popular trend of thought expressed in the search for a so-called new religion.

PEACEFUL COEXISTENCE

The dominant trend in all the addresses at the conference itself and in the current debate was a general mood of tolerance. It had been nurtured by the World's Parliament of Religions in 1893 and was strengthened after the Sino-Japanese War. After years of conflict, rapprochement was becoming a fact, featured in a number of religious and cultural journals.[45] Regarding the implications of peaceful coexistence, however, the opinions differed widely, from those who combined a reluctant tolerance with an unbending belief in the uniqueness of their own faith to those who wanted to embrace both Buddhism and Christianity in a vague synthesis.

Much of what was said at the meeting expressed the unsophisticated view that religious people, irrespective of doctrinal differences, should develop friendship and mutual understanding, not merely through the study of books and scriptures, but through personal contact.[46] The Unitarian principle of "the sympathy of religions," which had been so predominant at the Parliament of Religions, was shared by several of the participants.[47] As for the Buddhists, who were accustomed to the traditional Japanese coexistence of Buddhism, Shinto, and Confucianism, it seemed easy to accept Christianity as an additional religious element, so long as it did not threaten the established harmony.[48] As we shall see below, a popular solution was to conceive rapprochement in terms of cooperation about common concerns somewhat external to the strictly doctrinal issues.

The idea of peaceful competition between Buddhism and Christianity was not clearly expressed at the meeting, but it could be discerned between the lines even in the most highflown proclamations about cooperation and unity. Shaku Sōen's question has already been mentioned: Which religion will prevail over the other? In the debate preceding the conference, Christian participants had argued that the future of religion would be settled through the evolutionary struggle for existence.[49] Similar ideas were expressed by the liberal Buddhist journal, *Hansei zasshi*, which characterized the encounter between the two religions as "a living comparative religion," suggesting that the future religion would emerge as a result of personal encounter and peaceful competition.[50] Others advocated "gentlemanlike struggle" and confrontation as a sound element of interfaith relations.[51]

In this connection a comment should be made on the critical tolerance of those Christians who were regarded by liberal groups as hopelessly conservative and aggressive, notably the Presbyterians and Methodists who wrote in *Fukuin shinpō* and *Gokyō*. Uemura Masahisa, the editor of *Fukuin shinpō*, especially was regarded as the archenemy of rapprochement.[52] In spite of their orthodoxy and missionary zeal, however, the conservative Christians generally advocated tolerance and impartiality in relation to other religions.[53] Another conservative Christian journal, *Michi*, rejected both syncretism and exclusivism, and argued that Christians should recognize the truths existing in other religions.[54]

As for Uemura Masahisa, he certainly gave an extremely negative evaluation of contemporary Buddhism and of the religious spirit of Meiji Japan. On the other hand, he was fascinated by classical Japanese Buddhism, and referred to the great masters, Kūkai, Hōnen, Eisai, Nichiren, and Shinran, as "shooting stars" in the firmament.[55] He also recognized the need of comparative religion; referring to Paul's speech at Areopagos, he urged Christian evangelists to learn from Paul's sympathetic approach to other religions, his keen critical sense, and his comprehensive scope.[56] Thus the critical attitude of Uemura and other conservative Christians toward rapprochement did not necessarily imply a rejection of tolerance and reconciliation. Rather, Uemura was often regarded as narrow-minded and intolerant because his version of tolerance was accompanied by a keen critical sense that, in the Japanese context, was felt as exclusive and provocative. He criticized the current rapprochement by referring to the fate of the Metaphysical Society in London, a forum that included Christians, atheists, and agnostics. According to Uemura, its aim was to help the members to clarify their views through a tolerant and liberal dialogue with others. It had, however, become a society merely aiming at developing friendship, and the discussions had, consequently, become useless chatting. Uemura claimed that the Metaphysical Society finally died by an overdose of love, and he predicted that the Buddhist-Christian dialogue in Japan would face a similar situation.[57] Thus, with his critical sense, Uemura almost prophetically uncovered a tendency that has been a constant threat to all religious dialogue.

In this way, various notions of coexistence and tolerance existed side by side, often combined in somewhat contradictory ways. Rather than leading toward clarification and a solution of the basic problems involved in interfaith dialogue, the conglomerate of attitudes reflected a mood that to a great extent blurred the vital issues. They have been depicted here as representative of the confusing mixture of attitudes held by liberal Buddhists and Christians at that particular time. It could also be argued that the Buddhist-Christian dialogue up to the present time often has been marred by a similar ambiguity.

COOPERATION

Along with the mood of peaceful coexistence, the rapprochement between the two religions was often conceived in a pragmatic way as collaboration about common concerns, leaving out controversial issues. Shaku Sōen, for instance, argued that Buddhism and Christianity were incompatible at the theoretical level, but that unity could be realized at the practical level of social work.[58] Such cooperation was generally considered in three directions: nationalism, social concern, and cooperation against such "common enemies" as atheism and irreligion.

Nationalism was undoubtedly the most conspicuous aspect of the early Buddhist-Christian rapprochement. Ōuchi Seiran's appeal for cooperation "for the sake of the Emperor, for the sake of the Empire!" was cited above as a characteristic expression of the mood of the Buddhist-Christian Conference. Otis Cary was certainly right when he stated that "many of the addresses were permeated with nationalistic ideas."[59] Nationalism has already been described as a many-sided phenomenon, which for decades had nurtured the animosity between the two religions. After the Sino-Japanese War, however, Buddhists and Christians began to regard nationalism as a unifying concern: they had a common calling to solve the problems of the nation. Religious cooperation thus became a part of the all-inclusive service for the nation; and a basis was laid for an emotional recognition of Christianity as an equal partner, at least on the practical level. Expressed in the words of the Buddhist journal *Sōtō kyōhō,* the two religions should "entrench themselves in the same citadel of nationalism," and regard the opponents as common enemies, whoever they might be.[60] The conference in 1896 may be regarded as an open recognition of the patriotic spirit of the Christians and a manifestation of the cooperation between Buddhists and Christians for the sake of nationalism.

The Christian participants used a rather pompous language to express their nationalistic concern. Yokoi Tokio referred to the difficult relationship to the Imperial household as a problem of the past, and urged the Shinto representative, Shibata Reiichi, to teach the Christians how far they had to change in order to be in accord with the national polity. Matsumura Kaiseki appealed for a patriotic unification in order to cope with moral decay: "At the national level it is not a question of Christianity or Buddhism, Shinto or Confucianism, . . . all must be one."[61] Another pastor, probably Ebina Danjō, stated that the object of the meeting was to "adapt religion to this condition, to intensify the nationalistic spirit, and by showing that it is endorsed by the teaching of our creeds, to render those creeds a power in the world."[62] Referring to Japan's international role, he argued that a common front of religions, unified "under the spiritual power of nationalism," should play a leading role in the whole world.[63] Such emotional expressions of patriotic sentiment blurred some of the controversial issues that, if discussed, might have created problems.[64]

On the Buddhist side, Ōuchi Seiran referred to the change in Christian attitudes as the main reason for his consenting to be a promoter of the Buddhist-Christian Conference. Cooperation was possible "because the Christians had become Japanized,"[65] just as the excessive proforeign spirit and disloyalty of the Christians in previous years had provoked his anti-Christian activity. The indispensable condition for cooperation was still the reverence for the Emperor, he said, and he even expected the Christian participants of the meeting to make a common front with the Buddhists against other Christians who were in conflict with the national polity.[66] *Meikyō shinshi* suggested that the time of conflict had passed, and criticized the violent anti-Christian agitators as "fake Buddhists and fake nationalists."[67] Such sentiments were apparently shared by the participants, even though it was still difficult for some to overcome the deep-rooted emotional aversion to Christianity.

The recognition of Christian patriotism was graphically expressed in the Buddhist journal *Shimei yoka,* which described state and religion as the warp and the woof of the great "embroidered brocade of Yamato [Japan]." Hitherto Shinto, Confucianism, and Buddhism had sufficed as the religious woof, while Christianity had been excluded as destructive of the national warp. Now the time had come to include Christianity, and thus add colors to the brocade; however, the absolute condition was still that the national warp should not be destroyed.[68] The symbolism should not be strained; but it seemed to suggest that the state was of primary importance as the warp, while religious truth was acceptable as woof only insofar as it did not threaten the state. For Buddhism a conflict with the state was apparently inconceivable. And the Christian participants, on their part, were happy to be accepted as partners "under the spiritual power of nationalism."[69]

The social concern of Buddhists and Christians opened another area of cooperation. In the opening address the common standpoint was characterized as the concern for philanthropy and public welfare.[70] Shaku Sōen identified Buddhist compassion with Christian love and argued that these should be accomplished in society as philanthropic work; Ōuchi Seiran referred to his twenty years of cooperation with Christians. Both suggested a division of labor: just as Buddhism could offer guidance in problems related to doctrine and philosophy, Christianity could contribute to problems related to society; together they could deal more adequately with the urgent social problems.[71]

None of the speakers went beyond generalities and lofty proclamations. Nevertheless, considering that philanthropic work had been, and still was, the object of competition and conflict, the Buddhist statements were significant. Many Buddhists still regarded Christian philanthropic work with suspicion and animosity; they opposed and criticized Christian workers, censured their relief work, or attempted to exclude them from certain positions they regarded as a traditional monopoly of the Buddhists.[72] In contrast to such sentiments, the Buddhist-Christian Conference expressed an almost unanimous recognition of the unique contribution of the Christian philanthropic work.

A third area of cooperation was the front against what was conceived as a "common enemy." In the 1870s and 1880s Japanese Buddhists had actively introduced and promoted anti-Christian trends of Western thought in order to use them in their attacks against Christianity. In spite of some unsuccessful experiences, it was not until the 1890s that they discovered that the same arguments could be used against Buddhism as well. They never seemed to doubt that Buddhism was in complete harmony with science and reason, but they gradually realized that the alliance with Western atheism and irreligion was rather dubious. What they had introduced as anti-Christian thought proved to be almost equally antagonistic to Buddhism.

The problem had been accentuated in Japan a short time before the Buddhist-Christian Conference through the antireligious and anti-Buddhist polemics of Katō Hiroyuki of the Imperial University. Katō represented a one-sided evolutionism;[73] he regarded fear as the essential principle of religion, and its central motive as the quenching of fear and attainment of peace.[74] He was the first who responded to the questionnaire in *Nihon shūkyō* about the future of religion, rejecting faith as spiritual slavery, incompatible with science.[75] Even though he admitted the philosophical significance of Buddhism, he failed to recognize its religious value; and he urged the Buddhists to refrain from wasting their time discussing the metaphysical side of their religion.[76] Observing the Buddhist reaction, a Christian paper commented somewhat ironically that "a few years ago Buddhists boasted that their system was philosophical. Now that it is being made the object of attack on scientific and philosophical grounds, its supporters say that Buddhism is not philosophy but religion."[77]

Katō's views raised a storm in the Buddhist world, and were rebutted by both Buddhists and Christians.[78] Toki Hōryū, one of the Buddhist delegates to Chicago in 1893, supported the Buddhist-Christian Conference by referring specifically to the attack on religion from Katō and his associates. Such problems related to the development of science, he argued, "will more and more stimulate the rapprochement between the two religions."[79] Hence it was not surprising that the idea of a common front against irreligion and materialism became one of the focal points of the conference. It was most strongly advocated by the Orthodox participant, Konishi Masutarō: "In a time when materialism is flourishing and irreligion is swaggering in the world, the different religions must cultivate their skills in order to fight these ideologies. In such a time, should we worry about domestic squabbles? No, we should rather advance unitedly and attack materialism."[80] Yokoi Tokio even argued that the Christians should stimulate the interest in Buddhism in Japan in order to stem the tide of materialism.[81]

Anesaki Masaharu indicated some of the contradictory implications of such a Buddhist-Christian alliance. From a humanistic point of view, he agreed that Buddhists should cooperate with Christians against irreligion as a public enemy, hostile to humanity. On the other hand, he argued, if irreligion was merely understood as a rejection of traditional belief in a personal God and the immortality of the individual soul, the Buddhists should rather support irreligion against Christianity.[82] In spite of such profound differences regarding basic problems, the idea of a common front against irreligion and materialism was apparently not questioned at the meeting; it had become a popular idea, frequently advocated by Japanese religionists, and it was emphasized even more strongly at the second Buddhist-Christian Conference in 1897.[83]

SEARCH FOR A NEW RELIGION

Discontented with confining themselves to particular religions, an increasing number of religious intellectuals were looking for a synthesis beyond Buddhism and Christianity, a new religion in which they could appreciate both and even propagate both.[84] That is one of the reasons why the Buddhist-Christian Conference was characterized as a "consultation in order to establish a new religion"; and several observers argued that the conference could become "an incentive to a new religion."[85]

Before specific ideas of a new religion are examined, some points of more general character need clarification. First, the concept has nothing to do with what is presently called the New Religions of Japan.[86] Second, the idea of a new religion must be understood against the background of the contemporary belief in progress and evolution. "New" was contrasted to "old" as the final stage in the evolution toward the ideal religion.[87] Third, such religious evolutionism was frequently expressed in more traditional terms as reform (kakushin), reformation (kaikaku), or even revolution (kakumei),[88] and was closely related to the Buddhist search for a "new Buddhism" and the Christian search for a "new theology" or a "new Christianity."[89] Others advocated in similar terms a "new Shintoism," a scientific "new religion," or the "new gospel" of "eternal life in social revolution."[90]

Thus the idea of a new religion or a new development in religion was widely used about a variety of attempts to create an ideal future religion. Apart from such a general background and a rather ambiguous concept, however, there were great discrepancies as to the understanding of the future new religion.

Beyond Established Religion. The most natural solution to the search for a new religion seemed to be a sort of eclectic syncretism, in which a new unity in religion was found in a vague acceptance of the plurality of faiths.[91] Many religious liberals expected comparative religion to contribute toward this process. *Hansei zasshi,* for instance, argued that a synthesis of Buddhism and Christianity would include the best in both traditions; through comparative studies and actual encounter, by cutting away the defects and maintaining the virtues of the two religions, the foundation would be laid for the "ultimate, great harmony," or the "perfect, great, unified religion."[92] The fact that this sort of syncretism was severely criticized shows that the idea must have had sufficient support to be felt as a threat to more orthodox views.[93]

Parallel with the vague ideas of an eclectic syncretism, another, related notion of unity was expressed, for instance, by Anesaki Masaharu. He opposed the idea of a mere eclectic mixture of Buddhism and Christianity, and advocated a "fusion of the central spirit." According to Anesaki, such a unity would be possible only by overcoming and transcending the present limits of religions at the very basis; or, expressed in Zen terms: One had to "climb beyond the hundred foot pole."[94] Rather than expecting a new religion to be founded by priests and propagators, he trusted more in influential persons outside the religious establishment. As a concrete model he referred to Brahmo Samaj, the Indian movement that aimed at integrating Christianity, Hinduism, and other religions under the central principle of monotheism.[95] The idea of a fusion of the central spirit was somewhat abstract, so the reference to Brahmo Samaj is useful. It indicates that the search for a new religion did not aim at establishing a new religious sect, but rather a reform movement, in which the essential spirit in every religion could be integrated.[96]

Anesaki himself identified the common spirituality of religions as the Buddha nature in Buddhism and the Holy Spirit in Christianity.[97] Others referred to a common "a priori religiosity,"[98] or the common compassion and love.[99] Several hesitated to accept the idea of a new religion at the present stage but appreciated the idea as a vision for the future.[100] At a later stage Togawa expressed his view on the fundamental unity of Buddhism and Christianity through the Buddhist term *shinnyo* (True Thusness);[101] Anesaki attempted to realize his vision in the Association of Unity (Kiitsu Kyōkai);[102] and Matsumura Kaiseki founded the Society of the Way (Dōkai), which was characterized as a new religion based on the essence of all religions.[103]

In many cases the idea of a new religion was associated with expectations about a religious genius *(shūkyōteki tensai)* who could bring about a total change of the religious situation.[104] *Rikugō zasshi* commented that the religious world was expecting a "great man" *(ijin)* to arouse the human spirit.[105] *Hansei zasshi* reported that "the so-called *progressive religionists* are drifting about amid the whirling tide of scepticism, and the general voice is constantly calling for the forthcoming of a religious magnate."[106] *Nihon shūkyō* was convinced that a "great man" or "man of virtue" *(taijin)* was about to appear, and saw it as its calling to prepare the way for this man.[107] Others considered the advent of a religious genius as a necessary condition for establishing an ideal future religion,[108] or referred to a "pioneer" who would bring about religious reform.[109] At a later stage *Shūkyō* argued that religious unification could only happen through the appearance of a religious genius like Buddha, Jesus, or Mohammed.[110]

The idea seemed to be closely related to the romantic wave in the literary world, which also featured the genius.[111] As this romantic idea was introduced in the religious world, it was mixed with more traditional expectations of a religious reformer who could reverse the decay and bring about total renewal. Some of the advocates of the New Buddhism referred to Luther and the Protestant Reformation as a model for religious renewal. The leaders of new religious movements in the East, such as the Ceylonese monk H. Dharmapala, the Hindu reformer Swami Vivekananda, and the leaders of Brahmo Samaj, may have contributed to such expectations.[112]

Assimilation into Buddhism. The trends sketched above suggest a synthesis beyond established religion. Whenever the synthesis was described in some detail, however, the idea of a unity *beyond* yielded to a unity somewhat *within* the limits of one particular tradition, that is, in categories inseparably linked to either Buddhism or Christianity.[113] Ultimately, it became a question about supremacy: Buddhism or Christianity. Within Buddhism, therefore, the future religion was understood as a liberal Buddhism which assimilated other traditions, notably Christianity.

Shaku Sōen's view has already been mentioned. In spite of rhetoric about a common ground of compassion and love, and references to Jesus as an incarnate Bodhisattva, he hardly went beyond recognizing certain practical aspects of Christianity. He expected Buddhism ultimately to conquer Christianity.[114] Ōuchi Seiran was in general agreement with Sōen. As mentioned above, he found a basis for unification in the Lotus Sutra; but he also adopted Esoteric Buddhist terminology to clarify his standpoint. Esoteric Buddhism, introduced into Japan by Kūkai (774–835), is a magnificent religious synthesis, which established the supremacy of (Esoteric) Buddhism by demonstrating the inadequacy of all other doctrines. At the same time it integrates all philosophies and doctrines as secondary expressions of the ultimate truth. This is symbolically expressed in the *mandala,* which is a graphic representation of the truth of the universe. Referring to the various types of *mandalas,* Ōuchi suggested that the cross could be included in the *samaya mandala* as one of the symbols expressing the intention *(samaya)* of the Mahavairocana Buddha, who represented the ultimate truth. Likewise, the word "Amen" could, according to Ōuchi, be recited as a mantra of the *Dharma-mandala,* representing the letter *A,* the Esoteric expression of "the unborn truth."[115] By adopting the traditional Buddhist philosophy of assimilation, as it was developed in Esoteric Buddhism, Ōuchi suggested that his recognition of Christianity was never conceived in terms of equality. Christianity was to be assimilated into Buddhism, just as Shinto had been assimilated when Buddhism entered Japan.[116]

A similar idea was expressed by Shaku Unshō. He was unable to attend the Buddhist-Christian Conference, but he explained in a letter that he had intended to give an address about "Dual Aspect Christianity" (Ryōbu Yaso) and announced that he would develop this idea further in an article. The expression was borrowed from another concept, "Dual Aspect Shinto" (Ryōbu Shinto), which was the traditional way of assimilating Shinto into Buddhism by regarding Buddhas and Bodhisattvas as the "true nature" *(honji)* and Shinto deities as secondary "trace manifestations" *(suijaku)* of the truth. The announced article was apparently never published; but the expression "Dual Aspect Christianity" certainly suggested that he wanted Christianity to be assimilated into Buddhism as a secondary manifestation of the ultimate truth.[117] Anesaki Masaharu, who advocated a synthesis beyond both Buddhism and Christianity, followed the same pattern in his interpretation of Christianity. Reviewing and criticizing the Christian concept of God in the light of the deities of the Hindu-Buddhist pantheon, he gave Christianity a place in a synthesis that was thoroughly molded by Buddhism.[118]

Thus the apparently unlimited Buddhist tolerance had obvious limitations. It was based on well-trodden philosophical ground, mostly a traditional philosophy of assimilation. Even the most daring expressions about unity revealed a strong conviction that Buddhism was bound to conquer Christianity. The Buddhists were challenged by Christianity on the practical level, but they claimed that it had to be assimilated into Buddhism in order to attain its full meaning. The new religious synthesis was nothing but liberal Buddhism stimulated by some aspects of practical Christianity.

Fulfillment in Christianity. Similar attempts were made on the Christian side to integrate Buddhism into Christianity. While the Buddhists applied the well-established philosophy of assimilation, the Christians preferred to conceive the integration of Buddhism in terms of evolution toward fulfillment. The idea of fulfillment was well known in Western theology; especially after Schleiermacher, who conceived Christianity from the standpoint of "religion," it became natural to regard non-Christian religions as preparatory stages toward the highest expression of truth in Christianity. Such ideas were gaining popularity also in missionary thinking, supported by predominant trends in comparative religion and the evolutionary and optimistic spirit of the late nineteenth century.[119]

We have already observed how the new theological trends in Japan in the 1890s heightened the expectations of evolution in Christianity. The program of Japanization stimulated efforts to adapt Christianity to the spiritual climate of Japan, a concern that was accompanied by the conviction that true Christianity would integrate and fulfill the best in all religions. The Japanese Christian leaders tended to see their Christian faith as an organic development of their past. One of the most common patterns of relationship between Christianity and the old faith is characterized by Takeda Kiyoko as "grafting"; Christianity was grafted into the old; it did not destroy the old, but grew out of the old.[120] In his now almost classical *Bushido: The Soul of Japan,* Nitobe Inazō described Christianity as the fulfillment of Bushido spirituality. He also suggested the preparatory function of the non-Christian religions by characterizing them as a religious "Old Testament."[121]

In part because the samurai training and Confucian background of most Christian leaders tended to prejudice them against Buddhism, it was more difficult to discover a similar Christian fulfillment of Buddhism. In connection with the attempt to Japanize Christianity in the early 1890s, however, Buddhism was increasingly considered as one of the spiritual traditions relevant for further consideration. Matsumura Kaiseki argued that Christianity had to be "largely modified by Buddhist and Confucian ideas."[122] Ebina Danjō, who was characterized as a "Shinto Christian" because he found the ideals of Shinto inherited and fulfilled in Christianity,[123] also wanted to integrate Buddhism: "Shinto, Buddhism, and Confucianism have their respective God-given truth which must be swallowed up and well digested by Christianity, and become elements that transform Christianity." The ultimate aim for the Japanization of Christianity was the Christianization of the Japanese religions; only in Christianity would they have a viable future, for Christianity was destined to conquer the world.[124] In a later essay he suggested in similar terms that Christianity would "swallow up" Buddhism by making the "pantheistic element of Christianity" manifest.[125] Iwamoto Yoshiharu, one of the Christian promoters of the Buddhist-Christian Conference, argued that Christianity would have to integrate Buddhism and Bushido in order to succeed in its mission.[126] According to Kishimoto Nobuta, it was a matter of course that the various religions were developing toward fulfillment in liberal Christianity.[127] The Unitarians expected "rationalized Christianity to lead the future of the Empire," and regarded Christianity as the "larger faith and life" through which Buddhism would fulfill its deepest aims.[128] In a comment on the Buddhist-Christian Conference in 1896, *Kirisutokyō shinbun* summarized the view of liberal Christians in the following way: "The Christians should really have a spirit of tolerance and devote themselves to the great task of bringing about the Kingdom of Heaven by including and guiding the others [the Buddhists]."[129] Finally, the idea of fulfillment in Christianity was advocated as one of the central ideas at the second Buddhist-Christian Conference in April 1897, when the General Secretary of the World's Parliament of Religions, John Henry Barrows, was invited as the main speaker. He was firmly convinced that all religions, including Buddhism, would turn to Christianity; and he used the opportunity to express his hope that the time would come "when every one will turn to Christ."[130]

Compared to the traditional wholesale condemnation of heathendom and idol worship, the idea that Christ came to fulfill and not to destroy represented a great step toward a recognition of the values in other religions. On the other hand, this view was rather unsatisfactory from the standpoint of other religions, which were reduced to being stages toward fulfillment in Christianity. They were not evaluated on their own terms, and the criteria for evaluation and the categories in which they were discussed were thoroughly permeated by Christian ideas.

In sum, most of the proclamations about tolerance, religious unification, or synthesis of Buddhism and Christianity were, in the end, based on a firm belief in the supremacy of one of the respective religions: The Buddhists recognized Christianity by attempting to assimilate it into Buddhism, and the Christians accepted Buddhism by regarding it as a preparatory stage toward the final fulfillment in Christianity.

THE SIGNIFICANCE OF THE FIRST BUDDHIST-CHRISTIAN CONFERENCE

The Buddhist-Christian Conference was planned and carried out by a minority of reform-minded leaders representing primarily the liberal wings of their respective communities. Conservative Buddhists and Christians were generally reluctant and critical toward the conference, fearing that the mood of compromise would lead to a weakening of faith, and even to apostasy. Some of the radical ideas, such as the search for religious unity beyond established faiths, never reached beyond liberal circles. The fact that several prominent Christian participants in the conference later left the church, or had a remote relation to the church,[131] clearly indicates that their ideas created problems for traditional church life; they could more easily be realized outside the church.

Nevertheless, an increasing number of conservative leaders on both sides shared some of the central concerns, such as the awareness that struggle had to be replaced by tolerance, cooperation, and mutual recognition. Buddhist leaders regained their confidence and were willing to recognize the positive aspects of Christian practice. And among church leaders the somewhat tolerant interpretation of Buddhism and other religions as preparatory stages toward fulfillment in Christianity remained a dominant idea.[132]

The direct results of the Buddhist-Christian Conference were perhaps not as impressive as one might have expected from the proclamations of the participants. A few points should, nevertheless, be pointed out to indicate its significance.

The most significant contribution of the conference was that Buddhists and Christians had actually met face to face in peaceful dialogue. It proved beyond doubt that dialogue was possible between representatives of two religions that for decades had been in bitter conflict and still were engaging in hostilities in many provinces. The conference set an example of open encounter that was bound to influence later developments of Buddhist-Christian relations.

From the Christian point of view, it was an open recognition of Christianity. According to traditional thinking, Shinto, Confucianism, and Buddhism were the accepted faiths of Japan, often referred to as an established unity, the three faiths of *Shin-Ju-Butsu*. Now Buddhism and Christianity alone were singled out as the two religions relevant for the future Japan. The fact that leading Buddhists not only made theoretical proclamations about tolerance and coexistence but actually met with prominent Christians in a friendly atmosphere was seen by many Christians as an unmistakable sign of the position Christianity had won for itself in Japan. *Kirisutokyō shinbun,* concluding that Christianity had finally been recognized as "one of the great religions of Japan," added, with a badly hidden pride, that Christianity, after hardly thirty years' history, had reached the same level as Buddhism, with its history of more than a thousand years.[133]

Rather than being a direct result of the conference, the recognition of Christianity should be regarded as the conclusion of a long process which became manifest and was dramatically demonstrated at the conference. Considering the fact that several of the Buddhist participants until recently had been active in anti-Christian campaigns, and that many of the Christian participants had experienced personal pressure, attacks, and even violent persecution from the Buddhist side, the conference was certainly a dramatic expression of the new atmosphere of mutual recognition.

Another direct result of the conference was the promotion of the study of comparative religion. The conference, which had been inspired by such studies, also paved the way for a society that aimed at promoting dialogue on a scholarly level. The initiative was taken by two young scholars of religion, the Buddhist Anesaki Masaharu and the Christian Kishimoto Nobuta, who at the first conference agreed to organize such studies. After two preparatory meetings, on November 1 and 7, 1896, the first Japanese Society for the Study of Comparative Religion was founded with eight participants on December 14, 1896, in the Kanda YMCA building in Tokyo.[134]

The first Buddhist-Christian Conference was to be followed by biannual meetings every spring and autumn, but almost nothing is known about the further planning. The second conference was held on April 21, 1897, rather abruptly, in connection with the visit of John Henry Barrows, General Secretary of the World's Parliament of Religions, who was invited as the main speaker.

Barrows' address focused on his experience from the Parliament of Religions in 1893. He recapitulated some of the central concerns of the parliament: religious tolerance, search for common points of religious faiths, the common front against materialism, cooperation in social and moral problems, and so forth. He rejected the idea of creating a future religion based on eclecticism, and finally presented his favorite idea that all religions would develop toward Christianity, expressing his hope that "everyone would turn to Christ."[135] The address thus voiced rather traditional ideas; his utterance aroused the indignation of the Buddhist participants, but they were polite enough not to express their feelings directly. The debate also seemed rather commonplace; there was little that evoked the excitement and the expectations of the participants, as in the first conference. The participation was also disappointing; only thirty-six persons attended, of whom twenty-four were Christians and only seven Buddhists.[136] The Buddhist promoters of the first conference, as well as several other prominent participants, failed to attend.

The record does not indicate any plans for future meetings; no new committee was appointed, and no date fixed. The Buddhist-Christian Conference, which was scheduled to meet biannually to promote cooperation "for the sake of the Empire, for the sake of the Emperor," did not meet again. It seemed as if the most pessimistic evaluation had come true: The Buddhist-Christian Conference would disappear without a trace, like bubbles on the water. Even though it failed to accomplish its lofty visions, however, its significance went far beyond the momentary excitement of encounter; the conferences between religious leaders after the turn of the century, mentioned in the Epilogue, were regarded as a continuation of what had been initiated in 1896.

In conclusion, one could say that the Buddhist-Christian Conference in 1896 was not an isolated happening, but an outward manifestation of a long process, and thus had symbolic meaning far beyond the actual happening. It could be compared to a railway junction, where lines from different directions come together and then spread out again in many directions. That is, the conference was a meeting point where earlier developments in Buddhist-Christian relations were brought together and made manifest, positively or negatively, and then developed further in various directions. There were few ideas expressed at the meeting that had not somehow been anticipated at earlier stages. And most aspects of the further development of Buddhist-Christian relations can be traced back to this early stage of contact, as we shall see in the Epilogue. Thus the Buddhist-Christian Conference in 1896 was not only the first Buddhist-Christian dialogue on the public level, but is a key to understanding the positive and negative aspects of later religious dialogue and cooperation in Japan.

Retrospect and Prospect—the Buddhist-Christian Dialogue in Historical Perspective

CONSISTENT TRENDS AND CHANGING SITUATIONS

WE HAVE FOLLOWED the development of Buddhist-Christian relations from bitter conflict to open dialogue. The initial contact after the opening of Japan in 1854 presented no basis for dialogue. From the Buddhist point of view, dialogue was impossible: Christianity was a deadly enemy, and there was no room for concessions. From the Christian point of view, dialogue was superfluous: Buddhism posed no threat, and there was no need for contact. The one-sided Buddhist animosity toward Christianity was gradually replaced by a mutual concern, as the Christians discovered that Buddhism could not be ignored, but posed vigorous and sometimes violent challenges to Christian expansion. In the 1890s Buddhists and Christians confronted each other as equal adversaries. Both realized the potential power of the other religion, but each was still confident that it would eventually conquer the other. This confidence and feeling of superiority enabled them in a paradoxical way to deal with each other in a spirit of tolerance, and even friendship; they could learn from each other, and cooperate in working toward common goals.

The development that made these radical changes possible has been examined in great detail above, and will not be repeated here. I will only briefly comment on some of the consistent trends, which are still relevant for Buddhist-Christian relations, indicating how the central issues underwent changes in emphasis, applications, and impact, according to the changing situations.

The rejection of Christianity on the basis of nationalistic arguments, remained, for instance, one of the most popular themes in Buddhist apologetics from early Tokugawa until the end of the nineteenth century. In a monotonous propaganda barrage Christianity was denounced as an intruder threatening national independence and destroying traditional religion and culture. The impact of such propaganda, however, varied drastically. In the initial period, it was nurtured by the popular suspicion against the "evil religion" of Christianity inherited from the Tokugawa period and supported by the official ban on Christianity. The arguments were reinforced by up-to-date information about Western power politics and colonial expansion, but such arguments gradually lost their appeal, especially when the Westernizing trend gained momentum in the 1870s and 1880s. In the wake of the nationalistic reaction from the end of the 1880s, however, the old charges were revived and applied again with a tremendous force, supported by new and violent strategies to keep Christians out of public life. The specter of military aggression and colonial expansion was used by the Buddhists as late as 1899, in arguments against the coming mixed residence.[1] By then, however, the nationalistic anti-Christian propaganda had lost much of its appeal, primarily because the Christians had proved their patriotic spirit in connection with the Sino-Japanese War. The situation was reversed: rather than dividing Buddhists and Christians, nationalism became the basis for Buddhist-Christian reconciliation and cooperation.

The traditional Buddhist appeal to nationalistic sentiments had, of course, been intensified by the fact that the Christians generally identified themselves with Western ideas of civilization and modernization. Among missionaries, as well as among Japanese Christians, there was a strong feeling of cultural superiority, nurtured by the conviction that Christianity was the spiritual backbone of the civilized (Western) world. The naive identification between Westernization and Christianization was radically questioned in the 1890s, when Japanese Christians began to reject Western models and advocated the Japanization of Christianity. It is, however, significant that the feeling of cultural superiority remained intact: the patriotic Christians were still convinced that only Christianity, albeit Japanized Christianity, could offer a viable future for the Japanese people.

The fact that a concern having little to do with Christianity or Buddhism became such a predominant factor in the relationship between the two religions demonstrates that the Buddhist-Christian encounter was only to a limited degree a religious one. It was perhaps primarily a cultural and political confrontation, in which nationalism became the crucial issue, strongly affected by political and social changes. Ultimately it became a struggle about power and privileges. Buddhism defended its old position as a national religion and feared the Christian encroachment upon its traditional privileges. The Christians struggled for the right for free expansion and, ultimately, to take the lead in the formation of the future Japan.

The doctrinal rejection of Christianity, too, was surprisingly monotonous. There was among Buddhist priests and scholars an unbending belief in the doctrinal superiority of Buddhism over Christianity. Knowledge about Christianity increased radically after the opening of Japan, but the increase only added new arguments to the traditional charge that Christianity was in conflict with reason and modern knowledge. Three significant changes, however, added some nuances to the doctrinal criticism. First, the acquaintance with Western critical theology from the 1870s added new arguments to Buddhist polemics, enabling Buddhist apologists to distinguish critically between the Christian church and its doctrines of Christ on the one hand and the "real" Jesus on the other. Second, this distinction enabled them to appreciate the person of Jesus without abandoning their struggle against Christianity, a position that was dramatically expressed in the writings of Inoue Enryō. The admiration for the person of Jesus has continued since that time and has developed further as one of the most characteristic elements of the Buddhist relationship to Christianity.[2] Third, the influence of Unitarian and liberal ideas supported the Buddhist rejection of Christian dogmas; on the other hand, it also forced the Buddhists to undertake a critical examination of the basis of Buddhist doctrines, diverting interest from anti-Christian propaganda to preoccupation with inconsistencies in Buddhist thought and practices.

The dominant trend of Christian understanding of Buddhism was also quite consistent. The primary reason for ignoring or rejecting Buddhism was that Buddhism obviously was facing a serious crisis: the priesthood was corrupt and lacked spiritual vigor, and Buddhism was severely criticized by intellectual and political leaders. Such observations were combined with doctrinal arguments, the crisis of Buddhism being generally explained as a consequence of inherent fallacies in the Buddhist doctrines. In Buddhism there was no God and no soul, only ultimate annihilation. Mahayana Buddhism was an inauthentic deviation from the original teaching of the Buddha and could neither satisfy the spiritual needs nor create a basis for a sound society; it was pessimistic, passive, and powerless. In spite of some clamorous proclamations in the 1890s about relating Christianity to Buddhist and Confucian traditions, and a few attempts to harmonize Christian "theism" and Buddhist "pantheism" or otherwise to integrate Buddhist insights into Christian life and thought,[3] the majority of the Christians had few positive things to say about Buddhist doctrines.

Closely related to doctrinal controversies was the problem of modern science and philosophy. Both religions claimed to be in accordance with reason and scientific knowledge, but the argument changed over time. In the initial period, missionaries and Japanese Christians used their knowledge of modern science to prove the fallacies of the Buddhist world view. The Buddhists, on their part, mobilized all their apologetical skills to disprove first the geocentric (Ptolemaic), and then the heliocentric (Copernican) theories, defending the traditional Buddhist cosmology. As the Buddhists became involved in the enlightenment movement, however, they not only accepted Western scientific ideas, but utilized them in fervent attacks on Christianity. In the 1880s especially the Buddhists allied themselves with Western trends critical of Christianity, such as positivism, evolutionism, and materialism, which the missionaries desperately opposed as the modern "infidelity." A new stage was again reached in the 1890s, when Buddhists and Christians began to advocate a common front against such antireligious ideas.

What paved the way for Buddhist-Christian reconciliation in the 1890s was a development in various aspects of these trends that proved favorable to rapprochement. Nationalism became a basis for cooperation for the sake of the nation, primarily because Japanese Christianity changed its character and began to identify with the goals of the political authorities. The doctrinal divergencies were radically deemphasized for the sake of practical cooperation. And the threat from antireligious ideologies brought Buddhists and Christians together in a common front against irreligion and materialism. Their search for reform enabled them to learn from each other, and the strong conviction of Buddhists and Christians that their respective religions would finally conquer the other gave each of them a confidence that made dialogue possible.

FURTHER DEVELOPMENTS

A detailed examination of the further developments in Buddhist-Christian relations is outside the scope of the present study. It is, however, significant to see how the relationship between the two religions developed from what had been initiated and anticipated before the turn of the century. A rough sketch must suffice to indicate some characteristic trends. For the sake of clarity and convenience, I will indicate three areas of contact, well aware that the various types of dialogue were often combined: (1) the "establishment dialogue," (2) the "antiestablishment dialogue," and (3) various types of spiritual search and encounter.

THE "ESTABLISHMENT DIALOGUE"

I have already suggested that even though the first Buddhist-Christian Conference in 1896 was planned and carried out by liberal Buddhists and

Christians and criticized by conservatives, it expressed a concern that was rapidly gaining support also in conservative circles. What I have here characterized as the "establishment dialogue" is the contact and cooperation that developed among influential leaders in the mainstream of the Buddhist and Christian establishments. We have seen that nationalism, more than anything else, broke down the barriers between Buddhists and Christians in the 1890s, enabling them to cooperate "for the sake of the Emperor, for the sake of the Empire." As the Sino-Japanese War prepared the way for the recognition of Christian patriotism, the Russo-Japanese War (1904–1905) brought religious leaders together in a common effort to support the government and strengthen the unity of the Japanese people.

The Third Conference of Religionists (Daisankai Shūkyōka Kondankai) was convened in Tokyo on May 16, 1904, as a "War-time Conference of Religionists," gathering more than a thousand Buddhists, Christians, and Shintoists.[4] It was obviously felt that religious leaders needed to reach a consensus in order to provide guidance in a time of confusion and disorder. Some people argued for pacifism, which, after the Sino-Japanese War, had been openly advocated by both Christian and secular socialists, as well as by noted individuals who were neither, such as Uchimura Kanzō.[5] Others interpreted the war as a racial and religious conflict between the white and the yellow races, and between Christianity and Buddhism, represented by Russia and Japan. The conference rejected both pacifism and such allegations, justifying the war as a means to protect "the security of the Japanese Empire and the eternal peace of the Far East," aiming at "world civilization and humanity."[6]

A number of other conferences and organizations took up the trend. Prompted by the social and moral disorder after the Russo-Japanese War, influential religious leaders founded the Japanese Religionists' Concord Association (Nihon Shūkyōka Kyōwakai) in 1906. The association was to hold biannual meetings, fostering friendship among religious people, promoting the prosperity of the state, and providing moral leadership in a time of confusion.[7] In 1908 the Conference of Religions (Shūkyō Taikai) was held in Nagano City, with approximately six hundred participants. This and similar conferences were convened from time to time, promoting religious harmony and nurturing the patriotic spirit.[8] In 1912 the government sponsored the so-called Conference of the Three Religions (Sankyō kaidō), inviting Buddhists, Shintoists, and Christians. The initiative was taken by Tokonami Takejirō, vice-minister for home affairs, who had been concerned about the situation after the Russo-Japanese War; he regarded religionists as an unused resource for spiritual and moral guidance, and appealed for their cooperation. The Ministry of Home Affairs had to issue a statement to avoid the impression that the government supported an unconstitutional confusion of religion and state affairs. Nevertheless, the Conference of the Three Religions was attended by a number of sponsoring government ministers and officials, in addition to seventy-one religionists. A resolution urged all three religions to make their teachings manifest, support the Imperial Way, and increasingly plan for the promotion of the national morality. Cooperation between politics, religion, and education was also prescribed as a way to promote the prosperity of the country.[9] This conference stimulated other initiatives, such as the Conference for Educationalists and Religionists (Kyōikuka Shūkyōka Kondankai), which was held on June 28, 1912, and the Association of Unity (Kiitsu Kyōkai), founded in the same month, which aimed at concord between classes, nations, races, and religions.[10] In this way many influential leaders in the Buddhist and Christian establishments cooperated with each other to strengthen the state, fostering patriotic spirit, national unity, and moral strength in a time they perceived as fraught with disorder and crisis.

From the standpoint of the government and the religious establishment, the first decade of the twentieth century was characterized by a number of ominous tendencies, particularly in politics and ideology. Socialism had already been introduced; the first Society for the Study of Socialism was organized in 1898; and the first Social Democratic party was founded in 1901, only to be banned the day it was founded. The socialist movement gradually split into one branch that advocated a Christian socialism and a left wing of secular socialists who were inspired also by Marxism, anarchism, and syndicalism. The situation was aggravated when Kōtoku Shūsui returned from the United States in 1906, advocating "direct action." The plot to assassinate the Emperor in 1910 made a great impact upon the political situation: Kōtoku and eleven others were executed for their alleged leadership in the plot, and the socialist movement lost its momentum for a decade. We cannot go into details at this point, but there is no doubt that the government policy toward religions and its support of religious cooperation was stimulated by apprehensions about socialism and other "dangerous thoughts."[11]

Such semiofficial contact between Buddhists and Christians was renewed in the 1920s when Christian leaders joined other religionists in their criticism of the American Oriental Exclusion Act in 1924.[12] Another great Conference of Japanese Religions (Nihon Shūkyō Taikai) held in 1928 expressed concerns about social problems and peace, and took a stand against fascism; the basic trend, however, was characterized by the support of the national spirit and unity, and the fight against moral decay, political corruption, and "dangerous thoughts."[13]

Religious developments in the 1930s and during the war years were, of course, dominated by patriotic and Shintoistic indoctrination, and religious leaders had to adapt themselves to the circumstances. Further research is necessary to elucidate the religious cooperation and the trend of Japanized Christianity in those years.[14] In general, however, it can be said that the "establishment dialogue" failed to elucidate for religious leaders the ways in which politicians might use religion for nationalistic purposes.

I shall not here comment on what might presently be characterized as the "establishment dialogue." The above-mentioned development, however, is certainly a valuable reminder about latent trends in religious cooperation in Japan.

THE "ANTIESTABLISHMENT DIALOGUE"

Previously we have seen that various Buddhist reform movements dissociated themselves from the Buddhist establishment, advocating a radically new Buddhist life-style, including a revolution of the Buddhist organization and hierarchy and a new effort to break out of the political and social impasse. These efforts brought the Buddhist reformers into close contact with several Christian groups, mainly liberal Christians, Unitarians, and Christian socialists. Because of their critical attitudes to the religious establishment and to government interference in religious affairs, the New Buddhists questioned the close cooperation between the religious leadership and the government. Some of them also supported the socialists in their criticism of militaristic patriotism, and advocated pacifistic views. They did not become socialists, but they cooperated intimately with socialist leaders and promoted socialist literature; *Shin Bukkyō* [The New Buddhism] and other Buddhist journals carried articles that supported socialism. Suzuki Daisetsu, who was then in the United States, criticized the government for banning the Social Democratic Party in 1901. It is also significant that several Buddhists were involved in the Kōtoku incident in 1910; it was a Christian socialist, Ishikawa Sanshirō, who was with the Buddhist anarchist, Uchiyama Gudō, the last hours before he was executed for alleged participation in the plot.[15] The New Buddhists also opposed the Conference of the Three Religions in 1912 as an expression of political opportunism.[16]

A similar expression of antiestablishment contact can be seen between Buddhists and Christians in the years around 1930. Senō Girō, the leader of a Buddhist socialist movement, seems to have been especially influenced by Christian thought, and also by Christian individuals, such as Nitobe Inazō. In one period of his life he was a fervent student of both the Bible and the Lotus Sutra. The relationship between Buddhist socialism and social Christianity in those years has yet to be explored, but there was obviously both actual contact and ideological closeness. While the Christians were anticipating the "establishment of the Kingdom of God," the Buddhists advocated the "establishment of the Buddha-Land," not as a state of mind, but as an actual social reality.[17]

Compared to the "establishment dialogue," the contact between the small groups that were critical of established religion and nationalistic values may seem insignificant and may be easily forgotten. Nevertheless, they stand for a trend that deserves due consideration, particularly because of their critical function in the predominantly conservative religious world of Japan.

THE SPIRITUAL ENCOUNTER

The above-mentioned types of dialogue and contact were certainly expressions of a spiritual encounter, but here the term is used in a narrower sense to characterize various types of contact resulting from a spiritual search on the individual level.

Spiritual Search. The turn of the century in Japan was characterized by change and transition. It was a time of anguish and agony and spiritual restlessness.[18] Exposed to numerous new ideas and movements, many religious people shared the uprootedness of the time and searched desperately for new attitudes and approaches to the problems of the world. The apparent failure of established religions led many Buddhists and Christians to search for a spirituality that could offer a true alternative. They became spiritual pilgrims.

A few such pilgrims have already been introduced: Hirai Kinzō, a zealous Buddhist who also devoted himself to Unitarianism; Saji Jitsunen, an influential Buddhist who served as a Unitarian leader, but who, nevertheless, never abandoned his Buddhist faith; the Christian pastor and poet Togawa Yasuie, who later devoted himself to Buddhism; Yoshida Seitarō, a Christian who was "called by God" to receive three years of Zen training in Kyoto before he returned to his ministry; Matsumura Kaiseki, a prominent pastor and preacher who wanted to unify all religions in his Society of the Way (Dōkai); and a number of Christians who contributed to the initial Buddhist-Christian dialogue but later dissociated themselves from active church life. It could also be mentioned that one of the pioneers of Christian socialism, Kinoshita Naoe, left the church and oriented himself toward Buddhism.[19]

The two who most characteristically incorporated the spirit of the times were perhaps Takayama Chogyū and Tsunajima Ryōsen. Takayama (1871–1902) was an extremely talented poet and literary critic. He characterized himself as a "person of contradiction and of agony," and went through typical changes of attitudes, such as romanticism, Japanism, and a Nietzschean type of individualism and superhumanism. "There are only two ways to be great," he wrote. "One is to realize one's smallness and the other is to have confidence in one's greatness. . . . One is the doctrine of Christ and Buddha, the other of Napoleon and Nietzsche." He rejected religion, but admired Nichiren, Buddha, Socrates, Confucius, and Christ.[20] Tsunajima (1873–1907) was baptized in his youth, but as a philosopher he went through stages of serious doubt and skepticism. Faced with illness, he experienced ecstatic, mystical visions of God, and advocated a romantic, emotional mysticism that easily harmonized with Pure Land Buddhism.[21]

Among others who were inclined toward a spiritual unification of Buddhism and Christianity, a few names deserve mention: Nishida Tenkō, whose conversion was influenced by both religions, created in Ittōen (The Garden of Light) a religious community beyond the boundaries of church and temple.[22] Itō Shōshin created a similar community in Mugaen (The Garden of Selflessness), and advocated a "selfless love" *(muga-ai)*, which should unify Buddhist selflessness and Christian love.[23] Kurata Momozō (Hyakuzō) contributed to the boom of Pure Land Buddhism through his popular book about Shinran, *The Priest and His Disciples,* in which his description of Shinran was colored by Pauline Christianity; and he searched for ways to unify Buddhist and Christian spirituality.[24] The congregational pastor Kaneko Hakumu tried to develop what he had discovered as the Zen spirituality in Christianity.[25] And another pastor, Katayama Yūkichi, advocated what he called "Zen Christianity."[26]

The list of people who made such pilgrimages from one religion to the other, or searched for a synthesis of the two, could easily be enlarged. I have mentioned a few for whom the Buddhist-Christian dialogue became a spiritual search with profound consequences. There is no doubt that such efforts appealed to Japanese sentiments. And they still appeal. Among loyal Christians there are many who cannot simply abandon Buddhism; and a number of Buddhists are, likewise, drawn toward Christianity. They live in a constant dialogue with the other faith, their own hearts being the place of encounter. This quiet spiritual search is perhaps the most characteristic expression of the Buddhist-Christian dialogue in Japan.

A more direct testimony about conversions from Buddhism to Christianity is found in what might be called "pilgrimage literature." There are, in fact, numerous such books and pamphlets. Most of them are written with an obvious evangelical concern; they are often quite apologetical and biased, and would hardly impress Buddhist readers. But such a testimony as Kamegai Ryōun's book about his pilgrimage from Buddhism to Christ certainly exhibits a deep religious spirit.[27]

Comparative Religion. Comparative religion in Japan did not develop as an isolated academic speciality, but as an expression of spiritual search. In the beginning it was primarily used to refute competing religions, but it soon became a part of the actual encounter between the different religions, particularly Buddhism and Christianity. It is thus not surprising that the two founders of comparative religion in Japan were both engaged in the Buddhist-Christian dialogue.[28] Kishimoto Nobuta was a liberal Christian, closely related to the Unitarians, but he found spiritual support in the practice of a Buddhist way of meditation.[29] Anesaki Masaharu was a devoted Buddhist, but he also believed in a unification of the two religions. The Buddhists, he wrote, "are ready to accept Christianity; nay, more, our faith in Buddha is faith in Christ. *We see Christ because we see Buddha.*"[30]

Although there are an increasing number of recent comparative studies of Buddhism and Christianity in Japan, the only study that previously was fairly well known seems to be Masutani Fumio's *A Comparative Study of Buddhism and Christianity,*[31] probably because it was translated into English. Numerous comparative studies have been published in Japanese, however, since the turn of the century. In fact, comparative studies are so numerous that they might be regarded as a characteristic expression of the Buddhist-Christian dialogue. Most of these studies are not very original or penetrating, and tend to serve apologetical purposes; but as a phenomenon they tell very much about the spiritual climate and about how the Japanese seem to be drawn in the direction of both religions.[32]

The Philosophical Dialogue. The roots of the philosophical discussions between Buddhism and Christianity are old in Japan, but they did not really grow very deep until Nishida Kitarō tilled the ground and created a fertile soil for dialogue. What is taking place in Buddhist-Christian dialogue at the present time would be inconceivable without the influence of Nishida and his disciples, who in various ways have enriched the dialogue by discussing such issues as theism and atheism, the personal and impersonal character of the Ultimate (God), transcendence and immanence, the selfhood and selflessness of man, and similar matters.[33] The topics of such discussions, which took place between Nishida and leading Buddhists and Christians in the 1930s, have been in the focus of interest at most stages of Buddhist-Christian contact.[34]

The Missionary Dialogue. Christian mission is often regarded as incompatible with the spirit of dialogue. It is, however, a fact that missionary and apologetical concerns were among the decisive forces that brought Christians into direct contact and dialogue with Buddhists. We have also seen that at an early stage the conviction that Christ came "not to destroy, but to fulfill" created a climate for a positive evaluation of other religions.[35]

An interesting attempt along these lines was made by the American Episcopal missionary Arthur Lloyd, whose interest in Buddhism resulted in his writing many books and studies. He was one of the few foreigners who was prepared for engaging in the dialogue in the 1890s. His main concern, expressed in a poem dedicated to the Buddhist prophet Nichiren, was to demonstrate how Buddhism was fulfilled in Christianity.

> So peace be to thy soul, good Nichiren,
> And in that Unseen World, where thou art now,
> May'st thou behold the Christ thou knew'st not here,
> And so approach the highest realm of Truth,
> The knowledge of the Father and the Son,
> Wherein consists alone eternal life.[36]

He found that "the quarrel between Eastern Buddhism and Western Christianity is one to be best solved by the path of meditation and prayer," and he wanted to make a "new and perhaps dangerous missionary experiment" of discovering the way of Christianity through the Shin Buddhist teaching.[37] Among other missionaries who distinguished themselves as fervent students of Buddhism were A. K. Reischauer and Hans Haas.[38] In addition, one of the most respected German scholars of Buddhism, Wilhelm Gundert (1880–1971), worked as a missionary in Japan for many years before he left the ministry and devoted himself to Buddhism. He later acknowledged that it was "the light of the unfathomable mystery of God" that had opened his eyes to Buddhism, especially to the inscrutable mystery of Zen.[39] Among the many contemporary missionaries who have devoted themselves to the study of Buddhist philosophy and practice are such names as Henrich Dumoulin and H. M. Enomiya Lassalle; the radical openness in their search has in a characteristic way been combined with a strong Christian commitment.[40] A similar commitment to dialogue and mission is characteristic of a number of Christian study centers, such as the National Christian Council (NCC) Center for the Study of Japanese Religions in Kyoto, of which I have been a member for many years. A true dialogue—including that based on a missionary concern—opens itself to spiritual search and does not necessarily yield to the temptation of cheap apologetics.

THE PRESENT DIALOGUE

As indicated in the Preface, my interest in Buddhist-Christian relations is the result of involvement in dialogue with Buddhists in Japan. The change from conflict to dialogue is part of the history of the Christian church to which I belong. It could be argued that the hostile confrontation between the two religions released zeal and latent energies among religious people. It was, on the other hand, seldom creative, and it contradicted the basic tenets of both religions. The reconciliation between Buddhism and Christianity in the 1890s was, therefore, a joyful event in the history of the two religions. Whatever reservations one might have about the motives for rapprochement, or about the various types of contact that resulted from the early contact, the atmosphere of respect, friendship, and confidence that now characterizes interfaith relations in Japan is more creative than the earlier animosity. It has given religious people in Japan unique opportunities to live in peace with each other, to learn from each other, to cooperate with each other, and to witness to their faith without being offensive or feeling threatened.

The present dialogue is inconceivable without the long history of Buddhist-Christian contact. It has certainly reached a deeper level of philosophical penetration and spiritual sharing, but a historical perspective would help us to recognize the courage and wisdom of those who pioneered the dialogue more than eighty years ago.

It might also be wise to realize that religious dialogue does not only take place at organized meetings and conferences. Dialogue is a way of life that is rooted in faith and opens itself to other people's experiences and insights. To a great extent, therefore, it takes place as encounters between people who never appear in any reports. It is a part of the daily experience of pastors, missionaries, and other religious workers; it takes place wherever religious people encounter each other, as neighbors, colleagues, or in various types of social activity. This "hidden" dialogue, which is conducted at the everyday level and seldom is expressed in public statements, is certainly as important as the organized dialogue.

A careful study of the different types of relationships described above will offer abundant material for reflection, criticism, and admiration. I will limit myself here to a few observations that seem relevant to what is happening at the present time. First of all, the very fact that Buddhist-Christian relations were so strongly influenced by political and social changes may be a useful lesson for all interactions between the two religions. Rapprochement became possible when the Buddhists realized that Christianity could not deprive Buddhism of its power and would not challenge the dominant nationalistic way of thinking. Religious interactions are easily manipulated by those with nonreligious motives. Especially in a time of crisis and national emergency, religions might again be expected to join hands in support of the government or to avoid all issues likely to create political tension; and any critical or "antiestablishment dialogue" would be felt subversive. It might be useful to make a critical evaluation of the present dialogue from such a point of view.

Another trend that has characterized the Buddhist-Christian dialogue from the beginning is the attempt to foster harmony by deemphasizing doctrinal and philosophical differences or by blurring central issues. This is perhaps an expression of Japanese wisdom, according to which maintenance of harmony is more important than the insistence on particular religious truths. On the other hand, there seems to be a constant danger for religious dialogue in Japan to become so all-inclusive that it degenerates into superficial conversations and a production of vague statements. This pertains not only to the very basis for cooperation and the doctrinal issues involved, but also to the goals to which religionists agree to devote themselves, be it moral problems, social issues, peace, justice, or the like. Religionists tend to avoid issues that imply commitment to specific goals, preferring generalities agreeable to everybody. In the words of a Catholic observer, harmony is maintained by "blurring the point of controversy and keeping up appearances."[41] Uemura Masahisa's sarcastic comment in 1896 that the religious dialogue would "die by an overdose of love" is certainly a critical reminder to all who are engaged in such ventures.[42]

I have often met enthusiasts who describe the Buddhist-Christian encounter as the most important event in our century. Such an exaggeration is hardly warranted, but it is understandable as an expression of the excitement and joy of sharing with others in the search for truth. A similar excitement was also found among those who pioneered the dialogue in the 1890s, when the rapprochement was characterized as the beginning of a new age in religion. On the other hand, there is no doubt that the encounter between Buddhists and Christians is important and will continue to play a vital role. It was pioneered by outsiders, and it has often taken place as special ventures somewhere on the periphery of the two religions; however, at least in the Christian church the dialogue is more and more accepted as a central concern. It is supported by many church leaders and promoted by central organs in the World Council of Churches and the Vatican; and a number of Eastern and Western theologians are gradually abandoning the one-sided dependence on Western models and discovering that Buddhism poses unexpected challenges.

From my own point of view, it seems that a dialogue that takes place only on the periphery of the church, uncommitted to its traditional life and thinking, however interesting and challenging it might be, will fail to make any lasting impact upon the church. I am convinced that only when the dialogue is also taken seriously by committed and loyal Christians will it have significant consequences for Christian theology and spirituality. A Buddhist friend expressed the challenge in the following words:

> Christianity has been through many ordeals. It has endured the fire of persecution, and has through 2,000 years been exposed to various cultures and philosophies. It has been tried by the fire of science, philosophy, skepticism, and antireligious thought, and has somehow managed to get through. However, it has not yet been through the fire of Mahayana Buddhism. When that happens I have no doubt that Christianity will enter a melting pot in which it will be thoroughly transformed by Buddhism.[43]

I do not know to what extent Christianity will be transformed by Buddhism, but there are good reasons to believe that a true encounter will force Christians into a painful process through which faith has to be radically reshaped in order to attain meaning again. This is also part of a missiological quest: in a culture deeply influenced by Buddhist ideas and practices, the Christian faith cannot be transmitted in a meaningful way unless it is able to relate to Buddhism, with humility and confidence.

Abbreviations

DS	*Daidō shinpō* (Buddhist nationalistic journal)
FS	*Fukuin shūhō;* from 1891 *Fukuin shinpō* (Christian weekly newspaper)
HZ	*Hanseikai zasshi;* from 1892 *Hansei zasshi* (English title, *The Temperance;* reform Buddhist journal)
JE	*Japan Evangelist* (Christian bimonthly journal)
JK	*Jōdo kyōhō* (Buddhist journal)
JWM	*Japan Weekly Mail*
JZ	*Jogaku zasshi* (Christian journal)
KS	*Kirisutokyō shinbun* (Christian weekly newspaper)
MH	*Missionary Herald*
MK	*Mitsugon kyōhō* (Buddhist journal)
MS	*Meikyō shinshi* (Buddhist journal)
NS	*Nihon shūkyō* (liberal religious journal)
OS	Ozawa Saburō. In the footnotes (OS) refers to Ozawa's collections of excerpts from journals and newspapers, copied by hand, one for each year of the Meiji period.
ReiZ	*Reichikai zasshi* (Buddhist journal)
RZ	*Rikugō zasshi* (Christian journal)
SB	*Shin Bukkyō* (reform Buddhist journal)
SY	*Shimei yoka* (Buddhist journal)

Notes

CHAPTER ONE

1. J. H. Gubbins, *The Progress of Japan, 1853–1871* (Oxford: Clarendon Press, 1911), pp. 227, 266–284; John K. Fairbank, Edwin O. Reischauer, and Albert M. Craig, *East Asia: The Modern Transformation* (Boston: Houghton Mifflin Co., 1965), p. 205.

2. See, e.g., W. G. Beasley, *The Meiji Restoration* (Stanford, Calif.: Stanford University Press, 1973), pp. 172–213; Otis Cary, *A History of Christianity in Japan: Catholic, Greek Orthodox, and Protestant Missions*, new ed., 2 vols. in one (Rutland, Vermont, & Tokyo, Japan: Charles E. Tuttle Co., 1976; first publ. in 1909), 1:274–293, 2:43–66.

3. Quoted in Kishimoto Hideo, ed., *Japanese Religion in the Meiji Era*, trans. John F. Howes (Tokyo: Ōbunsha, 1956), p. 8.

4. Other schools later came into prominence. For further reference to Tokugawa Confucianism, see Warren W. Smith, Jr., *Confucianism in Modern Japan: A Study of Conservatism in Japanese Intellectual History*, 2d ed. (Tokyo: Hokuseido Press, 1973), pp. 1–40; Robert N. Bellah, *Tokugawa Religion: The Values of Pre-Industrial Japan* (Boston: Beacon Press, 1970).

5. C. R. Boxer, *The Christian Century in Japan, 1549–1650*, 2d, corrected printing (Berkeley and Los Angeles: University of California Press, 1967), pp. 362–397; Richard Henry Drummond, *A History of Christianity in Japan* (Grand Rapids, Mich.: William B. Eerdmans Publishing Co., 1971), pp. 87–94.

6. The ruthless persecution of Christianity has been described in detail in a number of studies. In addition to the above-mentioned works by Boxer and Cary, see George Elison, *Deus Destroyed: The Image of Christianity in Early Modern Japan* (Cambridge, Mass.: Harvard University Press, 1973); Joseph Jennes, *A History of the Catholic Church in Japan: From Its Beginnings to the Early Meiji Era (1549–1873)*, rev. ed. (Tokyo: Oriens Institute for Religious Research, 1973).

7. Quoted in Jennes, p. 162.

8. In spite of such strict measures, various types of intercourse with the Western world continued. See Donald Keene, *The Japanese Discovery of Europe, 1720–1830*, rev. ed. (Stanford, Calif.: Stanford University Press, 1969).

9. Drummond, p. 91.

10. Anesaki Masaharu, quoted in Jennes, p. 179.

11. Quoted from *Sources of Japanese Tradition*, comp. Ryusaku Tsunoda, Wm. Theodore de Bary, and Donald Keene, 4th printing, 2 vols. (New York: Columbia University Press, 1968), 2:95–96; see also Beasley, pp. 74–75. In Richard T. Chang, *From Prejudice to Tolerance: A Study of the Japanese Image of the West, 1826–1864* (Tokyo: Sophia University, 1970), pp. 55–56, the view of another political thinker, Fujita Tōko (1806–1855), is summarized as follows: "If foreign trade was a means for bringing about conquest of Japan by a Western power, Kirishitan was an even more potent instrument of Western aggression. It was an Evil Religion, subversive of the order and security of the Divine Country."

12. See, e.g., Kōsaka Masaaki, ed., *Japanese Thought in the Meiji Era*, trans. David Abosch (Tokyo: Pan-Pacific Press, 1958), pp. 17–48.

13. See Jennes, p. 184.

14. George B. Sansom, *A History of Japan, 1615–1867*, reprint ed. (Folkestone, Kent: Wm. Dawson & Sons, 1978; first publ. in 1963), pp. 228–229. See also Kōsaka, pp. 19–20.

15. The expressions are used by Tokushige Asakichi, *Ishin seiji shūkyōshi kenkyū*, reprint ed. (Tokyo: Rekishi Toshosha, 1974; first publ. in 1935), pp. 123, 126.

16. Boxer, p. 318. See also Elison, pp. 7–8.

17. Quoted in Boxer, p. 318.

18. Ibid., pp. 318–320.

19. Apart from Christianity, certain Buddhist sects were oppressed, such as the Fuju Fuse sect of Nichiren Buddhism and Shin Buddhism in certain areas. See Tamamuro Taijō, ed., *Nihon Bukkyōshi*, vol. 3: *Kinsei kindaihen* (Kyoto: Hōzōkan, 1975), pp. 70–72, 230–247.

20. Oliver Statler, *Shimoda Story*, new ed. (Rutland, Vermont, & Tokyo, Japan: Charles E. Tuttle Co., 1971), p. 324.

21. The ceremony was called *efumi;* the pictures used for the purpose were called *fumie,* or "stepping-pictures."

22. Jennes, pp. 166–167.

23. Ibid., p. 167. For further details, see Boxer, pp. 391–397; Elison, pp. 195–211.

24. Translated in Elison, pp. 257–291, under the title, "Deus Destroyed." For an easily available annotated compilation of anti-Christian writings in Japanese, see Ebisawa Arimichi et al., eds., *Kirishitansho, Hai-Yasho,* Nihon shisō taikei, vol. 25 (Tokyo: Iwanami Shoten, 1970).

25. *Myōtei* stands for two names, *Myōshū* and *Yūtei.*

26. For a further discussion of Fabian and his two books, see Elison, pp. 142–184.

27. Ibid., p. 282.

28. See ch. 2.

29. For further comments on *Taiji jashūron,* see Elison, pp. 230–232; Jennes, pp. 176–177. The quotation is from Elison, p. 231.

30. Jennes, pp. 176–177.

31. *Ha-Kirishitan* is translated in Elison, pp. 375–389, under the title "Chris-

tians Countered." *Kirishitan* was the common appellation of Christianity, the Jesuits, or the Christians. The quotation is from p. 377. Elison suggests that *Ha-Kirishitan* is the content of the sermons Shōsan preached in Amakusa between 1643 and 1645. Another work by Shōsan was *Deusu mondō* [A dispute about Deus]. Further comments on these and other Buddhist tracts are found in Nakamura Hajime, *A History of the Development of Japanese Thought from A.D. 592 to 1868,* 2 vols. (Tokyo: Kokusai Bunka Shinkokai, 1969), 1:111–149.

32. Quoted from Elison, pp. 379–380.

33. Quoted in Jennes, p. 177.

34. *Kirishitan monogatari* is translated in Elison, pp. 319–374, under the title "Kirishitan Monogatari: Anonymous Chapbook." For *Kirishitan taiji monogatori,* see ibid., pp. 213–214; Jennes, p. 180.

35. Quoted from Elison, p. 374.

36. Ibid., p. 232.

37. Translated in Elison, pp. 149–153, under the title "The Anti-Jesuit."

38. For further references to Confucian criticism of Christianity or popular anti-Christian tales, see Jennes, pp. 176–179, 180; Elison, pp. 212–247.

39. Quoted from Cary, 2:30.

40. According to Cary, 2:31–32, Perry had not been so strict about transactions on Sundays.

41. William Elliot Griffis, *Dux Christus: An Outline Study of Japan* (New York: Macmillan Co., 1904), pp. 139–140. A similar sentiment is expressed in Cary, 2:31: "Thus did America call upon Japan, not only to have friendly relations with Western nations, but also to know and serve the Lord."

42. Yoshiya Abe, "From Prohibition to Toleration: Japanese Government Views regarding Christianity, 1854–1873," *Japanese Journal of Religious Studies* 5 (June–Sept. 1978): 111.

43. Cary, 2:30.

44. Abe, "From Prohibition," p. 112. A similar demand was also made by Townsend Harris; see Cary, 2:38.

45. Abe, "From Prohibition," p. 113.

46. Quoted from Gubbins, p. 275; see also Abe, "From Prohibition," p. 114; Cary, 2:39.

47. Abe, "From Prohibition," p. 114.

48. See Cary, 2:36–37.

49. Ibid., p. 37.

50. Ibid., p. 101.

51. Kishimoto Hideo, p. 197; *MH* (April 1873), pp. 114, 126. The year would still be reckoned in the traditional way, from the date of the foundation of Japan, 660 B.C.

52. Kishimoto Hideo, p. 197; Cary, 2:101–103. A notice by the medical missionary, Dr. J. C. Berry, indicates how problematic the issue was felt to be from the government point of view: "As foreigners form but a small portion of the civil staff, it would be, or was thought to be, impracticable to close the public offices on their (the foreigners') account alone; and it would be equally impracticable to keep the offices open on the native holidays, to be occupied by the few foreign laborers only." *MH* (Dec. 1873), p. 390.

53. Quoted in Cary, 2:38.

54. Ibid., p. 39. Cary indicates that this perhaps was based on a misunderstanding, as the instruction is not found in any official correspondence.

55. Ibid., p. 51.

56. Ibid., p. 53.

57. This board was actually the third of the so-called three notice boards *(sadame sansatsu)*, the first aiming at disseminating Confucian virtues and warning against crimes like homicide and arson, the second warning against various forms of conspiracy. The three boards corresponded to the three edicts issued by the shogunate in 1664. See Ishii Ryosuke, ed., *Japanese Legislation in the Meiji Era,* trans. William J. Chambliss (Tokyo: Pan-Pacific Press, 1958), pp. 43–44; Thomas W. Burkman, "The Urakami Incidents and the Struggle for Religious Toleration in Early Meiji Japan," *Japanese Journal of Religious Studies* 1 (June–Sept. 1974): 209; Sakurai Masashi, *Meiji shūkyōshi kenkyū* (Tokyo: Shunjūsha, 1971), pp. 54–57.

58. Quoted in Suzuki Norihisa, *Meiji shūkyō shichō no kenkyū* (Tokyo: Tōkyō Daigaku Shuppankai, 1979), p. 16.

59. Ishii, p. 44; Sakurai, p. 57.

60. For details about the discovery of the hidden Christians and their subsequent persecution and deportation, see Burkman, pp. 148–166, 183–206; Jennes, pp. 216–229; Cary, 1:274–331.

61. Jennes, p. 227.

62. Ibid.

63. Cary, 1:311; see also Burkman, pp. 187–188.

64. Burkman, p. 183. For details about diplomatic efforts, see ibid., pp. 157–165, 185–190; Abe, "From Prohibition," pp. 125–132.

65. Abe, "From Prohibition," pp. 128–132; Burkman, pp. 190–206.

66. See, e.g., Jennes, p. 215; Sakurai, pp. 58–59, 69–70.

67. Cary, 1:375–404.

68. See Cary, 2:11–27. The characteristic title of the chapter was "Waiting before the Closed Gates."

69. Ibid., pp. 28–29.

70. *MH* (Jan. 1859), pp. 13–14.

71. Ibid.

72. Cary, 2:49, 55; Kishimoto Hideo, pp. 176–177. See also H. J. Jones, "*Bakumatsu* Foreign Employees," *Monumenta Nipponica* 29 (Autumn 1974): 320–321.

73. Cary, 1:281, 377.

74. John Liggins, quoted in Cary, 2:45. For a further description of such books, see Ebisawa Arimichi, *Ishin henkakuki to Kirisutokyō* (Tokyo: Shinseisha, 1968), pp. 271–292.

75. Ebisawa Arimichi, "*Shakkyō seibyū* to sono hankyō," *Shien* 13 (Jan. 1940): 40, 48–49.

76. Quoted in Cary, 2:90.

77. Jennes, p. 215; Sakurai, pp. 58–59, 69–70.

78. See ch. 2 for further references to such activity.

79. A characteristic comment is found in a missionary report from 1873: "Their repugnance to foreigners, too largely founded on their fear of Jesuitical treachery and mercantile rapacity, will quickly yield to the more genuine and just procedure of Americans and Europeans promoting trade and propagating Christianity. The unscrupulous cupidity of Portuguese and Dutch traders, and the political ambition and tortuous policy of Jesuits, under the guise of Christianity, cannot repeat themselves." Quoted from *MH* (May 1873), p. 144. Townsend Harris argued that "the Portuguese who came to Japan 250 years ago apparently had three objectives in view, that is, trade, conquest and proselytization, and that at the present day no nation desired to propagate its religious faith by force of arms." Quoted from Abe, "From Prohibition," p. 113.

CHAPTER TWO

1. Kishimoto Hideo, pp. 10–13, 107–110.
2. See examples in ibid., p. 108. A lengthy description of Buddhist decay and priestly corruption is found in Tsuji Zennosuke, *Nihon Bukkyōshi*, vol. 9: *Kinseihen*, no. 4 (reprint ed., Tokyo: Iwanami Shoten, 1970; first publ. in 1955), pp. 404–489.
3. Cited in Kishimoto Hideo, p. 10.
4. Tsuji, pp. 493–494.
5. Kishimoto Hideo, p. 110.
6. Smith, p. 13.
7. The five relationships were those of ruler and minister, father and son, husband and wife, elder and younger brother, and friend and friend. The five virtues were humaneness (benevolence), righteousness, wisdom, propriety, and sincerity. See ibid., p. 14.
8. Critics belonging to the Wang Yang-ming school include Nakae Tōju (1608–1648) and Kumazawa Bansan (1619–1691); critics belonging to the Kogaku school include Yamaga Sokō (1623–1685), Itō Jinsai (1627–1705), Ogyū Sorai (1666–1728), Dazai Shuntai (1680–1747), among others. See Kashiwabara Yūsen and Fujii Manabu, eds., *Kinsei Bukkyō no shisō,* Nihon shisō taikei, vol. 57 (Tokyo: Iwanami Shoten, 1973), pp. 519–521.
9. Ibid., pp. 521–522, 527–530.
10. Ibid., pp. 525–527. Concerning Buddhist cosmology, see also Alicia Matsunaga, *The Buddhist Philosophy of Assimilation: The Historical Development of the Honji-Suijaku Theory* (Tokyo: Sophia University, 1969), pp. 38–39.
11. Kishimoto Hideo, p. 15.
12. Kashiwabara and Fujii, p. 523.
13. Tamamuro, pp. 271–274.
14. Quoted from Tamamuro, p. 271; the translation is fairly free, but the word *shukke* (bonzes) bears the implication of the phrase in brackets.
15. Kashiwabara and Fujii, pp. 527–530; Tamamuro, pp. 257–271, 274–276.
16. Tamamuro, pp. 271–274, 276–279; Kishimoto Hideo, pp. 43–64, 128–132.
17. For details about this development, see Kishimoto Hideo, pp. 43–73; Shigeyoshi Murakami, *Japanese Religion in the Modern Century,* trans. H. Byron Earhart (Tokyo: University of Tokyo Press, 1980), pp. 27–32.
18. Kishimoto Hideo, p. 70; Murakami, p. 29; Sakurai, p. 45. See fig. 2.
19. Kishimoto Hideo, pp. 128–135; Sakurai, pp. 42–54; Tamamuro, pp. 289–293.
20. Kishimoto Hideo, p. 118; Tamamuro, pp. 282–283.
21. Tamamuro, pp. 284–289.
22. Ibid., pp. 288–289. Kishimoto Hideo, p. 121, cites slightly different numbers.
23. *Kōza kindai Bukkyō,* vol. 2: *Rekishihen* (Kyoto: Hōzōkan, 1961), p. 13.
24. Quoted from Kishimoto Hideo, p. 111.
25. The great variety of apologetical concerns is clearly demonstrated in Tokushige Asakichi's analysis of Buddhist apologetical literature in the Meiji era. Tokushige suggests the following categories of apologetical concerns: general works; self-examination and discipline; the national benefit of Buddhism; the coexistence of Shinto, Confucianism, and Buddhism; criticism of Shinto; criti-

cism of Confucianism; criticism of Christianity; and responses to the actual historical situation in Meiji Japan. See *Meiji Bukkyō zenshū,* vol. 8: *Gohōhen,* ed. Tokiwa Daijō (Tokyo: Shunyōdō, 1935), pp. 47–50; see also Kashiwabara and Fujii, pp. 533–549.

26. Kishimoto Hideo, pp. 147–148; Tamamuro, pp. 113–116, 324–325.

27. See, e.g., Tamamuro, pp. 117–120.

28. Quoted from Kishimoto Hideo, p. 126.

29. As we shall see below, a certain impact can be observed in the reform of Buddhist studies and temple administration.

30. See, e.g., the aims of the Association of Buddhist Sects in Kyoto and Tokyo in 1868–1869, quoted in Kishimoto Hideo, pp. 127–128.

31. Ikeda Eishun, *Meiji no shin Bukkyō undō* (Tokyo: Yoshikawa Kōbunkan, 1976), pp. 99–100. Ikeda quotes a later statement of Gyōkai, but this was probably representative also of his attitude in the initial stage of encounter with Christianity.

32. Tokushige, p. 273; Kashiwabara and Fujii, pp. 535, 546–547. In spite of the great variety of apologetical concerns referred to in n. 25 above, it is characteristic that comparatively few writings were devoted specifically to defense against Confucianism and Shinto, while the number of anti-Christian writings increased drastically after 1854. See *Meiji Bukkyō zenshū,* 8:47–50; Kashiwabara and Fujii, pp. 533–549.

33. *Ha-Daiusu* was republished in 1868, with a foreword by Ugai Tetsujō. For the other titles see Kashiwabara and Fujii, 534–535; Kashiwabara Yūsen, *Nihon kinsei kindai Bukkyōshi no kenkyū* (Kyoto: Heirakuji Shoten, 1965), pp. 332–333. Sessō's treatise was included in *Heikja kankenroku,* referred to later in the same paragraph.

34. Published by Tokugawa Nariaki. It was also called *Minchō hajashū* or *Seichō hajashū, Minchō* meaning the Ming dynasty, and *Seichō* meaning the "sacred dynasty." The Chinese original, written by Hsü Ch'ang chih, was published in Peking in 1640.

35. Ugai belonged to the Jōdo sect and later became chief abbot of Chion'in, the powerful head temple of the sect. See Sakurai, p. 109. For the collections mentioned, see Ebisawa, "*Shakkyō,*" p. 40; Kashiwabara and Fujii, p. 535. Ugai also published a number of other anti-Christian treatises in Chinese and Japanese.

36. For a detailed examination of the remarkable Buddhist-Christian controversy in China, see Ōchō Enichi, "Minmatsu Bukkyō to Kirisutokyō to no sōgō hihan," *Ōtani gakuhō* 29 (Dec. 1949): 1–20; 29 (May 1950): 18–38. The controversy was not restricted to writing. Buddhists instigated persecutions against the Christians in some areas and attempted to unite Buddhism, Taoism, and Confucianism against Christianity. For contemporary Confucian-Christian controversies, see Gotō Yumi, *Min-Shin shisō to Kirisutokyō* (Tokyo: Kenbun Shuppan, 1979), notably pp. 95–121.

37. According to Abe Shinzō, a Catholic who had been converted when he was spying on the missionary activity in Nagasaki, the critics of Christianity lacked knowledge of Christian literature and depended one-sidedly on Chinese anti-Christian sources. See Sakurai, pp. 114–115; Ebisawa, *Ishin,* pp. 181–223.

38. Tokushige, pp. 326–327; Ashikaga Zuigi, *Ryūkoku Daigaku sanbyaku-nenshi* (Kyoto: Ryūkoku Daigaku Shuppanbu, 1939), pp. 588–589.

39. Motoda Sakunoshin, *Rōkantoku Uiriamusu* (Tokyo: Bunshōdō, 1914), pp. 66–67; Tokushige, pp. 318–320.

40. His notes included a list of more than eighty Chinese books on Christian-

ity, registered at Nagasaki; an account of his notes from C. M. Williams' instructions on the Ten Commandments, heaven and hell, etc., is included in Tokushige, pp. 321–325.

41. *Meiji Bukkyō zenshū,* vol. 8, "General Introduction," pp. 23–24, 30–32; several of Ryuōn's writings are included in this volume. See also Kashiwabara and Fujii, pp. 105–146; *Kōza kindai Bukkyō,* 2:135–136.

42. *Kōza kindai Bukkyō,* 2:153–157; Tsunemitsu Kōnen, *Meiji no Bukkyōsha,* 2 vols. (Tokyo: Shunjūsha, 1968), 1:164–165.

43. The treatise was *Shakkyō seibyū* [Correcting the errors of Buddhism], written by Joseph Edkins. See further comments later in this section.

44. *Kōza kindai Bukkyō,* 2:135–136; Sakurai, p. 124; Saba Wataru, ed., *Uemura Masahisa to sono jidai,* new ed., 5 vols. and 3 supp. vols. (Tokyo: Kyōbunkan, 1976; 5 vols. and 2 supp. vols. first publ. in 1938–1943), 1:379, 2:423, 433. The activities of the spies were in accordance with the system of espionage common in the Tokugawa period. The government cooperated with the Buddhists as well as sending their own spies to the missionaries.

45. Quoted from William Elliot Griffis, *Verbeck of Japan: A Citizen of No Country* (New York: Fleming H. Revell Co., 1900), pp. 134–135; see also Tokushige, pp. 369–370. A translation of the tract is found in Cary, 2:89–94. In Tokushige, p. 372, the tract is identified as *Sakiyō chabanashi: Yasokyō no shimatsu* [Tales of Nagasaki: The state of Christianity], written by a priest named Ryōgen. Another similar tract was *Nagasaki kenmon* [Observations in Nagasaki]; see Ebisawa, "*Shakkyō,*" p. 50.

46. "The study and refutation of Christianity" was also recommended as the second topic for study by the Association of Buddhist Sects in Kyoto in 1868. See Kishimoto Hideo, pp. 127–128.

47. Ashikaga, pp. 593–594; Ebisawa, "*Shakkyō,*" p. 58.

48. *Meiji Bukkyō zenshū,* 8:45; Yoshida Kyūichi, *Nihon kindai Bukkyōshi kenkyū* (Tokyo: Yoshikawa Kōbunkan, 1959), pp. 44–45 (hereafter cited as Yoshida, *Bukkyōshi*).

49. Ebisawa, "*Shakkyō,*" p. 59.

50. See the recommendations by J. Liggins to missionaries in 1861: "They can dispose by sale of a large number of the historical, geographical, and scientific works prepared by the Protestant missionaries in China. Faithful histories of Christian countries tend to disarm prejudice and to recommend the religion of the Bible; while works on true science are very useful in a country where astrology, geomancy, and false teachings on scientific subjects generally, are so interwoven with their religious beliefs." Quoted from Cary, 2:54. Reacting to such methods, the Buddhists warned: "The priests of the Jesus doctrine live mostly in private houses, and under the pretence of teaching astronomy, geography, and the use of fire-arms, and medicine desire in actual fact to spread about the abominable poison of Jesus." Quoted from ibid., p. 90. A detailed analysis of the Buddhist response to the use of Western scientific literature is found in Ebisawa, *Ishin,* pp. 271–292; Ozawa Saburō, *Bakumatsu Meiji Yasokyōshi kenkyū* (Tokyo: Nihon Kirisuto Kyōdan Shuppankyoku, 1973), pp. 141–204.

51. In 1855, the year after the opening of Japan, Nishi Honganji approved the production of instruments for astronomical observations to be used by their scholars to substantiate traditional Buddhist cosmology. The most famous representative of such apologetics was Sada Kaiseki. See Ashikaga, pp. 590, 592.

52. Among his works about Christianity, Ishikawa Shuntai even left an unpublished manuscript on Mormonism. See Tsunemitsu, 1:166–167; *Kōza kindai Bukkyō,* 2:156–157.

53. Tsunemitsu, 1:54, 69.
54. Yoshida, *Bukkyōshi*, p. 46; *Kōza kindai Bukkyō*, 2:136–137.
55. See, e.g., examples in Sakurai, pp. 118, 120, 121, 124.
56. Tamamuro, p. 121. Even though the shogunate accepted the opening of Japan, the ultimate aim had been to learn sufficiently about Western science and technology to expel the foreigners.
57. Ibid., pp. 121–122. The domains of Choshu and Satsuma were the dominant powers behind the Meiji Restoration.
58. Kashiwabara and Fujii, p. 546; Tamamuro, p. 122.
59. Kishimoto Hideo, pp. 127–128.
60. Kashiwabara, p. 362.
61. Ibid.
62. Tamamuro, pp. 132–134.
63. Griffis, *Verbeck,* pp. 134–135.
64. See Cary, 2:291.
65. Ibid., pp. 91–92.
66. Ibid., p. 96. For similar writings, see Sakurai, pp. 118–125.
67. Yoshida Kyūichi distinguishes between three types of thinking in relation to the national benefit of Buddhism: (1) the "enlightenment type" *(kaimeiteki),* represented by Shimaji Mokurai, Ishikawa Shuntai, and Ōuchi Seiran; (2) the "conservative type" *(hoshuteki),* based on the old Buddhist idea of *chingo kokka,* "to pacify and protect the nation" by the power of Buddha or religious ceremonies; and (3) the "nationalistic type" *(kokusuiteki),* represented by Sada Kaiseki, who opposed foreign influence and advocated protection of national traditions at all levels of society in religious, political, economic, and social life. See Tamamuro, pp. 332–335; Yoshida, *Bukkyōshi,* pp. 81–82.
68. Sakurai, pp. 118, 128–129.
69. In addition to the examples in ibid., see also *Meiji Bukkyō zenshū,* 8:117–128, 153–178, 192–225, 293–306, 314–334.
70. Sakurai, pp. 118–125; Cary, 1:89–94, 103–104.
71. The main themes included for study at the Institute for Apologetical Studies were, e.g., Genesis, Exodus, a Catholic book about the Ten Commandments, and a criticism of Buddhism written by Joseph Edkins, a missionary in China. See *Kōza kindai Bukkyō,* 2:136. Edkins' book will be discussed later in this section.
72. On this point Buddhism was also attacked by Confucian and Shinto scholars. See Kashiwabara and Fujii, p. 540.
73. Ibid., pp. 540–544; Kashiwabara, pp. 333–336, 365–372. See also Matsunaga, pp. 38–39.
74. *MH* (Sept. 1870), p. 294.
75. Kashiwabara and Fujii, p. 543.
76. Ibid., p. 544.
77. Ibid.; see also ch. 6. One problem that remained unresolved until it was taken up by Buddhist reformers in the 1890s was the historical criticism that Mahayana was not the authentic teaching of Buddha. See ch. 12.
78. For a detailed analysis of the impact of Edkins' book in Japan, see Ebisawa, "*Shakkyō,*" pp. 40–68; idem, *Ishin,* pp. 293–338. Even though it was a Chinese book, the Japanese rendering of the title is used, as we are concerned with its impact in Japan. Apart from having a remarkable linguistic talent and interest, Edkins distinguished himself as a devoted student of Chinese Buddhism. In 1854–1855 he wrote a series of Buddhist studies in the weekly *N. C. Herald,* entitled "Notices of Chinese Buddhism." In addition to his *Notices of Buddhism*

in China, published in Shanghai in 1855–1856, this formed the basis for *Shakkyō seibyū* (Ebisawa, *"Shakkyō,"* pp. 47–48). Edkins had obviously a considerable knowledge about Buddhism; however, the book was limited by the strong bias of Western Buddhologists against Mahayana Buddhism and by his own missionary concern, which made him emphasize the negative aspects of Chinese Buddhism. His criticism was systematically developed in twenty chapters, dealing with such topics as Buddhist sutras and doctrines, the historical Buddha, transmigration, the three treasures, and monks. He questioned the historical value of most Buddhist sutras which, in his opinion, were written by hundreds of different persons during a period of more than eleven centuries. He found Buddha's original teaching in Theravada Buddhism and rejected the authenticity of Mahayana. He argued that the doctrine of Nirvana was inhuman; the idea of Emptiness neglected the empirical reality; monkhood was useless and incompatible with the moral obligations to one's lord, parents, and spouse; Buddhist cosmology was in conflict with modern theories (Tamamuro, p. 131; Ebisawa, *"Shakkyō,"* pp. 43–48). See also Edkins' *Chinese Buddhism: A Volume of Sketches (Historical, Descriptive, and Critical),* reprint ed., (New York: Paragon Book Reprint Corp., 1968; first publ. in 1880).

79. Ebisawa, *"Shakkyō,"* p. 49. The first reference to the book was made in *Gohō sōron* [An introduction to Buddhist apologetics], where it was listed among 96 other books imported from China.

80. Ebisawa, *"Shakkyō,"* p. 56.

81. Ibid., pp. 56–61. The first lectures were held at the Institute for Apologetical Studies in January 1869.

82. Ibid., pp. 60–61. Ebisawa suggests that the text was either printed as a textbook by one of the two above-mentioned temples or made by Buddhist bookshops at the request of Buddhist scholars.

83. See Sakurai, pp. 109–111; Ebisawa, *"Shakkyō,"* pp. 46–47.

84. A corresponding treatise on ancestor worship, written by the American missionary J. L. Nevius, was also imported from China, but it apparently did not provoke such vehement reactions. See Tamamuro, pp. 131–132; Kashiwabara and Fujii, p. 531.

85. See ch. 3.

86. *Kōza kindai Bukkyō,* 2:12–15.

87. Sakurai, p. 107.

88. Ibid., p. 98; Kishimoto Hideo, p. 127.

89. Ozawa Saburō, *Nihon Purotesutantoshi kenkyū* (Tokyo: Tōkyō Daigaku Shuppankai, 1964), p. 48.

90. Fukushima Hirotaka, "Kaigai kyōjō shisatsu: Hai-Butsu jōkyōka no Seiō," *Ryūkoku Daigaku ronshū,* no. 413 (Oct. 1978), p. 46.

91. It should, however, be mentioned that Aoki Shūzō, who wrote the first draft, was warned by the German advisor, Professor Rudolf von Gneist, that foreign religions represented a danger; the Japanese were advised to stipulate the prohibition of Catholicism and the establishment of Buddhism. See Yoshiya Abe, "Religious Freedom under the Meiji Constitution," part 2, *Contemporary Religions in Japan* 10 (March–June 1969): 60–61.

92. Cary, 1:294–298; Jennes, pp. 223–225.

93. See references in ch. 1, n. 60.

94. Tokushige, pp. 407–418; Cary, 1:314.

95. A detailed study of such activities is found in Tokushige, pp. 389–610.

96. Cary, 1:310.

97. Cary, 2:83.

CHAPTER THREE

1. Even though some of the Catholic missionaries in the sixteenth century engaged in dialogues with Buddhist priests and obtained some knowledge of Buddhist doctrines, the general attitude toward Buddhism was rather negative; in most cases Buddhism was condemned as the work of the Devil. See, e.g., Elison, pp. 13, 29, 36–43, 52–53; Boxer, pp. 38–40, 43–45, 69–71, 221; Michael Cooper, ed., *They Came to Japan: An Anthology of European Reports on Japan, 1543–1640* (Berkeley and Los Angeles: University of California Press, 1965), pp. 309–352; Georg Schurhammer, *Die Disputationen des P. Cosme de Torres, S.J., mit den Buddhisten in Yamaguchi im Jahre 1551* (Tokyo, 1929). The persecution during the Tokugawa period has been referred to before.

2. Father Nicolai seemed to have established a good relationship with a Buddhist priest in 1872, but was greatly disturbed about his role as a spy; see Cary, 1:402–403. The Buddhist reformer Ōuchi Seiran wrote a tract against the Orthodox Church in 1872; see *Kōza kindai Bukkyō*, 2:236. The real confrontation seemed to start later, mainly in connection with the nationalistic reaction around 1890, when the Orthodox Church was attacked along with other churches.

3. *MH* (May 1873), p. 144.

4. *MH* (July 1871), p. 207.

5. W. A. Russell of the English Church Missionary Society, in *MH* (March 1870), pp. 75–76.

6. Report from the Committee on the Japan Mission, in *MH* (Nov. 1872), p. 356. Many similar reports could be cited.

7. *MH* (Nov. 1869), p. 380.

8. William Elliot Griffis, *A Maker of the New Orient: Samuel Robbins Brown* (New York: Fleming H. Revell Co., 1902), p. 147.

9. *MH* (Nov. 1869), p. 381.

10. Ibid.

11. R. S. Maclay at a missionary conference in 1883. See *Proceedings of the General Conference of the Protestant Missionaries of Japan, Held at Osaka, Japan, April, 1883* (Yokohama: R. Meiklejohn & Co., 1883), pp. 135–137 (hereafter cited as *Proceedings 1883*); also see the debate in ibid., pp. 145–152.

12. For further comments on these issues, see ch. 10.

13. John F. Howes, "Japanese Christians and American Missionaries," in *Changing Japanese Attitudes toward Modernization,* ed. Marius B. Jansen (Princeton, N.J.: Princeton University Press, 1965), pp. 344–345. For the following sketch of missionary attitudes, see ibid., pp. 340–349.

14. Ibid., p. 342. For nuances in missionary traditions, see Cyril H. Powles, "Foreign Missionaries and Japanese Culture in the Late Nineteenth Century: Four Patterns of Approach," *Northeast Asia Journal of Theology* 1 (Sept. 1969): 14–28.

15. See, e.g., Uchimura Kanzō's characteristic experience depicted in his autobiographical *How I Became a Christian: Out of My Diary,* in *The Complete Works of Kanzō Uchimura,* 7 vols. (Tokyo: Kyobunkwan, 1971), 1:28–29.

16. This was particularly the case during the Tokugawa period, when not only Christianity but also certain sects of Nichiren Buddhism and Shin Buddhism were forbidden and suppressed as subversive; see Tamamuro, pp. 64–65, 70–72, 230–247. For a more general examination of religious conflicts in Japan, see Wilbur M. Fridell, "Notes on Japanese Tolerance," *Monumenta Nipponica* 27 (Autumn 1972): 253–271.

17. See Ōhama Tetsuya, *Meiji Kirisuto kyōkaishi no kenkyū* (Tokyo: Yoshikawa Kōbunkan, 1979), pp. 80–87, 89. This problem was, of course, most strongly felt in the provincial cities and towns. For the problems in the rural areas, see notably Morioka Kiyomi, *Chihō shōtoshi ni okeru Kirisuto kyōkai no keisei: Jōshū Annaka Kyōkai no kōzō bunseki* (Tokyo: Nihon Kirisuto Kyōdan Senkyō Jimusho, 1959); idem, "Christianity in the Japanese Rural Community: Acceptance and Rejection," in *Religion in Changing Japanese Society,* ed. Kiyomi Morioka (Tokyo: University of Tokyo Press, 1975), pp. 117–133. See also my examination in ch. 9.

18. Dohi Akio, *Nihon Purotesutanto Kirisutokyōshi* (Tokyo: Shinkyō Shuppansha, 1980), pp. 52–55.

19. Howes, "Japanese Christians," pp. 345–346.

20. Winburn T. Thomas, *Protestant Beginnings in Japan: The First Three Decades, 1859–1889* (Rutland, Vermont, & Tokyo, Japan: Charles E. Tuttle Co., 1959), p. 84.

21. Howes, "Japanese Christians," p. 342.

22. This point cannot be dealt with here, but a careful look at, e.g., the contributors to the *Transactions of the Asiatic Society of Japan,* published from 1872, demonstrates the breadth and depth of the missionaries' interest in things Japanese. Howes is perhaps too critical in his evaluation of the Meiji missionaries.

23. William Elliot Griffis, who was closely related to the missionary movement in Japan in the early 1870s, was perhaps an exception. He recollected that during his stay in Fukui he had ample opportunities for learning both the scholastic and the popular forms of Shinto and Buddhism, and concluded: "During my four years' residence and travel in the Empire, I perceived that in all things the people of Japan were *too* religious." See his *The Religions of Japan: From the Dawn of History to the Era of Méiji,* reprint ed. (Freeport, N.Y.: Books for Libraries Press, 1972; first publ. in 1895), pp. viii–ix.

24. Quoted from Cary, 2:58.

25. Ibid., p. 64.

26. Ibid., p. 66. Townsend Harris commented on the religious indifference of the Japanese leaders: "I must say that I never was in a country so abounding with priests, temples, *miya* [shrines], statues, etc., etc., where there was so great indifference on religious subjects as there is in Japan. I believe all the higher classes are in reality *atheists.*" Quoted from Statler, p. 366. Basil Hall Chamberlain commented: "Ask an educated Japanese a question about Buddhism, and ten to one he will smile in your face,—a hundred to one that he knows nothing about the subject, and glories in his nescience." See his *Things Japanese: Being Notes on Various Subjects Connected with Japan* (London: Kegan Paul, Trench, Trubner & Co., 1939; first publ. in 1890), p. 78.

27. According to a missionary report in 1873, "Many [temples] are deserted and unfrequented, or possessed by a few solitary priests, who are ready to let the building for a very small rental." *MH* (Oct. 1873), p. 310.

28. Griffis, *A Maker,* p. 148. Griffis was not a missionary, but he was closely related to the missionary community in the early 1870s and probably expressed their sentiment on this point. See also his *Sunny Memories of Three Pastorates: With a Selection of Sermons and Essays* (Ithaca, N.Y.: Andrus and Church, 1903); and Edward R. Beauchamp, *An American Teacher in Early Meiji Japan* (Honolulu: University Press of Hawaii, 1976).

29. C. F. Pascoe, *Two Hundred Years of the S.P.G.: An Historical Account of the Society for the Propagation of the Gospel in Foreign Parts, 1701–1900,* 2

vols. (London: S.P.G., 1901), 2:718. See also Griffis, *A Maker,* p. 161; Cary, 2:99; Statler, pp. 60–63.

30. Cary, 2:64.
31. Cary, 1:294–335.
32. See Griffis, *Verbeck,* pp. 134, 136; Tokushige, pp. 368–371.
33. *MH* (Sept. 1870), p. 294.
34. Griffis, *A Maker,* p. 153.
35. *MH* (March 1870), p. 77.
36. *MH* (July 1871), p. 206.
37. *MH* (Oct. 1873), p. 310.
38. J. D. Davis in *MH* (Sept. 1873), p. 292.
39. Quoted in *MH* (Aug. 1873), p. 265.
40. *MH* (July 1871), p. 206.
41. Ibid., p. 207. Calling for a reexamination of the unsuccessful government policy, Ōkuma Shigenobu referred to the view of many officials, which he supported: "Therefore, Christianity is bound to become, sooner or later, a strong religion in Japan, particularly since there is nothing to take the place of Buddhism." Quoted from Kishimoto Hideo, p. 55.
42. One of D. C. Greene's closest associates, Matsuyama Takayoshi, a prominent Christian who distinguished himself as a Bible translator, made this characteristic comment on Buddhism: "As for Buddhism, it teaches little that is of use in the daily life of men, and its priests, content with an outward conformity to its precepts, have deceived themselves and others, and thus led the way in sin, and through their roundabout teaching and wonders, the foolish people have been confirmed in their folly." *MH* (July 1873), p. 226.
43. *Meiji bunka zenshū,* vol. 23: *Shisōhen,* ed. Meiji Bunka Kenkyūkai, 2d ed. (Tokyo: Nihon Hyōronsha, 1967; first publ. in 1929), pp. 8, 207–221. The treatise was translated by J. H. Gubbins in 1875; see Cary, 2:103–104; Kishimoto Hideo, pp. 184–185; Saba, 4:296–299.
44. Kuyama Yasushi, ed., *Kindai Nihon to Kirisutokyō: Meijihen* (Tokyo: Sōbunsha, 1956), pp. 72–73.
45. Ibid., pp. 66–70; Sumiya Mikio, *Kindai Nihon no keisei to Kirisutokyō* (Tokyo: Shinkyō Shuppansha, 1974; first publ. in 1961), pp. 26–28. Two of Yasui Sokken's disciples, Nakamura Keiu (Masanao) and Matsumura Kaiseki, became prominent Christians; see Saba, 4:299; Sakurai, p. 272.
46. See notably Takeda Kiyoko, *Ningenkan no sōkoku* (Tokyo: Kōbundō, 1967; first publ. 1959), pp. 65–88; Howes, "Japanese Christians," pp. 347–348.
47. Statler, p. 366; see also *Proceedings 1883,* pp. 35–36.
48. Fukuzawa Yukichi, *The Autobiography of Fukuzawa Yukichi,* trans. Eiichi Kiyooka (Tokyo: Hokuseido Press, 1960), p. 68.
49. Thomas R. H. Havens, *Nishi Amane and Modern Japanese Thought* (Princeton, N.J.: Princeton University Press, 1970), pp. 182–183.
50. Evarts Boutell Greene, *A New-Englander in Japan: Daniel Crosby Greene* (Boston: Houghton Mifflin Co., 1927), p. 121.
51. *MH* (Jan. 1873), p. 33.
52. *MH* (July 1871), p. 206.
53. Greene, p. 117.
54. Ibid., p. 120.

CHAPTER FOUR

1. See ch. 1.
2. Kōsaka, pp. 26–27, 34.

3. The missionaries especially regarded the adoption of the "Christian" calendar as a major victory. See, e.g., *MH* (April 1873), pp. 114, 126; *Proceedings 1883*, p. 54.

4. For further reference, see *Meiroku Zasshi: Journal of the Japanese Enlightenment*, trans. William Reynolds Braisted (Tokyo: University of Tokyo Press, 1976); Kōsaka, pp. 61–133.

5. Kōsaka, p. 117. Nakamura himself received baptism and made important contributions to the expansion of the Christian church; see ibid., pp. 113–122; Cary, 2:74–76, 103. For other supporters of Christianity among the members of Meirokusha, see Kōsaka, pp. 163–165.

6. See ch. 6 for further comments.

7. For the former, see Saba, 2:90–91, 363–364; for the latter, Kishimoto Hideo, p. 191.

8. In addition to missionary observations about Buddhism discussed in ch. 3, see also ch. 6.

9. Cary, 2:156–157; *Chrysanthemum* 2 (May 1882): 226.

10. Quoted in Cary, 2:172–173; see also Wayne H. Oxford, *The Speeches of Fukuzawa: A Translation and Critical Study* (Tokyo: Hokuseido Press, 1973), p. 240.

11. See, e.g., Daikichi Hirokawa, "Freedom and the Concept of People's Rights," in *Modern Japan: An Interpretive Anthology*, ed. Irwin Scheiner (New York: Macmillan Co., 1974), pp. 190–201; Roger W. Bowen, *Rebellion and Democracy in Meiji Japan: A Study of Commoners in the Popular Rights Movement* (Berkeley and Los Angeles: University of California Press, 1980).

12. Kōsaka, pp. 134–135.

13. Kuyama, p. 102; Kōsaka, pp. 135, 152–159.

14. Dohi, p. 90; Fairbank, Reischauer, and Craig, pp. 284–285.

15. A detailed analysis of the Christian involvement in the Popular Rights Movement is found in Dohi, pp. 90–103; see also Sumiya, pp. 52–56; Kōsaka, pp. 165–166.

16. Chitoshi Yanaga, *Japan since Perry* (New York: McGraw-Hill Book Co., 1949), pp. 126–127; Ernest E. Best, *Christian Faith and Cultural Crisis: The Japanese Case* (Leiden: E. J. Brill, 1966), p. 45.

17. Cary, 2:174–175.

18. These changes will be discussed in chs. 7 and 8.

19. This in spite of oppression of the press and political critics; see Sumiya, pp. 28–29.

20. Ibid., pp. 57–77; Fairbank, Reischauer, and Craig, pp. 285–291.

21. Kishimoto Hideo, p. 241; Sumiya, pp. 83–96.

22. Fairbank, Reischauer, and Craig, pp. 263–264.

23. *MH* (Dec. 1885), p. 522.

24. Uemura Masahisa, quoted in Kishimoto Hideo, p. 241.

25. *Fragments of Fifty Years: Some Lights and Shadows of the Work of the Japan Mission of the American Board, 1869–1919* (n.p., n.d.), p. 36.

26. J. L. Atkinson in *MH* (Oct. 1888), p. 442.

27. According to *Proceedings 1883*, pp. 56–57, twenty-nine new missionaries arrived in 1873, one more than the entire number of missionaries in 1872, and two less than the total number that had arrived during the previous fourteen years. See also Cary, 2:104–105; Ebisawa Arimichi and Ōuchi Saburō, *Nihon Kirisutokyōshi* (Tokyo: Nihon Kirisuto Kyōdan Shuppankyoku, 1970), p. 185.

28. See statistics in Cary, 2:105, 163; Ebisawa and Ōuchi, pp. 194, 250.

29. Cary, 2:97–163.

30. Verbeck in *Proceedings 1883*, p. 25.

31. Cary, 2:164–211.

32. The numbers are cited from Ebisawa and Ōuchi, p. 296. The statistics from this period show slight differences, but the general trend is quite obvious. See statistics in ibid., p. 194; Kishimoto Hideo, pp. 237, 247–249. According to Kuyama, p. 126, the membership in the Congregational Churches (Kumiai Kyōkai) increased 68 percent in 1883 and 53 percent in 1884.

33. See *Proceedings 1883,* pp. 161*, 135–152.

34. Detailed information about this expansion is found, e.g., in the *Missionary Herald,* which included almost monthly reports and letters from the missionaries of the American Board.

35. G. F. Verbeck's historical review of the years after 1873, in *Proceedings 1883,* pp. 53–185*, includes brief but exact records of the increasing involvement of the missionary societies and the gradual expansion of their work.

36. See the discussion in *Proceedings 1883,* pp. 144–147, 150 (p. 144).

37. Isabella L. Bird, *Unbeaten Tracks in Japan: An Account of Travels in the Interior, Including Visits to the Aborigines of Yezo and the Shrine of Nikko,* 2 vols. (New York: G. P. Putnam's Sons, 1880), 2:309. For a report of the first years of the Home Missionary Society, see *Nihon Kirisuto Dendō Kaisha ryakushi* (Osaka: Nihon Kirisuto Dendō Kaisha, 1898). In 1880 a similar mission board was organized by the (Presbyterian) United Church of Christ; see Ebisawa and Ōuchi, pp. 198–199.

38. *Proceedings 1883,* pp. 147*–148*. In the initial years the Chinese Bible had been used in Japan. Several missionaries published early translations of parts of the Bible, in cooperation with Japanese co-workers. The translation of the New Testament was completed in 1880, and of the entire Bible in 1888.

39. *MH* (March 1883), p. 112. It is significant that Japanese evangelists and pastors soon outnumbered foreign missionaries. In 1882 there were 145 foreign missionaries and 137 Japanese workers in the churches, while in 1885 there were 179 foreigners and 242 Japanese. See Ōhama, p. 59. Verbeck concluded his survey of the history of Protestant missions in Japan until 1883 by regretting the paucity of Japanese names in the sketches he had received from missionary colleagues, prophesying that Japanese names would greatly outnumber foreign names in the history of the next missionary period. See *Proceedings 1883,* p. 180*.

40. Cary, 2:167–172; *MH* (June 1884), p. 224; (Aug. 1883), p. 286.

41. Cary, 2:171; rendered by Cary as *rebaibaru.*

42. J. L. Atkinson in *MH* (June 1884), p. 223.

43. Cary, 2:166; Kuyama, pp. 125–126; Bird, 2:309. Such expectations were, of course, further enhanced by the trend of Westernization.

44. Kishimoto Hideo, pp. 219–222.

45. See, e.g., Cary, 2:77, 98–99, 107–108, 134–136, 205–208.

46. Further information about these developments can be found in most standard works about the Christian church in Japan.

47. An English translation of the aims of *Rikugō zasshi* is found in *Chrysanthemum* 1 (April 1881): 151.

48. Kōsaka, p. 135.

49. A review of a number of Christian journals and newspapers is included in Saba, 3:404–419; see also Kishimoto Hideo, pp. 224–225. Kōsaka Masaaki argues in Kuyama, pp. 103–104, that *Rikugō zasshi* had the same kind of position in the 1880s as *Meiroku zasshi* in the 1870s, *Kokumin no tomo* in the late 1880s and early 1890s, and *Taiyō* in the decade after 1897.

50. For further comments on the apologetical vigor of the Christians, see, e.g., Cary, 2:175–177; Kōsaka, pp. 177–186; Saba, 4:308.

51. *Proceedings 1883,* pp. 117*–119*, 125, 134–135; Cary, 2:152–154; Saba, 2:527–545.

52. Quoted in Charlotte B. DeForest, *The Evolution of a Missionary: A Biography of John Hyde DeForest, for Thirty-Seven Years Missionary of the American Board, in Japan* (New York: Fleming H. Revell Co., 1914), p. 83.

53. *Kyōdōshoku,* or "official priesthood," as it was sometimes called. See, e.g., *MH* (Nov. 1884), pp. 456, 462; Cary, 2:177.

54. *MH* (Nov. 1884), pp. 421, 456–457; Cary, 2:177. A Catholic observer, Father A. Villion, regarded the abolishment of the "ecclesiastical investiture" as a coup by the political authorities, and described the effect in Kyoto as a "clap of thunder," resulting in fervent but vain opposition from the Buddhist headquarters. See his *Cinquante ans d'apostolat au Japon* (Hong Kong: Société des Missions-Étrangères, 1923), pp. 276–277.

55. *MH* (Nov. 1881), p. 444. The pamphlet was entitled *Yasokyō kokugairon* [Christianity a national injury].

56. *MS* (April 24, 1881), p. 5.

57. Quoted from *Chrysanthemum* 2 (April 1882): 179.

58. Bird, 2:250.

59. *Chrysanthemum* 1 (Oct. 1881): 408. See also his speech about religious reformation, recorded in *Nōjunkai zasshi,* no. 3 (Nov. 1885), pp. 30–34; no. 4 (Dec. 1885), pp. 44–51.

60. Tajima Shōji, *Bukkyō metsubōron* (Nagoya: Kichūdō, 1888; first publ. in 1887), pp. 100–102.

61. Inoue Enryō (Fusui), *Haja shinron* (Tokyo: Meikyōsha, 1885), p. 1.

62. *Nihonjin,* no. 1 (April 3, 1888) (OS). In a similar way, Christianity and Buddhism were compared to the rising sun and the setting sun in Shimada Gunkichi, *Butsu-Ya yūshō reppaiben* (Iisakachō, Fukushima: Yuishindō, 1889), Preface.

63. *Taiyō,* translated in *JE* 3 (June 1896): 277.

64. *Japan Mail,* cited in *MH* (Nov. 1881), p. 444; (Nov. 1885), p. 423.

65. *MH* (March 1884), pp. 97–98; (April 1885), pp. 157–158; (Sept. 1885), p. 341.

66. Quoted in Cary, 2:159. See also Fukuzawa's criticism in *Jiji shinpō,* quoted in *MH* (Nov. 1885), p. 423.

67. *MH* (Nov. 1885), p. 423; *JWM* (March 12, 1887), p. 239.

68. For further reference, see Ikeda, pp. 112–116, 135–143.

69. For further information about Ōuchi Seiran, see chs. 7 and 14.

70. These two points will be further examined in ch. 6.

CHAPTER FIVE

1. *MH* (March 1885), p. 53.

2. Cited in the *Missionary Review of the World,* n.s., 2 (June 1889): 464; *JWM* (March 9, 1889), pp. 233–234. See also *MH* (April 1876), p. 129; (Feb. 1884), p. 65.

3. J. L. Atkinson in *MH* (Aug. 1884), p. 311.

4. G. M. Meacham in *Proceedings 1883,* p. 105.

5. J. H. Pettee in *MH* (July 1886), p. 262.

6. Yamamoto Kakuma, a lay Christian from Kyoto, in *MH* (Aug. 1878), p. 242.

7. Ise (Yokoi) Tokio in *Proceedings 1883,* p. 165. See also the discussion about Buddhism at the General Conference of Protestant Missionaries in 1883, in ibid., pp. 101–105. I have registered references to Buddhism in the monthly letters and

reports from Japan in the *Missionary Herald* during the 1870s and 1880s, as well as in a number of books written by missionaries and Japanese Christians. Space does not allow further references, but the above quotations seem representative. Comments on Buddhism were generally short and monotonous, and often functioned merely as the gloomy background of reports about the brilliant performances of Christian preachers.

8. See the section on "The Potential of Buddhism" in ch. 3.

9. Greene was, however, one of the first foreigners to make a serious study of such new religions as Tenrikyo and Renmonkyo. See, e.g., *Transactions of the Asiatic Society of Japan,* no. 23 (1895), pp. 24–74; no. 29 (1901), pp. 17–33.

10. Apart from quotations, these terms will be used without the derogatory implications so common in missionary literature. The background of the missionaries and their emphasis on the biblical rejection of idol worship have already been commented on in ch. 3.

11. "The folly of idolatry" had apparently constituted a basic element in Japanese preaching. See, e.g., *MH* (June 1884), p. 224.

12. Tamamuro, pp. 131–132; Kashiwabara and Fujii, p. 531. The tract was written by the American missionary J. L. Nevius.

13. Recorded in *Meiji bunka zenshū,* vol. 19: *Shūkyōhen,* ed. Meiji Bunka Kenkyūkai, 2d ed. (Tokyo: Nihon Hyōronsha, 1967; first publ. in 1928), pp. 279–291. For details about Ballagh and Okuno, see ibid., p. 23.

14. Ibid., pp. 247–251, 23.

15. See, e.g., his articles in *MH* (Sept. 1881), pp. 371–374; (Aug. 1883), pp. 321–324.

16. *MH* (Sept. 1881), p. 371. Some were also sent to his alma mater, Yale University; see ibid., p. 374.

17. *MH* (Aug. 1883), p. 321.

18. C. B. DeForest, p. 74.

19. *MH* (April 1881), p. 141.

20. *MH* (May 1881), pp. 181–182.

21. Published by Beikoku Haken Dengyōshi Jimukyoku [American Board of Commissioners for Foreign Missions] in 1880, and reprinted a number of times.

22. C. B. DeForest, p. 103.

23. Ibid.

24. J. H. DeForest, *Kareki,* p. 8 and pp. 4–9. DeForest of course referred to the scientific and technological superiority of the West. See also his statement in *MH* (Feb. 1881), p. 58: "Idolatry stultifies the people who practice it."

25. J. H. DeForest, *Kareki,* p. 10.

26. Ibid., pp. 10–11. See also *MH* (May 1877), p. 158; (May 1881), pp. 180–182; *Proceedings 1883,* pp. 35–36, 105; *Chrysanthemum* 2 (May 1882): 227–228.

27. J. H. DeForest, *Kareki,* pp. 12–13. The use of *hōben* (Skt., *upāya*), or "skillful means," was here understood to have only negative connotations.

28. *MH* (Sept. 1878), p. 292.

29. C. B. DeForest, p. 82.

30. Ibid., pp. 125–128, 133. His new attitude developed primarily after his return from furlough in 1883.

31. *MH* (May 1881), p. 181.

32. C. B. DeForest, p. 239.

33. Ibid., p. 230. The statement was made in 1892.

34. Ibid.

35. Ibid., pp. 244–245.

36. *Proceedings 1883*, pp. 90–105.

37. In a characteristic statement in *Bukkyō tanomu ni tarazu* (n.p.; Kirisuto-kyō Shorui Kaisha, 1882), p. 2, Gordon emphasized that his purpose was not to expose or to ridicule the miserable state of Buddhism but only to explain the reason for its inadequacy, without exasperating the Buddhists. His rhetoric about "searching the truth together without partiality," however, could hardly conceal his apologetical concern: to demonstrate the inadequacy of Buddhism and the perfection of Christianity.

38. *Proceedings 1883*, p. 91.

39. Ibid., p. 93.

40. *Chrysanthemum* 1 (April 1881): 110.

41. Ibid.

42. For further comments on this development, see ch. 13.

43. See, e.g., his article, "John Stuart Mill's Use of Buddhism," in *Chrysanthemum* 3 (April 1883): 175–177.

44. *MH* (April 1881), pp. 133–134; *Chrysanthemum* 1 (April 1881): 109–115.

45. See his article, "The Legend of Amida Buddha," in *Chrysanthemum* 2 (Jan. 1882): 3–10; and *Bukkyō tanomu ni tarazu*.

46. *Chrysanthemum* 1 (April 1881): 111–112; Edward J. Reed, *Japan: Its History, Traditions and Religions, with the Narrative of a Visit in 1879*, 2 vols., 2d ed. (London: John Murray, 1880), 1:83–84.

47. *MH* (April 1881), p. 133.

48. *Proceedings 1883*, p. 105.

49. These scholars are mentioned in the material referred to below. For further comments on the influence of comparative religion in Japan, see ch. 13.

50. *Chrysanthemum* 2 (Jan. 1882): 3–10. Gordon's article was based on *Muryōjukyō* [The Larger Sukhāvatī-vyūha], one of the three major Pure Land sutras.

51. The Japanese tract was published in 1881 by Beikoku Haken Dendōshi Jimukyoku [American Board of Commissioners for Foreign Missions]; for the English, see *Chrysanthemum* 2 (March 1882): 104–110.

52. See n. 37 above.

53. *Chrysanthemum* 2 (March 1882): 104, 106–107.

54. Ibid., p. 108. A lengthy explanation of the development of Buddhism is included in *Bukkyō tanomu ni tarazu*, pp. 3–34; see also *Proceedings 1883*, p. 99; *Chrysanthemum* 3 (April 1883): 175–177; *MH* (April 1881), pp. 133–134.

55. *Chrysanthemum* 2 (March 1882): 109. See also *Bukkyō tanomu ni tarazu*, pp. 31–32; *Proceedings 1883*, p. 97. Max Müller commented on another Pure Land sutra in *The Sacred Books of the East*, vol. 49, part 2 (Oxford: Clarendon Press, 1894), p. xxi: "I was so much disappointed at the contents of this Sutra, that I hesitated for a time whether I ought to publish it in this volume."

56. *Chrysanthemum* 2 (Jan. 1882): 4.

57. *Proceedings 1883*, pp. 94–99.

58. *Chrysanthemum* 1 (April 1881): 112–115.

59. M. L. Gordon, *An American Missionary in Japan* (Boston: Houghton, Mifflin and Co., 1892), p. 209. See also his further arguments in ibid., pp. 213–220.

60. *Chrysanthemum* 2 (March 1882): 109. Even though he tended to contrast Buddhism negatively with Christianity, his expressions at least indicated the recognition of a certain relationship between the two, in terms of preparation and fulfillment.

61. *Proceedings 1883,* pp. 200–210; *MH* (May 1875), pp. 131–133.
62. *MH* (Feb. 1878), p. 47. It is not clear whether or not he actually taught the course.
63. *MH* (Feb. 1883), p. 51.
64. *Proceedings 1883,* p. 202.
65. This was the main concern of the series of public lectures held in the Meiji Kaidō in 1883, recorded in *Daiichi Tōkyō enzetsu: Gakujutsu ni yotte Kirisutokyō o ronzu,* ed. Charles Eby (Yokohama: Eikoku Seisho Kaisha, Beikoku Seisho Kaisha, 1884).
66. Translated as "Meditations of a Recluse," and published in several installments, beginning in *Chrysanthemum* 3 (Feb. 1883): 87–90.
67. *Daiichi Tōkyō enzetsu,* pp. 269–342. An English version is found in *Chrysanthemum* 3 (April 1883): 181–197, to which I shall refer later.
68. Quoted passages are from ibid., pp. 181, 184, and 196, respectively.
69. Ibid., pp. 196, 197.
70. In *Yūbin hōchi* (Feb. 21, 1889) (OS), Eby was characterized as "the opponent of Buddhist lectures."
71. See, e.g., *Chrysanthemum* 2 (March 1882): 115–119.
72. In *MH* (Aug. 1884), p. 311, he rejected Japanese religions as "a dense mass of unenlightened, besotted heathenism." On the other hand, he also wanted to stress the good elements in Confucianism and Buddhism, as, e.g., in *MH* (Nov. 1877), p. 373.
73. Published in Boston by the Congregational Sunday-school Society, 1893. According to J. H. DeForest, the book was also used to a great extent by Buddhists in Japan; see *JE* 1 (April 1894): 190–191. Atkinson later published a series of studies about the Ten Buddhist Precepts, in *Transactions of the Asiatic Society of Japan,* no. 33, part 2 (1905), pp. 159–184; no. 35, part 1 (1907), pp. 33–70; no. 36, part 1 (1908), pp. 9–22.
74. Published in Tokyo by Jūjiya in 1880. It was apparently first published under the title *Bukkyō shinron* [A new treatise on Buddhism], but it is usually known as *Butsudō shinron;* it appeared in several editions in the 1880s. This examination is based on the fourth edition (1883).
75. Saba, 4:160–164.
76. Many of these articles are collected in Ikemoto Yoshiharu, ed., *Kirisutokyō oyobi Bukkyō* (Tokyo: Keiseisha, 1889). The following discussion is to a great extent based on this collection.
77. Takahashi published *Bukkyō shinkai* in Tokyo in 1883. For the original charge, see Nōjin Hakugon, *Mukai nanshin* (Hyogo, 1881); the author was a Soto Zen priest from Hyogo (within the present Kobe).
78. The former was published in Tokyo by Jūjiya, 1881; the latter and other books were advertised in *Bukkyō shinkai.* In the foreword to the third edition of *Butsudō shinron,* Takahashi referred to his history of India as a "great snake" or "dragon," prepared to swallow up the Buddhist snakes of opposition to his previous work.
79. Saba, 4:160–166. For a bibliography of his works, see Ebisawa Arimichi, "Takahashi Gorō chosakusho mokuroku," *Shien,* vol. 23, no. 2 (1958).
80. See ch. 8 below.
81. See notably Takahashi, *Shoshū benran,* Preface, pp. 1–4.
82. Recorded in Ikemoto, p. 16.
83. For this point, see notably Takahashi, *Bukkyō shinkai,* chs. 9 and 15.
84. Ibid., chs. 13, 14. A similar emphasis is found in *Butsudō shinron.*
85. Ibid., ch. 12.

86. Ibid., ch. 16.

87. Ibid., chs. 16, 17, 18, 19. For an explanation of the philosophy of Tendai Buddhism, see Junjirō Takakusu, *The Essentials of Buddhist Philosophy,* 3d ed., ed. Wing-Tsit Chan and Charles A. Moore (Honolulu: Office Appliance Co., 1956; first publ. in 1947), pp. 126–141.

88. In addition to previous references, see, e.g., Takahashi, *Butsudō shinron,* pp. 27–36; Ikemoto, p. 44.

89. Ikemoto, p. 41.

90. Ibid., p. 31. This was actually cited as a summary of his conclusion in an earlier essay, entitled "The Basis of Buddhism." See Ikemoto, pp. 1–17.

91. See quotations in Aasulv Lande, "Meiji shoki no okeru shūkyōteki taiwa no jittai," in *Gendai ni okeru shūkyō no taiwa,* ed. Takenaka Masao (Tokyo: Seibunsha, 1979), pp. 73–74.

92. This was especially emphasized in an article in *Rikugō zasshi* about Buddhism and morality. See Ikemoto, pp. 57–83; Lande, pp. 71–73.

93. Takahashi, *Bukkyō shinkai,* pp. 197–198, 243.

94. Ikemoto, pp. 230–238.

95. Apart from the above-mentioned *Mukai nanshin,* such opposition is referred to in the preface of the third edition of *Butsudō shinron;* articles in *Meikyō shinshi* critical of Takahashi are referred to in Ikemoto, p. 30.

96. Articles by these are included in Ikemoto's collection.

97. See notably the article by Ibuka in Ikemoto, pp. 193–214.

98. Among tracts that included comparisons between Buddhism and Christianity could be mentioned *Shaka to Kirisuto* [Buddha and Christ] (Yokohama: London Religious Tract Society, 1886; publ. in several editions); William Muirhead, *Ju Shaku Dō Kai Yaso gokyō tsūkō* [The five religions of Confucianism, Buddhism, Taoism, Islam, and Christianity], (Tokyo: Jūjiya, 1879); *Ka: Bukkyō to Kirisutokyō to izure ga ze naru* [Which is right: Buddhism or Christianity?], (n.p.; Beikoku Haken Senkyōshi Jimusho [American Board of Commissioners for Foreign Missions], 1888).

99. See Albert Felix Verwilghen, "The Buddhist Studies of Father A. Villion," *Japan Missionary Bulletin* 25 (June 1971): 252; Villion, p. 205.

100. Villion, p. 205.

101. Ibid., pp. 211, 213–217.

102. Ibid., pp. 205, 226.

103. Ibid., pp. 206–207, 212, 215, 217. He followed consistently the advice given by Bishop Bigandet of Rangoon: "If you want to follow the best method for studying the religion of the Japanese, I tell you, translate their books and nothing else than that!" See Verwilghen, p. 253.

104. Villion, pp. 209, 216.

105. Ibid., pp. 209–211.

106. Ibid., p. 211.

107. Ibid., pp. 212–213.

108. Ibid., p. 247.

109. He might have published something in *Missions Catholiques,* which I have been unable to check.

110. For these projects, see Villion, pp. 451–452, 457–460, 476–480.

111. He also compiled a Buddhist lexicon. The manuscripts are presently kept at the Oriens Institute for Religious Research in Tokyo; see Verwilghen, pp. 254–255.

112. Villion, pp. 209, 452–453.

113. Ibid., p. 209.

114. Ibid., pp. 215–216.

115. See, e.g., ibid., pp. 478–480.

116. The most positive statement about Buddhism from a Christian point of view that I have found in this context, is in a small tract entitled *Kirisutokyō no teki* [The enemy of Christianity], written by George Eves and published in 1889. Eves argued that rather than being an enemy, true Buddhism should be regarded as an ally against moral corruption: "Sakyamuni would be the first to respect and love Jesus, and Christ would be the first to love and respect the Buddha. Except Christ alone, no one is as venerable as Buddha." Eves, pp. 5–6.

CHAPTER SIX

1. Sakurai, p. 87; *Kirisutokyō to Bukkyō,* Fukyō shinjitsu, no. 2 (Kyoto: Hōzōkan, [1899]), p. 92.

2. See Fukushima, "Kaigai kyōjō," pp. 45–65.

3. Tsunemitsu, 1:40–42, 165–166.

4. It was translated by Higashi Kan'ichi as *Ryōyaku zensho jigo sōi,* and published in two volumes in 1875. See Higashi's comments in the Preface; Saba, 5:12.

5. *Shimaji Mokurai zenshū,* ed. Futaba Kenkō and Fukushima Hirotaka, 5 vols. (Kyoto: Honganji Shuppan Kyōkai, 1973–1978), 2:84–97.

6. On the incompatibility with modern science, see ibid.; on the criticism of the stories about Eden, see ibid., pp. 105–112; for the criticism of biblical scriptures, see ibid., pp. 113–144.

7. See ch. 2.

8. The volume was published in Tokyo by Hōchisha in 1875; originally it appeared in the journal *Hōchi sōdan;* see the Preface, p. 2, for comments on the distortion of Jesus' image. Ishikawa was probably acquainted with the writings of D. F. Strauss and F. C. Baur as well. See Saba, 5:18–19.

9. *Kōza kindai Bukkyō,* 2:156–157.

10. See *MH* (Sept. 1875), p. 267; Bird, 2:242–243; *Chrysanthemum* 1 (Oct. 1881): 404.

11. *Chrysanthemum* 2 (March 1882): 110.

12. *Proceedings 1883,* pp. 103–104.

13. *Chrysanthemum* 2 (March 1882): 109.

14. The following is based on a Japanese translation of the article, found in *Yuniterian* 1 (May 1890): 37–40.

15. Kasahara died in 1883, the year after he returned to Japan.

16. Recorded in Kanzaki Issaku, *Haja sōsho,* 2 vols. (Tokyo: Tetsugaku Shoin, 1893), 2:138, 153.

17. Unfortunately I have no similar material available concerning Nanjō Bunyū. He seemed to be in general agreement with the anti-Christian policy of his closest colleagues at Higashi Honganji. He wrote the foreword to Saji Jitsunen's refutation of Christianity, *Hajaketsu* (Tokyo: Kōmeisha, 1885), and engaged from time to time in anti-Christian propaganda. See, e.g., *KS* (Oct. 21, 1892), p. 3 (OS).

18. See, e.g., his article about Christian "idol worship," included in Kanzaki, 2:191–197.

19. Suga's criticism of Christianity is included in ibid., pp. 197–202.

20. For his criticism of Christianity, see the section on "Buddhist Arguments against Christianity" in this chapter; for his activity in the 1890s, see the end of ch. 8.

21. See the section on "A. Villion: A Catholic Inquirer" in ch. 5.

22. *MH* (Nov. 1881), p. 444.

23. *MH* (Sept. 1884), p. 359.

24. In addition to previous references, see also *MH* (March 1885), p. 114; (Sept. 1885), p. 341; (Feb. 1888), p. 79. Most of the anti-Christian writings referred to in n. 48 below were based on more or less thorough studies of the Bible and Christian doctrines.

25. See, e.g., *MH* (May 1875), pp. 131–133; Robert S. Schwantes, "Christianity *versus* Science: A Conflict of Ideas in Meiji Japan," *Far Eastern Quarterly* 12 (Feb. 1952): 123–132.

26. *MH* (April 1881), p. 133.

27. Paine's *The Age of Reason* was translated into Japanese in 1876 as *Dōri no yo;* the foreword was written by the Shin Buddhist Higashi Kan'ichi. Draper's *History of the Conflict between Religion and Science* was translated in 1883 by the prominent Buddhist Ogurusu Kōhei as *Gakugyōshiron: Yasokyō to jitsugaku no sōtō* (Tokyo: Aikoku Gohōsha, 1883); forewords were written by two other Buddhists, Torio Tokuan and Ōuchi Seiran. For Ingersoll, see Saba, 4:309, 313.

28. J. D. Davis in *MH* (May 1875), p. 132.

29. J. T. Gulick in *MH* (June 1878), p. 196; similar statements are found in *MH* (Nov. 1880), p. 471; (Feb. 1885), p. 53–55; *Proceedings 1883*, pp. 118–135; Cary, 2:161–162.

30. See, e.g., J. D. Davis' statement in *MH* (June 1878), p. 197: "We are in the midst of a mighty battle here in Japan. The battle which I saw was coming when I landed here six and a half years ago, and which I told you was coming, is upon us. It is a battle between Christianity and infidelity." See also Schwantes, pp. 123–132.

31. See, e.g., *Chrysanthemum* 1 (Oct. 1881): 392–396; 2 (April 1882): 181–183; *MH* (Sept. 1881), p. 361; Ōhama, pp. 63–64.

32. Hirai Kinzō, *Shinyaku zensho danpaku* (Kyoto, 1883), Preface. The Preface is partly translated in *MH* (Sept. 1883), p. 353.

33. J. T. Gulick in *MH* (Feb. 1880), p. 63. The evolutionism of Darwin and Spencer was, for instance, used to defend the doctrine of karma. See Villion, pp. 307–308.

34. H. Faulds in *Chrysanthemum* 2 (March 1882): 115–116.

35. This happened in some cases in the 1880s, as, e.g., reported in *MH* (Sept. 1884), pp. 359–360; but it was not felt as a serious problem until the 1890s.

36. He compared his position to that of a cardinal in the Roman Catholic Church. See *MH* (April 1881), p. 133; *Chrysanthemum* 1 (April 1881): 110.

37. Tsunemitsu, 1:21.

38. *Chrysanthemum* 1 (April 1881): 115.

39. *MH* (April 1881), p. 133; see also Villion, pp. 212–213.

40. Reed, 1:84–86; *Chrysanthemum* 1 (April 1881): 111–112.

41. Reed, 1:83.

42. Ibid., p. 84.

43. He later founded Musée Guimet in Lyon, which was taken over by the state and moved to Paris in 1885. His writings included two volumes of *Promenades japonaises,* published in 1878 and 1880. See *Encyclopaedia Britannica,* 11th ed., s.v., "Guimet, Jean Baptiste."

44. The dialogue is recorded in *Shimaji Mokurai zenshū,* 5:818–849.

45. See Bird, 2:242–253.

46. Ibid., pp. 249, 250.

47. Ibid., pp. 250, 253. Another visitor Akamatsu received was King Oscar II

of Sweden-Norway, with whom in 1884 he had a quite interesting discussion about issues related to Buddhism and Christianity. See *ReiZ,* no. 8 (Nov. 1884), pp. 47–50.

48. Among such rather commonplace anti-Christian writings were, e.g., Aoyagi Takatomo, *Mataiden benbyū* [Clarifying the fallacies of the Gospel of Matthew], (Osaka, 1882), and *Hakuja tettsui* [An iron hammer against the evil religion], (Tokyo: Yōtokukai, 1889); Hirai Kinzō, *Shinyaku zensho danpaku* [Refutation of the New Testament], (Kyoto, 1883); Kawai Kiyomaru, *Kyūyaku zensho fukashinron* [The Old Testament unbelievable], (Kyoto, 1882); Mekata Sakae, *Benseki makyōron* [Refutation of the diabolic religion], 2 vols. (Kobe, 1886); Nishida Kaichirō, *Bakujaron* [Refutation of the evil religion], (Kyoto: Hōkyōsha, 1881); Sada Kaiseki, *Bukkyō sōseiki* [The Buddhist Genesis], (Musashi, Kanagawa Prefecture, 1880; first publ. in 1878); Saji Jitsunen, *Hajaketsu* [Methods of refuting the evil religion], (Tokyo: Kōmeisha, 1885); Tajima Shōji, *Yaso ichidai benmōki* [Refutation of the life of Jesus], (Tokyo, 1874), and *Yasokyō-i mondō* [A dispute about the meaning of Christianity], (Tokyo, 1875); Yoshioka Nobuyuki, *Haja kenshōron* [Refuting errors and demonstrating the truth], (Tokyo, 1882), and *Haja kenshō jashō mondō* [Refuting errors and demonstrating the truth: A dispute on error and truth], (Tokyo, 1884). In the foreword to Yoshioka's *Haja kenshōron,* Ōuchi Seiran rightly questioned the quality of this type of literature, indicating the lack of differentiation in the treatment of Catholicism and Protestantism and the one-sided dependence on Genesis for criticism.

49. Written by Saitō Goichirō and published in many different editions in 1881.

50. A summary of Saitō's lecture in English is found in *Chrysanthemum* 1 (Oct. 1881): 394–396. The above quotations are taken from this translation, but have been checked and slightly altered according to the Japanese original.

51. See ch. 2.

52. Ōhama, pp. 85–86; Yoshida Kyūichi, *Nihon kindai Bukkyō shakaishi kenkyū* (Tokyo: Yoshikawa Kōbunkan, 1964), pp. 59–64 (hereafter cited as Yoshida, *Bukkyō shakaishi*).

53. Villion, pp. 269, 270. Similar criticism is mentioned in C. B. DeForest, pp. 78–79. Sada's vehement anti-Western spirit was even expressed on his tombstone. According to *JWM* (Dec. 28, 1889), p. 589, the inscription had attracted police attention, and part of it had been obliterated, perhaps because it could mislead "people of almost equally misguided patriotism," as the newspaper put it.

54. Fujishima stayed in France from 1882 to 1889; see *ReiZ,* no. 67 (Oct. 1889), p. 36.

55. See figs. 10–13.

56. Kishimoto Hideo, p. 233; *Chrysanthemum* 2 (May 1882): 227.

57. See, e.g., *Ajia Bukkyōshi,* 20 vols., ed. Nakamura Hajime, Kasahara Kazuo, and Kanaoka Shūyū, (Tokyo: Kōsei Shuppansha, 1973–1976), *Nihonhen,* vol. 8: *Gendai Bukkyō,* pp. 111–112 (hereafter cited as *Ajia Bukkyōshi*); *MH* (Oct. 1880), p. 393; Ōhama, p. 64. It is characteristic that the type of propaganda mentioned in the previous section on "Buddhist Arguments against Christianity" to a great extent was used in such confrontations.

58. For the opposition to the Doshisha College in Kyoto, see, e.g., Cary, 2:118–119; *MH* (March 1876), pp. 83–84; (April 1876), p. 129.

59. *MH* (Sept. 1881), p. 361; *Chrysanthemum* 1 (Oct. 1881): 392–396; 2 (April 1882): 181–183; Ōhama, pp. 63–64; Saba, 4:309–338; 5:17–19.

60. Villion, p. 269.
61. For further reports from Kyoto, see ibid., pp. 269–281; *MH* (Sept. 1884), p. 359.
62. *Yaso taiji* was apparently also adopted as the name of Buddhist associations; see H. Ritter, *A History of Protestant Missions in Japan*, trans. George E. Albrecht (Tokyo: Methodist Publishing House, 1898), p. 133. See also the humorous picture of *taiji jakensō*, "the priest who is extinguishing the heretic view" (fig. 14).
63. According to Miyatake Gaikotsu, *Meiji enzetsushi* (Tokyo: Seikōkan, 1929), p. 214, earlier Buddhist propaganda had made only a minor impact outside the limited circle of devoted Buddhists.
64. Kuyama, pp. 118–119. A detailed account of the persecutions in the city of Takahashi in Okayama Prefecture is found in Matsumura Kaiseki, *Shinkō gojūnen* (Tokyo: Dōkai Jimusho, 1926), pp. 71–106; see also Yūasa Yosō, *Kirisuto ni aru jiyū o motomete: Nihon Kumiai Kirisuto Kyōkaishi* (Tokyo: Sōbunsha, 1958), pp. 116–117. Numerous incidents of persecutions and confrontations are reported in Ōhama, pp. 59–79; Yoshida, *Bukkyōshi*, pp. 180–199; see also Kuyama, 117–121. Additional information about similar campaigns can be found in historical studies from local churches and in the monthly reports in the *Missionary Herald*.
65. See, e.g., descriptions in Villion, p. 270; Gordon, *An American*, pp. 72–75; *MH* (Aug. 1881), pp. 297–300; Saji Jitsunen, *Nihon Yuniterian-shugi kōbōshi* (Tokyo, 1910), pp. 6–7.
66. Cited in *Chrysanthemum* 2 (April 1882): 179.
67. This was strongly emphasized in missionary circles. See, e.g., *MH* (Nov. 1884), pp. 456–457, 462; Villion, pp. 276–277.
68. *MH* (Nov. 1884), p. 421.
69. *MH* (Jan. 1885), pp. 19–20.
70. *MH* (March 1886), p. 110.

CHAPTER SEVEN

1. See, e.g., *JWM* (April 27, 1889), pp. 404–405.
2. Tokyo: Meikyōsha, 1885. The book was based on articles previously published in *Meikyō shinshi*.
3. Kōsaka, pp. 243–244.
4. Inoue published more than a hundred books. Kishimoto Hideo, p. 148, refers to 122 books.
5. Published in Kyoto, 1886–1887; the following references are based on an edition from 1890.
6. *Bukkyō katsuron* was first published by Tetsugaku Shoin in Tokyo in 1887, and later appeared in several editions; the following references are based on editions from 1887 and 1888.
7. Kōsaka, p. 243. Apart from specific references, the following account is based on the biographical sketch in Tsunemitsu, 1:174–181.
8. Kōsaka Masaaki argues in Kuyama, p. 173, that Inoue was temporarily a Christian, mainly from philosophical interest.
9. Inoue, *Bukkyō katsuron joron*, quoted from Kishimoto Hideo, p. 149.
10. Inoue, *Haja shinron*, p. 1; *Shinri kinshin*, 1:1.
11. Inoue, *Bukkyō katsuron joron*, pp. 60–61.
12. *Nihonjin*, no. 1 (April 3, 1888) (OS).
13. Inoue, *Bukkyō katsuron joron*, pp. 60–61.

14. Inoue, *Shinri kinshin,* vol. 2, Preface, pp. 1–4. Actually, the prospect of political change had stimulated Buddhists to a critical review of the state of Buddhism and to a consequent call for reform since around 1881, when the preparation for the Constitution had begun. See, e.g., Imakita Kōsen's appeal to Buddhist chief abbots in 1882, recorded in *Suzuki Daisetsu zenshū,* vol. 26 (Tokyo: Iwanami Shoten, 1970), pp. 126–132. The Buddhist apprehensions were not groundless, for the Christians were conscious about their intellectual and political strength and were much better prepared for the change than the Buddhists. For an expression of the Christian sense of superiority concerning the future political influence, see, e.g., the characteristic statement by D. C. Greene, quoted in Cary, 2:210.

15. Inoue, *Bukkyō katsuron joron,* p. 13; the translation is taken from Kishimoto Hideo, p. 149.

16. Inoue, *Haja shinron,* p. 2.

17. Inoue, *Shinri kinshin,* 2:4, 5–6.

18. Inoue, *Bukkyō katsuron joron,* pp. 1–5; idem, *Kyōiku shūkyō kankeiron* (Tokyo: Tetsugaku Shoin, 1893), p. 29; Miyamoto Shōson, *Meiji Bukkyō no shichō: Inoue Enryō no jiseki* (Tokyo: Kōsei Shuppansha, 1975), pp. 229–231.

19. Inoue, *Haja shinron,* pp. 191–196.

20. Inoue Enryō, *Ōbei kakkoku seiji nikki,* 2 vols. (Tokyo: Tetsugaku Shoin, 1889), 2:72–75; Miyamoto, pp. 232–234.

21. Yoshida, *Bukkyōshi,* p. 194.

22. See *Nori no ame,* no. 22 (Oct. 20, 1889), pp. 32–33 (OS).

23. See, e.g., Inoue, *Kyōiku shūkyō kankeiron.*

24. Inoue, *Shinri kinshin,* 3:18; *Bukkyō katsuron joron,* Preface and pp. 43–46.

25. Inoue, *Shinri kinshin,* 3:16–17; *Bukkyō katsuron joron,* pp. 43–44.

26. Inoue, *Shinri kinshin,* 3:15–48; see notably pp. 15–17.

27. Sakurai, p. 373.

28. See Kenneth B. Pyle, *The New Generation in Meiji Japan: Problems of Cultural Identity, 1885–1895* (Stanford, Calif.: Stanford University Press, 1969), p. 64.

29. Kōsaka, pp. 245–248.

30. For a further discussion of the character of *Nihonjin* and Seikyōsha, see Pyle, pp. 53–98.

31. See Kashiwabara, pp. 388–389. According to Pyle, p. 65, few others in the group regarded Buddhism as an essential aspect of Japanese civilization.

32. Such a concern was eloquently expressed by Tokutomi Soho in *Kokumin no tomo:* "The present day world is one in which civilized people tyrannically destroy savage peoples. . . . The European countries stand at the very pinnacle of violence and base themselves on the doctrine of force. . . . India, alas, has been destroyed, Annam has been destroyed, Burma will be next. The remaining countries will be independent in name only." Quoted from Kōsaka, p. 209.

33. See Kōsaka, pp. 215–217, 245–247.

34. *JWM* (April 27, 1889), pp. 404–405.

35. *Nihonjin,* no. 14 (Oct. 18, 1888), pp. 6–9.

36. *Nihonjin,* no. 19 (Jan. 3, 1889), pp. 14–17.

37. See ch. 10.

38. A similar development toward exclusionist views can also be observed among other pioneers of liberal views, such as, e.g., Nishimura Shigeki and Toyama Masakazu. See Donald H. Shively, "Nishimura Shigeki: A Confucian View

of Modernization," in *Changing Japanese Attitudes toward Modernization,* ed. Marius B. Jansen (Princeton, N.J.: Princeton University Press, 1965), pp. 193–241; Saba, 5:995–998; Ikeda, pp. 150–156; Kishimoto Hideo, p. 144.

39. See *Yomiuri shinbun* (Jan. 6, 1889), p. 3 (OS); Sakurai, pp. 388–389; Tamamuro, pp. 340–344.

40. *JWM* (March 3, 1889), pp. 233–234, quoted in Cary, 2:212–213. The translation is rather free. An easily available copy of the original text of the prospectus is found in Sakurai, p. 388.

41. Ōuchi Seiran, *Sonnō hōbutsuron* (Tokyo: Kōmeisha, 1889), p. 13.

42. Ibid., pp. 1–4, 7.

43. *DS,* no. 1 (March 11, 1889), pp. 3–5; *ReiZ,* no. 58 (Jan. 1889), pp. 150–154.

44. *DS,* no. 1 (March 11, 1889), p. 17; see fig. 15.

45. *JWM,* quoted in Cary, 2:213.

46. Robert A. Scalapino, *Democracy and the Party Movement in Prewar Japan: The Failure of the First Attempt* (Berkeley and Los Angeles: University of California Press, 1967), p. 113. Scalapino rendered the party name as "Union of Like Thinkers."

47. *ReiZ,* no. 58 (Jan. 1889), pp. 165–175. Other Buddhists criticized such cooperation.

48. Ōuchi, pp. 16–17; Mishima Yoshitada, *Shin Nihon kokutairon: Shinkyō jiyūron* (Tokyo: Kōyūsha, 1889), pp. 34–36; see also *SY,* no. 13 (Jan. 1889), pp. 19–20, 51.

49. Reports on the expansion are found in every issue of *Daidō shinpō.*

50. *FS* (Nov. 28, 1890), p. 5 (OS). See also *JK,* no. 23 (Jan. 5, 1890), p. 5 (OS); Yoshida, *Bukkyōshi,* p. 188; and frequent reports in *Daidō shinpō.*

51. Yoshida, *Bukkyōshi,* p. 178. Minoda was also involved in campaigns for Sonnō Hōbutsu Daidōdan; see *DS,* no. 3 (April 5, 1889), p. 107.

52. See the harsh criticism referred to in Mishima, p. 33.

53. *Thirteenth Report of the Council of Missions Coöperating with the United Church of Christ in Japan* (Tokyo: Council of Missions Coöperating with the United Church of Christ in Japan, 1890), pp. 24–25. For a further discussion of the politicization of religious struggle, see ch. 8.

54. *Chōya shinbun* (April 5, 1889), p. 2 (OS).

55. *JWM* (April 27, 1889), pp. 404–405.

56. *JWM* (Jan. 25, 1890), pp. 74–75.

57. *JWM* (March 9, 1889), pp. 233–234.

58. *KS* (Feb. 13, 1889), p. 1; see also Yoshida, *Bukkyōshi,* pp. 176–178.

59. Cited in *JWM* (March 9, 1889), pp. 233–234.

60. Tamamuro, p. 341.

61. *KS* (July 18, 1890), p. 4 (OS); *Kokumin shinbun* (July 2, 1890) (OS).

62. *DS,* no. 31 (July 21, 1890), pp. 373–377.

63. *SY,* no. 52 (April 1892), p. 20.

64. Apart from the Buddhist associations mentioned in Sakurai, pp. 384–412, there were numerous minor organizations that engaged in anti-Christian campaigns, especially in the provinces, as described in ch. 9.

65. *JE* 1 (April 1894): 233.

66. See, e.g., Ohara Masao, *Bukkyō daishōri Yasokyō daihaiboku: Butsu-Ya katsumondō* (Osaka, 1889), p. 41. Ōuchi Seiran called himself a "wild Buddhist" because he was independent from denominational ties and wanted to cooperate with all; see *HZ* 11 (Oct. 2, 1896): 72; Tsunemitsu, 1:188.

67. *ReiZ*, no. 75 (June 1890), pp. 32–33; *SY*, no. 28 (April 1890), p. 24; no. 30 (June 1890), p. 44; Sakurai, pp. 396–397.

68. *SY*, no. 41 (May 1891), pp. 23–24; *ReiZ*, no. 86 (May 1891), pp. 33–34. The meeting in Tokyo in the previous year did not pass any resolutions against Christianity.

69. *SY*, no. 52 (April 1892), p. 43; *Zenkoku Bukkyōsha Daisan Konwakai gijiroku* (Kyoto: Dōmei Bukkyōdan Honbu, 1892), p. 1.

70. *SY*, no. 20 (Aug. 1889), no page number; no. 26 (Feb. 1890), p. 39. The plan of a Buddhist university was finally abandoned, and only a minor institute, Tōyōkan, or Oriental Hall, was established in the precincts of Chishakuin, a temple in southern Kyoto; see *SY*, no. 33 (Sept. 1890), pp. 38–39; no. 34 (Oct. 1890), p. 38; no. 45 (Sept. 1891), p. 17.

71. *SY*, no. 49 (Jan. 1892), pp. 2–3.

72. *SY*, no. 64 (April 1893), pp. 1–5.

73. *SY*, no. 49 (Jan. 1892), p. 3; no. 51 (March 1892), p. 37.

74. *DS*, no. 6 (June 1, 1889), pp. 191–196; Mishima, pp. 27–28.

75. Sakurai, p. 373, classifies Seikyōsha as a Shinto organization.

76. *Daidō sōshi* 1 (July 1888): 13, 24, 30.

77. See Kanzaki, 2:422–440; Sakurai, pp. 344–346.

78. Torio Tokuan (Koyata), *Shinsei tetsugaku: Mushinron* ([Tokyo]: Nihon Kokkyō Daidōsha, 1894; first publ. in 1887).

79. Sakurai, pp. 386–387; Tamamuro, pp. 340–341.

80. Nakanishi Ushio, *Shūkyō kakumeiron* (Tokyo: Hakubunkan, 1889), pp. 132–134.

81. *HZ*, no. 1 (Aug. 1887); Nakanishi Ushio, *Shin Bukkyōron* (Kyoto: Kōkyō Shoin, 1892), Appendix, p. 50.

82. Sakurai, pp. 387–388.

83. For further comments on contacts with Western Buddhists and Buddhist scholars, see chs. 6 and 13.

84. *ReiZ*, no. 60 (March 1889), pp. 257–268, 303–307; *RZ*, no. 98 (Feb. 1889), pp. 78–81 (OS); *JWM* (March 16, 1889), pp. 249–250; Nakanishi, *Shūkyō kakumeiron*, pp. 133–142; Cary, 2:224–225.

85. *The Orient* 14 (July 1899): 13; Nakanishi, *Shin Bukkyōron*, Appendix, pp. 52–54.

86. C. Pfoundes, *Bukkyō enzetsushū*, ed. Uchimiya Torasuke (Kyoto: Kōbundō, 1893), pp. 1–4, 33–36.

87. *MS* (Feb. 18, 1893), pp. 7–8; *SY*, no. 62 (Feb. 1893), pp. 36–37, 41–43; no. 63 (March 1893), pp. 33–38; Yoshida, *Bukkyōshi*, pp. 178–179. For a discussion of the role of the World's Parliament of Religions in this connection, see ch. 13.

88. Cary, 2:224–225; Otto Schmiedel, *Kultur- und Missionsbilder aus Japan* (Berlin: A. Haack, 1891), p. 22; *MS* (May 12, 1893), p. 6.

89. *Koji* is the Japanese rendering of the Sanskrit *gṛhapati*, which literally means landlord, or a man who resides in a house. In Japan it was generally used about dedicated lay Buddhists, and is also a posthumous title attached to male Buddhists.

90. Ikeda, p. 123.

91. *Kōza kindai Bukkyō*, 2:232–239; *Ajia Bukkyōshi, Nihonhen*, 8:251.

92. *SY*, no. 1 (Jan. 1888), p. 28; his anti-Christian writings have already been mentioned.

93. *Kōza kindai Bukkyō*, vol. 1: *Gaisetsuhen*, (Kyoto: Hōzōkan, 1963), pp. 79–80.

94. *MS* (July 28, 1896), p. 1 (OS).
95. See ch. 12.
96. *ReiZ,* no. 63 (June 1889), p. 3.
97. Tamamuro, pp. 352–353; Sakurai, pp. 391–394.

CHAPTER EIGHT

1. Cary, 2:183–185; W. T. Thomas, pp. 179–180. The problem was serious enough to provoke strong Buddhist opposition; see, e.g., Inoue, *Bukkyō katsuron joron,* pp. 40–42.

2. W. T. Thomas, pp. 187–188; Saba, 5:36–37 and *Shin ho'i* [New additional volume], pp. 165–166. See also George B. Sansom, *The Western World and Japan: A Study in the Interaction of European and Asiatic Cultures* (London: Cresset Press, 1950), pp. 359–361.

3. W. T. Thomas, p. 205.

4. Ibid., pp. 183–184; Kuyama, p. 205; *KS* (Dec. 27, 1889), pp. 1–2 (OS); *FS* (Nov. 28, 1890), p. 5 (OS).

5. *MH* (Aug. 1884), pp. 304–306.

6. *JWM* (Oct. 25, 1890), pp. 402–403.

7. *Yomiuri shinbun* (Sept. 24, 1890), p. 1 (OS); (Sept. 30, 1890), p. 1 (OS); *JWM* (Oct. 25, 1890), pp. 409–410.

8. *Dentō,* no. 10 (Oct. 21, 1890), p. 41 (OS).

9. *MK,* no. 27 (Nov. 12, 1890), p. 34 (OS). When the British Buddhist C. Pfoundes, in one of his anti-Christian speeches in 1893 blamed the missionaries for the failure of treaty revision, even the Buddhist reporter hesitated to accept his view. See *MS* (Feb. 18, 1893), pp. 7–8.

10. *JWM* (Oct. 12, 1889), p. 325. *JWM* has Tōryô instead of Torio.

11. Ishii, pp. 366–389; see also *Sources of Japanese Traditions,* 2:155–172; Kuyama, p. 180.

12. Fairbank, Reischauer, and Craig, pp. 295–296.

13. Tasuku Harada, *The Faith of Japan* (New York: Macmillan Co., 1914), p. 163. Hiyane Antei suggests, in his *Nihon kinsei Kirisutokyō jinbutsushi* (Tokyo: Kirisutokyō Shisō Sōsho Kankōkai, 1935), pp. 263–270, that Mori Arinori, who was assassinated on the day the new Constitution was promulgated, was the first victim of the conservative reaction, and Uchimura Kanzō the second. For further comments on Uchimura, see the section on "The Uchimura Incident" later in this chapter.

14. Kuyama, pp. 180–181; Sumiya, pp. 109–110; *Sources of Japanese Tradition,* 2:170–171. Such views were shared by many others, such as, e.g., Nishimura Shigeki; see Sakurai, pp. 367–370.

15. Representative expressions of Buddhist attitudes are found in, e.g., Ōuchi, *Sonnō hōbutsuron,* pp. 7–8; Ashitsu Jitsuzen, *Kenpō seigan: Tōyō shin Buppō* (Osaka: Kyōgaku Shoin, 1890), pp. 147–148.

16. Quoted from Cary, 2:222.

17. Ozawa, *Nihon Purotesutantoshi kenkyū,* pp. 50–52. See also the detailed examination of the article on religious freedom in Yoshiya Abe, "Religious Freedom under the Meiji Constitution," part 2, *Contemporary Religions in Japan* 10 (March–June 1969): 57–97.

18. *KS* (Feb. 27, 1889), pp. 1–2. For this and many of the following references to the relationship between Christianity and the Constitution, see Ozawa Saburō, "Kenpō happu to Kirisutokyō: Meiji nijūninen," n.p., n.d., a collection of excerpts from magazines and newspapers, copied by hand.

19. Numerous celebrations were reported in, e.g., *KS* (Feb. 13, 1889), Appendix 2, pp. 1–2; (Feb. 20, 1889), pp. 2–3; (Feb. 27, 1889), pp. 2–4, etc. See also *Doyō shinbun* (Feb. 13, 1889), p. 2.

20. *JK*, no. 4 (March 25, 1889), p. 5.

21. *KS* (Feb. 6, 1889), p. 2; (Feb. 13, 1889), Appendix 2, pp. 1–2.

22. *MS* (April 6, 1889), pp. 6–7; *JK*, no. 2 (Feb. 25, 1889), pp. 1–2; no. 3 (March 10, 1889), p. 6.

23. *JK*, no. 3 (March 10, 1889), p. 6; *ReiZ*, no. 59 (Feb. 1889), pp. 193–202.

24. *Sōtō fushūkai zasshi*, no. 13 (Feb. 28, 1889), p. 16; *JK*, no. 2 (Feb. 25, 1889), pp. 1–2; *ReiZ*, no. 80 (Nov. 1890), pp. 28–30.

25. *SY*, no. 15 (March 1889), pp. 13–14.

26. *MS* (April 6, 1889), pp. 6–7.

27. *DS*, no. 2 (April 1, 1889), pp. 33–37; no. 6 (June 1, 1889), pp. 191–196; no. 7 (June 16, 1889), pp. 232–234; see also *ReiZ*, no. 59 (Feb. 1889), pp. 201–202; no. 73 (April 1890), pp. 1–5; no. 80 (Nov. 1890), p. 28; *JK*, no. 59 (Jan. 5, 1891), p. 14; no. 60 (Jan. 15, 1891), p. 14.

28. *JK*, no. 9 (June 10, 1889), p. 13; Kamata Enkai, *Bukkyō daitōronkai*, 4th ed. (Kyoto: Kendō Shoin, 1894), pp. 17–18. For a further discussion of this problem, see ch. 10.

29. See, e.g., Itō Hirobumi's comment on the Constitution, recorded in *Sources of Japanese Tradition*, 2:161, 166. A somewhat restrictive trend can be observed in the response to the above-mentioned letter from the German missionaries Spinner and Schmiedel; see *JK*, no. 4 (March 25, 1889), p. 5.

30. *SY*, no. 25 (Jan. 1890), pp. 1–2. A characteristic example of such politicization was the anti-Christian association Sonnō Hōbutsu Daidōdan.

31. *ReiZ*, no. 73 (June 1890), pp. 32–33.

32. *Yūbin hōchi* (Jan. 15, 1890), p. 1 (OS); *Mainichi shinbun* (May 31, 1890), p. 2 (OS); *Chōya shinbun* (May 27, 1893), p. 2 (OS). See also the section about Sonnō Hōbutsu Daidōdan in ch. 7.

33. *KS* (July 18, 1890), p. 4 (OS); see also *KS* (Nov. 18, 1892), p. 4 (OS).

34. *Yomiuri shinbun* (March 7, 1889), p. 2 (OS). The suspicion of Christian influence in the party was in this case based on a misunderstanding.

35. Walter Wallace McLaren, *A Political History of Japan during the Meiji Era, 1867–1912* (New York: Russell & Russell, 1965; first publ. in 1916), pp. 204–208; Fairbank, Reischauer, and Craig, pp. 299–302.

36. Fairbank, Reischauer, and Craig, p. 301; W. T. Thomas, p. 238.

37. Sansom, *The Western World and Japan*, p. 361. See also McLaren, pp. 205–206; Scalapino, pp. 104, 157, 219.

38. *JWM* (Oct. 11, 1890), p. 360. Scalapino, p. 104, suggests "strong-arm men."

39. Quoted from *JWM* (Jan. 18, 1890), p. 46.

40. *JWM* (Oct. 12, 1889), p. 326.

41. *Kokumin no tomo*, cited in *JWM* (Oct. 11, 1890), pp. 348–349.

42. *JWM* (March 2, 1889), p. 203; McLaren, p. 206.

43. See *JWM* (Jan. 18, 1890), pp. 60–63; (Oct. 26, 1889), p. 374.

44. *JWM* (Oct. 11, 1890), pp. 348–349.

45. *JWM* (June 28, 1890), p. 646.

46. Fairbank, Reischauer, and Craig, p. 301.

47. *SY*, no. 41 (May 1891), pp. 7–8; *DS*, no. 5 (May 15, 1889), pp. 168–189.

48. Kishimoto Hideo, pp. 253–254; Cary, 2:228–230.

49. See descriptions in, e.g., *FS* (Dec. 5, 1890), p. 2 (OS); (Dec. 12, 1890), pp. 5–6 (OS); (Dec. 19, 1890), p. 12 (OS); *Seikyō shinpō*, no. 204 (Dec. 1, 1890), Appendix, p. 2 (OS).

50. *KS* (Feb. 27, 1889), pp. 1–2.

51. Kuyama, p. 205; W. T. Thomas, p. 183.

52. Recorded in *Sources of Japanese Tradition,* 2:139–140; see also W. T. Thomas, p. 200; John Whitney Hall and Richard K. Beardsley, *Twelve Doors to Japan* (New York: McGraw-Hill, 1965), pp. 400–402.

53. Hall and Beardsley, p. 402; Kishimoto Hideo, p. 254; Ozawa Saburō, *Uchimura Kanzō fukei jiken* (Tokyo: Shinkyō Shuppansha, 1961), pp. 39–41.

54. Hiyane, *Nihon kinsei,* pp. 266–267.

55. See Honda Yōichi's report in *Mainichi shinbun* (Oct. 26, 1895), p. 1 (OS).

56. *JK,* no. 23 (Jan. 5, 1890), p. 5 (OS). Doshisha denied that this was true; see Yoshida, *Bukkyōshi,* p. 264.

57. *FS* (Nov. 14, 1890), p. 6 (OS); (Nov. 21, 1890), p. 3 (OS). See also the discussion of Christian patriotism in ch. 11.

58. Cary, 2:227.

59. Quoted from *JWM* (March 9, 1889), pp. 233–234. Even Uemura Masahisa, with his keen critical sense, supported the rescript as a positive force for the sake of moral education. He just found it insufficient, lacking the necessary inspiration so indispensable for educational purposes. See *Nihon hyōron,* no. 17 (Nov. 8, 1890), included in *Uemura Masahisa chosakushū,* 7 vols. (Tokyo: Shinkyō Shuppansha, 1966–1967), 1:283–288. For a discussion of Ōnishi Hajime's criticism of the rescript, see Kōsaka, pp. 259–260.

60. *KS* (March 21, 1890), p. 1 (OS).

61. See, e.g., *ReiZ,* no. 73 (April 1890), pp. 1–5.

62. Ozawa, *Uchimura Kanzō,* pp. 39–41.

63. Similar ceremonies at other Higher Middle Schools included semimilitary ceremonials by the students; see ibid., pp. 43–44. For further comments on the background, see Yoshiya Abe, "Religious Freedom," part 3, *Contemporary Religions in Japan* 10 (Sept.–Dec. 1969): 189–196.

64. Suzuki Norihisa, *Uchimura Kanzō to sono jidai: Shiga Jūkō to no hikaku* (Tokyo: Nihon Kirisuto Kyōdan Shuppankyoku, 1975), p. 137.

65. Saba, 5:769–770; Ozawa, *Uchimura Kanzō,* pp. 52–53.

66. Ozawa, *Uchimura Kanzō,* pp. 52–54, 69–73.

67. Ibid., p. 76; Suzuki, *Uchimura Kanzō,* pp. 137–141.

68. Such a representative newspaper as *Yūbin hōchi* considered the problem solved when the letter of apology was written; for discussion of that and the letter of resignation, see Ozawa, *Uchimura Kanzō,* pp. 77–78.

69. This was one of the reasons for his conflict with missionaries in Niigata in 1888. See, e.g., John F. Howes, "Kanzo Uchimura: Teacher and Writer," *Japan Christian Quarterly* 23 (April 1957): 150–156; Suzuki, *Uchimura Kanzō,* pp. 113–128. Uchimura's opposition to the missionaries was reported favorably by the nationalistic magazine *Nihonjin,* no. 20 (Jan. 16, 1889), pp. 18–19.

70. Saba, 5:769–770.

71. See, e.g., *The Complete Works of Kanzō Uchimura,* 4:54–55.

72. Ozawa, *Uchimura Kanzō,* pp. 159–211.

73. Saba, 5:766–768.

74. Yoshida, *Bukkyōshi,* p. 210.

75. The five were Oshikawa Masayoshi, Uemura Masahisa, Minami Hajime, Maruyama Tsūichi, and Iwamoto Yoshiharu; see Ozawa, *Uchimura Kanzō,* pp. 191–193.

76. *FS* (Feb. 20, 1891), recorded in *Uemura Masahisa chosakushū,* 1:288–291; Ozawa, *Uchimura Kanzō,* pp. 205–207.

77. For details, see Ozawa, *Uchimura Kanzō,* pp. 204–208.

78. Ibid., pp. 78–79.

79. Yoshida, *Bukkyōshi,* p. 211.
80. Ibid., pp. 204–205.
81. *MS,* cited in ibid., p. 205.
82. *ReiZ,* cited in ibid., p. 209.
83. For a detailed study of the newspaper coverage of the incidents, see Ozawa, *Uchimura Kanzō,* pp. 133–156.
84. This tendency was continued by Inoue Tetsujirō, who in 1893 based his criticism of Uchimura mainly on the report of the Buddhist journal *Reichikai zasshi.* Further comments in the section on "Inoue Tetsujirō and the Controversy about Education and Religion" later in this chapter.
85. Yoshida, *Bukkyōshi,* p. 212.
86. Ibid., pp. 213–214.
87. Ibid.
88. Cary, 2:239.
89. Yoshida, *Bukkyōshi,* pp. 215–217; *MK,* no. 73 (Oct. 12, 1892), p. 20 (OS).
90. Several such incidents are dealt with in Yoshida, *Bukkyōshi,* pp. 219–221.
91. *Bukkyō kōron,* no. 26 (April 10, 1893), p. 29 (OS); Yoshida, *Bukkyōshi,* p. 220.
92. *SY,* no. 39 (March 1892), p. 24.
93. Some random examples can be mentioned from the mainstream Buddhist journal, *Meikyō shinshi.* It reported on a Christian who killed a child (April 2, 1893, p. 9); Christians who obstructed parents in connection with a funeral (May 20, 1893, pp. 5–6); Christians who were "selling the country" by selling land to foreigners (June 24, 1893, p. 5); etc. According to Yoshida, *Bukkyōshi,* p. 221, the sale of land to foreigners was a common charge against Christians in Japan.
94. Ohara, pp. 1–4.
95. Hiyane, *Nihon kindai,* pp. 270–273; Saba, 5:759–760.
96. See, e.g., *MS* (Aug. 30, 1893), p. 7; (Sept. 4, 1893), p. 7; (Sept. 6, 1893), pp. 7–8; (Oct. 2, 1893), p. 5. It is also noteworthy that Tamura was severely criticized by his Christian colleagues as well, and finally the general assembly of his church divested him of his pastorate. See Hiyane, *Nihon kindai,* pp. 272–273; Saba, 5:759–760.
97. Yoshida, *Bukkyōshi,* pp. 219–221.
98. For an examination in English of Inoue Tetsujirō's thinking, see Winston Davis, "The Civil Theology of Inoue Tetsujirō," *Japanese Journal of Religious Studies* 3 (March 1976): 5–40; Masakazu Yamazaki and Tōru Miyakawa, "Inoue Tetsujirō: The Man and His Works," *Philosophical Studies of Japan,* no. 7 (1966), pp. 111–125.
99. According to Suzuki, *Uchimura Kanzō,* pp. 142–143, the articles were published, wholly or partially, in 28 different journals and newspapers; Yoshida, *Bukkyōshi,* p. 224, refers to 15 Buddhist journals and newspapers that published the essays.
100. I have used an edition from 1902, *Kyōiku to shūkyō no shōtotsu* (Tokyo: Keigyōsha, 1902).
101. Sakurai, p. 183.
102. Hiyane, *Nihon kinsei,* pp. 280–281.
103. Suzuki, *Meiji shūkyō,* p. 94.
104. Ibid., pp. 93–96.
105. Inoue Tetsujirō, *Naichi zakkyo zokuron* (Tokyo: Tetsugaku Shoin, 1891), pp. 63–70.

106. In *Tensoku,* cited in Suzuki, *Meiji shūkyō,* pp. 95–96. For a further discussion of mixed residence, see ch. 10.

107. Sakurai, pp. 166–167.

108. Inoue Tetsujirō, *Kyōiku,* p. 4.

109. Ibid., pp. 5–8.

110. Ibid., pp. 40–45.

111. Ibid., p. 73.

112. Ibid., pp. 85, 87.

113. Ibid., p. 99.

114. Sakurai, pp. 166–167.

115. Ibid., pp. 169–183. See also the section on Christian patriotism in ch. 11.

116. *Chōya shinbun* (June 6, 1893), p. 2 (OS).

117. Inoue Tetsujirō, *Kyōiku,* pp. 169–183.

118. Yoshida, *Bukkyōshi,* p. 227.

119. Ibid., pp. 224–225; Inoue Tetsujirō, *Kyōiku,* p. 8.

120. In this respect he differed from Inoue Enryō, whose criticism of Christianity was based on Buddhist views; see Yoshida, *Bukkyōshi,* p. 227.

121. Sakurai, p. 189.

122. Yoshida, *Bukkyōshi,* p. 224.

123. Takahashi Gorō, *Hai-gitetsugakuron* (Tokyo: Minyūsha, 1893), pp. 39–40; Takahashi's charges were based on reports in *Kokkai shinbun.*

124. Fujishima Ryōon (Tangaku), *Yasokyō matsuro* (Tokyo: Tetsugaku Shoin, 1893), pp. 1, 44. Furukawa Rōsen was an exception; see ch. 12.

125. *Dentō,* no. 44 (April 28, 1893), p. 27 (OS).

126. *MS* (Aug. 6, 1893), p. 11; see also *MS* (Sept. 19, 1893), cited in Yoshida, *Bukkyōshi,* p. 243.

127. *Bukkyō kōron,* no. 26 (April 10, 1893), p. 29 (OS).

128. Yoshida, *Bukkyōshi,* p. 222; see also Seki Kōsaku, *Inoue Hakase to Kirisutokyōto* (Tokyo, 1893).

129. See n. 123 above and the section on Takahashi Gorō in ch. 5 above.

130. Takahashi, *Hai-gitetsugakuron,* Preface, pp. 1–2, and main part, pp. 7–8, 10–11.

131. Ibid., pp. 39–42. Takahashi referred to the Buddhists' ordering two thousand copies of Inoue's book in advance.

132. Published by Tetsugaku Shoin in Tokyo, 1893. See the picture of the front cover, fig. 17.

133. Yoshida, *Bukkyōshi,* p. 234.

134. See, e.g., Urasato, pp. 77, 84, 123.

135. Ibid., pp. 90–96; *MS* (May 24, 1893), cited in Yoshida, *Bukkyōshi,* p. 241.

136. See n. 124 and the section on "Buddhist Arguments against Christianity" in ch. 6; *ReiZ,* no. 67 (Oct. 1889), p. 36.

137. All three were published by Tetsugaku Shoin in Tokyo in 1893.

138. *Bukkyō chūkōhen,* p. 5.

139. Yoshida, *Bukkyōshi,* pp. 231–232.

140. For Nakanishi's attraction to Unitarianism, see ch. 12 below. *Kyōiku shūkyō shototsu dan'an* was published by Hakubunkan in Tokyo in 1893. *Sekai sanseiron* was published by Okajima Hōbunkan in Osaka in 1893; the Preface was written by Inoue Tetsujirō; his argument that Buddhism fostered a patriotic spirit is found in this work, pp. 148–149. Several other Buddhist writings on the controversy are examined in Yoshida, *Bukkyōshi,* pp. 231–236; Sakurai, pp. 183–190.

141. Yoshida, *Bukkyōshi*, pp. 236–248.
142. For further references, see the section on Furukawa Rōsen in ch. 12.
143. His article is included in *Rōsen ikō*, ed. Sugimura Kōtarō (Jūō) (Tokyo: Bukkyō Seito Dōshikai, 1901), pp. 87–95.
144. Hiyane, *Nihon kindai*, p. 285.
145. In *Shūkyō to kokka* [Religion and the state], the sale of which was prohibited; see Yoshida, *Bukkyōshi*, pp. 254–255; Ebisawa, *Ishin*, pp. 447–466.
146. Maruyama Tsūichi in *Shinri*, cited in Yoshida, *Bukkyōshi*, p. 261.
147. See Yoshida, *Bukkyōshi*, pp. 253–258, 260, 262, 265.
148. Cited in ibid., p. 263.
149. Cited in ibid., p. 264.
150. Kuyama, p. 203; Hiyane, *Nihon kindai*, p. 285.
151. Kuyama, p. 188; Kishimoto Hideo, pp. 257–258.
152. See, e.g., *JE* 2 (April 1895): 221; *Kokumin shinbun* (Jan. 1, 1894), Appendix, p. 3 (OS).
153. *Jūzen hōkutsu*, no. 56 (1894), pp. 14–28.
154. See ch. 11.
155. *Chōya shinbun* (June 6, 1893), p. 2 (OS).
156. For instance, in May 1895 the Minister of Home Affairs issued instructions criticizing the intellectual and moral standard of Buddhist and Shinto priests and ordering reform of their education. See *Kanpō*, no. 3573 (May 30, 1895), p. 1 (OS); *Mainichi shinbun* (July 27, 1895), p. 1 (OS); Cary, 2:262–263. In August 1899 the government issued regulations concerning private schools, favoring total separation between religion and education. These regulations affected Buddhist as well as Christian schools; see Cary, 2:285–286. For further comments, see the examination of Buddhist attempts to establish "state Buddhism" in ch. 10.

CHAPTER NINE

1. Thelle, "From Conflict," ch. 14.
2. As mentioned in the Preface, I have depended heavily on Ozawa Saburō's editions of excerpts from the contemporary press, copied by hand, especially from *Fukuin shūhō/Fukuin shinpō* and *Kirisutokyō shinbun*, but also from the daily press and such Buddhist publications as *Bukkyō shinundō*, *Bukkyō kōron*, *Dentō*, *Jōdo kyōhō*, *Meikyō shinshi*, *Mitsugon kyōhō*, and *Shimei yoka*. Apart from material mentioned specifically below, I refer to studies of local churches, such as *Kanazawa Nihon Kirisuto Kyōkai gojūnenshi*, ed. Nakazawa Shōshichi (Kanazawa: Kanazawa Nihon Kirisuto Kyōkai, 1930); *Matsuyama Kyōkai kyūjūnen ryakushi* (Matsuyama: Nihon Kirisuto Kyōdan Matsuyama Kyōkai, 1975); *Meiji shoki no Kinan Kirisutokyō: Tanabe Kyōkaishi*, vol. 1, ed. Tadokoro Sōgorō (Tanabe: Nihon Kirisuto Kyōdan Tanabe Kyōkai, [1974]); *Nihon Kirisuto Kyōdan Imabari Kyōkai hachijūnen kinenshi* (Imabari: Nihon Kirisuto Kyōdan Imabari Kyōkai, 1959); *Nihon Kirisuto Kyōdan Tosa Kyōkai hachijūnenshi* (Kochi: Nihon Kirisuto Kyōdan Tosa Kyōkai, 1976); *Nihon Kirisuto Niigata Kyōkai ryakushi* (Niigata: Nihon Kirisuto Niigata Kyōkai, 1933); *Nihon Kumiai Kyōto Kirisuto Kyōkai gojūnenshi*, ed. Nakai Saichirō (Kyoto: Nihon Kumiai Kyoto Kirisuto Kyōkai, 1935); *Nihon Seikōkai Kyōto chihōbu: Rekishi hensan shiryō*, 2 vols. ([Kyoto]: Nihon Seikōkai Kyōto Chihōbu, [1937]); *Ōmi Hachiman Kirisuto Kyōkai ryakushi*, ed. Ōmi Hachiman Kirisuto Kyōkai Rekishi Hensan Iin (Shiga: Ōmi Hachiman Kirisuto Kyōkai, 1926); *Onchō hachijūnen: Nihon Kirisuto Kyōdan Nagoya Chūō Kyōkai hachijūnen ryakushi* (Nagoya: Nihon Kirisuto Kyōdan Nagoya Chūō Kyōkai, 1960); *Saijō Kumiai*

Kirisuto Kyōkai, Komatsu Kumiai Kirisuto Kyōkai enkaku ryakushi, ed. Hoshino Mitsuo (Saijo, Ehime Prefecture, 1934); *Sōritsu hachijūnen o mukaete: Nihon Kirisuto Kyōdan Aichi Kyōkai shiryō* (Nagoya: Nihon Kirisuto Kyōdan Aichi Kyōkai, 1972). Other material is found in the *Missionary Herald, Japan Weekly Mail, Japan Evangelist,* and *Jogaku zasshi.* For details I refer to my dissertation, mentioned in n. 1 above, where I have also tried to evaluate the validity of the reports in the Christian press, compared with Buddhist reports. In general, the facts described in the Christian press seem to be correct, while the interpretation of the happenings obviously has an anti-Buddhist bias.

3. Among the new groups were Southern Baptists (1889), (American) Lutherans (1891), the Scandinavian Alliance Mission (1892), and the Salvation Army (1895). See Ebisawa and Ōuchi, p. 638.

4. Through the vehement opposition in the years after 1889, however, several Christians gradually realized that they had to contend with Buddhism as a strong rival for the spiritual leadership of Japan. For an early recognition of the potential power of Buddhism, see ch. 5.

5. See chs. 6 and 12.

6. See notably ch. 7.

7. See, e.g., Nakamura Hajime, *Bukkyō daijiten,* 3 vols. (Tokyo: Tōkyō Shoseki Kabushiki Kaisha, 1975), s.v. *"Haja kenshō."*

8. Tenrikyo was a new religion that, expanding rapidly in the 1890s, was suffering severe persecution.

9. The most common expressions were *bari, zanbō, waruguchi, hibō* (abuse, slander, defamation), *kōgeki* (attack), *bakugeki* (attack, refutation).

10. It is indicated in 19 of 64 cases that such meetings were accompanied by other, more aggressive, forms of anti-Christian activity.

11. *Kokumin shinbun* (Jan. 1, 1894), Appendix, p. 3 (OS).

12. For earlier references, see chs. 2 and 6. Among the activists in the 1890s, Ohara Masao claimed to have studied Christianity and even to know some of the leaders of the Orthodox Church; see Ohara, p. 57. Umehara Kitarō, who clashed with Christians in Nagoya, claimed to have studied Christianity for seven years; see his *Butsu-Ya zessen: Yaso daihaiboku* (Nagoya: Kichūdō, 1892), Preface. We have seen in ch. 7 that Inoue Enryō had quite extensive knowledge of Christianity. Another activist, Minoda Kakunen, is discussed later in this chapter.

13. Respectively, these were written by Nagaoka Jō and published in Kokura in 1892; written by Imai Tōgorō and published in Tokyo in 1891; written by Shimada Gunkichi and published in Iisakacho, Fukushima, by Yuishindō in 1889; and published in three small volumes by Minoda Kakunen (Tokyo: Seinenkai, 1888–1889).

14. For the former, see Shimada Gunkichi, *Shakagatake to Yasogawa ōzumō* [The great sumo tournament between Shakagatake and Yasogawa], introduced in Shimada's above-mentioned book; for the latter, see Honda Zuien, *Yasokyō shinpan* (Tokyo, 1887).

15. Most of the above-mentioned publications were based on actual anti-Christian speeches. In addition to books and pamphlets, comparative studies appeared frequently in Buddhist journals.

16. See chs. 7 and 8. The development of anti-Christian ideas, depicted in ch. 8 above, certainly made a great impact on Buddhist propagation.

17. See n. 22 below.

18. See *Seikyō shinpō,* no. 214 (Nov. 1, 1889), pp. 27–28 (OS); *KS* (Oct. 10, 1890), p. 3 (OS); *Kanazawa Nihon Kirisuto Kyōkai gojūnenshi,* pp. 17–18, and Yoshida, *Bukkyōshi,* p. 188; and *FS* (July 6, 1894), pp. 14–15 (OS).

19. The material includes 17 such cases. It should be noted that references are also made to violence on the part of the Christians.

20. The Buddhist use of *sōshi* and other ruffians is specifically mentioned in 15 cases. In spite of possible exaggerations on the part of the Christian reporters, it seemed to be generally acknowledged and in several cases confirmed by Buddhist reports that the Buddhist priests often instigated the crowd in order to obstruct Christian activity.

21. *KS* (Oct. 21, 1892), p. 3 (OS).

22. Edited by Tajima Kyōkei, and published in Kyoto by Hōzōkan in 1893. The missionaries were G. Allchin, C. S. Eby (American Protestants), W. Spinner (German Protestant), A. M. Knapp (American Unitarian), and a French Roman Catholic priest. Minoda was also called *bakuja hakase*, "Dr. Refutation." Further reports about Minoda's activities are found in Tajima Kyōkei, ed., *Nōben taika Kakunen Koji: Bakuja enzetsu hikki* (Kyoto: Hōzōkan, 1892).

23. See also Ama Tokumon, *Ikyō taiwa* (Osaka, 1897), which is a record of disputes between the author and the French Catholic Father Villion, seen from the Buddhist point of view.

24. The material refers to 14 cases of such public discussions. It is not always clear, however, whether or not the discussions were actually held. In some cases Christian meetings developed into such discussions.

25. The former was written by Ohara Masao, and published in Osaka in 1889; the latter by Umehara Kitarō, and published in Nagoya by Kichūdō in 1892. A comparison between Umehara's account and a thorough report about the confrontation in Nagoya in *JZ* no. 303 (Feb. 6, 1892), Appendix, reveals interesting differences in the interpretation of the happenings.

26. *Seikyō shinpō*, no. 214 (Nov. 1, 1889), pp. 27–28 (OS).

27. *KS* (Nov. 25, 1892), pp. 4–5 (OS); *Dentō*, no. 38 (Jan. 28, 1893), pp. 30–31 (OS).

28. See *Nihon Seikōkai Kyōto chihōbu*, 1:22–26.

29. The material tends to include only the more dramatic expressions of anti-Christian agitation; pressure from the household was probably too common to be mentioned.

30. [Herbert Moore], *The Christian Faith in Japan*, 2d ed. (Westminster: Society for the Propagation of the Gospel in Foreign Parts, 1904), p. 99.

31. Further comments below. The illustration in fig. 19 expresses somewhat humorously the popular notion that religious divergence among family members would lead to disruption of family ties.

32. *KS* (Nov. 25, 1892), p. 3 (OS).

33. See examples in Yoshida, *Bukkyōshi*, pp. 187–193; Ōhama, pp. 66–67, 82–84.

34. See *FS* (Nov. 3, 1893), pp. 5–6 (OS).

35. *MK*, no. 17 (June 2, 1890), p. 32 (OS).

36. *FS* (June 25, 1894), p. 15 (OS).

37. See Cary, 1:415–416.

38. See ch. 8.

39. See, e.g., Yoshida, *Bukkyōshi*, pp. 180, 187; Cary, 2:225.

40. [Moore], *The Christian Faith in Japan*, p. 99.

41. Ibid.

42. See ch. 8.

43. Cary, 2:239–240.

44. See *Nihon Seikōkai Kyōto chihōbu*, vol. 2, page no. missing.

45. See Yoshida, *Bukkyōshi*, pp. 213–214; *FS* (Nov. 3, 1893), pp. 5–6 (OS); (Jan. 19, 1894), p. 14. For details, see ch. 8.

46. The material refers to 34 cases of police action. Cases of police oppression of Christians were, however, reported in the 1880s; see ch. 6.

47. *Nihon Seikōkai Kyōto chihōbu,* vol. 2, page no. missing.

48. Thelle, "From Conflict," ch. 14.

49. *Nihon Seikōkai Kyōto chihōbu,* 1:217–228.

50. Yoshida, *Bukkyōshi,* p. 197. Numerous reports appeared in *Fukuin shinpō* during the summer of 1894. Father Villion referred to the influence of Shin Buddhism in Hagi as "this oppressive tyranny." See Villion, p. 453.

51. Tamamuro, p. 243.

52. *Nihon Seikōkai Kyōto chihōbu,* 1:22–26.

53. John W. Saunby, *The New Chivalry in Japan: Methodist Golden Jubilee* (Toronto: Missionary Society of the Methodist Church, 1923), p. 277.

54. *JE* 2 (Feb. 1895): 135–137.

55. Yoshida Kyūichi has concentrated his analysis of the Buddhist-Christian conflict in the field of propagation to the years of 1891 to 1893, with the Inoue controversy as the focal point. He thus leaves the impression that the Buddhist campaigns took place primarily in that period. See Yoshida, *Bukkyōshi,* pp. 166–201. Those years were certainly of central importance, and provided the Buddhists with strong arguments against the Christians. The anti-Christian campaigns were, however, equally frequent both before and after that period.

56. Support for continued anti-Christian propaganda was, for instance, voiced in a characteristic way by Oda Tokunō at the first Buddhist-Christian Conference in 1896; see ch. 14.

57. Such expressions became almost standard refrains in reports in the Christian press.

58. According to *Dentō,* no. 38 (Jan. 28, 1893), pp. 30–31 (OS), this was the case in the district of Tajima in northern Hyogo Prefecture.

CHAPTER TEN

1. The common term was *kōninkyō,* which literally means "officially recognized religion." Since the official recognition implied state supervision and protection, I will use the term "state-recognized religion," which was one of the translations used in the contemporary press. See, e.g., *JE* 7 (Jan. 1900): 11. The term *kokkyō,* or "state religion," was also common.

2. *Chōya shinbun* (Jan. 20, 1889), p. 2 (OS); Cary, 2:253; *Brief Survey of Christian Work in Japan, 1892: With Special Reference to the Kumi-ai Churches and the American Board's Mission,* ed. J. H. DeForest (Yokohama, [1892]), pp. 22–23. For references to missionary itineracy in the 1880s, see the section on "Christian Expansion" in ch. 4.

3. See Pyle, pp. 110–111. A second, revised edition of Inoue's book was published in 1891.

4. Pyle, p. 110.

5. Ibid., p. 111.

6. *JWM* (Oct. 12, 1889), p. 325.

7. *Jiyū shinbun* (Jan. 11, 1894), p. 2 (OS); (Jan. 13, 1894), p. 2 (OS).

8. *Sōtō fushūkai zasshi,* no. 13 (Feb. 28, 1889), pp. 4–5. See also *ReiZ,* no. 63 (June 1889), p. 38, where economic and industrial implications were also considered.

9. See the section on "Buddhist Cooperation" in ch. 7.

10. *Dentō,* no. 39 (Feb. 13, 1893), pp. 27–28 (OS); no. 45 (May 13, 1893), p. 28 (OS); *MS* (April 22, 1893), pp. 4–5; (April 24, 1893), pp. 3–4; (April 26, 1893), pp. 1–3.

11. Katō Totsudō (Taiichirō), *Naichi zakkyo ni tai-suru Bukkyō shinto no kokoroe: Naichi zakkyo to Bukkyō* (Tokyo: Kokubosha, 1897), p. 1.

12. Takada Dōken, *Naichi zakkyo Butsu-Ya mondō* (Tokyo: Tsūzoku Bukkyōkan, 1899; first publ. in 1897), pp. 4–6.

13. For a review of various organizations and publications, see Kashiwabara, p. 380.

14. Katō, *Naichi zakkyo,* pp. 2, 23–26, 38–42.

15. See the Bibliography for further details on Katō's numerous writings.

16. Katō, *Naichi zakkyo,* pp. 17–19.

17. See n. 12 above.

18. Takada, pp. 7, 12–15, 21, 31, 42. Similar ideas were expressed in the description of an actual debate between a missionary and a Japanese Buddhist, in Itō Masahiko, *Naichi zakkyo Butsu-Ya tōronkai* (Tokyo: Kokubosha, 1898).

19. See, e.g., *Seikyō jihō,* no. 12 (June 1, 1899), p. 9 (OS); no. 4 (Feb. 15, 1899), p. 6 (OS); *Gokyō* (June 11, 1898), p. 6 (OS).

20. Cited in Yoshida Kyūichi, *Nihon kindai Bukkyō shakaishi kenkyū* (Tokyo: Yoshikawa Kōbunkan, 1964), p. 191 (hereafter cited as Yoshida, *Bukkyō shakaishi*).

21. See ch. 7.

22. See his essay on the preparation for mixed residence, in Tan Reigen, ed., *Naichi zakkyo junbi: Bukkyō enzetsushū* (Tokyo: Kokubosha, 1897).

23. Ibid., pp. 5–9.

24. Yoshida, *Bukkyō shakaishi,* pp. 193–194, 196.

25. Ibid., p. 193.

26. See, e.g., Inoue's characteristic description of the "wrestling tournament" between Buddhism and Christianity in the section on "The First Buddhist-Christian Conference" in ch. 14.

27. See Ōuchi's preface in Katō Totsudō, *Teikoku kenpō shinkyō jiyū no ben: Kokutai to Yasokyō* (Tokyo: Kokubosha, 1898).

28. See Ōuchi's essay on mixed residence in Tan Reigen, pp. 1–3, 9–13, 15–17.

29. Fujishima Ryōon (Tangaku), *Seikyō shinron* (Kyoto: Kōkyō Shoin, 1899), pp. 88–91, 93–94, 96–103.

30. See Katō Totsudō, *Bukkyō kokumin zakkyogo no kokoroe* (Tokyo: Kōmeisha, 1899).

31. *JK,* no. 9 (June 10, 1889), p. 13.

32. Quoted from Cary, 2:173.

33. Ibid., pp. 172–175; Suzuki, *Meiji shūkyō,* pp. 44–46.

34. Cary, 2:174.

35. *MS* (Sept. 30, 1889), p. 8 (OS); (Oct. 18, 1889), p. 10 (OS).

36. *Nori no ame,* no. 22 (Oct. 20, 1889), pp. 32–33 (OS).

37. Kashiwabara, p. 378.

38. *SY,* no. 29 (May 1890), p. 25 (OS); *JE* 6 (Jan. 1899): 10.

39. *Nihon* (Oct. 18, 1898), p. 1 (OS).

40. *Jiji shinpō* (Jan. 21, 1898), p. 3 (OS).

41. Kashiwabara, pp. 381–382. For a detailed examination of the religions bill, its defeat, and the ordinances issued in that connection, see Abe, "Religious Freedom," part 4, *Contemporary Religions in Japan* 11 (March–June 1970): 27–53.

42. Cited in Kashiwabara, p. 382.

43. *Seikyō jihō,* no. 1 (Jan. 4, 1899), p. 6.

44. Ibid., pp. 6–7.

45. Quoted from *Seikyō jihō*, no. 2 (Jan. 15, 1899), p. 1.
46. Other versions read "religion" *(shūkyō)* instead of "non-recognized religion" *(hikōninkyō)*; see, e.g., Cary, 2:283; *Jiji shinpō* (Nov. 1, 1898), p. 2 (OS). In either case the front against Christianity was obvious.
47. The translation is based on the prospectus of the Alliance, quoted from *Seikyō jihō*, no. 2 (Jan. 15, 1899), p. 1. The translation in Cary, 2:283, is used with some minor changes.
48. Quoted from *JE* 7 (Jan. 1900): 10.
49. Cary, 2:283. The chaplain, Tomeoka Kōzuke, later obtained an important position, training officials for reformatory work.
50. Kashiwabara, p. 382; *Tenchijin*, no. 19 (July 2, 1899), p. 102 (OS); *MK*, no. 233 (June 12, 1899), p. 33 (OS).
51. Kashiwabara, p. 382.
52. Cited in ibid. See also *Chūō kōron* 15 (Jan. 1900): 87–91; *The Orient* 14 (July 1899): 34–35.
53. Cary, 2:292.
54. Abe, "Religious Freedom," part 4, pp. 52–53.
55. Kashiwabara, pp. 383–384.
56. See Epilogue.
57. See notably chs. 11–13.
58. See Yoshida Kyūichi's analysis of Buddhist concerns in the years 1891–1893, in Yoshida, *Bukkyōshi*, pp. 153–163.
59. Ibid.
60. This was boldly expressed by Furukawa Rōsen, who in 1891 argued that the apparent restoration of Buddhism was merely the result of the nationalistic reaction. As Christianity had flourished during the period of Westernization in the 1880s, the emphasis on the national essence had drawn people's attention to Buddhism. Without a radical reformation, however, Buddhism was bound for decay. Unfortunately, few Buddhists had the keenly critical ability of Furukawa. See notably Mori Ryūichi, ed., *Shinshū shiryō shūsei*, vol. 13: *Shinshū shisō no kindaika* (Kyoto: Dōbōsha, 1977), pp. 229–230, and ch. 12 of this volume.

CHAPTER ELEVEN

1. The expression "New Christianity" was not so commonly used as the Buddhist concept of a "New Buddhism," but is introduced here as a common denominator of several new developments within the Christian churches. The term is used in, e.g., *Bukkyō*, no. 83 (Jan. 5, 1894), p. 3; *JE* 3 (June 1896): 279.
2. The word "patriotism," the English equivalent of *aikoku-shugi*, will be used here to distinguish Christian attitudes from Buddhist ideas of nationalism. The reason will be clarified in the following pages.
3. Most standard works on Japanese Buddhism explain the close connection between Buddhism and nationalism. See, e.g., Watanabe Shoko, *Japanese Buddhism: A Critical Appraisal*, rev. ed. (Tokyo: Kokusai Bunka Shinkokai, 1968; first publ. in 1964), pp. 60–71.
4. See ch. 2.
5. A number of popular terms and catchwords expressed this trend, such as *gohō aikoku*, "Buddhist apologetics and patriotism"; *sonnō hōbutsu*, "revering the Emperor and worshipping the Buddha"; *gokoku airi*, "protection of the nation and love of reason"; *gokoku Bukkyō*, "state-protecting Buddhism," etc. The developments described in chs. 7 and 8 above were concrete manifestations of such ideas.

6. Kamata, pp. 1–10.
7. Kōsaka, p. 185.
8. For a further examination of such trends in Japanese Protestantism, see Irwin Scheiner, *Christian Converts and Social Protest in Meiji Japan* (Berkeley and Los Angeles: University of California Press, 1970), pp. 41–66.
9. Kōsaka, p. 183.
10. Quoted from ibid., pp. 183–184. For a further examination of various conceptions of nationalism and social ideas among Christians, see ibid., pp. 183–186, 198–234; Pyle, pp. 53–117; Scheiner, *Christian Converts*, pp. 100–126, 188–247.
11. *RZ*, no. 109 (Jan. 1890), pp. 1–3; the translation is rather free. The term "nationality" for *kokumin-shugi* was suggested by *Rikugō zasshi* itself. See also Uemura Masahisa's essay on nationalism in *Nihon hyōron*, no. 40 (Feb. 25, 1892), included in *Uemura Masahisa chosakushū*, 1:295–298.
12. The Inoue controversy examined in ch. 8 was a characteristic expression of this conflict.
13. Quoted from Kōsaka, p. 209.
14. *The Complete Works of Kanzō Uchimura*, 1:105–106, 118–119.
15. Cary, 2:216.
16. Matsumura, *Shinkō gojūnen*, pp. 24, 50–51.
17. *RZ*, no. 109 (Jan. 1890), pp. 1–3.
18. Yokoi Tokio, *Waga kuni no Kirisutokyō mondai* (Tokyo: Keiseisha, 1894), pp. 195–196.
19. Cary, 2:219.
20. Ibid., p. 241.
21. *Fragments of Fifty Years*, p. 40.
22. J. H. DeForest in *MH* (Oct. 1890), p. 404; *JWM* (Dec. 20, 1890), pp. 615–616.
23. *RZ*, no. 120 (Dec. 1890), pp. 7–12.
24. The former conflict was described in detail from Matsumura's point of view in his *Shinkō gojūnen*, pp. 127–143. The two incidents are commented on in Howes, "Japanese Christians," pp. 354–355; see also idem, "Kanzo Uchimura: Teacher and Writer," pp. 150–153.
25. James H. Pettee, *A Chapter of Mission History in Modern Japan* ([Okayama], n.d. [ca. 1895], pp. 102, 174. The principal of the school, Kurahara Korehiro, belonged to the so-called Kumamoto Band, but abandoned his Christian faith. In fact, a great number of Christians left the church or abandoned their faith in the wake of the nationalist react⌐n, probably because Christianity lost its attraction for many of those who had become Christians in the time of Westernization when the popular sentiment turned against the West.
26. Characteristic examples of such a spirit of independence are the activities of Paul Sawayama and of the indigenous Home Missionary Society, founded in 1878. See Cary, 2:132, 139, 165; and ch. 4 of this volume.
27. Cary, 2:240–241, 252, 274–276; *JZ* (Feb. 25, 1893), p. 1620.
28. See, e.g., *Nihonjin*, no. 20 (Jan. 16, 1889), pp. 18–19 (OS); *Dentō*, no. 15 (March 1891), p. 19 (OS).
29. *JK*, no. 23 (Jan. 5, 1890), p. 5 (OS).
30. Quoted from Pyle, pp. 82–83.
31. *Nihonjin*, no. 20 (Jan. 16, 1889), pp. 18–19 (OS).
32. *JK*, no. 23 (Jan. 5, 1890), p. 5 (OS); see also *FS* (Nov. 14, 1890), p. 6 (OS); (Nov. 21, 1890), p. 3 (OS).
33. See ch. 8 of this volume; and notably *FS* (Dec. 19, 1890), p. 12 (OS).

34. See, e.g., Yoshida, *Bukkyōshi,* pp. 263–264; and ch. 8 of this volume.

35. Cited in *JE* 3 (June 1896): 299.

36. *HZ* 10 (Feb. 1895): 10; written with reference to Yokoi Tokio. It was further suggested that even God or the Roman Catholic pope would have to kowtow to the *Yamato-damashii* [Japanese spirit] in order to be accepted in Japan.

37. Quoted from Cary, 2:266–267.

38. Ibid., pp. 277–279.

39. Tomo Tanaka in *JE* 2 (April 1895): 216–219.

40. *Mainichi shinbun* (Aug. 12, 1894), p. 3 (OS).

41. *JK,* no. 191 (Sept. 5, 1894), p. 11 (OS).

42. See, e.g., *Mainichi shinbun* (Aug. 14, 1894) (OS); *FS* (Jan. 18, 1895), p. 13 (OS); (Jan. 11, 1895), pp. 10, 12 (OS); (Jan. 25, 1895), p. 14 (OS); *KS* (Feb. 1, 1895), pp. 1–4 (OS).

43. In addition to the references in n. 42 above, see also *FS* (Feb. 22, 1895), pp. 13, 14 (OS); (March 1, 1895), p. 15 (OS).

44. Cary, 2:250; *FS* (Feb. 1, 1895), p. 11 (OS).

45. Cary, 2:251.

46. *FS* (Nov. 2, 1894), p. 2 (OS); (Nov. 16, 1894), p. 13 (OS); *Shūkyō,* no. 37 (Nov. 1894), pp. 342–343 (OS).

47. Pettee, p. 99.

48. Tomo Tanaka in *JE* 2 (April 1895): 220.

49. See, e.g., *FS* (Feb. 22, 1895), pp. 14–15 (OS).

50. *FS* (Oct. 12, 1894), p. 10 (OS); (Nov. 2, 1894), pp. 1–2 (OS); (Jan. 11, 1895), p. 10 (OS); (Jan. 25, 1895), p. 14 (OS); *KS* (Nov. 15, 1895), pp. 4–5 (OS).

51. *JK,* no. 191 (Sept. 5, 1894), p. 11 (OS).

52. *Kokkai* (Sept. 11, 1894), p. 1 (OS). "Demons" is here a free translation of *shura.*

53. Yanaga, p. 252; Best, pp. 114–115.

54. *MK,* cited in *JE* 3 (April 1896): 246.

55. *JZ,* no. 411 (June 25, 1895), pp. 1–3.

56. Cited in Sumiya, p. 131.

57. See Kōsaka, p. 132; Pyle, pp. 44–45.

58. See Sumiya, p. 132; Pyle, pp. 163–187; Takeda Kiyoko, *Ningenkan no sōkoku,* rev. ed. (Tokyo: Kōbundō, 1967; first publ. in 1959), pp. 179–182.

59. See Suzuki, *Meiji shūkyō,* pp. 132 (Matsumura), 150–151 (Honda), and 155–158, 162 (Miyakawa).

60. A collection of Hiraiwa's essays was published in 1894, with the characteristic title, *Waga kokutai to Kirisutokyō* [Our national polity and Christianity] (Tokyo: Keiseisha, 1895; first publ. in 1894); see pp. 16–23 for his views on Shinto. Further expressions of this trend among Japanese Christians will be discussed in the section on "Nationalism" in ch. 14.

61. *HZ* 10 (Feb. 1895): 10.

62. Sumiya, pp. 132–133.

63. See, e.g., the tendencies described in ch. 10.

64. *JK,* no. 230 (Oct. 5, 1895), pp. 1–2 (OS); Saba, 5:869–873.

65. Kutsumi Sokuchū (Kesson), *Yasokyō shōtotsuron* (Tokyo, 1893), pp. 72–74.

66. Sumiya, pp. 134–135.

67. See *Sōtō kyōhō,* no. 23 (March 5, 1896), pp. 1–3 (OS). The translation "citadel" is somewhat inaccurate, as the character used is not *shiro* (citadel, castle), but *iki* (region). Since the two characters are very similar, and the context

refers to the defense of the citadel of nationalism, the use of the character for *iki* is probably a misprint.

68. The most common expressions were *Nihonka*, "Japanization," *Nihonteki* or *Nihonfū*, "Japanese," and *dōka*, "assimilation," "adaptation," or "integration."

69. See Yokoi Tokio's essay in *RZ*, no. 114 (June 1890), pp. 1–6; see also idem, *Kirisutokyō shinron* (Tokyo: Keiseisha, 1891), pp. 1–2; *RZ*, no. 116 (Aug. 1890), pp. 12–14; Cary, 2:218–219.

70. Examples are mentioned in Cary, 2:233–234, 259–260; Sumiya, pp. 133–134.

71. W. E. Griffis, cited in *Brief Survey of Christian Work in Japan*, p. 42.

72. *RZ*, no. 114 (June 1890), p. 5.

73. It was emphasized in *RZ*, no. 118 (Oct. 1890), pp. 39–40, that Yokoi avoided the expression of the Unitarians, "on the basis of Confucian and Buddhist doctrines," and merely argued that Christianity should "stand on Confucian and Buddhist civilization."

74. Yokoi, *Kirisutokyō shinron*, p. 9.

75. Yokoi, *Christianity—What Is It? A Question in the Far East* (a pamphlet printed by the *Japan Mail* office, [1893]), p. 3.

76. *JE* 1 (Oct. 1893): 34–35; Matsumura, *Shinkō gojūnen*, pp. 50–51.

77. See, e.g., Matsumura Kaiseki, *Tenchijin* (Tokyo: Keiseisha, 1912), p. 96.

78. The classical expression is Nitobe Inazō's *Bushido: The Soul of Japan* (Rutland, Vermont, & Tokyo, Japan: Charles E. Tuttle Co., 1970; first publ. in 1900).

79. See, e.g., *RZ*, no. 198 (June 1897), pp. 259–269.

80. See ch. 5.

81. See, e.g., *MS* (Feb. 10, 1892), p. 5; see also ch. 13 in this volume.

82. Numerous articles were published in *Rikugō zasshi*.

83. *Bukkyō shinundō*, no. 12 (Sept. 1890), p. 24.

84. In Japanese, *Bukkyōteki Kirisutokyō*; in some cases *Busshōteki Kirisutokyō*, literally "Buddha-nature Christianity." See *Dentō*, no. 51 (Aug. 13, 1893), p. 31 (OS); *MS* (May 18, 1893), p. 6; Kuyama, p. 223.

85. *Kokumin shinbun* (Jan. 1, 1894), Appendix, p. 3 (OS).

86. For Togawa's interest in Eastern religion, particularly in Zen, see *NS* 1 (Sept. 1895): 159–163; 1 (May 1896): 655–657; Kuyama, p. 223; *Nihon kindai bungaku daijiten*, ed. Nihon Kindai Bungakkai, 6 vols. (Tokyo: Kōdansha, 1977), s.v. "Togawa Yasuie." A critic characterized him as a Christian who always talked about Buddhism; see *Kokumin shinbun* (Sept. 26, 1896), p. 5 (OS). Later in life he apparently devoted himself to Buddhism; see *Bungei shunjū* 14 (April 1936): 226–229. For Iwamoto, see *NS* 1 (July 1895): 9; 1 (Dec. 1895): 273–274; Hiyane, *Nihon kinsei*, p. 296; Kuyama, p. 223; *Nihon kindai bungaku daijiten*, s.v. "Iwamoto Yoshiharu." For both, see also ch. 14.

87. *JZ*, no. 325 (Aug. 13, 1892), pp. 1262–1265; no. 326 (Aug. 27, 1892), pp. 1290–1293.

88. A visit to Shaku Sōen in Kamakura is described by Togawa Yasuie in *NS* 1 (Sept. 1895): 159–163. For further references to Hoshino Tenchi and trends in *Jogaku zasshi* and *Bungakkai*, see Michael C. Brownstein, "*Jogaku Zasshi* and the Founding of *Bungakkai*," *Monumenta Nipponica* 35 (Autumn 1980): 319–336. According to Brownstein, pp. 328, 332–333, Baba Kochō characterized some trends in *Bungakkai* as part of a movement "beyond the realm of Christian faith or Christian morality."

89. Yoshida Seitarō, *Kami o miru* (Tokyo: Keiseisha, 1931), pp. 215–216.

90. Japanese, *jiyū shingaku;* sometimes called *shin shingaku,* or "the new theology."

91. Cary, 2:216–217.

92. Charles H. Germany, *Protestant Theologies in Modern Japan: A History of Dominant Theological Currents from 1920–1960* (Tokyo: International Institute for the Study of Religions, 1965), pp. 9–10; Cary, 2:180–181; Suzuki, *Meiji shūkyō,* pp. 24–43.

93. Saba, 5:201. For further references to Brahmo Samaj, see M. M. Thomas, *The Acknowledged Christ in the Indian Renaissance* (Bangalore and Madras: C.L.C., The Christian Institute for the Study of Religion and Society, 1970).

94. Suzuki, *Meiji shūkyō,* pp. 27–28.

95. Not immediately after Spinner's arrival as indicated in Cary, 2:181, and Germany, p. 9.

96. Cited in Cary, 2:181.

97. See Suzuki, *Meiji shūkyō,* pp. 29–36, for a review of *Shinri* and the differences between liberal and Unitarian views.

98. Ibid., pp. 38–40.

99. Cited in Yoshida, *Bukkyōshi,* p. 160.

100. Tajima Kyōkei, *Butsu-Ya kessen,* pp. 11, 16.

101. Saba, 5:200–205.

102. Kuyama, pp. 208–209.

103. *RZ,* no. 119 (Nov. 1890), pp. 1–6.

104. Yokoi, *Waga kuni no Kirisutokyō mondai,* p. 127.

105. Yokoi eventually withdrew from active church life. But in the 1880s and 1890s he was regarded as one of the most prominent Protestant leaders in Japan: a successful pastor, an eloquent speaker, a progressive theologian and thinker. In spite of his liberal views, he maintained a close relationship with such conservative Christians as Uemura Masahisa and Uchimura Kanzō. He published his views on liberal theology in various books and journals, notably in *Rikugō zasshi.* Several of his essays were collected in *Kirisutokyō shinron* [A new treatise on Christianity] and *Waga kuni no Kirisutokyō mondai* [The problems of Christianity in our country], which have already been introduced. They will hereafter be referred to as *Shinron* and *Waga kuni.*

106. *Shinron,* Preface, pp. 1–2; *Waga kuni,* pp. 127–128.

107. *Waga kuni,* pp. 157–164.

108. *Shinron,* pp. 1–2; *RZ,* no. 116 (Aug. 1890), pp. 12–13.

109. *Shinron,* Preface, pp. 1–2, and main text, pp. 1–2; *Waga kuni,* p. 127.

110. *Waga kuni,* pp. 152, 154–155.

111. Ibid., pp. 149, 152.

112. *RZ,* no. 120 (Dec. 1890), pp. 1–6.

113. *Shinron,* p. 73; *Waga kuni,* pp. 149–150, 190.

114. *RZ,* no. 120 (Dec. 1890), pp. 3–5.

115. *Shinron,* pp. 11–12, 15, 21, 73–74; *Waga kuni,* p. 190.

116. *Shinron,* pp. 15, 37.

117. *Waga kuni,* p. 127.

118. *Shinron,* p. 73.

119. The Confucian influence was obvious in his use of such concepts as "benevolence," "Heaven," etc., and probably also in his emphasis on the conscience and inherent goodness of human beings.

120. Sumiya, pp. 130–135; Cary, 2:216–221; W. T. Thomas, pp. 193–195.

121. Universalism will not be specifically examined in this context. It was

introduced into Japan in 1890, but its influence was not comparable to that of Unitarianism; and it represented, in spite of some differences and nuances, a trend of liberal Christianity very similar to Unitarianism. For further comments on some of the differences, see Suzuki, *Meiji shūkyō,* pp. 60–63, 66–70.

122. Cited in Cary, 2:199.

123. Suzuki, *Meiji shūkyō,* p. 44.

124. Ibid., pp. 45–47.

125. Clay MacCauley, *Memories and Memorials: Gatherings from an Eventful Life* (Tokyo, 1914), pp. 503–504.

126. Suzuki, *Meiji shūkyō,* pp. 47–48; *Nihon no kyōgaku,* no. 11 (July 10, 1888), pp. 42–45 (OS).

127. MacCauley, pp. 504–505; Suzuki, *Meiji shūkyō,* pp. 54–55.

128. See the section on "Unitarianism and Buddhism" in ch. 12.

129. MacCauley, pp. 505–506.

130. Ibid., pp. 487–491, 511, 516.

131. The title of Saji's historical record of the Unitarian movement clearly expressed the problematic development of Unitarianism in Japan: *Nihon Yuniterian-shugi kōbōshi* [The history of the rise and fall of Japanese Unitarianism], (Tokyo: Suieisha, 1910).

132. Suzuki, *Meiji shūkyō,* pp. 49, 63.

133. MacCauley, p. 508; see also Cary, 2:199.

134. Cited in Suzuki, *Meiji shūkyō,* pp. 50–51.

135. MacCauley, p. 508.

136. Suzuki, *Meiji shūkyō,* p. 52. Suzuki is somewhat misleading when he summarizes the three points as (1) the study of Japanese religions, (2) propagation of Unitarianism, and (3) mutual cooperation between religions. Knapp limited his interest to the study of and cooperation with religious trends among the intellectuals.

137. MacCauley, p. 507.

138. Ibid., pp. 494, 498.

139. Ibid., p. 509.

140. Suzuki, *Meiji shūkyō,* pp. 46–47, 53–54; *Yuniterian* 1 (March 1890): 4–5.

141. See notably ch. 6.

142. MacCauley, p. 478.

143. Sakurai, p. 236.

144. Urasato, p. 46; *Yuniterian* 1 (Sept. 1890): 16–18.

145. MacCauley, p. 499.

146. The former remark is cited in Cary, 2:199–200. The latter is Kishimoto Nobuta, cited in ibid., p. 201.

147. *RZ,* no. 117 (Sept. 1890), p. 5.

148. *RZ,* no. 118 (Oct. 1890), pp. 33–35; Saba, 5:105–107; Cary, 2:201.

149. Suzuki, *Meiji shūkyō,* p. 53.

150. MacCauley, pp. 474–508 passim. The quoted passage (p. 509) is very similar to the brief Unitarian creed, cited in Sakurai, pp. 237–238, and Suzuki, *Meiji shūkyō,* pp. 53–54.

151. Suzuki, *Meiji shūkyō,* p. 54.

152. *Yuniterian* 1 (July 1890): 12. Knapp published a pamphlet with the characteristic title *The God of Evolution;* see MacCauley, p. 487.

153. MacCauley, pp. 511–512.

154. Ibid., p. 491.

155. Cary, 2:201.

156. *Yuniterian* 1 (July 1890): 12–15. Knapp had some time before advocated similar views in a public speech in the Rokumeikan in Tokyo; see *RZ*, no. 117 (Sept. 1890), p. 1.

157. *Yuniterian* 1 (July 1890): 12–15.

158. On this point he claimed that both orthodox Christianity and traditional Buddhism were in conflict with a scientific faith, for both gave the human realization of the ideal (Buddha, Christ) a divine status.

159. Ibid., pp. 16–19. In a dispute with Minoda Kakunen, Knapp emphasized the common points of Unitarianism and Buddhism. He agreed to the adoption of the good points in such scriptures as the Lotus Sutra and the Amida Sutra. He further argued that prayer and worship in Japan should be adapted to indigenous forms, and found it justified to chant *nenbutsu* and *daimoku,* the Buddhist incantations according to Pure Land and Nichiren Buddhist traditions. As for theism, the point was, according to Knapp, to foster a Unitarian spirit in people, irrespective of the question of God's existence. See Tajima Kyōkei, *Butsu-Ya kessen,* pp. 37–39.

160. *RZ*, no. 117 (Sept. 1890), pp. 1–5. See also *JWM* (Oct. 4, 1890), pp. 322–323.

161. *RZ*, no. 118 (Oct. 1890), pp. 33–35; a slight difference between Knapp's and Yokoi's views on Buddhism is indicated in ibid., pp. 39–40.

162. Takahashi Gorō commented, e.g., in *RZ*, no. 117 (Sept. 1890), p. 1, that the Buddhist-related journals and newspapers eagerly endorsed the Unitarian view.

163. *Yuniterian* 1 (April 1890): 32–36. The author was probably a Buddhist.

164. *Yuniterian* 1 (Aug. 1890): 41–42. The word used was *sendatsu,* meaning "pioneer," "guide," "religious leader."

165. MacCauley, p. 494.

166. Ibid., p. 493. A more negative evaluation of the students was given in, e.g., *HZ* 10 (March 25, 1895): 9.

167. MacCauley, p. 493; Suzuki, *Meiji shūkyō,* p. 60.

168. *Yuniterian* 1 (Sept. 1890): 16–19.

169. *MS* (June 6, 1893), pp. 2–3; *Shūkyō,* no. 30 (April 1894), pp. 249–250. Nakanishi's ideas will be examined in greater detail in ch. 12.

170. MacCauley, p. 516.

171. *SY,* no. 56 (Aug. 1892), p. 41–42.

172. MacCauley, pp. 516–552 passim.

173. Saji, *Nihon Yuniterian-shugi kōbōshi,* pp. 9–10.

174. See, e.g., his *Hajaketsu* (Tokyo: Kōmeisha, 1885), in which he gave a critical review of Western religions, especially criticizing Christianity for being in conflict with reason and science.

175. Ibid., pp. 19–30, 36–42.

176. Saji, *Nihon Yuniterian-shugi kōbōshi,* pp. 6, 9–10.

177. Ibid., pp. 12–14.

178. Ibid., pp. 7–9; *Nōjin shinpō* (Oct. 20, 1890) (OS).

179. Saji, *Nihon Yuniterian-shugi kōbōshi,* pp. 12–13, 15–16; *MK,* no. 71 (Sept. 12, 1892), p. 14 (OS).

180. Saji, *Nihon Yuniterian-shugi kōbōshi,* pp. 18–20.

181. Ibid., p. 72. Murai and Abe were also among those invited to lecture.

182. Ibid., pp. 79–103.

183. See, e.g., *MS* (Jan. 12, 1896), pp. 1–2; (Jan. 14, 1896), pp. 1–2.

184. See, e.g., Saji Jitsunen, *Shūkyō enzetsu hikki* (Tokyo: Nihon Yuniterian Kyōkai, 1895), pp. 17–18, 24–25, 28–29, 42–79 passim.

185. Saji, *Nihon Yuniterian-shugi kōbōshi,* pp. 110, 113–114; similar expressions are found in *Yuniterian* 1 (May 1890): 17–19.
186. In Takashima En (Beihō), ed., *Shōrai no shūkyō* (Tokyo: Shin Bukkyōto Dōshikai, 1903), p. 210.
187. Ibid., p. 212. He was particularly concerned about the problem of poverty.
188. *Yuniterian* 1 (Sept. 1890): 6; MacCauley, p. 478.
189. MacCauley, pp. 474, 535–536, 548 (quoted passage).
190. Suzuki, *Meiji shūkyō,* pp. 60–61.
191. *Dentō,* no. 91 (April 13, 1895), p. 48.
192. Tajima, *Butsu-Ya kessen,* pp. 34, 39–40; literally, "like catching a catfish in an empty gourd."
193. Cited in MacCauley, p. 513.

CHAPTER TWELVE

1. See, e.g., *HZ* 5 (April 10, 1890): 1–4; Sakaino Kōyō, ed., *Shin Bukkyō jūnenshi* (Tokyo: Shin Bukkyōto Dōshikai, 1910), p. 2. In *Kōza kindai Bukkyō,* 2:82, Yoshida Kyūichi emphasizes the radical discontinuity between the reform movements before the Sino-Japanese War and the formation of the New Buddhism at the time of the war. In spite of obvious differences and changes, this distinction should not be exaggerated. Further, the primary concern here is not the Buddhist reform movements as such, but their contribution to the development of Buddhist-Christian relations. On this point there is no radical change before and after the Sino-Japanese War, and it is natural to regard the more radical attitudes of Furukawa Rōsen and his followers as a development of inherent trends in the older reform movements.
2. *Kyō* stands for doctrine, religion, or -ism in the religious sense.
3. It should be remembered that the Buddhists were acquainted with the Reformation and the differences between Catholicism and Protestantism from fervent studies since the opening of Japan; see ch. 2. The first serious description of the life of Luther was perhaps the essay written by Nakamura Keiu in *Dōninsha bungaku zasshi,* no. 4 (July 1876); for this and other studies of Luther, see Saba, 2:589–593.
4. Published respectively in Tokyo by Kōkyō Shorin; in Tokyo by Hakubunkan; and in Kyoto by Kōkyō Shorin.
5. Mizutani, *Shin Bukkyō,* Epilogue, pp. 1–9.
6. See notably Nakanishi, *Shūkyō kakumeiron,* pp. 86–97, 169–192. Nakanishi's views will be commented on later.
7. *SY,* no. 24 (Dec. 1889), pp. 6–7.
8. The book was published in Nagoya by Kichūdō in 1888; see pp. 1–2 and the Preface.
9. Two of his anti-Christian booklets have already been mentioned: *Yaso ichidai benmōki* [Refutation of the life of Jesus] and *Yasokyō-i mondō* [Dispute about the meaning of Christianity], published in 1874 and 1875 respectively.
10. Tajima, *Bukkyō metsubōron,* p. 108.
11. Ibid., chs. 2 and 3, pp. 100–104.
12. See ch. 7 above; Inoue, *Shinri kinshin,* 2:6–7, 18–19.
13. Ashitsu Jitsuzen, *Nihon shūkyō miraiki* (Hyogo, 1889), p. 120.
14. *Nōjunkai zasshi,* no. 4 (May 12, 1885), p. 49.
15. *JE* 3 (June 1896): 280.
16. Ibid., p. 279.

17. *JE* 3 (Oct. 1895): 45.
18. Cary, 2:263.
19. Yoshida, *Bukkyō shakaishi,* pp. 209–213.
20. *JE* 3 (June 1896): 280.
21. *JE* 2 (June 1895): 301.
22. *Sōtō fushūkai zasshi,* cited in Yoshida, *Bukkyō shakaishi,* p. 213.
23. See, e.g., *Kokumin shinbun* (Jan. 1, 1894), Appendix, p. 3 (OS); *JE* 1 (Feb. 1894): 150; 2 (April 1895): 221.
24. *Hansei* in Hanseikai means literally "self-examination."
25. Tsunemitsu, 1:363.
26. *HZ* 1 (Feb. 1888), inside cover.
27. *HZ* 1 (Nov. 1887): 1–4.
28. See the basic principles of Hanseikai, cited in Tsunemitsu, 1:363. For further references to Hanseikai and Buddhist temperance movements, see Yoshida, *Bukkyō shakaishi,* pp. 365–374.
29. In 1892 it was renamed *Hansei zasshi,* and in 1899 *Chūō kōron.*
30. *HZ* 1 (March 1888): 18–24.
31. See *Rōsen ikō,* p. 260.
32. Tsunemitsu, 1:363–364.
33. Yoshida, *Bukkyō shakaishi,* p. 370.
34. *Bukkyō,* no. 101 (April 10, 1895), p. 153. The fact that the above-mentioned Buddhist leaders were members of Hanseikai suggests that the new reform movement was regarded as a legitimate continuation of the reform efforts described here in ch. 6.
35. *Rōsen ikō,* p. 260.
36. *HZ* 1 (May 1888): 2.
37. Sakurai, pp. 387–388; Mori Ryūkichi, ed., *Shinshū shiryō shūsei,* vol. 13: *Shinshū shisō no kindaika* (Kyoto: Dōbōsha, 1977), p. 17.
38. See, e.g., the editorials in *Hanseikai zasshi* during the first half of 1891, written by Furukawa Rōsen; included in Mori, notably pp. 222–223.
39. Cary, 2:188.
40. Yoshida, *Bukkyō shakaishi,* pp. 365–366, 369.
41. *HZ* 1 (Nov. 1887): 1–4.
42. *HZ* 5 (Oct. 1890): 12–13.
43. Tsunemitsu, 1:349–350.
44. *HZ* 1 (June 1888): 1.
45. Yoshida, *Bukkyōshi,* pp. 243–244.
46. *HZ* 8 (Dec. 1893): 1–2.
47. See chs. 13 and 14.
48. *JE* 3 (Feb. 1896): 184.
49. See announcement in *The Hansei Zasshi* 12 (March 1897).
50. Mori, p. 17.
51. *HZ* 13 (Nov. 1898): 57–58. On this point the journal was in agreement with the leadership of Nishi Honganji.
52. *HZ* 11 (Oct. 2, 1896), back cover.
53. Nakanishi, *Shūkyō kakumeiron,* pp. 19–21. The entire book was based on this idea; the remainder of this discussion is based on pp. 22–24, 28–29, 91–92, 152–158, 163, 168–169.
54. Nakanishi, *Shin Bukkyōron,* p. 116.
55. Nakanishi, *Shūkyō taiseiron* (Kyoto: Kōkyō Shoin, 1891), pp. 172–175.
56. *MS* (June 6, 1893), pp. 2–3.
57. *Shūkyō,* no. 30 (April 1893), pp. 249–250.

58. Nakanishi, *Shūkyō kakumeiron,* p. 159.
59. Ibid., pp. 170–192; quotation from p. 170. It is worth noticing that Furukawa Rōsen at an early stage identified his own view on the New Buddhism with Nakanishi's ideas; see notably Furukawa's editorials in *Hanseikai zasshi* in 1891, recorded in Mori, pp. 219–235.
60. Nakanishi makes numerous references to Unitarianism in his *Shūkyō kakumeiron* from 1889; see notably pp. 106–107, 167–168.
61. Nakanishi, *Shin Bukkyōron,* pp. 94–98, 114.
62. Nakanishi, *Shin Bukkyōron,* Appendix, pp. 18–32, notably pp. 30–32. He found a characteristic expression of such an unsuccessful attempt to harmonize Buddhism and Christianity in Sir Edwin Arnold's poetry. Arnold, who had once aroused the enthusiasm of the Buddhists with his great poem about the Buddha, *The Light of Asia: The Great Renunciation,* later disappointed them by writing a similar work about Christ, *The Light of the World: The Great Consummation,* finding in Christianity the fulfillment of Buddhism. This was, according to Nakanishi, a total failure, which resulted from the tendency of Christians to interpret Christianity by the help of Buddhism, adding "Buddhist colors to the Christian black-and-white drawing."
63. *The Young East* 1 (July 1925): 40–44.
64. His original name was Furukawa Isamu, but he was best known under his pseudonym Rōsen.
65. The following data are primarily based on Sugimura Jūō's biographical sketch in *Rōsen ikō,* pp. 407–416.
66. See his recollections of his Kyoto years in *HZ,* recorded in *Rōsen ikō,* pp. 257–261.
67. Mori, p. 56. This issue preceded the publication of *HZ,* vol. 1, no. 1 (Dec. 1887).
68. Mori, pp. 222–223.
69. *Rōsen ikō,* p. 408.
70. Ibid.
71. See, e.g., Mori, pp. 221–223, 235.
72. *Bukkyō* (May 1893), recorded in *Rōsen ikō,* p. 94. For similar expressions of his consistent rejection of Christianity, see his comparison of Buddhism and Christianity in connection with the Sino-Japanese War, in *MK* (Dec. 1894), recorded in *Rōsen ikō,* pp. 152–157; and his criticism of missionaries as a "nuisance," in *HZ* (March 1898), recorded in *Rōsen ikō,* pp. 345–347. His relationship to Unitarianism will be examined later.
73. *HZ* (Oct. 1898), recorded in *Rōsen ikō,* pp. 310–325; see also pp. 365–367.
74. *Bukkyō,* no. 83 (Jan. 5, 1894), pp. 1–5 The theme was further developed in the consecutive issues of the journal.
75. *Hihyō,* or "criticism," has in this context positive connotations, probably alluding to the so-called higher criticism in contemporary theology.
76. Furukawa used the word *setchū,* or "compromise," which was a popular catchword. As "compromise" now has several negative connotations, I have used the word "synthesis" in this connection.
77. *Bukkyō,* no. 83 (Jan. 5, 1894), p. 5.
78. Cited in Yoshida, *Bukkyōshi,* p. 365.
79. *Bukkyō,* no. 97 (Dec. 10, 1894), pp. 5–8, 10–11; no. 98 (Jan. 17, 1895), p. 2.
80. Yoshida, *Bukkyōshi,* pp. 365–366. Keiikai cannot easily be rendered into English; *kei-i* stands for warp and woof, or longitude and latitude, and refers to the two basic principles of the association.

81. More accurately, *shinshū fukyū no nen,* literally, "the untiring pursuit of [progressive] learning and virtue."
82. Yoshida, *Bukkyōshi,* pp. 365–366.
83. Furukawa also referred to historical studies by Shimaji Mokurai, Oda Tokunō, Fujii Senshō, and Nakanishi Ushio; see his article in *Shūkyō* (March 1895), recorded in *Rōsen ikō,* pp. 168–180.
84. *Bukkyō* (April 1894), recorded in *Rōsen ikō,* pp. 123–124.
85. See Fukushima Hirotaka's comments in *"Shin Bukkyō" ronsetsushū,* vol. 2, ed. Futaba Kenkō, Akamatsu Tesshin, and Fukushima Hirotaka (Kyoto: Nagata Bunshōdō, 1979), pp. 1397–1398.
86. See references to Sakaino Kōyō in the following section.
87. See, e.g., *Bukkyō,* no. 83 (Jan. 5, 1894), pp. 1–5; no. 98 (Jan. 17, 1895), p. 2; *Rōsen ikō,* pp. 116–124.
88. Ikeda, pp. 276–277.
89. Recorded in *Rōsen ikō,* pp. 116–124.
90. Similar views were expressed in an article about the past, present, and future of Unitarianism, in *Bukkyō,* no. 98 (Jan. 17, 1895), pp. 3–7.
91. *HZ* (an editorial in 1891), recorded in Mori, p. 235. On this point Furukawa was perhaps influenced by Nakanishi Ushio.
92. Recorded in *Rōsen ikō,* pp. 253–257.
93. *Bukkyō,* no. 147 (Feb. 15, 1899), p. 85.
94. Yoshida, *Bukkyōshi,* pp. 365–366.
95. The exact date was February 12, not October, 1899, as indicated in Ikeda, p. 282, and *Kōza kindai Bukkyō,* 1:95. The information given in Yoshida, *Bukkyōshi,* p. 368 is correct. See *Bukkyō,* no. 148 (March 15, 1899), pp. 101–103. The main principles were published in March 1899, as indicated in every issue of the journal *Shin Bukkyō.*
96. The designation Dōshikai will be used for both names of the association.
97. See comments on the "antiestablishment dialogue" in the Epilogue.
98. *Bukkyō,* no. 150 (May 21, 1899), pp. 173–174.
99. Sakaino, p. 4. We have observed similar trends in Hanseikai more than a decade earlier.
100. *SB* 1 (July 1900): 1–5.
101. The Manifesto is published in ibid. *Nenbutsu* and *daimoku* are invocations according to Pure Land and Nichiren Buddhist traditions respectively.
102. Ibid.
103. Sakaino, p. 7.
104. *SB* 1 (July 1900): 1–5; Yoshida, *Bukkyōshi,* pp. 369, 377.
105. *SB* 1 (July 1900): 1–5.
106. Tsunemitsu, 2:97; Ikeda, pp. 87–89.
107. Yoshida, *Bukkyōshi,* p. 379.
108. Among the Christians were Ebina Danjō, Uchimura Kanzō, Kozaki Hiromichi, Uemura Masahisa, and others. The articles were collected in Takashima, *Shōrai no shūkyō;* see the Appendix, p. 17.
109. There were two versions of the Dōshikai principles; the first was formulated in February 1899, when Dōshikai was founded, but later appeared in a slightly revised version as part of the Manifesto, published in the first issue of *Shin Bukkyō.* I have quoted the latter version, where the Unitarian influence is most obvious. See also Yoshida, *Bukkyōshi,* pp. 359, 368–369; Sakurai, pp. 352–353.
110. Yoshida, *Bukkyōshi,* pp. 359–360; Ikeda, pp. 284–285.
111. Sakaino, p. 25.
112. See *Chūō kōron* 16 (June 1901): 62.

113. *RZ*, no. 235, cited in Yoshida, *Bukkyōshi*, p. 378.
114. *SB* 3 (Jan. 1902): 22–24.
115. *RZ*, no. 244 (April 1901), pp. 66–67.
116. *Chūō kōron* 16 (May 1901): 70–71.
117. *RZ*, no. 245 (May 1901), pp. 71–72.
118. *SB* 2 (May 1901): 217–224.
119. *SB* 1 (Nov. 1900): 223–226. For other views on pantheism, see *SB* 2 (Sept. 1901): 434–446, and 4 (Dec. 1903): 978–981.
120. See notably *SB* 1 (Nov. 1900): 225–226.
121. Yoshida, *Bukkyōshi*, p. 379. See also the section on "Unitarianism and Buddhism" in ch. 11 of this volume.

CHAPTER THIRTEEN

1. Guy Richard Welbon, *The Buddhist Nirvāna and Its Western Interpreters* (Chicago: University of Chicago Press, 1968), p. 102.
2. Cited in ibid., p. 105.
3. Suzuki, *Meiji shūkyō*, p. 18.
4. See *Encyclopedia Americana*, 1963 ed., s.v. "Muller, Friedrich Max."
5. Ibid.; William Peiris, *The Western Contribution to Buddhism* (Delhi: Motilal Banarsidass, 1973), pp. 26–30.
6. Tsunemitsu, 1:245–255. See also the section on "Apologetical Study and Travels to the West" in ch. 6.
7. Welbon, pp. 223–240; Peiris, pp. 10–19.
8. For a comprehensive review of Western scholars of Buddhism in this period, see J. W. de Jong, A Brief History of Buddhist Studies in Europe and America," part 1, *The Eastern Buddhist*, n.s., 7 (May 1974): 55–106.
9. Peiris, pp. 31–36.
10. *Ajia no kōki*, trans. Nakagawa Tarō (Kyoto: Kōkyō Shoin, 1890).
11. See, e.g., Stanley Cook's article "Religion," in *Encyclopaedia of Religion and Ethics,* ed. James Hastings.
12. W. Brede Kristensen, *The Meaning of Religion,* 3d ed. (The Hague: Martinus Nijhoff, 1971), p. 2.
13. See, e.g., the critical review of such studies in Paul Carus, *Buddhism and Its Christian Interpreters,* rev. ed. (Chicago: Open Court, 1905; first publ. in 1894).
14. Peiris, p. 10.
15. Cited in *Chrysanthemum* 2 (Jan. 1882): 4.
16. See the section on M. L. Gordon in ch. 5.
17. Frank S. Dobbins in *Chrysanthemum* 2 (June 1882): 257–259.
18. Ibid.
19. See ch. 5 above for an examination of M. L. Gordon, Takahashi Gorō, and other Christians in Japan who used Buddhist studies in their criticism of Japanese Pure Land Buddhism. Similar views were expressed in Ibuka Kajinosuke's essay, "The Light of Asia and the Light of the World," in *RZ*, nos. 69–72, recorded in Ikemoto, pp. 193–214; see also Tanaka Tatsu, *Bukkyō kanken* (Tokyo: Mesojisuto Shuppansha, 1895); *Uemura Masahisa chosakushū,* 4:289–290.
20. M. L. Gordon, *An American,* p. 209.
21. See my section on "Liberal Theology" in ch. 11.
22. MacCauley, p. 150; see my section on "Unitarianism" in ch. 11.
23. Norihisa Suzuki, "Nobuta Kishimoto and the Beginnings of the Scientific

Study of Religion in Modern Japan," *Contemporary Religions in Japan* 11 (Sept.–Dec. 1970): 157.

24. Cited in ibid., pp. 157–158. It is dubious whether the technical term "science of religion" was first introduced into Japan by Ishikawa Shuntai in 1884, as Suzuki suggests. Considering the popularity of comparative religion among missionaries and foreigners in Japan in the early 1880s, it is probable that the term had been used also in the Japanese context; see, e.g., *Chrysanthemum* 2 (March 1882): 115–119. It is also inconceivable that Takahashi Gorō, with his mastery of foreign languages and extensive religious studies, should not be acquainted with the Western science of religion. In a series of apologetical lectures in Tokyo in 1883, Charles Eby spoke on the comparison between Christianity and other faiths, and criticized Spencer's ideas on religious evolution by introducing the views of Max Müller and others; see ch. 5.

25. *HZ* 10 (April 1895): 13–17; 10 (May 1895): 7–11.

26. See, e.g., Nakanishi Ushio, *Sekai sanseiron* (Osaka: Okajima Hōbunkan, 1893). See also my references to Nakanishi in ch. 12.

27. Suzuki, "Nobuta Kishimoto," pp. 158–159.

28. *HZ* 5 (Dec. 1890): 32.

29. *HZ* 11 (Oct. 2, 1896): 17–19; Carus, pp. 209–216.

30. See Peiris, pp. 35–36.

31. Joseph M. Kitagawa, "The History of Religions in America," in *The History of Religions: Essays in Methodology,* ed. Mircea Eliade and Joseph M. Kitagawa (Chicago: University of Chicago Press, 1959), pp. 4–5.

32. Carus, p. 310.

33. A full report of the parliament is found in John Henry Barrows, *The World's Parliament of Religions,* 2 vols. (Chicago: Parliament Publishing Co., 1893).

34. For a complete definition of the aims of the parliament, see Barrows, 1:18.

35. Ibid., 2:1558.

36. Ibid., 1:11.

37. Ibid., p. 72.

38. It is characteristic that, e.g., the addresses by Thomas W. Higginson on "The Sympathy of Religions" and J. Estlin Carpenter on "The Need of a Wider Conception of Revelation" seemed to stir the greatest interest during the parliament. See ibid., pp. 122–123. Among the Oriental delegates, those who stressed the basic unity of religions—such as Hirai Kinzō and Shibata Reiichi from Japan and Swami Vivekananda and Protar Chunder Mozoomdar from India—also made the strongest impression. Ibid., pp. 101, 114–116.

39. Ibid., 2:1557–1558.

40. Only the Nichiren Buddhist delegate disturbed the image of harmony, as he attacked even the other Buddhists to demonstrate the unique truth of his own sect; see ibid., 2:1290–1293.

41. See *Bukkyō,* no. 83 (Jan. 5, 1894), p. 40.

42. *Meikyō shinshi,* for instance, gave a broad coverage of the various aspects of the parliament throughout the year 1893. *MS* (July 6, 1893), pp. 2–4, referred to fourteen Buddhist journals that supported the parliament.

43. Matsuyama Rokuin, *Bankoku Shūkyō Taikaigi,* 2 vols. (Kyoto: Kōbundō, 1893–1894), 1:10–11; Nakanishi Ushio in *Bukkyō,* no. 83 (Jan. 5, 1894), p. 39; Barrows, 2:1285.

44. Matsuyama, 1:93–99; *Bukkyō,* no. 83 (Jan. 5, 1894), p. 39.

45. Matsuyama, 1:71–77.

46. Nakanishi Ushio in Matsuyama, vol. 1, Appendix, pp. 4–7.

47. *JE* 2 (April 1895): 221; see also *Bukkyō,* no. 83 (Jan. 5, 1894), pp. 39–40. It could be argued that the parliament occurred at a time when Buddhist reformers were already developing more positive relationships to Christians, as described in ch. 12 above. But the parliament was certainly one of the factors that contributed to a change of climate; and it had, moreover, a great symbolic value.

48. *MS* (March 16, 1893), pp. 1–2.

49. Even though representatives of other faiths were invited as advisors in preparation of the parliament, the General Committee appointed in 1891 consisted of sixteen Christians and one Jew; see Barrows, 1:6–8.

50. Ibid., p. 18, Article 5.

51. See, e.g., the general trend in the closing addresses of the American delegates; ibid., pp. 173–184, 249–250.

52. The motto, taken from Mal. 2:10, was suggested by H. Adler, the Chief Rabbi of the British Empire.

53. Ibid., p. ix.

54. Ibid., pp. 66–67, 112–113.

55. Matsuyama, 1:100.

56. Barrows, 2:1569.

57. Ibid., pp. 1581–1582. For other similar expressions, see ibid., pp. 1572–1580 passim.

58. Ibid., pp. 1283–1296.

59. Ibid., pp. 1013–1014.

60. Ibid., p. 1282.

61. Ibid., p. 1374.

62. Ibid., p. 1273.

63. Ibid., pp. 1280–1282.

64. See, e.g., Matsuyama, 1:131–140, and Appendix, p. 10; *MS* (Oct. 22, 1893), pp. 5–6; (Dec. 12, 1893), pp. 2–4; H. Dharmapala in Barrows, 2:1557.

65. Barrows, 2:1557; Ōhara Kakichi, trans., *Bankoku Shūkyō Taikai enzetsu-shū* (Osaka: Kanekawa Shoten, 1893), pp. 99–100.

66. Barrows, 2:1559; Tamamuro, p. 352; Tsunemitsu, 1:215. The Japanese pamphlets were written by Shaku Sōen, Akamatsu Renjō, Kiyozawa Manshi, and others. Sōen's pamphlet was translated by Suzuki Daisetsu.

67. Barrows, 2:1559; Yatsubuchi Banryū, *Shūkyō Taikai hōdō,* ed. Hayashi Denji (Kyoto: Kōkyō Shoin, 1894), p. 45; *MS* (Dec. 12, 1893), p. 3. According to Yatsubuchi, Hirai even had problems finding time for meals.

68. *HZ* 8 (Dec. 30, 1893): 1–2.

69. According to Barrows, 1:64, "The most gorgeous group was composed of the Chinese and Japanese delegates, great dignitaries in their own country, arrayed in costly silk vestments of all colors of the rainbow, and officially representing the Buddhist, Taoist, Confucian and Shinto forms of worship."

70. Ibid., pp. 121, 136, 716–723; 2:1038–1040.

71. According to *St. Louis Observer* (Sept. 21, 1893), "one trembled to know that such a figure stood at the head of the movement to consolidate all the disciples of Buddha and spread 'the light of Asia' throughout the civilized world" (cited in Barrows, 1:95). See also Ōhara, p. 98.

72. *Chicago Herald* (Sept. 14, 1893), cited in Barrows, 1:115–116.

73. Barrows, 1:449; see also ibid., 2:1288.

74. Japanese, *rekishijō misou naru kūzen no dekigoto.*

75. Ōhara, pp. 5–6.

76. Yatsubuchi, p. 57.

77. *HZ* 8 (Dec. 30, 1893): 1–2.

78. Yatsubuchi, pp. 14–16, 56; Matsuyama, 1:77–89.
79. *MS* (Nov. 22, 1893), p. 6.
80. Nakanishi Ushio in *Bukkyō*, no. 83 (Jan. 5, 1894), p. 39; see also Matsuyama, 1:65–66 and Appendix, pp. 10–11.
81. Yatsubuchi, pp. 35–40, 44–45.
82. See ch. 14.
83. Suzuki, "Nobuta Kishimoto," pp. 160–166. The lectures were later included in a Buddhist collection of essays, entitled *Kirisutokyō to Bukkyō* (Kyoto: Hōzōkan, [1899]).
84. *Kirisutokyō to Bukkyō,* pp. 15–17, 19.
85. Ibid., p. 44.
86. Ibid., pp. 46–51.
87. *Shūkyō kenkyū* was published in Tokyo by Keiseisha in 1899; see pp. 258 and 263–264.
88. Ibid., pp. 268–280.
89. Suzuki, "Nobuta Kishimoto," p. 175.
90. See ch. 14.
91. Masaharu Anesaki, *History of Japanese Religion: With Special Reference to the Social and Moral Life of the Nation* (Rutland, Vermont, & Tokyo, Japan: Charles E. Tuttle Co., 1963; first publ. in 1930). For further information about Anesaki's life and work, see his *Waga shōgai,* new ed. (Tokyo: Anesaki Masaharu Sensei Seitan Hyakunen Kinenkai, 1974), and *Anesaki Masaharu Sensei no gyōseki: Kinen kōenshū chosaku mokuroku* (Tokyo: Anesaki Masaharu Sensei Seitan Hyakunen Kinenkai, 1974).
92. Anesaki's contribution will be further commented on in ch. 14 and the Epilogue.

CHAPTER FOURTEEN

1. Two of the participants were, in fact, Shintoists: Shibata Reiichi, head of a reform Shinto sect named Jikkokyo, and Maruyama Masahiko. Among the non-affiliated participants, one was a distinguished Confucian diviner, Takashima Gayuemon. In addition to the forty-two registered participants, six observers attended the meeting; see *NS* 2 (Oct. 1896): 203–205.
2. *JE* 3 (Oct. 1895): 60, introduced *Nihon shūkyō* as "The Review of Religious Reviews," its intention being to give its readers an "intelligent and comprehensive grasp of the content of the forty-four Christian, fifty-eight Buddhist, and four Shinto periodicals in Japan." It was a liberal journal, dominated by Christians. One of its aims was to arouse the vitality of the religious world in Japan by maintaining the spirituality of the East and at the same time adding something new to the universal "Great Way." See *NS* 1 (July 1895): 1–2.
3. *NS* 1 (May 1896): 642; see also *JE* 3 (June 1896): 298–299.
4. See, e.g., *HZ* 11 (Aug. 25, 1896): 1–4, and Inoue Enryō's essay mentioned below. Similar ideas are expressed in Uchimura Kanzō's essay from 1892, "Japan: Her Mission," in *The Complete Works of Kanzō Uchimura,* 5:54–65.
5. Inoue's essay was published in *SY,* and is included in *Kirisutokyō to Bukkyō,* pp. 86–91.
6. The responses are found in *NS* 1 (June 1896): 697–712; 2 (July 1896): 33–39.
7. *NS* 1 (June 1896): 699. For "friendly talk" he used the phrase *kondan kaiwa; kondan* was later used for the Buddhist-Christian Conference.
8. *JE* 3 (June 1896): 277.

9. Ibid., p. 279.

10. Sōen had participated in the Parliament of Religions in 1893. The liberal Buddhist journal *Hansei zasshi* had in March 1896 suggested that a similar Parliament of Religions should be convened in Japan, and that a Conference of Japanese Religions should be held as a preparation for such a meeting; see *JE* 2 (April 1896): 245; *NS* 2 (Aug. 1896): 85.

11. *NS* 1 (June 1896), and 2 (July, Aug., Sept., Oct., Nov. 1896) include numerous clippings from and reviews of reactions in the contemporary press. The strongest skepticism was voiced in *Fukuin shinpō* (Christian) and *Tsūzoku Bukkyō shinbun* (Buddhist).

12. Sōen was, for instance, censured by Buddhists in certain districts because of his initiative; see *Taiyō* 2 (Oct. 20, 1896): 198; *Tsūzoku Bukkyō shinbun* (Sept. 26, 1896), p. 11 (OS); *Kokumin shinbun* (Sept. 26, 1896), p. 5 (OS).

13. For further references to Iwamoto and Togawa, see ch. 11, n. 86.

14. Hirota Ichijō in *SY*, recorded in *Kirisutokyō to Bukkyō*, pp. 95–101.

15. Ibid., pp. 98–99. The name of Tsunashima (Kakichi) is misprinted as Amishima. Another description of the participants is found in *KS* (Oct. 2, 1896), p. 7.

16. Ōuchi Seiran, who until recently had agitated against Christianity, expressed his amazement in the words, "It is a miraculous world!" "Miraculous" *(myō)* has the connotation of "strange," "wonderful," "fantastic." See *HZ* 11 (Oct. 2, 1896): 72.

17. *NS* 2 (Oct. 1896): 195.

18. For the following review, see mainly ibid., pp. 195–196; *MS* (Sept. 30, 1896), pp. 2–3. Kishida apparently turned toward Buddhism later.

19. See *Myōhō-Renge-Kyō: The Sutra of the Lotus Flower of the Wonderful Law*, trans. Bunnō Katō (Tokyo: Risshō Kōsei-kai, 1971), p. 408.

20. *MS* (Sept. 28, 1896), p. 6.

21. *Kirisutokyō to Bukkyō*, p. 99.

22. Hirota Ichijō in ibid.

23. Ibid., pp. 99–100.

24. *NS* 2 (Oct. 1896): 196–197; *HZ* 11 (Oct. 2, 1896): 69.

25. *NS* 2 (Oct. 1896): 173–177; quote from p. 175.

26. He referred to the story of Barlaam and Ioasaph; see *Barlaam and Ioasaph*, St. John Damascene, trans. G. R. Woodward, H. Mattingly, and D. M. Lang (London: William Heinemann, 1967; first publ. in 1914).

27. See the short biography of Shibata in *NS* 1 (Sept. 1895): 1.

28. *NS* 2 (Oct. 1896): 197.

29. Ibid., p. 198.

30. See Tsunemitsu, 1:277, 280; *NS* 1 (Dec. 1895): 341–343. Murakami characterized Buddhists and Christians as mutual "enemies."

31. *NS* 2 (Oct. 1896): 198.

32. Ibid., pp. 198–199.

33. *HZ* 11 (Oct. 2, 1896), English supplement.

34. Ibid., p. 68.

35. Oda later distinguished himself through the compilation of the Buddhist dictionary, *Bukkyō daijiten* (Tokyo: Daizō Shuppan, 1957; first publ. in 1916). See also Tsunemitsu, 1:332–342.

36. *NS* 2 (Oct. 1896): 199.

37. *HZ* 11 (Oct. 2, 1896): 70.

38. *NS* 2 (Oct. 1896): 202.

39. *KS* (Oct. 2, 1896), p. 7.

40. *HZ* 11 (Oct. 2, 1896): 68–69.
41. Ibid., p. 69.
42. *RZ,* no. 190 (Oct. 1896), p. 492; similar expressions were used in, e.g., *Mainichi shinbun* (Sept. 29, 1896), p. 2 (OS); *Shūkyō,* cited in *NS* 2 (Oct. 1896): 206; *KS* (Oct. 1896), p. 7; *SY,* no. 106 (Oct. 1896), pp. 25–26 (OS).
43. *RZ,* no. 190 (Oct. 1896), p. 492.
44. *Kirisutokyō to Bukkyō,* p. 101. A similar mood was expressed in *MS* (Sept. 28, 1896), pp. 6–7: "The moon was reflected in the water of Shiba Bay, sending forth the light of universal brotherhood."
45. See *NS* 1 (April 1896): 617–622; 1 (Aug. 1895): 122–124; *Sōtō kyōhō,* no. 23 (March 5, 1896), pp. 1–3 (OS).
46. This was one of the main purposes of the meeting, and was repeatedly expressed by the speakers. See notably Togawa Yasuie's opening address in *NS* 2 (Oct. 1896): 195; see also Anesaki's review in *Taiyō* 2 (Oct. 20, 1896): 197–202.
47. See notably the address by the Unitarian Clay MacCauley in *NS* 2 (Oct. 1896): 200.
48. See, e.g., ibid., pp. 173–176, 195–197. This was a tendency that, particularly since the Tokugawa period, had characterized the relationship between religions in Japan; the maintenance of harmony was more important than the insistence upon the uniqueness of one's own religion.
49. See, e.g., Ebina Danjō and Watase Tsunekichi in *NS* 1 (June 1896): 700–701, 705.
50. *HZ* 11 (Aug. 25, 1896): 3.
51. Such views were voiced in *Guze,* cited in *NS* 2 (Nov. 1896): 257; *Nihonjin,* 3d s., no. 22 (May 20, 1896), pp. 18–21; *Mitsugon kyōhō,* cited in *NS* 2 (Aug. 1896): 92–93.
52. *NS* 1 (April 1896): 620.
53. See quotation in *NS* 1 (Aug. 1895): 123–124.
54. See *NS* 2 (July 1896): 35–36.
55. *FS* (March 6, 1896), pp. 1–2. See also Uemura's essay on Hōnen, included in *Uemura Masahisa chosakushū,* 3:154–167.
56. *FS,* cited in *NS* 1 (Sept. 1895): 188.
57. *FS* (Sept. 18, 1896), pp. 1–2.
58. *NS* 2 (Oct. 1896): 174–175.
59. Cary, 2:268.
60. Discussed in *Sōtō kyōhō,* no. 23 (March 5, 1896), pp. 1–3 (OS).
61. *NS* 2 (Oct. 1896): 196–199.
62. Cary, 2:268.
63. *NS* 2 (Oct. 1896): 198. In a similar way, Togawa Yasuie had earlier argued that Christianity had to be harmonized with the patriotic spirit and become a nationalistic Christianity; see *NS* 1 (May 1896): 656–657.
64. The patriotic Christians, for instance, still maintained their universalistic outlook, a standpoint that had been one of the main targets of criticism. Matsumura Kaiseki had recently been attacked for lese majesty when he publicly argued that the Emperor should worship God "through Christ, through the cross, holding the eternal faith with a consciousness of sin." See *MK,* no. 155 (March 12, 1896), pp. 74–79 (OS).
65. *MS* (Sept. 28, 1896), p. 6.
66. *NS* 2 (Oct. 1896): 195–196.
67. *MS* (Sept. 28, 1896), p. 1.
68. *SY* (Nov. 1896), pp. 15–16.
69. See n. 63 above.

70. *NS* 2 (Oct. 1896): 195; expressed in a letter from Shimaji Mokurai, quoted in Togawa Yasuie's opening address.

71. Ibid., pp. 175–176, 195–196; see also *MK,* no. 165 (Aug. 12, 1896), pp. 11–12 (OS); *MS* (Sept. 30, 1896), p. 3.

72. Numerous examples of such negative attitudes and activities are mentioned in chs. 7–10.

73. See, e.g., Kōsaka, pp. 153–159. *JE* 2 (June 1895): 337–338, characterized Katō in the following way: "All his thinking begins and ends in the principle of evolution, the struggle for existence, and the right of the stronger."

74. *JE* 3 (April 1896): 244.

75. *NS* 1 (June 1896): 697.

76. *JE* 3 (April 1896): 244–246.

77. See *JE* 3 (June 1896): 313.

78. *JE* 3 (April 1896): 246.

79. *Dentō,* no. 127 (Oct. 13, 1896), p. 13. A number of liberal Buddhists obviously felt that cooperation was necessary in order to overcome "the irreligious spirit of the times"; see review in *JE* 3 (Feb. 1896): 154; 3 (April 1896): 245. According to *Bukkyō,* cited in *JE* 2 (Feb. 1895): 176, "Science and philosophy are assailing the foundations of religion. Buddhism, which was believed to stand on a firm philosophical foundation, has met difficulty. . . . Religious workers, in order to meet the situation, should be thoroughly united in spirit, liberal in their views, and earnest and faithful in practical work."

80. *NS* 2 (Oct. 1896): 202; see also ibid., pp. 177–179.

81. Ibid., pp. 196–197.

82. *Taiyō* 2 (Oct. 20, 1896): 199–200.

83. *NS* 2 (April 1897): 526–531; *Taiyō* 3 (April 12, 1897): 178–179.

84. *NS* 2 (Nov. 1896): 252; see also *NS* 1 (June 1896): 703; 2 (July 1896): 39–40.

85. *NS* 2 (Nov. 1896): 259; similar views were expressed in *Shūkyō,* no. 60 (Oct. 1896), pp. 33–35; *Bukkyō,* cited in *NS* 2 (Nov. 1896): 258.

86. Several of these new religions existed in the 1890s, such as Tenrikyo, Konkokyo, Kurozumikyo, and Renmonkyo. At that time, however, they were not called New Religions, but were denounced and persecuted as dangerous superstitions. The concept of a new religion had positive connotations, and the term was not used in the derogatory sense as it is sometimes today. For further references to these, see Harry Thomsen, *The New Religions of Japan* (Rutland, Vermont, & Tokyo, Japan: Charles E. Tuttle Co., 1963); H. Neill McFarland, *The Rush Hour of the Gods: A Study of the New Religious Movements in Japan* (New York: Harper & Row, 1967).

87. For a characteristic expression of such a view, see Ōnishi Hajime's response in *NS* 2 (Aug. 1896): 63–64. Similar ideas were expressed by Kishimoto Nobuta and Togawa Yasuie; see *NS* 2 (Oct. 1896): 183–186; 2 (Nov. 1896): 236–242; *NS* 1 (May 1896): 653–658.

88. In this case "revolution" hardly implied more than a radical reform.

89. See chs. 11 and 12.

90. *NS* 2 (March 1897): 479–482; Motora Yūjirō in *NS* 2 (July 1896): 6–20; Toyama Masakazu in *NS* 2 (Sept. 1896): 144–145.

91. In addition to the views of Shibata Reiichi and Matsumura Kaiseki, described above, we should notice the characteristic idea of the Orthodox priest, Konishi Masutarō, according to whom the particular religions were like different colors, which could be harmonized without destroying the features of the individual colors; see *NS* 2 (Oct. 1896): 177–178.

92. *HZ* 11 (Aug. 25, 1896): 3; see also *RZ*, no. 190, cited in *NS* 2 (Nov. 1896): 253–254; *Bukkyō*, cited in *NS* 2 (Nov. 1896): 258.

93. A Christian critic, Ibuka Kajinosuke, even compared the syncretistic tendency to the threat of gnosticism in the early church; see *FS*, reviewed in *NS* 2 (Oct. 1896): 191–192. Similar criticism was also raised in *NS* 1 (Aug. 1895): 124.

94. *Taiyō* 2 (Oct. 20, 1896): 200; see also Anesaki's comment in *Tetsugaku zasshi*, cited in *NS* 2 (Nov. 1896): 254.

95. Anesaki in *Taiyō*, cited in *NS* 2 (Aug. 1896): 89–90.

96. Brahmo Samaj seemed to have made a strong impression in Japan. It was frequently mentioned as a model for religious reform, and was introduced in great detail by *Nihon shūkyō* as a synthesis of old and new religions, of Eastern and Western traditions; see *NS* 1 (July 1895), Appendix; 1 (May 1896): 657. Mozoomdar had visited Japan as a representative of Brahmo Samaj as early as 1882; see Clara Denison Loomis, *Henry Loomis: Friend of the East* (New York: Fleming H. Revell Co., 1923), pp. 57–58; for further references, see M. M. Thomas, *The Acknowledged Christ in the Indian Renaissance.*

97. *NS* 2 (Sept. 1896): 116–120.

98. Japanese, *sententeki shūkyōshin;* Konishi Masutarō in *NS* 2 (Oct. 1896): 178.

99. Shimada Bankon in ibid., pp. 199–200. Shaku Sōen used the same words to define the common ground of the two religions, but drew different conclusions; see *NS* 2 (Oct. 1896): 173–177.

100. Togawa Yasuie in *NS* 1 (May 1896): 657–658; Watase Tsunekichi in ibid., pp. 705–706.

101. See Matsumura, *Tenchijin,* p. 207.

102. See the description of further developments in the Epilogue.

103. Matsumura, *Shinkō gojūnen,* pp. 169–193; Kuyama, p. 223.

104. *MK,* cited in *NS* 2 (Aug. 1896): 93.

105. *RZ*, no. 190, cited in *NS* 2 (Nov. 1896): 254.

106. *HZ* 11 (Aug. 25, 1896), English appendix, pp. 2–3.

107. *NS* 1 (July 1895): 2.

108. Ōnishi Hajime in *NS* 2 (Aug. 1896): 65–66; *KS* (June 19, 1896), pp. 2–3.

109. *MS* (Sept. 12, 1896), p. 1.

110. *Shūkyō*, no. 68 (June 1897), pp. 44–49.

111. *NS* 2 (Aug. 1896): 93; both Togawa Yasuie and Iwamoto Yoshiharu were closely related to literary circles. See also Kōsaka, pp. 261–269; *KS* (June 19, 1896), pp. 2–3.

112. Nakanishi, *Shin Bukkyōron,* pp. 64, 69. For further references, see the examination of the New Buddhism in ch. 12, and of the World's Parliament of Religions in ch. 13. Western Buddhists, such as Colonel Olcott and C. Pfoundes, were also regarded as pioneers of Buddhist reform and unification. Olcott was called the "Bodhisattva (the coming Buddha) of the nineteenth century," a "Buddhist Luther," and a "representative of a new religion"; see *Missionary Review of the World,* n.s., 2 (Nov. 1889): 818 (has "Bodhisat" instead of "Bodhisattva"); *Bukkyō enzetsukai*, no. 2, ed. Ozawa Yoshiyuki (Nagoya, 1889), p. 75; Nakanishi, *Shūkyō kakumeiron,* pp. 133–142; idem, *Shin Bukkyōron,* pp. 103, 108, Appendix, pp. 48–57.

113. There were also similar tendencies to define the unity in Shinto or other categories, but only Buddhism and Christianity will be discussed here.

114. *NS* 2 (Oct. 1896): 173–177; *JE* 3 (June 1896): 277–280; see also the review above of Sōen's speech at the Buddhist-Christian Conference.

115. *Daidō shinshi,* cited in *NS* 1 (Aug. 1895): 123. For further references to the Buddhist philosophy of assimilation and the symbolism of the *mandala,* see Matsunaga, *The Buddhist Philosophy of Assimilation,* and Yoshito S. Hakeda, *Kūkai: Major Works, Translated, with an Account of His Life and a Study of His Thought* (New York: Columbia University Press, 1972).

116. *MS* (Sept. 24, 1896), pp. 2–3.

117. *Jūzen hōkutsu,* cited in *NS* 2 (Nov. 1896): 258. Shaku Unshō had, in fact, expressed similar views as early as 1894, in *Jūzen hōkutsu,* no. 54 (1894), pp. 14–28; see also no. 73 (1896), pp. 37–38. The limitation of Unshō's and Ōuchi's recognition of Christianity is seen in their strong emotional reactions against attempts to compare Buddha and Christ on an equal level, as reported in Takashima, Appendix, p. 7.

118. *Kirisutokyō to Bukkyō,* pp. 110–120.

119. Such trends have already been mentioned in chs. 5 and 13. For further references, see, e.g., Ernst Troeltsch, *The Absoluteness of Christianity and the History of Religions* (Richmond, Va.: John Knox Press, 1971; originally publ. in German in 1901), notably pp. 63–83; Hendrik Kraemer, *Religion and the Christian Faith* (London: Lutterworth Press, 1956), pp. 35–95. A thorough study of similar trends in India is found in Eric J. Sharpe, *Not to Destroy But to Fulfil: The Contribution of J. N. Farquhar to Protestant Missionary Thought in India before 1914* (Uppsala: Gleerup, 1965).

120. Takeda Kiyoko, *Dōchaku to haikyō* (Tokyo: Shinkyō Shuppansha, 1967), pp. 3–26.

121. Nitobe, p. 190. Nitobe's book was published in 1900, but it reflected a sentiment that was widespread in the 1890s. Religious and cultural journals abounded in articles featuring the relationship between Christianity and Bushido, especially after the Sino-Japanese War. For the "preparatory function," see p. xiv.

122. *JE* 1 (Oct. 1893): 34–35.

123. *RZ,* no. 198 (June 1897), pp. 268–269.

124. *NS* 1 (May 1896): 700–701.

125. In Takashima, p. 66.

126. *NS* 1 (Dec. 1895): 273–274.

127. See Barrows, 2:1280–1282, and further comments in ch. 13.

128. MacCauley, pp. 508, 516, 535–536, 548.

129. *KS,* no. 686 (1896), cited in *NS* 2 (Oct. 1896): 207.

130. *NS* 2 (April 1897): 528.

131. Among the participants the following later withdrew from active church life: Yokoi Tokio, Matsumura Kaiseki, Iwamoto Yoshiharu, Kishimoto Nobuta, Togawa Yasuie, and Konishi Masutarō. As for the latter, see *HZ* 12 (May 1897): 70.

132. Such a trend was, e.g., predominant in the reports from missionaries and pastors from Japan, represented at the World Missionary Conference in Edinburgh in 1910. See *World Missionary Conference, 1910. Report of Commission IV: The Missionary Message in Relation to Non-Christian Religions* (Edinburgh: Oliphant, Anderson & Ferrier, 1910), pp. 73–121. The complete collection of unpublished reports from Japan is still available, a detailed study of which will substantiate the above observation.

133. *KS* (Oct. 2, 1896), p. 6; see also *KS* (Jan. 22, 1897), pp. 2–3; *JE* 4 (Nov. 1896): 62–63; 4 (Jan. 1897): 107.

134. *NS* 2 (Dec. 1896): 328; Sakurai, pp. 430–434; Suzuki, *Meiji shūkyō,* pp. 261–269. The most detailed reports of the activities of the society are found in *Shūkyō,* no. 62 (Dec. 1896), and the following issues: nos. 63, 64, 66, 69, 72,

75, 76. The activity continued until 1898, when, for some reason, it stopped functioning.

135. *NS* 2 (April 1897): 526–528; Sakurai, p. 436.

136. According to *NS* 2 (April 1897): 530–531, the Buddhist Anesaki was registered as unaffiliated.

EPILOGUE

1. See ch. 10.

2. See Notto R. Thelle, "Foe and Friend: The Changing Image of Christ in Japanese Buddhism," *Japanese Religions* 12 (July 1982), esp. pp. 37–45.

3. See ch. 11.

4. There were 747 Buddhists, 365 Christians, and 18 Shintoists at the meeting. For further reference, see Sakurai, pp. 436–441.

5. For further information about the relationship between Christianity, socialism, and pacifism, see Dohi, pp. 203–225; Cary, 2:330–331; Kōsaka, pp. 322–330. The relationship between Buddhism, socialism, and pacifism is examined in Yoshida, *Bukkyōshi,* pp. 388–416; *Kōza kindai Bukkyō,* 2:112–130. The pacifistic trend was further stimulated by the translation during the war of Tolstoi's writings on pacifism; see Yoshida, *Bukkyō shakaishi,* p. 433.

6. Sakurai, pp. 436–441; Cary, 2:318–319.

7. Sakurai, pp. 441–443; see also Cary, 2:328.

8. Sakurai, pp. 443–444.

9. Ibid., pp. 444–449; Dohi, pp. 132–136. See also the report written by Motoda Sakunoshin, *Sankyō Kaidō to Kirisutokyō* (Tokyo: Torakuto Kankōkai, 1912).

10. Sakurai, pp. 450–455.

11. For further information, see F. G. Notehelfer, *Kōtoku Shūsui: Portrait of a Japanese Radical* (Cambridge: Cambridge University Press, 1971); Yoshida, *Bukkyōshi,* pp. 395–415, 434–548; Kōsaka, pp. 330–344.

12. *The Young East* 1 (July 1925): 57–59; 1 (Sept. 1925): 99–105, 117–118.

13. *Nihon Shūkyō Taikai kiyō* (Tokyo: Nihon Shūkyō Konwakai, 1928).

14. It seems, e.g., as if Japanese Buddhism became a model for efforts among Christians to compromise with the ultranationalistic way of thinking; see *Kōza kindai Bukkyō,* 2:143–146.

15. Yoshida, *Bukkyōshi,* pp. 385–388; idem, *Bukkyō shakaishi,* pp. 412–416.

16. Yoshida, *Bukkyōshi,* pp. 385–388.

17. See, e.g., Inagaki Masami, *Butsuda o seoite gaitō e* (Tokyo: Iwanami Shoten, 1974): idem, *Henkaku o motometa Bukkyōsha* (Tokyo: Daizō Shinsho, 1975); Dohi, pp. 377–382; Ebisawa and Ōuchi, pp. 500–508.

18. See, e.g., Kōsaka, pp. 289–299.

19. Yoshida, *Bukkyōshi,* pp. 412–414.

20. Kōsaka, pp. 299–312; Tamamuro, p. 370; see also Thelle, "Foe and Friend," p. 41.

21. Kōsaka, pp. 312–321. See Tsunajima's two books, *Byōkenroku* and *Kaikōroku,* both published in Tokyo by Kanao Bun'endō, in 1905 and 1909 respectively.

22. Tamamuro, pp. 369–370; Thomsen, 221–234.

23. Yoshida, *Bukkyō shakaishi,* pp. 603–633; Tamamuro, pp. 366–369.

24. *The Priest and His Disciples* was translated by Glenn W. Shaw in 1922; a new edition was published by The Hokuseidō Press in 1950, and has appeared in

several printings. See also *Kurata Momozō senshū,* 5 vols. (Tokyo: Shunjūsha, 1963); *Kōza kindai Bukkyō,* 2:130–131.

25. Kaneko Hakumu, *Taiken no shūkyō* (Tokyo: Kyōbunsha, 1922).

26. Katayama Yūkichi, *Zenteki Kirisutokyō* (Hakodate, 1944). It is also significant that a contemporary Protestant theologian who has been involved in dialogue with Buddhism, Doi Masatoshi, has entitled one of his books *Search for Meaning through Interfaith Dialogue* (Tokyo: Kyo Bun Kwan, 1976).

27. Kamegai Ryōun, *Bukkyō kara Kirisuto e* (Tokyo: Fukuinkan, 1952). See also, e.g., Imai Kaku, *Yo ga jikken no shūkyō: From Buddhism to Christianity: A Personal Experience* (Tokyo: Nihon Kirisutokyō Kōbun Kyōkai, 1917); idem, *Yo ga kaishū no tenmatsu: Why I Left Buddhism and Became a Christian* (Tokyo: Nihon Kirisutokyō Kōbun Kyōkai, 1914); Tanaka Hisahiko, *Nehan yori Kami no kuni e* (Okayama: Takaya Kirisuto Kyōkai Dendōbu, 1922).

28. See chs. 13 and 14.

29. See Kishimoto Nobuta, *Okada-shiki seiza sannen* (Tokyo: Dai Nihon Tosho Kabushiki Kaisha, 1916).

30. *Hibbert Journal* 4 (Oct. 1905): 10.

31. Published by Bukkyō Dendo Kyōkai in Tokyo in 1957, and reprinted several times.

32. Innumerable comparative studies, both popular and scholarly, have been published in religious and cultural journals. Among major comparative studies in the Japanese language can be mentioned Iino Norimoto, *Kirisuto to Butsuda: Tōzai shūkyō no rikai* (Tokyo: Risōsha, 1957); Iwamoto Yasunami, *Kirisutokyō to Bukkyō no taihi* (Tokyo: Sōbunsha, 1974); Michihata Taisei, *Amida Butsu to Kirisuto* (Tokyo: Kyūdōsha Shuppanbu, 1932); idem, *Shina no Jōdoshū no kaiso Zendō Daishi ni ataeshi Keikyō no kanka* (Niigata: Kyūdōsha Shuppanbu, 1927); Oka Hōshun, *Shinkan to kyūseikan: Bukkyō to Kirisutokyō* (Kyoto: Hyakkaen, 1952); Shiozu Jun'ichi, *Kirisuto to Nichiren* (Tokyo: Genshōdō, 1948); Tanaka Tatsu, *Kirisutokyō to Bukkyō* (Tokyo: Nihon Kirisutokyō Kōbun Kyōkai, 1915); Yamakawa Chio, *Kirisutokyō to Nichiren Shōnin no shūkyō* (Tokyo: Sōgensha, 1951). Yamakawa explained that his spiritual search had led him to Nichiren Buddhism via Confucianism and Christianity. His comparative study of Nichiren Buddhism and Christianity was an attempt to follow the advice of his master, Tanaka Chigaku (1861–1939), the Nichiren Buddhist reformer; see Yamakawa, pp. 1–2.

33. Some of the central issues in the contemporary dialogue are examined in Hans Waldenfels, *Absolute Nothingness: Foundations for a Buddhist-Christian Dialogue,* trans. J. W. Heisig (New York: Paulist Press, 1980); Joseph J. Spae, *Buddhist-Christian Empathy* (Tokyo: Oriens Institute for Religious Research, 1980). *Japanese Religions,* the journal of the National Christian Council (NCC) Center for the Study of Japanese Religions, includes numerous studies and essays related to the above-mentioned issues.

34. There was, e.g., a vivid discussion in the daily *Yomiuri shinbun* in 1931 and 1932; see also Ojima Saneharu, *Ki-Butsu ronsen* (Tokyo: Shinraisha, 1932).

35. See chs. 5 and 11.

36. *Transactions of the Asiatic Society of Japan* 22 (1894): 505–506.

37. Arthur Lloyd, *Shinran and His Work: Studies in Shinshu Theology* (Tokyo: Kyo Bun Kwan, 1910), pp. 1–8. Among his other studies were, e.g., *The Higher Buddhism in the Light of the Nicene Creed* (Tokyo, 1893); *Buddhist Meditations from the Japanese: With an Introductory Chapter of Modern Japanese Buddhism* (Tokyo, 1905); *The Wheat among the Tares: Studies of Buddhism in*

Japan (London: Macmillan and Co., 1908). In addition, numerous studies were published in the *Transactions of the Asiatic Society in Japan.*

38. August Karl Reischauer, *Studies in Japanese Buddhism* (New York: Macmillan Co., 1917); Hans Haas, *Japans Zukunftsreligion* (Berlin: Verlag von Karl Curtius, 1907); idem, *Amida Buddha unsere Zuflucht: Urkunden zum Verständnis des japanischen Sukhāvatī-Buddhismus* (Leipzig: Dieterich'sche Verlagsbuchhandlung, 1910). Interest in Buddhism was also expressed in the study of another Japan missionary, Robert Cornell Armstrong, *Buddhism and Buddhists in Japan* (New York: Macmillan Co., 1927).

39. Quoted in *The Eastern Buddhist,* n.s., 5 (May 1972): 162.

40. Both have published numerous studies. For orientation, see Heinrich Dumoulin, *Christianity Meets Buddhism* (LaSalle: Open Court, 1974); H. M. Enomiya Lassalle, *Zen Meditation and Christian Mysticism* (LaSalle: Open Court, 1974). Much more negative views have been expressed by Tucker N. Callaway in *Japanese Buddhism and Christianity* (Tokyo: Shinkyo Shuppansha, 1957), and *Zen Way—Jesus Way* (Rutland, Vermont, & Tokyo, Japan: Charles E. Tuttle Co., 1976).

41. Father Jan Swyngedouw in a conference sponsored by the Ecumenical Group for the Study of Interfaith Dialogue in Atami, Japan, in March 1979.

42. See *FS* (Sept. 18, 1896), pp. 1–2.

43. The late Inagaki Saizō in a private discussion with the writer.

Glossary

bakuja 駁邪
Bakujaron 駁邪論
Benmō 辯妄
Benseki makyōron 辨斥魔教論
bōja 防邪
bokumetsu 撲滅
Bukkyō katsuron 仏教活論
Buppō gyōshōka 仏法暁鐘歌
Butsu-Ya 仏耶
Byōkenroku 病間録
Byō-Shuku mondō 廟祝問答

chingo kokka 鎮護国家
chū 中
chūdō jissō 中道実相
Chūkō katsuron 忠孝活論

Daidōdan 大同団
Daidō shinpō 大同新報
Daidō sōshi 大道叢誌
Dai Nihon Kokkyō Daidōsha
  大日本国教大道社

Dentō 伝灯
dokudan jidai 独断時代

Fukkatsu shinwa 復活新話

Gakurin 学林
gedō 外道
gegaku 外学
gekyō 外教
gohō 護法
Gohōjō 護法場
gokoku 護国
gokyō 護教
Gūzō hishinron 偶像非神論

haibutsu kishaku 排仏毀釈
Hai-gitetsugakuron 排偽哲学論
Hai-Yaso 排耶蘇
hajagaku 破邪学
haja kenshō 破邪顕正
Hajaketsu 破邪訣
Hekija kankenroku 闢邪管見録

323

Hekijashū 闢邪集
hihyō jidai 批評時代
honji suijaku 本地垂迹

ijin 偉人
Ikyō taiwa 異教対話
Ikyō sōsetsu 異教勧説

jakyō taiji 邪教退治
jashū 邪宗
jin 仁
jinkakuteki jitsuzai 人格的実在
Jūzen hōkutsu 十善法窟

kaigi jidai 懐疑時代
ke 仮
keirei 敬礼
keisei 経世
Kenpō seigan 憲法正眼
kinnōsō 勤王僧
kiyūsō 杞憂僧
koji 居士
kokueki 国益
kokutai 国体
kōkyo 公許
kōnin 公認
kū 空
kyōto 教徒
kyōyū 教友

Meikyō shinshi 明教新誌
meiroku 明六
minri 民利
Mitsugon kyōhō 密厳教報
Mukai nanshin 霧海南針

naichi zakkyo 内地雑居
Nōjunkai zasshi 能潤会雑誌

Reichikai zasshi 令知会雑誌
Rōsen ikō 老川遺稿
Ryōbu Yaso 両部耶蘇

Sakiyō chabanashi 崎陽茶話
santai 三諦
seikyō(to) 清教（徒）
Seikyō jihō 政教時報
Seikyōsha 政教社
Seikyō shinpō 正教新報
Shakkyō seibyū (shoha) 釈教正謬（初破）
shikyōkai 私協会
Shimei yoka 四明餘霞
shinnyo jissō 真如実相
Shinri kinshin 真理金針
shinshū 進修
sonnō hōbutsu 尊王奉仏
sonnō jōi 尊王攘夷
sōshi 壮士
suijaku, see *honji suijaku*

taiji 退治
Taiji jashūron 退治邪執論
taijin 大人

uchū banyū no hongen 宇宙万有の本源

Yaso ichidai benmōki 耶蘇一代辨妄記
Yasokyō-i mondō 耶蘇教意問答
Yasokyō issekiwa 耶蘇教一夕話
Yaso taiji 耶蘇退治
yōgaku 洋学

zettai mugen no sonzai (junrei) 絶対無限の存在（純霊）

Bibliography

BOOKS AND PAMPHLETS

Abe, Yoshiya. "From Prohibition to Toleration: Japanese Government Views regarding Christianity, 1854–1873." *Japanese Journal of Religious Studies* 5 (June–Sept. 1978): 107–138.

——. "Religious Freedom under the Meiji Constitution." *Contemporary Religions in Japan* 9 (Dec. 1968): 268–338; 10 (March–June 1969): 57–97; 10 (Sept.–Dec. 1969): 181–203; 11 (Sept.–Dec. 1970): 27–79; 11 (March–June 1970): 223–296.

Adachi Fumei. *Yasokyō bōkokuron* [Christianity a national ruin]. Tokyo: Nyozesha, 1893.

Ajia Bukkyōshi [A history of Buddhism in Asia]. 20 vols. Edited by Nakamura Hajime, Kasahara Kazuo, and Kanaoka Shūyū. *Nihonhen* [Japan], vol. 8: *Gendai Bukkyō* [Modern Buddhism]. Tokyo: Kōsei Shuppansha, 1973–1976.

Ama Tokumon. *Ikyō taiwa* [A dialogue on the heretic faith]. Osaka, 1897.

Anesaki, Masaharu. *History of Japanese Religion: With Special Reference to the Social and Moral Life of the Nation.* Rutland, Vermont, & Tokyo, Japan: Charles E. Tuttle Co., 1963; first published in 1930.

——. *Religious Life of the Japanese People.* Tokyo: Kokusai Bunka Shinkokai, 1970; first published in 1936.

——. *Waga shōgai* [My life]. New ed. Tokyo: Anesaki Masaharu Sensei Seitan Hyakunen Kinenkai, 1974.

Anesaki Masaharu Sensei no gyōseki: Kinen kōenshū chosaku mokuroku [The work of Anesaki Masaharu: A collection of memorial lectures and an index of his writings]. Tokyo: Anesaki Masaharu Sensei Seitan Hyakunen Kinenkai, 1974.

Aoki Kunijirō. *Shūkyō kyōshinkai* [Religious propagation contest]. Tokyo: Bunpōdō, 1885.

Aoyagi Takatomo. *Hakuja tettsui* [An iron hammer against the evil religion]. Tokyo: Yōtokukai, 1889.
————. *Mataiden benbyū* [Clarifying the fallacies of the Gospel of Matthew]. Osaka, 1882.
Armstrong, Robert Cornell. *Buddhism and Buddhists in Japan.* New York: Macmillan Co., 1927.
Arnold, Edwin. *Ajia no kōki* [The light of Asia]. Translated by Nakagawa Tarō. Kyoto: Kōkyō Shoin, 1890.
Ashikaga Zuigi. *Ryūkoku Daigaku sanbyakunenshi* [A three hundred years' history of Ryukoku University]. Kyoto: Ryūkoku Daigaku Shuppanbu, 1939.
Ashitsu Jitsuzen. *Kenpō seigan: Tōyō no shin Buppō* [The aim of the Constitution: The new Buddhism of the East]. Osaka: Kyōgaku Shoin, 1890.
————. *Nihon shūkyō miraiki* [Notes on the future of religion in Japan]. Hyogo, 1889.
Atkinson, J. L. *Prince Siddhartha, the Japanese Buddhist.* Boston: Congregational Sunday-school Society, 1893.
Baago, Kaj. *Pioneers of Indigenous Christianity.* Bangalore and Madras: Christian Institute for the Study of Religion and Society, Christian Literature Society, 1969.
Barlaam and Ioasaph. St. John Damascene. Translated by G. R. Woodward, H. Mattingly, and D. M. Lang. London: William Heinemann, 1967; first published in 1914.
Barrows, John Henry. *The World's Parliament of Religions.* 2 vols. Chicago: Parliament Publishing Co., 1893.
Beasley, W. G. *The Meiji Restoration.* Stanford, Calif.: Stanford University Press, 1973.
Beauchamp, Edward R. *An American Teacher in Early Meiji Japan.* Honolulu: University Press of Hawaii, 1976.
Bellah, Robert N. *Tokugawa Religion: The Values of Pre-Industrial Japan.* Boston: Beacon Press, 1970.
Berry, Catherine Fiske. *A Pioneer Doctor in Old Japan: The Story of John C. Berry, M.D.* New York: Fleming H. Revell Co., 1940.
Best, Ernest E. *Christian Faith and Cultural Crisis: The Japanese Case.* Leiden: E. J. Brill, 1966.
A Bibliography of Christianity in Japan: Protestantism in English Sources (1859–1959). Compiled by Fujio Ikado and James R. McGovern. Tokyo: Committee on Asian Cultural Studies, International Christian University, 1966.
Bird, Isabella L. *Unbeaten Tracks in Japan: An Account of Travels in the Interior, Including Visits to the Aborigines of Yezo and the Shrine of Nikko.* 2 vols. New York: G. P. Putnam's Sons, 1880.
Blacker, Carmen. *The Japanese Enlightenment: A Study of the Writings of Fukuzawa Yukichi.* Cambridge: Cambridge University Press, 1964.
Bowen, Roger W. *Rebellion and Democracy in Meiji Japan: A Study of Commoners in the Popular Rights Movement.* Berkeley and Los Angeles: University of California Press, 1980.
Boxer, C. R. *The Christian Century in Japan, 1549–1650.* 2d, corrected printing. Berkeley and Los Angeles: University of California Press, 1967.
Brief Survey of Christian Work in Japan, 1892: With Special Reference to the Kumi-ai Churches and the American Board's Mission. Edited by J. H. DeForest. Yokohama, [1892].

Brown, Delmer. *Nationalism in Japan: An Introductory Historical Analysis.* New York: Russell & Russell, 1955.

Brownstein, Michael C. *"Jogaku Zasshi* and the Founding of *Bungakkai." Monumenta Nipponica* 35 (Autumn 1980): 319–336.

Bukkyō enzetsukai [Buddhist oratorical meeting], no. 1. Edited by Tajima Shōji. Nagoya, 1888.

———, no. 2. Edited by Ozawa Yoshiyuki. Nagoya, 1889.

———, no. 3. Edited by Kobayashi Shinji. Nagoya, 1891.

Burkman, Thomas W. "The Urakami Incidents and the Struggle for Religious Toleration in Early Meiji Japan." *Japanese Journal of Religious Studies* 1 (June–Sept. 1974): 143–216.

Caldarola, Carlo. *Christianity: The Japanese Way.* Leiden: E. J. Brill, 1979.

Callaway, Tucker N. *Japanese Buddhism and Christianity.* Tokyo: Shinkyo Shuppansha, 1957.

———. *Zen Way—Jesus Way.* Rutland, Vermont, & Tokyo, Japan: Charles E. Tuttle Co., 1976.

Carus, Paul. *Buddhism and Its Christian Critics.* Revised ed. Chicago: Open Court, 1905; first published in 1894.

Cary, Otis. *A History of Christianity in Japan: Roman Catholic, Greek Orthodox, and Protestant Missions.* New ed. (2 vols. in one). Rutland, Vermont, & Tokyo, Japan: Charles E. Tuttle Co., 1976; first published in 1909.

Chamberlain, Basil Hall. *Things Japanese: Being Notes on Various Subjects Connected with Japan.* London: Kegan Paul, Trench, Trubner & Co., 1939; first published in 1890.

Chang, Richard T. *From Prejudice to Tolerance: A Study of the Japanese Image of the West, 1826–1864.* Tokyo: Sophia University, 1970.

Christianity in Japan: A Bibliography of Japanese and Chinese Sources. Part 1 (1543–1858). Compiled by Arimichi Ebisawa. Tokyo: Committee on Asian Cultural Studies, International Christian University, 1960.

Clement, Ernest W. *Christianity in Modern Japan.* Philadelphia: American Baptist Publication Society, 1905.

Cooper, Michael, ed. *They Came to Japan: An Anthology of European Reports on Japan, 1543–1640.* Berkeley and Los Angeles: University of California Press, 1965.

Daiichi Tōkyō enzetsu: Gakujutsu ni yotte Kirisutokyō o ronzu [The first Tokyo lectures: Discussing Christianity on the basis of science]. Edited by Charles Eby. Yokohama: Eikoku Seisho Kaisha, Beikoku Seisho Kaisha, 1884.

Davis, J. Merle. *Davis—Soldier, Missionary: A Biography of Rev. Jerome D. Davis, D.D., Lieut-Colonel of Volunteers and for Thirty-Nine Years a Missionary of the American Board of Commissioners for Foreign Missions in Japan.* Boston: Pilgrim Press, 1916.

Davis, Winston. "The Civil Theology of Inoue Tetsujirō." *Japanese Journal of Religious Studies* 3 (March 1976): 5–40.

DeForest, Charlotte B. *The Evolution of a Missionary: A Biography of John Hyde DeForest, for Thirty-Seven Years Missionary of the American Board, in Japan.* New York: Fleming H. Revell Co., 1914.

DeForest, John Hyde. *Kareki o ogamu no gai* [The evil of worshipping dried wood]. N.p.: Beikoku Haken Dengyōshi Jimukyoku [American Board of Commissioners for Foreign Missions], 1880.

———. *Naichi zakkyoron* [Mixed residence]. Tokyo, 1898.

de Jong, J. W. "A Brief History of Buddhist Studies in Europe and America." *The Eastern Buddhist*, n.s., 7 (May 1974): 55–106; 7 (Oct. 1974): 49–82.

Dilworth, David A., and Hirano, Umeyo, trans. *Fukuzawa Yukichi's "An Encouragement of Learning."* Tokyo: Sophia University, 1969.

Dilworth, David A., and Hurst, G. Cameron, trans. *Fukuzawa Yukichi's "An Outline of a Theory of Civilization."* Tokyo: Sophia University, 1973.

Dohi Akio. *Nihon Purotesutanto Kirisutokyōshi* [A history of Protestant Christianity in Japan]. Tokyo: Shinkyō Shuppansha, 1980.

Doi, Masatoshi. *Search for Meaning through Interfaith Dialogue*. Tokyo: Kyo Bun Kwan, 1976.

Dōshisha Kyōkai kyūjūnen shōshi [A brief history of the ninety years of the Doshisha church]. Kyoto: Dōshisha Kyōkai, 1966.

Drummond, Richard Henry. *A History of Christianity in Japan*. Grand Rapids, Mich.: William B. Eerdmans Publishing Co., 1971.

Dumoulin, Heinrich. *Christianity Meets Buddhism*. LaSalle, Ill.: Open Court, 1974.

Earhart, H. Byron. *Japanese Religion: Unity and Diversity*. Encino, Calif.: Dickenson Publishing Co., 1974.

Ebisawa Arimichi. *Ishin henkakuki to Kirisutokyō* [The revolutionary time of the Meiji Restoration and Christianity]. Tokyo: Shinseisha, 1968.

————. "*Shakkyō seibyū* to sono hankyō" [Responses to *Correcting the errors of Buddhism*]. *Shien* 13 (Jan. 1940): 40–68.

————. "Takahashi Gorō chosakusho mokuroku" [A bibliography of Takahashi Gorō]. *Shien*, vol. 23, no. 2 (1958).

Ebisawa Arimichi; Cieslik, Hubert; Doi Tadao; and Ōtsuka Mitsunobu, eds. *Kirishitansho, Hai-Yasho* [Christian writings, anti-Christian writings]. Nihon shisō taikei [An outline of Japanese thought], vol. 25. Tokyo: Iwanami Shoten, 1970.

Ebisawa Arimichi and Ōuchi Saburō. *Nihon Kirisutokyōshi*. [A history of Christianity in Japan]. Tokyo: Nihon Kirisuto Kyōdan Shuppankyoku, 1970.

Eby, C. S. "Christianity and Other Religions." *Chrysanthemum* 3 (April 1883): 181–197.

Edkins, Joseph. *Chinese Buddhism: A Volume of Sketches (Historical, Descriptive, and Critical)*. Reprint ed. New York: Paragon Book Reprint Corp., 1968; first published in 1880.

Eliade, Mircea, and Kitagawa, Joseph M., eds. *The History of Religions: Essays in Methodology*. Chicago: University of Chicago Press, 1959.

Elison, George. *Deus Destroyed: The Image of Christianity in Early Modern Japan*. Cambridge, Mass.: Harvard University Press, 1973.

Eves, George. *Kirisutokyō no teki* [The enemy of Christianity]. Tokyo, 1889.

Fairbank, John K.; Reischauer, Edwin O.; and Craig, Albert M. *East Asia: The Modern Transformation*. Boston: Houghton Mifflin Co., 1965.

Fragments of Fifty Years: Some Lights and Shadows of the Work of the Japan Mission of the American Board, 1869–1919. N.p., n.d.

Fridell, Wilbur M. "Notes on Japanese Tolerance." *Monumenta Nipponica* 27 (Autumn 1972): 253–271.

Fujishima Ryōon (Tangaku). *Seikyō shinron* [A new treatise on politics and religion]. Kyoto: Kōkyō Shoin, 1899.

————. *Yasokyō matsuro* [The end of Christianity]. Tokyo: Tetsugaku Shoin, 1893.

————. *Yasokyō no mudōri* [The unreasonableness of Christianity]. 3 vols. Kyoto, 1881.

Fukushima Hirotaka. "Kaigai kyōjō shisatsu: Hai-Butsu jōkyōka no Seiō" [Observations on the religious situation abroad: Western Europe at the time of the anti-Buddhist movement in Japan]. *Ryūkoku Daigaku ronshū,* no. 413 (Oct. 1978), pp. 45–65.

Fukuzawa Yukichi. *The Autobiography of Fukuzawa Yukichi.* Translated by Eiichi Kiyooka. Tokyo: Hokuseido Press, 1960.

Germany, Charles H. *Protestant Theologies in Modern Japan: A History of Dominant Theological Currents from 1920–1960.* Tokyo: International Institute for the Study of Religions, 1965.

Gordon, M. L. *An American Missionary in Japan.* Boston: Houghton, Mifflin and Co., 1892.

———. *Bukkyō tanomu ni tarazu* [Buddhism is unreliable]. N.p.: Kirisutokyō Shorui Kaisha, 1882.

———. "The Doctrine of Amida Unauthentic." *Chrysanthemum* 2 (March 1882): 104–110.

———. "The Legend of Amida Buddha." *Chrysanthemum* 2 (Jan. 1882): 3–10.

———. *Mida monogatari* [The story of Amida]. N.p.: Beikoku Haken Dendōshi Jimukyoku, 1881.

———. *Thirty Eventful Years: The Story of the American Board's Mission in Japan, 1869–1899.* Boston: Congregational House, 1901.

Gotō Yumi. *Min-Shin shisō to Kirisutokyō* [Ming and Ching thought and Christianity]. Tokyo: Kenbun Shuppan, 1979.

Greene, Evarts Boutell. *A New-Englander in Japan: Daniel Crosby Greene.* Boston: Houghton Mifflin Co., 1927.

Griffis, William Elliot. *Dux Cristus: An Outline Study of Japan.* New York: Macmillan Co., 1904.

———. *A Maker of the New Orient: Samuel Robbins Brown.* New York: Fleming H. Revell Co., 1902.

———. *The Religions of Japan: From the Dawn of History to the Era of Méiji.* Reprint ed. Freeport, N.Y.: Books for Libraries Press, 1972; first published in 1895.

———. *Sunny Memories of Three Pastorates: With a Selection of Sermons and Essays.* Ithaca, N.Y.: Andrus and Church, 1903.

———. *Verbeck of Japan: A Citizen of No Country.* New York: Fleming H. Revell Co., 1900.

Gubbins, J. H. *The Progress of Japan, 1853–1871.* Oxford: Clarendon Press, 1911.

Gulick, Addison. *Evolutionist and Missionary: John Thomas Gulick, Portrayed through Documents and Discussions.* Chicago: University of Chicago Press, 1932.

Haas, Hans. *Amida Buddha unsere Zuflucht: Urkunden zum Verständnis des japanischen Sukhāvatī-Buddhismus.* Leipzig: Dieterich'sche Verlagsbuchhandlung, 1910.

———. *Japans Zukunftsreligion.* Berlin: Verlag von Karl Kurtius, 1907.

Hakeda, Yoshito S. *Kūkai: Major Works, Translated, with an Account of His Life and a Study of His Thought.* New York: Columbia University Press, 1972.

Hall, John Whitney, and Beardsley, Richard K. *Twelve Doors to Japan.* New York: McGraw-Hill, 1965.

Hanayama, Shinsho, ed. *Bibliography on Buddhism.* Tokyo: Hokuseido Press, 1961.

Harada, Tasuku. *The Faith of Japan.* New York: Macmillan Co., 1914.

Hardy, Arthur Sherburne, ed. *Life and Letters of Joseph Hardy Neesima.* Reprint ed. Kyoto: Doshisha University Press, 1980; first published in 1891.

Hashimoto Kagami. *Inmanueru: Fukuinteki shōmyō* [Immanuel: An evangelical invocation of the name]. Tokyo: Shinkyō Shuppansha, 1966.

Havens, Thomas R. H. *Nishi Amane and Modern Japanese Thought.* Princeton, N.J.: Princeton University Press, 1970.

Higashi Kan'ichi, trans. *Ryōyaku zensho jigo sōi* (translation of Henry Ball's *Self-Contradiction of the Bible*). 2 vols. Tokyo, 1875.

Hikone Kirisuto Kyōkai ryakushi [A brief history of Hikone Church]. Edited by Itō Masayoshi. Hikone: Hikone Kirisuto Kyōkai, 1939.

Hirai Kinzō. *Shinyaku zensho danpaku* [Refutation of the New Testament]. Kyoto, 1883.

Hiraiwa Yoshiyasu. *Waga kokutai to Kirisutokyō* [Our national polity and Christianity]. Tokyo: Keiseisha, 1895; first published in 1894.

Hirokawa, Daikichi. "Freedom and the Concept of People's Rights." In *Modern Japan: An Interpretive Anthology.* Edited by Irwin Scheiner. New York: Macmillan Co., 1974.

Hiyane Antei. *Kirisutokyō no Nihonteki tenkai* [The Japanese development of Christianity]. Tokyo: Kirisutokyō Shisō Sōsho Kankōkai, 1938.

———. *Kyōkai sanjūgoninzō* [Portraits of thirty-five church personalities]. Tokyo: Nihon Kirisuto Kyōdan Shuppanbu, 1959.

———. *Nihon kinsei Kirisutokyō jinbutsushi* [A history of Christian personalities in modern Japan]. Tokyo: Kirisutokyō Shisō Sōsho Kankōkai, 1935.

———. *Nihon Kirisutokyōshi* [A history of Christianity in Japan]. 5 vols. Tokyo: Kyōbunkan, 1940–1941.

Honda Zuien. *Yasokyō shinpan* [Christianity on trial]. Tokyo, 1887.

Howes, John F. "Kanzo Uchimura: Teacher and Writer." *Japan Christian Quarterly* 23 (April 1967): 150–156.

———. "Japanese Christians and American Missionaries." In *Changing Japanese Attitudes toward Modernization.* Edited by Marius B. Jansen. Princeton, N.J.: Princeton University Press, 1965.

Ienaga Saburō. *Kindai Nihon no shisōsha* [Modern Japanese thinkers]. Tokyo: Yūshindō, 1970.

———, ed. *Kindai Nihon shisōshi kōza* [Essays in the history of modern Japanese thought], vol. 1: *Rekishiteki gaikan* [Historical survey]. Tokyo: Chikuma Shobō, 1959.

Iino Norimoto. *Kirisuto to Butsuda: Tōzai shūkyō no rikai* [Christ and Buddha: Understanding Eastern and Western religions]. Tokyo: Risōsha, 1957.

Ikeda Eishun. *Meiji no shin Bukkyō undō* [The new Buddhist movement in the Meiji period]. Tokyo: Yoshikawa Kōbunkan, 1976.

Ikemoto Yoshiharu, ed. *Kirisutokyō oyobi Bukkyō* [Christianity and Buddhism]. Tokyo: Keiseisha, 1889.

Imai Kaku. *Yo ga jikken no shūkyō: From Buddhism to Christianity: A Personal Experience.* Tokyo: Nihon Kirisutokyō Kōbun Kyōkai, 1917.

———. *Yo ga kaishū no tenmatsu: Why I left Buddhism and Became a Christian.* Tokyo: Nihon Kirisutokyō Kōbun Kyōkai, 1914.

Imai Tōgorō. *Shūkyō yūretsuron* [Merits and demerits of religions]. Tokyo, 1891.

Inagaki Masami. *Butsuda o seoite gaitō e* [Bringing Buddha to the streets]. Tokyo: Iwanami Shoten, 1974.

———. *Henkaku o motometa Bukkyōsha* [Buddhists who sought revolution]. Tokyo: Daizō Shinsho, 1975.

Inoue Enryō (Fusui). *Bukkyō katsuron* [On the renewal of Buddhism]. 4 vols. Tokyo: Tetsugaku Shoin, 1887. Includes *Bukkyō katsuron joron* [On the renewal of Buddhism: introduction], and *Bukkyō katsuron honron* [On the renewal of Buddhism: main part], vols. 1–3.

———. *Chūkō katsuron* [About the renewal of loyalty and filial piety]. Tokyo: Tetsugaku Shoin, 1893.

———. *Haja shinron* [A new refutation of the evil religion]. Tokyo: Meikyōsha, 1885.

———. *Kyōiku shūkyō kankeiron* [The relationship between education and religion]. Tokyo: Tetsugaku Shoin, 1893.

———. *Ōbei kakkoku seiji nikki* [A diary of political and religious affairs in Europe and America]. 2 vols. Tokyo: Tetsugaku Shoin, 1889.

———. *Shinri kinshin* [The guiding principle of truth]. 3 vols. Kyoto, 1890; first published in 1886–1887.

Inoue Tetsujirō. *Kyōiku to shūkyō no shōtotsu* [The conflict between education and religion]. Tokyo: Keigyōsha, 1902; first published in 1893.

———. *Naichi zakkyo zokuron* [About mixed residence, continued]. Tokyo: Tetsugaku Shoin, 1891.

Ishii Ryosuke, ed. *Japanese Legislation in the Meiji Era*. Translated by William J. Chambliss. Tokyo: Pan-Pacific Press, 1958.

Ishikawa Kisaburō. *Nihon Seikyō dendōshi* [A record of the propagation of the Orthodox Church in Japan]. 2 vols. Tokyo: Seikyōkai Henshūkyoku, 1901.

Ishikawa Shuntai. *Yasokyō himitsusetsu* [About the secret of Christianity]. Tokyo: Hōchisha, 1875.

Itō Masahiko. *Naichi zakkyo Butsu-Ya tōronkai* [Mixed residence: a Buddhist-Christian dispute]. Tokyo: Kokubosha, 1898.

Iwamoto Yasunami. *Kirisutokyō to Bukkyō no taihi* [A comparison of Christianity and Buddhism]. Tokyo: Sōbunsha, 1974.

The Japan Biographical Encyclopedia and Who's Who. Edited by the Japan Biographical Research Department. Tokyo: Rengo Press, 1958.

Japanese Religion: A Survey by the Agency for Cultural Affairs. Tokyo: Kodansha International, 1972.

Jennes, Joseph. *A History of the Catholic Church in Japan: From Its Beginnings to the Early Meiji Era (1549–1873)*. Revised ed. Tokyo: Oriens Institute for Religious Research, 1973.

Jones, H. J. "*Bakumatsu* Foreign Employees." *Monumenta Nipponica* 29 (Autumn 1974): 305–327.

Ka: Bukkyō to Kirisutokyō to izure ga ze naru [Which is right, Buddhism or Christianity?]. N.p.: Beikoku Haken Senkyōshi Jimusho [American Board of Commissioners for Foreign Missions], 1888.

Kaigo Tokiomi. *Japanese Education: Its Past and Present*. Tokyo: Kokusai Bunka Shinkokai, 1968.

Kamata Enkai. *Bukkyō daitōronkai* [A great Buddhist dispute]. 4th ed. Kyoto: Kendō Shoin, 1894.

Kamegai Ryōun. *Bukkyō kara Kirisuto e* [From Buddhism to Christ]. Tokyo: Fukuinkan, 1952.

Kanazawa Nihon Kirisuto Kyōkai gojūnenshi [A history of the fifty years of Kanazawa Church of Christ]. Edited by Nakazawa Shōshichi. Kanazawa: Kanazawa Nihon Kirisuto Kyōkai, 1930.

Kaneko Hakumu. *Taiken no shūkyō* [Experiential religion]. Tokyo: Kyōbunsha, 1922.

Kanzaki Issaku. *Haja sōsho* [A library of anti-Christian writings]. 2 vols. Tokyo: Tetsugaku Shoin, 1893.

Kashiwabara Yūsen. *Nihon kinsei kindai Bukkyōshi no kenkyū* [Studies in the history of early modern and modern Buddhism in Japan]. Kyoto: Heirakuji Shoten, 1965.

Kashiwabara Yūsen and Fujii Manabu, eds. *Kinsei Bukkyō no shisō* [Early modern Buddhist thought]. Nihon shisō taikei [An outline of Japanese thought], vol. 57. Tokyo: Iwanami Shoten, 1973.

Katayama Yūkichi. *Zenteki Kirisutokyō* [Zen Christianity]. Hakodate, 1944.

Katō Totsudō (Taiichirō). *Bukkyō kokumin no kokoroe* [Directions for the Buddhist nation]. Tokyo: Meikyōsha, 1896.

———. *Bukkyō kokumin zakkyogo no kokoroe* [Direction for the Buddhist nation concerning mixed residence]. Tokyo: Kōmeisha, 1899.

———. *Chokugo to Bukkyō* [The Imperial Rescript and Buddhism]. Tokyo: Gohō Shoin, 1893.

———. *Hai-Yasokyō* [Refutation of Christianity]. Tokyo: Tsūzoku Bukkyōkan, 1899.

———. *Naichi zakkyo ni tai-suru Bukkyō shinto no kokoroe: Naichi zakkyo to Bukkyō* [Directions for Buddhists concerning mixed residence: Mixed residence and Buddhism]. Tokyo: Kokubosha, 1897.

———. *Teikoku kenpō shinkyō jiyū no ben: Kokutai to yasokyō* [The Imperial Constitution and the freedom of religion: The national polity and Christianity]. Tokyo: Kokubosha, 1898.

———. *Yamato-damashii* [The Japanese spirit]. Tokyo: Kokubosha, 1899.

———. *Zakkyo kokoroe: Bukkyō to aikokushin* [Directions for mixed residence: Buddhism and patriotism]. Tokyo: Kōmeisha, 1898.

Kawai Kiyomaru. *Kyūyaku zensho fukashinron* [The Old Testament unbelievable]. Kyoto, 1882.

Keene, Donald. *The Japanese Discovery of Europe, 1720–1830.* Revised ed. Stanford, Calif.: Stanford University Press, 1969.

Kindai Ōtaniha nenpyō [A chronology of the modern Ōtani sect]. Edited by Shinshū Kyōgaku Kenkyūsho. Kyoto: Higashi Honganji, 1977.

Kirisutokyō to Bukkyō [Christianity and Buddhism]. Fukyō shinjitsu [The truth of propagation], no. 2. Kyoto: Hōzōkan, [1899].

Kishimoto Hideo, ed. *Japanese Religion in the Meiji Era.* Translated by John F. Howes. Tokyo: Ōbunsha, 1956.

Kishimoto Nobuta. *Hikaku shūkyō ippan* [An outline of comparative religion]. Tokyo: Keiseisha, 1902.

———. *Okada-shiki seiza sannen* [Three years of meditation according to the Okada method]. Tokyo: Dai Nihon Tosho Kabushiki Kaisha, 1916.

———. *Shūkyō kenkyū* [The study of religion]. Tokyo: Keiseisha, 1899.

Kitagawa, Joseph M. *Religion in Japanese History.* New York: Columbia University Press, 1966.

Kitō Sokun. *Koji hikkei haja kinben* [The iron rod for refutation of Christianity indispensable for *koji*]. Nagoya: Kichūdō, 1892.

Kōsaka Masaaki, ed. *Japanese Thought in the Meiji Era.* Translated by David Abosch. Tokyo: Pan-Pacific Press, 1958.

Kōza kindai Bukkyō [Essays on modern Buddhism], vol. 1: *Gaisetsu* [Introduction]. Kyoto: Hōzōkan, 1963.

Kōza kindai Bukkyō [Essays on modern Buddhism], vol. 2: *Rekishihen* [History]. Kyoto: Hōzōkan, 1961.

Kozaki, Hiromichi. *Reminiscences of Seventy Years: The Autobiography of a Japanese Pastor.* Tokyo: Kyo Bun Kwan, 1928.

Kraemer, Hendrik. *Religion and the Christian Faith.* London: Lutterworth Press, 1956.

Kristensen, W. Brede. *The Meaning of Religion.* 3d ed. The Hague: Martinus Nijhoff, 1971.

Kurata Momozō senshū [Selected works of Kurata Momozō]. 5 vols. Tokyo: Shunjūsha, 1963.

Kutsumi Sokuchū (Kesson). *Yasokyō shōtotsuron* [On the conflict with Christianity]. Tokyo, 1893.

Kuyama Yasushi, ed. *Kindai Nihon to Kirisutokyō: Meijihen* [Modern Japan and Christianity: The Meiji period]. Nishinomiya: Kirisutokyō Gakuto Kyōdaidan, 1956.

Lande, Aasulv. "Meiji shoki ni okeru shūkyō taiwa no jittai" [The religious dialogue in the early Meiji period]. In *Gendai ni okeru shūkyō no taiwa* [Religious dialogue in the modern era]. Edited by Takenaka Masao. Tokyo: Seibunsha, 1979.

Lassalle, H. M. Enomiya. *Zen Meditation and Christian Mysticism.* LaSalle, Ill.: Open Court, 1974.

Laures, Johannes. *The Catholic Church in Japan: A Short History.* Rutland, Vermont, & Tokyo, Japan: Charles E. Tuttle Co., 1954.

Lee, Kun Sam. *The Christian Confrontation with Shinto Nationalism.* Philadelphia: Presbyterian and Reformed Publishing Co., 1966.

Lloyd, Arthur. *Buddhist Meditations from the Japanese: With an Introductory Chapter on Modern Japanese Buddhism.* Tokyo, 1905.

———. *The Higher Buddhism in the Light of the Nicene Creed.* Tokyo, 1893.

———. *Shinran and His Work: Studies in Shinshu Theology.* Tokyo: Kyobunkwan, 1910.

———. *The Wheat among the Tares: Studies of Buddhism in Japan.* London: Macmillan and Co., 1908.

Loomis, Clara Denison. *Henry Loomis: Friend of the East.* New York: Fleming H. Revell Co., 1923.

MacCauley, Clay. *Memories and Memorials: Gatherings from an Eventful Life.* Tokyo, 1914.

McFarland, H. Neill. *The Rush Hour of the Gods: A Study of the New Religious Movements in Japan.* New York: Harper & Row, 1967.

McLaren, Walter Wallace. *A Political History of Japan during the Meiji Era, 1867–1912.* New York: Russell & Russell, 1965; first published in 1916.

Marnas, Fransisque. *La "Religion de Jésus" (Yaso ja-kyō) ressuscitée au Japon dans la seconde moitié du XIXe siècle.* Paris: Séminaire des Missions Étrangères, 1931; first published in 1896.

Maruyama Masao. *Nihon no shisō* [Japanese thought]. Tokyo: Iwanami Shoten, 1961.

———. *Studies in the Intellectual History of Tokugawa Japan.* Translated by Mikiso Hane. Tokyo: University of Tokyo Press, 1974.

Masutani, Fumio. *A Comparative Study of Buddhism and Christianity.* Tokyo: Bukkyo Dendo Kyokai, 1957.

Matsumura Kaiseki. *Shinkō gojūnen* [Fifty years of faith]. Tokyo: Dōkai Jimusho, 1926.

———. *Tenchijin* [Heaven, earth, and man]. Tokyo: Keiseisha, 1912.

Matsunaga, Alicia. *The Buddhist Philosophy of Assimilation: The Historical*

Development of the Honji-Suijaku Theory. Tokyo: Sophia University, 1969.

Matsuyama Kyōkai kyūjūnen ryakushi [An outline of the ninety years' history of Matsuyama Church]. Matsuyama: Nihon Kirisuto Kyōdan Matsuyama Kyōkai, 1975.

Matsuyama Rokuin. *Bankoku Shūkyō Taikaigi* [The World's Parliament of Religions]. 2 vols. Kyoto: Kōbundō, 1893–1894.

Meiji Bukkyō zenshū [Collected works of Meiji Buddhism], vol. 8: *Gohōhen* [Apologetics]. Edited by Tokiwa Daijō. Tokyo: Shunyōdō, 1935.

Meiji bunka zenshū [Collected works of Meiji culture], vol. 19: *Shūkyōhen* [Religion]. Edited by Meiji Bunka Kenkyūkai. 2d ed. Tokyo: Nihon Hyōronsha, 1967; first published in 1928.

Meiji bunka zenshū [Collected works of Meiji culture], vol. 23: *Shisōhen* [Thought]. Edited by Meiji Bunka Kenkyūkai. 2d ed. Tokyo: Nihon Hyōronsha, 1967; first published in 1929.

Meiji shoki no Kinan Kirisutokyō: Tanabe Kyōkaishi [Christianity in southern Kii in early Meiji: The history of Tanabe Church]. Vol. 1. Edited by Tadokoro Sōgorō. Tanabe: Nihon Kirisuto Kyōdan Tanabe Kyōkai, [1974].

Meiroku Zasshi: Journal of the Japanese Enlightenment. Translated by William Reynolds Braisted. Tokyo: University of Tokyo Press, 1976.

Mekata Sakae. *Benseki Makyōron* [Refutation of the diabolic religion]. 2 vols. Kobe, 1886.

Michalson, Carl. *Japanese Contributions to Christian Theology.* Philadelphia: Westminster Press, 1960.

Michihata Taisei. *Amida Butsu to Kirisuto* [Amida Buddha and Christ]. Tokyo: Kyūdōsha Shuppanbu, 1932.

———. *Amida Butsu yori Kirisuto e* [From Amida Buddha to Christ]. Tokyo: Keiseisha, 1924.

———. *Butsu Bosatsu yori Kirisuto no Kami e* [From Buddhas and Bodhisattvas to the God of Christ]. Tokyo: Kyūdōsha, 1959.

———. *Shina no Jōdoshū no kaiso Zendō Daishi ni ataeshi Keikyō no kanka* [The influence on Nestorianism upon Zendō (Shan-tao) Daishi, the founder of the Pure Land sect in China]. Niigata: Kyūdōsha Shuppanbu, 1927.

Minami Hajime. *Nihon ni okeru jiyū Kirisutokyō no senkusha* [Pioneers of liberal Christianity in Japan]. Tokyo, 1935.

Minoda Kakunen. *Bukkyō Yasokyō shinkō kajō* [Buddhist and Christian articles of faith]. 3 vols. Tokyo: Seinenkai, 1888–1889.

Mishima Yoshitada. *Shin Nihon kokutairon: Shinkyō jiyūron* [On the national polity of the new Japan: Freedom of religion]. Tokyo: Kōyūsha, 1889.

Miyamoto Shōson. *Meiji Bukkyō no shichō: Inoue Enryō no jiseki* [Trends in Meiji Buddhism: The achievements of Inoue Enryō]. Tokyo: Kōsei Shuppansha, 1975.

Miyatake Gaikotsu. *Meiji enzetsushi* [A history of Meiji oratory]. Tokyo: Seikōkan, 1929.

Mizutani Jinkai. *Shin Bukkyō* [The New Buddhism]. Tokyo: Tōkyō Shorin, 1888.

[Moore, Herbert]. *The Christian Faith in Japan.* 2d ed. Westminster: Society for the Propagation of the Gospel in Foreign Parts, 1904.

Mori Ryūkichi, ed. *Shinshū shiryō shūsei* [A compilation of historical material on Shin Buddhism], vol. 13: *Shinshū shisō no kindaika* [The modernization of Shin Buddhist thought]. Kyoto: Dōbōsha, 1977.

Morioka Kiyomi. *Chihō shōtoshi ni okeru Kirisuto kyōkai no keisei: Jōshū Annaka Kyōkai no kōzō bunseki* [The formation of the Christian church in a minor provincial city: An analysis of the structure of Annaka church in the province of Kōzuke]. Tokyo: Nihon Kirisuto Kyōdan Senkyō Kenkyūsho, 1959.

————. "Christianity in the Japanese Rural Community: Acceptance and Rejection." In *Religion in Changing Japanese Society.* Edited by Kiyomi Morioka. Tokyo: University of Tokyo Press, 1975.

Morioka, Kiyomi, and Newell, William, eds. *The Sociology of Japanese Religion.* Leiden: E. J. Brill, 1968.

Moriwaki Sugayoshi (or Kankichi). *Shaka Yaso sōron no saiban* [The controversy between Buddha and Jesus on trial]. Kyoto, 1881.

Motoda Sakunoshin. *Rōkantoku Uiriamusu* [The aged Bishop Williams]. Tokyo: Bunshōdō, 1914.

————. *Sankyō Kaidō to Kirisutokyō* [The Conference of the Three Religions and Christianity]. Tokyo: Torakuto Kankōkai, 1912.

Muirhead, William. *Ju Shaku Dō Kai Yaso gokyō tsūkō* [The five religions of Confucianism, Buddhism, Taoism, Islam, and Christianity]. Tokyo: Jūjiya, 1879.

Müller, F. Max, ed. *The Sacred Books of the East,* vol. 49: *Buddhist Mahayana Texts.* Oxford: Clarendon Press, 1894.

Murakami Senshō. *Bukkyō chūkōron* [Buddhist loyalty and filial piety]. Tokyo: Tetsugaku Shoin, 1893.

Murakami, Shigeyoshi. *Japanese Religion in the Modern Century.* Translated by H. Byron Earhart. Tokyo: University of Tokyo Press, 1980.

Muraoka Tsunetsugu. "Kirisutokyō to Nihon shisō" [Christianity and Japanese thought]. *Katorikku kenkyū* (Jan.–Feb. 1942).

Myōhō-Renge-Kyō: The Sutra of the Lotus Flower of the Wonderful Law. Translated by Bunnō Katō. Tokyo: Risshō Kōsei-kai, 1971.

Nagahama Kyōkaishi [A history of Nagahama Church]. Nagahama, Shiga Prefecture: Nagahama Kirisuto Kyōkai, 1915.

Nagaoka Jō. *Butsu-Ya hikakuron* [Comparison of Buddhism and Christianity]. Kokura, 1892.

Nakamura Hajime. *Bukkyōgo daijiten* [A comprehensive dictionary of Buddhist terminology]. 3 vols. Tokyo: Tōkyō Shoseki Kabushiki Kaisha, 1975.

————. *A History of the Development of Japanese Thought from A.D. 592 to 1868.* 2 vols. Tokyo: Kokusai Bunka Shinkokai, 1969.

Nakanishi Ushio. *Kyōiku shūkyō shōtotsu dan'an* [The last word about the conflict between education and religion]. Tokyo: Hakubunkan, 1893.

————. *Sekai sanseiron* [The three sages of the world]. Osaka: Okajima Hōbunkan, 1893.

————. *Shin Bukkyōron* [The New Buddhism]. Kyoto: Kōkyō Shoin, 1892.

————. *Shūkyō kakumeiron* [Religious revolution]. Tokyo: Hakubunkan, 1889.

————. *Shūkyō taiseiron* [General trends in religion]. Kyoto: Kōkyō Shoin, 1891.

Nakazawa Shōshichi. *Nihon no shito: Tomasu Uin-den* [The apostle of Japan: The story of Thomas Winn]. Tokyo: Nagasaki Shoten, 1932.

Nihon jinmei daijiten [A comprehensive dictionary of Japanese names]. 7 vols. Edited by Shimonaka Kunihiko. Tokyo: Heibonsha, 1979; 6 vols. first published in 1937–1938.

Nihon kindai bungaku daijiten [A comprehensive dictionary of modern Japanese literature]. 6 vols. Edited by Nihon Kindai Bungakkai. Tokyo: Kōdansha, 1977.

Nihon kindai to Kirisutokyō [Modern Japan and Christianity]. Edited by Dōshisha Daigaku Jinbun Kagaku Kenkyūsho, Kirisutokyō Shakai Mondai Kenkyūkai. Tokyo: Shinkyō Shuppankai, 1973.

Nihon Kirisuto Dendō Kaisha ryakushi [A brief history of the Home Missionary Society]. Osaka: Nihon Kirisuto Dendō Kaisha, 1898.

Nihon Kirisutokyō bunken mokuroku: Meijiki [A bibliography of Christianity in Japan: The Meiji period]. *Part 2 (1859–1912)*. Edited by Ajia Bunka Kenkyū Iinkai. Tokyo: Kokusai Kirsutokyō Daigaku, 1965.

Nihon Kirisuto Kyōdan Imabari Kyōkai hachijūnen kinenshi [A commemorative record of the eighty years of Imabari Church of Christ in Japan]. Imabari: Nihon Kirisuto Kyōdan Imabari Kyōkai, 1959.

Nihon Kirisuto Kyōdan Tosa Kyōkai hachijūnenshi [A history of the eighty years of Tosa Church of Christ in Japan]. Kochi: Nihon Kirisuto Kyōdan Tosa Kyōkai, 1976.

Nihon Kirisuto Niigata Kyōkai ryakushi [An outline of the history of Niigata Church of Christ in Japan]. Niigata: Nihon Kirisuto Niigata Kyōkai, 1933.

Nihon Kumiai Kyōto Kirisuto Kyōkai gojūnenshi [A history of the fifty years of Kyoto Congregational Church of Christ in Japan]. Edited by Nakai Saichirō. Kyoto: Nihon Kumiai Kyōto Kirisuto Kyōkai, 1935.

Nihon Seikōkai Kyōto chihōbu: Rekishi hensan shiryō [The Kyoto district of the Anglican Church in Japan: A compilation of historical material]. 2 vols. [Kyoto]: Nihon Seikōkai Kyōto Chihōbu, [1937].

Nihon Shūkyō Taikai kiyō [Proceedings of the Conference of Japanese Religions]. Tokyo: Nihon Shūkyō Konwakai, 1928.

Nishida Kaichirō. *Bakujaron* [Refutation of the evil religion]. Kyoto: Hōkyōsha, 1881.

Nishikata Kandō. *Buppō gyōshōka* [Buddhist songs at the morning bell]. Tokyo, 1889.

Nitobe, Inazo. *Bushido: The Soul of Japan*. Rutland, Vermont, & Tokyo, Japan: Charles E. Tuttle Co., 1970; first published in 1900.

Nōjin Hakugon. *Mukai nanshin* [Guidance in the foggy sea]. Hyogo: 1881.

Nonomura Naotarō. *Naichi zakkyo to shūkyō* [Mixed residence and religion]. Kyoto: Kendō Gakkai Shihonkai, 1898.

Notehelfer, F. G. *Kōtoku Shūsui: Portrait of a Japanese Radical*. Cambridge: Cambridge University Press, 1971.

Ōchō Enichi. "Minmatsu Bukkyō to Kirisutokyō to no sōgō hihan" [The mutual criticism of Buddhism and Christianity in the late Ming period]. *Ōtani gakuhō* 29 (Dec. 1949): 1–20; 29 (May 1950): 18–38.

Oda Tokunō. *Bukkyō daijiten* [A comprehensive dictionary of Buddhism]. Tokyo: Daizō Shuppan, 1957; first published in 1916.

Ogurusu Kōhei, trans. *Gakukyōshiron: Yasokyō to jitsugaku no sōtō* (translation of John William Draper's *A History of the Conflict between Religion and Science*). Tokyo: Aikoku Gohōsha, 1883.

Ōhama Tetsuya. *Meiji Kirisuto kyōkaishi no kenkyū* [Studies in Meiji church history]. Tokyo: Yoshikawa Kōbunkan, 1979.

Ōhara Kakichi, trans. *Bankoku Shūkyō Taikai enzetsushū* [A collection of speeches from the World's Parliament of Religions]. Osaka: Kanekawa Shoten, 1893.

Ohara Masao. *Bukkyō daishōri Yasokyō daihaiboku: Butsu-Ya katsumondō*

[The great victory of Buddhism and the great defeat of Christianity: An actual Buddhist-Christian dispute]. Osaka, 1889.

Ojima Saneharu. *Ki-Butsu ronsen* [A Christian-Buddhist debate]. Tokyo: Shinraisha, 1932.

Oka Hōshun. *Shinkan to kyūseikan: Bukkyō to Kirisutokyō* [The understanding of God and salvation: Buddhism and Christianity]. Kyoto: Hyakkaen, 1952.

Ōmi Hachiman Kirisuto Kyōkai ryakushi [A brief history of Ōmi Hachiman church]. Edited by Ōmi Hachiman Kirisuto Kyōkai Rekishi Hensan Iin. Shiga: Ōmi Hachiman Kirisuto Kyōkai, 1926.

Onchō hachijūnen: Nihon Kirisuto Kyōdan Nagoya Chūō Kyōkai hachijūnen ryakushi [Eighty years of grace: An outline of the eighty years' history of Nagoya Central Church of Christ in Japan]. Nagoya: Nihon Kirisuto Kyōdan Nagoya Chūō Kyōkai, 1960.

O'Neill, P. G. *Japanese Names: A Comprehensive Index by Characters and Readings.* New York: John Weatherhill, 1972.

Ōtsuka Yūei (or Sukehide). *Shin Butsu Yaso fukyō seiryaku hibunroku* [A secret record of propaganda tactics of Shinto, Buddhism, and Christianity]. Tokyo, 1884.

Ōuchi Seiran. *Sensō to Bukkyō* [War and Buddhism]. Tokyo: Kokubosha, 1904; first published in 1894.

———. *Sonnō hōbutsuron* [Revering the emperor and worshipping the Buddha]. Tokyo: Kōmeisha, 1889.

Oxford, Wayne H. *The Speeches of Fukuzawa: A Translation and Critical Study.* Tokyo: Hokuseido Press, 1973.

Ozawa Saburō. *Bakumatsu Meiji Yasokyōshi kenkyū* [Studies in the history of Christianity in late Tokugawa and early Meiji]. Tokyo: Nihon Kirisuto Kyōdan Shuppankyoku, 1973.

———. "Kenpō happu to Kirisutokyō: Meiji nijūninen" [The promulgation of the Constitution and Christianity: 1889]. N.p., n.d. Excerpts from newspapers and magazines, copied by hand.

———. "Meiji nijūichinen no Kirisutokyō" [Christianity in 1888]. N.p., n.d. Ozawa compiled a series of collections of excerpts from newspapers and magazines, copied by hand, one or two volumes for each year of the Meiji period. I have particularly made use of the volumes from 1888 to 1899.

———. *Nihon Purotesutantoshi kenkyū* [Studies in the history of Japanese Protestantism]. Tokyo: Tōkyō Daigaku Shuppankai, 1964.

———. *Uchimura Kanzō fukei jiken* [The Uchimura Kanzō incident of lese majesty]. Tokyo: Shinkyō Shuppansha, 1961.

Ozawa Yoshiyuki. *Sonnō Hōbutsu Daidōdan* [The Great Association for Revering the Emperor and Worshipping the Buddha]. Nagoya: Kichūdō, 1889.

Papinot, E. *Historical and Geographical Dictionary of Japan.* Rutland, Vermont, & Tokyo, Japan: Charles E. Tuttle Co., 1972; first published in 1910.

Pascoe, C. F. *Two Hundred Years of the S.P.G.: An Historical Account of the Society for the Propagation of the Gospel in Foreign Parts, 1701–1900.* 2 vols. London: S.P.G., 1901.

Peiris, William. *The Western Contribution to Buddhism.* Delhi: Motilal Banarsidass, 1973.

Pettee, James H. *A Chapter of Mission History in Modern Japan.* [Okayama], n.d. [ca. 1895].

Pfoundes, C. *Bukkyō enzetsushū* [A collection of Buddhist lectures]. Edited by Uchimiya Torasuke. Kyoto: Kōbundō, 1893.

Piovesana, Gino K. *Recent Japanese Philosophical Thought, 1862–1962: A Survey.* Revised ed. Tokyo: Enderlee Bookstore, 1968.

Powles, Cyril H. "Foreign Missionaries and Japanese Culture in the Late Nineteenth Century: Four Patterns of Approach." *Northeast Asia Journal of Theology* 1 (Sept. 1969): 14–28.

Proceedings of the General Conference of the Protestant Missionaries of Japan, Held at Osaka, Japan, April, 1883. Yokohama: R. Meiklejohn & Co., 1883.

Proceedings of the General Conference of Protestant Missionaries in Japan, Held in Tokyo October 24–31, 1900. Tokyo: Methodist Publishing House, 1901.

Pyle, Kenneth B. *The New Generation in Meiji Japan: Problems of Cultural Identity, 1885–1895.* Stanford, Calif.: Stanford University Press, 1969.

Reed, Edward J. *Japan: Its History, Traditions and Religions, with the Narrative of a Visit in 1879.* 2 vols. 2d ed. London: John Murray, 1880.

Reischauer, August Karl. *Studies in Japanese Buddhism.* New York: Macmillan Co., 1917.

Ritter, H. *A History of Protestant Missions in Japan.* Translated by George E. Albrecht. Tokyo: Methodist Publishing House, 1898.

Rōsen ikō [Posthumous works of Furukawa Rōsen]. Edited by Sugimura Kōtarō (Jūō). Tokyo: Bukkyō Seito Dōshikai, 1901.

Saba Wataru, ed. *Uemura Masahisa to sono jidai* [Uemura Masahisa and his time]. New ed. 5 vols. and 3 supp. vols. Tokyo: Kyōbunkan, 1976; 5 vols. and 2 supp. vols. first published 1938–1943.

Sada Kaiseki. *Bukkyō sōseiki* [The Buddhist Genesis]. Musashi, Kanagawa Prefecture, 1880; first published in 1878.

Saijō Kumiai Kirisuto Kyōkai, Komatsu Kumiai Kirisuto Kyōkai enkaku ryakushi [A brief history of Saijō Congregational Church and Komatsu Congregational Church]. Edited by Hoshino Mitsuo. Saijo, Ehime Prefecture, 1934.

Saitō Goichirō. *Yasokyō kokugairon* [Christianity a national injury]. Osaka, 1881.

Saji Jitsunen. *Hajeketsu* [Methods of refuting the evil religion]. Tokyo: Kōmeisha, 1885.

———. *Nihon Yuniterian-shugi kōbōshi* [The history of the rise and fall of Japanese Unitarianism]. Tokyo: Suieisha, 1910.

———. *Shūkyō enzetsu hikki* [Notes of lectures on religion]. Tokyo: Nihon Yuniterian Kyōkai, 1895.

Sakaino Kōyō, ed. *Shin Bukkyō jūnenshi* [The ten years' history of the New Buddhism]. Tokyo: Shin Bukkyōto Dōshikai, 1910.

Sakurai Masashi. *Meiji shūkyōshi kenkyū* [Studies in the history of religions in Meiji]. Tokyo: Shunjūsha, 1971.

Sansom, George B. *A History of Japan, 1615–1867.* Reprint ed. Folkestone, Kent: Wm Dawson & Sons, 1978; first published in 1963.

———. *The Western World and Japan: A Study in the Interaction of European and Asiatic Cultures.* London: Cresset Press, 1950.

Saunby, John W. *The New Chivalry in Japan: Methodist Golden Jubilee.* Toronto: Missionary Society of the Methodist Church, 1923.

Scalapino, Robert A. *Democracy and the Party Movement in Prewar Japan: The Failure of the First Attempt.* Berkeley and Los Angeles: University of California Press, 1967.

Scheiner, Irwin. *Christian Converts and Social Protest in Meiji Japan.* Berkeley and Los Angeles: University of California Press, 1970.

Schmiedel, Otto. *Kultur- und Missionsbilder aus Japan.* Berlin: A. Haack, 1891.

Schurhammer, Georg. *Die Disputationen des P. Cosme de Torres, S.J., mit den Buddhisten in Yamaguchi im Jahre 1551.* Tokyo, 1929.

Schwantes, Robert S. "Christianity *versus* Science: A Conflict of Ideas in Meiji Japan." *Far Eastern Quarterly* 12 (Feb. 1952): 123–132.

Seki Kōsaku. *Inoue Hakase to Kirisutokyōto* [Dr. Inoue and the Christians]. Tokyo, 1893.

Shaka to Kirisuto [Buddha and Christ]. Yokohama: London Religious Tract Society, 1886; apparently published also in 1884.

Shaku Sōen. *Bankoku Shūkyō Taikai ichiran* [A summary of the World's Parliament of Religions]. Tokyo: Kōmeisha, 1893.

——— (Soyen Shaku). *Zen for Americans: Including the Sutra of Forty-Two Chapters.* LaSalle, Ill.: Open Court, 1974; originally published in 1906 under the title *Sermons of a Buddhist Abbot.*

Sharpe, Eric J. *Not to Destroy but to Fulfil: The Contribution of J. N. Farquhar to Protestant Missionary Thought in India before 1914.* Uppsala: Gleerup, 1965.

Shimada Gunkichi. *Butsu-Ya yūshō reppaiben* [Distinguishing between merits and demerits of Buddhism and Christianity]. Iisakacho, Fukushima: Yuishindō, 1889.

Shimaji Mokurai zenshū [The complete works of Shimaji Mokurai]. Edited by Futaba Kenkō and Fukushima Hirotaka. 5 vols. Kyoto: Honganji Shuppan Kyōkai, 1973–1978.

"Shin Bukkyō" ronsetsushū [A collection of articles from *Shin Bukkyō*]. Vol. 2. Edited by Futaba Kenkō, Akamatsu Tesshin, and Fukushima Hirotaka. Kyoto: Nagata Bunshōdō, 1979.

Shiozu Junichi. *Kirisuto to Nichiren* [Christ and Nichiren]. Tokyo: Genshōdō, 1948.

Shively, Donald H. "Nishimura Shigeki: A Confucian View of Modernization." In *Changing Japanese Attitudes toward Modernization.* Edited by Marius B. Jansen. Princeton, N.J.: Princeton University Press, 1965.

Smith, Warren W., Jr. *Confucianism in Modern Japan: A Study of Conservatism in Japanese Intellectual History.* 2d ed. Tokyo: Hokuseido Press, 1973.

Sōritsu hachijūnen o mukaete: Nihon Kirisuto Kyōdan Aichi Kyōkai shiryō [In preparation of the eightieth anniversary: Historical records of the Aichi United Church of Christ in Japan]. Nagoya: Nihon Kirisuto Kyōdan Aichi Kyōkai, 1972.

Sources of Japanese Tradition. Compiled by Ryusaku Tsunoda, Wm. Theodore de Bary, and Donald Keene. 4th printing. 2 vols. New York: Columbia University Press, 1968.

Spae, Joseph J. *Buddhist-Christian Empathy.* Tokyo: Oriens Institute for Religious Research, 1980.

Statler, Oliver. *Shimoda Story.* New ed. Rutland, Vermont, & Tokyo, Japan: Charles E. Tuttle Co., 1971.

Sumiya Mikio. *Kindai Nihon no keisei to Kirisutokyō* [Christianity and the formation of the modern Japan]. Tokyo: Shinkyō Shuppansha, 1974; first published in 1961.

Suzuki Daisetsu zenshū [The complete works of Suzuki Daisetsu]. Vol. 26. Tokyo: Iwanami Shoten, 1970.

Suzuki Norihisa. *Meiji shūkyō shichō no kenkyū* [A study of religious trends in the Meiji period]. Tokyo: Tōkyō Daigaku Shuppankai, 1979.

————. "Nobuta Kishimoto and the Beginnings of the Scientific Study of Religion in Modern Japan." *Contemporary Religions in Japan* 11 (Sept.–Dec. 1970): 155–180.

————. *Uchimura Kanzō to sono jidai: Shiga Jūkō to no hikaku* [Uchimura Kanzō and his time: A comparison with Shiga Jūkō]. Tokyo: Nihon Kirisuto Kyōdan Shuppankyoku, 1975.

Tajima Kyōkei. *Butsu-Ya kessen* [A bloody battle between Buddhism and Christianity]. Kyoto: Nishimura Hōzōkan, 1893.

————. *Nōben taika Kakunen Koji: Bakuja enzetsu hikki* [The great orator Kakunen *Koji:* Notes from lectures refuting the evil religion]. Kyoto: Hōzōkan, 1892.

Tajima Shōji. *Bukkyō metsubōron* [The ruin of Buddhism]. Nagoya: Kichūdō, 1888; first published in 1887.

————. *Yaso ichidai benmōki* [Refutation of the life of Jesus]. Tokyo, 1874.

————. *Yasokyō-i mondō* [A dispute about the meaning of Christianity]. Tokyo, 1875.

Takada Dōken. *Naichi zakkyo Butsu-Ya mondō* [Mixed residence: A Buddhist-Christian dispute]. Tokyo: Tsūzoku Bukkyōkan, 1899; first published in 1897.

Takahashi Gorō. *Bukkyō shinkai* [A new interpretation of Buddhism]. Tokyo, 1883.

————. *Butsudō shinron* [A new treatise on Buddhism]. 4th ed. Tokyo: Jūjiya, 1883; first published in 1880.

————. *Hai-gitetsugakuron* [Refutation of the false philosophy]. Tokyo: Minyūsha, 1893.

————. *Sekai sanseiron* [The three sages of the world]. Tokyo: Bun'eikaku, 1903.

————. *Shoshū benran* [A compendium of religions]. Tokyo: Jūjiya, 1881.

Takakusu, Junjirō. *The Essentials of Buddhist Philosophy.* 3d ed. Edited by Wing-Tsit Chan and Charles A. Moore. Honolulu: Office Appliance Co., 1956; first published in 1947.

Takashima En (Beihō), ed. *Shōrai no shūkyō* [The future religion]. Tokyo: Shin Bukkyōto Dōshikai, 1903.

Takeda Kiyoko. *Dochaku to haikyō* [Indigenization and apostasy]. Tokyo: Shinkyō Shuppansha, 1967.

————. *Ningenkan no sōkoku* [Rivalry about the view of man]. Revised ed. Tokyo: Kōbundō, 1967; first published in 1959.

Tamamuro Taijō. *Nihon Bukkyōshi* [History of Japanese Buddhism], vol. 3: *Kinsei kindaihen* [The early modern and modern period]. Kyoto: Hōzōkan, 1975.

Tan Reigen, ed. *Naichi zakkyo junbi: Butsu-Ya enzetsushū* [Preparation for mixed residence: A collection of Buddhist speeches]. Tokyo: Kokubosha, 1897.

Tanaka Hisahiko. *Nehan yori Kami no kuni e* [From Nirvana to the Kingdom of God]. Okayama: Takaya Kirisuto Kyōkai Dendōbu, 1922.

Tanaka Tatsu. *Bukkyō kanken* [A personal view on Buddhism]. Tokyo: Mesojisuto Shuppansha, 1895.

————. *Kirisutokyō to Bukkyō* [Christianity and Buddhism]. Tokyo: Nihon Kirisutokyō Kōbun Kyōkai, 1915.

Thelle, Notto R. "A Barthian Thinker between Buddhism and Christianity: Takizawa Katsumi." *Japanese Religions* 8 (Oct. 1975): 54–86.

———. "Buddhist-Christian Encounter: From Animosity to Dialogue." *Japan Christian Quarterly* 42 (Spring 1976): 96–104.

———. "Foe and Friend: The Changing Image of Christ in Japanese Buddhism." *Japanese Religions* 12 (July 1982): 19–46.

———. "From Anathema to Dialogue: Buddhist-Christian Relations in Japan." *Japanese Religions* 10 (Dec. 1978): 53–74.

———. "From Conflict to Dialogue: Buddhism and Christianity in Japan, 1854–1899." Th.D. Dissertation, University of Oslo, 1983 (published in a limited number).

———. "Prospects and Problems of the Buddhist-Christian Dialogue in Japan." *Japanese Religions* 10 (July 1979): 51–65.

Thirteenth Report of the Council of Missions Coöperating with the United Church of Christ in Japan. Tokyo: Council of Missions Coöperating with the United Church of Christ in Japan, 1890.

Thomas, M. M. *The Acknowledged Christ of the Indian Renaissance.* Bangalore and Madras: C.L.S., The Christian Institute for the Study of Religion and Society, 1970.

Thomas, Winburn T. *Protestant Beginnings in Japan: The First Three Decades, 1859–1889.* Rutland, Vermont, & Tokyo, Japan: Charles E. Tuttle Co., 1959.

Thomsen, Harry. *The New Religions of Japan.* Rutland, Vermont, & Tokyo, Japan: Charles E. Tuttle Co., 1963.

Togawa Zanka (Yasuie). *Sekai sandaishūkyō* [The three great religions of the world]. Tokyo: Hakubunkan, 1895.

Tokushige Asakichi. *Ishin seiji shūkyōshi kenkyū* [Studies in the political and religious history of the Meiji Restoration]. Reprint ed. Tokyo: Rekishi Toshosha, 1974; first published in 1935.

Torio Tokuan (Koyata). *Shinsei tetsugaku: Mushinron* [The true philosophy: Atheism]. [Tokyo]: Nihon Kokkyō Daidōsha, 1894; first published in 1887.

Troeltsch, Ernst. *The Absoluteness of Christianity and the History of Religions.* Richmond, Va.: John Knox Press, 1971; originally published in German in 1901.

Tsuji Zennosuke. *Nihon Bukkyōshi* [The history of Japanese Buddhism], vol. 9: *Kinseihen* [The early modern period], no. 4. Reprint ed. Tokyo: Iwanami Shoten, 1970; first published in 1955.

Tsunajima Ryōsen. *Byōkenroku* [Notes from a sickbed]. Tokyo: Kanao Bun'endō, 1905.

———. *Kaikōroku* [Notes on the returning light]. Tokyo: Kanao Bun'endō, 1909.

Tsunemitsu Kōnen. *Meiji no Bukkyōsha* [Meiji Buddhists]. 2 vols. Tokyo: Shunjūsha, 1968.

Uchimura Kanzō. *The Complete Works of Kanzō Uchimura.* 7 vols. Tokyo: Kyobunkwan, 1971–1973.

Uemura Masahisa chosakushū [A collection of Uemura Masahisa's writings]. 7 vols. Tokyo: Shinkyō Shuppansha, 1966–1967.

Umehara Kitarō. *Butsu-Ya zessen: Yaso daihaiboku* [A Buddhist-Christian battle of tongues: The great defeat of Christianity]. Nagoya: Kichūdō, 1892.

Urasato Rōen. *Yasokyō no kiki* [The crisis of Christianity]. Tokyo: Tetsugaku Shoin, 1893.

Verwilghen, Albert Felix. "The Buddhist Studies of Father A. Villion." *Japan Missionary Bulletin* 25 (June 1971).

Villion, A. *Cinquante ans d'apostolat au Japon.* Hong Kong: Société des Missions-Étrangères, 1923.

Waldenfels, Hans. *Absolute Nothingness: Foundations for a Buddhist-Christian Dialogue.* Translated by J. W. Heisig. New York: Paulist Press, 1980; originally published in German in 1976.

Watanabe, Shoko. *Japanese Buddhism: A Critical Appraisal.* Revised ed. Tokyo: Kokusai Bunka Shinkokai, 1968; first published in 1964.

Welbon, Guy Richard. *The Buddhist Nirvāna and Its Western Interpreters.* Chicago: University of Chicago Press, 1968.

World Missionary Conference, 1910. Report of Commission IV: The Missionary Message in Relation to Non-Christian Religions. Edinburgh: Oliphant, Anderson & Ferrier, 1910.

Yamaji Aizan. *Kirisutokyō hyōron* [A review of Christianity]. Tokyo: Iwanami Shoten, 1966; first published in 1906.

Yamakawa Chio. *Kirisutokyō to Nichiren Shōnin no shūkyō* [Christianity and the religion of Saint Nichiren]. Tokyo: Sōgensha, 1951.

Yamamoto Hideteru. *Nihon Kirisutokyōshi* [A history of Christianity in Japan]. Tokyo: Nihon Kirisuto Kyōkai Jimusho, 1929.

Yamazaki, Masakazu, and Miyakawa, Tōru. "Inoue Tetsujirō: The Man and His Works." *Philosophical Studies of Japan,* no. 7 (1966), pp. 111–125.

Yanaga, Chitoshi. *Japan since Perry.* New York: McGraw-Hill Book Co., 1949.

Yatsubuchi Banryū. *Shūkyō Taikai hōdō* [Report on the Parliament of Religions]. Edited by Hayashi Denji. Kyoto: Kōkyō Shoin, 1894.

Yokoi Tokio. *Christianity—What Is It? A Question in the Far East.* Yokohama: *Japan Mail* office [1893].

———. *Kirisutokyō shinron* [A new treatise on Christianity]. Tokyo: Keiseisha, 1891.

———. *Waga kuni no Kirisutokyō mondai* [The problem of Christianity in our country]. Tokyo: Keiseisha, 1894.

Yoshida Kyūichi. *Nihon kindai Bukkyō shakaishi kenkyū* [Studies in the social history of Buddhism in modern Japan]. Tokyo: Yoshikawa Kōbunkan, 1964.

———. *Nihon kindai Bukkyōshi kenkyū* [Studies in the history of Buddhism in modern Japan]. Tokyo: Yoshikawa Kōbunkan, 1959.

Yoshida Seitarō. *Kami o miru* [Seeing God]. Tokyo: Keiseisha, 1931.

Yoshioka Nobuyuki. *Haja kenshōron* [Refuting errors and demonstrating the truth]. Tokyo, 1882.

———. *Haja kenshō jashō mondō* [Refuting errors and demonstrating the truth: A dispute on error and truth]. Tokyo, 1884.

Young, John M. L. *The Two Empires in Japan: A Record of the Church-State conflict.* Tokyo: Bible Times Press, 1958.

Yūasa Yosō. *Kirisuto ni aru jiyū o motomete: Nihon Kumiai Kirisuto Kyōkaishi* [In search of freedom in Christ: The history of the Congregational Church in Japan]. Tokyo: Sōbunsha, 1958.

Zenkoku Bukkyōsha Daisan Konwakai gijiroku [Minutes of the Third All-Japan Meeting of Buddhists]. Kyoto: Dōmei Bukkyōdan Honbu, 1892.

JOURNALS AND NEWSPAPERS

Journals and newspapers recorded only in other sources or in Ozawa Saburō's unpublished collections are excluded here.

Bukkyō (Buddhist monthly journal).
Bukkyō shinundō (second series, Buddhist journal published twice a month).
The Chrysanthemum (monthly journal).
Chūō kōron (Buddhist monthly journal; see *Hanseikai zasshi*).
Daidō shinpō (Buddhist monthly journal devoted to nationalistic issues).
Daidō sōshi (monthly journal devoted to nationalistic issues).
Dentō (Buddhist monthly journal).
Fukuin shinpō (Christian weekly paper; see *Fukuin shūhō*).
Fukuin shūhō (Christian weekly paper; in 1891 its name was changed to *Fukuin shinpō*).
Hanseikai zasshi (Buddhist monthly journal; from 1892 it was named *Hansei zasshi,* and from 1899 *Chūō kōron;* its English title was *The Temperance*).
Hansei zasshi (see *Hanseikai zasshi*).
The Hansei Zasshi (monthly English edition of *Hansei zasshi;* from 1899 it was named *The Orient*).
The Japan Evangelist (Christian bimonthly journal).
The Japan Weekly Mail (sometimes called only the *Weekly Mail*).
Jogaku zasshi (Christian weekly journal; its English title was *The Woman's Magazine*).
Jūzen hōkutsu (Buddhist monthly journal).
Kirisutokyō shinbun (Christian weekly newspaper).
Mainichi shinbun (daily newspaper).
Meikyō shinshi (Buddhist newspaper published every second day).
The Missionary Herald (monthly journal of the American Board of Commissioners for Foreign Missions).
Nihonjin (journal published twice a month advocating nationalistic ideas).
Nihon-shugi (nationalistic journal).
Nihon shūkyō (monthly journal, advocating liberal religious views).
Nōjunkai zasshi (Buddhist monthly journal).
The Orient (see *The Hansei Zasshi*).
Reichikai zasshi (Buddhist monthly journal).
Rikugō zasshi (Christian monthly journal; its English title was *The Cosmos*).
Seikyō jihō (Buddhist nationalistic journal published twice a month).
Shimei yoka (Buddhist monthly journal).
Shin Bukkyō (Buddhist monthly journal devoted to reform).
Shūkyō (Unitarian monthly journal; see *Yuniterian*).
Taiyō (journal published twice a month; its English title was *The Sun*).
Transactions of the Asian Society of Japan.
The Young East (Buddhist monthly; the first series from 1925).
Yuniterian (Unitarian monthly journal; from 1891 it was named *Shūkyō*).

Index

Abe Isoo, 191
Abe Shinzō: on anti-Christian literature, 268n.37
Abe Yoshiya: on treaties, 12
"Age of doubt," 205–207
Aizawa Seishisai: *Shinron,* 5–6
Akamatsu Renjō, 35; on Buddhist crisis, 57; on Buddhist mission, 110; dialogue with Westerners, 85–86; and the enlightenment, 58; and Hanseikai, 200; mediator between Buddhists and Christians, 85; and missionaries, 68, 74–75; in the West, 79, 85
Akamatsu Seiichi, 74
All-Japan Buddhist Meeting, 108
All-Japan Meeting of Buddhists, 108, 152
American Board of Commissioners for Foreign Mission, 54
Anesaki Masaharu, 201; and Buddhist-Christian dialogue, 238–239, 241, 256; and comparative religion, 223–224, 245; *History of Japanese Religion,* 224; on Suzuki Shōsan, 9
Anti-Buddhist activity. *See* Buddhism; Buddhist apologetics
Anti-Christian activity: Buddhist campaigns, 105, 132, 135–149; and Buddhist cooperation, 108; in Buddhist meetings, 138–139; in China, 268n.36; decreasing after the Sino-Japanese War, 148; emotional background of, 2, 78; and the expansion of Christianity, 136–137; extent and results of, in the 1890s, 147–149; failure of, 161–162; literature,

8–10, 27–35, 87–90, 284n.48; politicization of, 117–119, 139–140; and Sonnō Hōbutsu Daidōdan, 103–107; terminology, 138; Tokugawa background, 4, 6–10; types of, 139–140, 143; violent confrontations, 90, 105, 132, 141–143
Apologetics: and comparative religion, 214–224 passim. *See also* Buddhist apologetics; Christian apologetics
Arnold, Edwin: on Christ's superiority, 218; *The Light of Asia,* 67, 215, 218; *The Light of the World,* 218; relationship to Buddhism and Christianity, 308n.62
Ashitsu Jitsuzen, 103, 197
Assimilation: of Christianity into Buddhism, 240–241; philosophy of, 241. *See also* Integration
Association of Buddhist Sects, 34, 108
Association of Christian Comrades, 170
Association for the Defense of the Country, 109
Association of Unity (Kiitsu Kyōkai), 239
Atheism: in Buddhism, 109; among Japanese intellectuals, 44; religious cooperation against, 237–238
Atkinson, J. L.: *Prince Siddhartha, the Japanese Buddhist,* 71
Atsumi Kaien: dialogue with Westerners, 85

Ball, Henry, 82; *Self-Contradiction of the Bible,* 79
Ballagh, J. H., 62
Barrows, John Henry, 243; on Christianity and other religions, 245

About the Author

Notto R. Thelle was born in Hong Kong of Norwegian missionary parents. He was educated in Norway and received a doctorate in theology from the University of Oslo. After training in Japanese studies (Sheffield, England) and Buddhist studies (Ōtani University, Kyoto), he became associate director of the National Christian Council Center for the Study of Japanese Religions in Kyoto, a position he held for over ten years.

Thelle's personal and scholarly interest in Buddhist-Christian dialogue is grounded in a missionary tradition that views Asian religious practitioners as fellow truth-seekers and friends. He has actively promoted interfaith interaction through seminars, lectures, and study projects, and as editor of the journal *Japanese Religions*. His publications have dealt with specific studies of Japanese Buddhism, new religions, the contemporary religious scene in Japan, as well as theological reflections on the implications of interfaith dialogue.